M000290417

Lean Software Strategies

Lean Software Strategies

Proven Techniques for
Managers and Developers

by
Peter Middleton
and
James Sutton

Productivity Press
NEW YORK, NEW YORK

© 2005 by Productivity Press, a division of Kraus Productivity Organization, Ltd.

All rights reserved. No part of this book may be reproduced or utilized in any form or by any means, electronic or mechanical, including photocopying, recording, or by any information storage and retrieval system, without permission in writing from the publisher.

Most Productivity Press books are available at quantity discounts when purchased in bulk. For more information, contact our Customer Service Department (888-319-5852). Address all other inquiries to:

Productivity Press
444 Park Avenue South, Suite 604
New York, NY 10016
United States of America
Telephone: 212-686-5900
Fax: 212-686-5411
E-mail: info@productivitypress.com

Page composition by William H. Brunson Typography Services
Printed and bound by Malloy Lithographing in the United States of America

Library of Congress Cataloging-in-Publication Data

Middleton, Peter, 1953–
     Lean software strategies : proven techniques for managers and developers /
   co-authors: Peter Middleton and James Sutton.
         p. cm.
      ISBN 1-56327-305-5 (alk. paper)
      1. Computer software industry.   2. Computer software industry—Management.
   3. Customer service—Data processing.   I. Sutton, James.   II. Title.
   HD9696.63.A2M53   2005
   005'.068'4—dc22
                                                                          2005005983

09 08 07 06 05   5 4 3 2 1

To Maura, Barbara, and Maeve
Peter Middleton

To my best friend and wisest advisor,
Yeshua Hamashiach
James Sutton

CONTENTS

Part IV: Experiences of Lean Software Producers

PREFACE

"IF THE AUTOMOBILE HAD FOLLOWED the same development as the computer, a Rolls-Royce would today cost $100, get a million miles per gallon, and explode once a year killing everyone inside," or so wagged tech commentator Robert Cringely. We laugh: The idea of $100 luxury cars is ridiculous. Yet, if lean production had not taken hold in automobile manufacture, today you and I would be shelling our $40,000 for an economy car that now costs us under $20,000. If lean hadn't been adopted by other industries, our bill for buying a nondescript kitchen stove would be $1,869 rather than the now-typical $300. And we'd work up to several weeks to earn a whopping $3,050 for a 27″ color TV for the back bedroom, almost ten times the actual current price of $325.[1]

Ironically for the software industry, the hardware we use has gotten cheaper and better far more quickly than have our own products. The cost of computing platform capability has effectively halved every 18 months since the 1960s per Moore's Law, an approximately 4,000,000 times bigger price drop than that of automobiles since 1970. Yet, the programs we write to execute on those platforms haven't dropped very much at all in time-adjusted price over the last three and a half decades . . . certainly not as much as the automobile. And software reliability still significantly lags that of hardware.[2]

Until now, as an industry we've ruled out the one thing that could have helped us significantly improve our development performance; recognizing our fraternity with all other industries so we could learn from them. Software has always assumed it was fundamentally different than traditional production industries.

We the authors of this book have found, through both experience and research, that the opposite is true. Software is like other industries in fundamental ways that have not been commonly recognized. Furthermore, lean production has transformed enough software projects to prove that it works with all kinds of software. When applied as thoughtfully and enthusiastically as it is every day in other sectors, lean has shown that it improves the cost, quality, and user-satisfaction of software programs just as dramatically as it does for more tangible products like cars, ranges, and TVs.

So whether you want to improve your company's bottom line or just to improve the consistency and performance of your in-house software team, read on. We're in the early days of lean software development, and there's still plenty of room left for you to gain a great competitive advantage over your nonlean counterparts. Come join us in the lean software-production journey!

ENDNOTES

1. These hypothetical prices were projected by taking actual 1970 prices and applying the rate of inflation since that time. Lean production hadn't yet made a big difference in most manufacturing in 1970, and mass production was very mature by that date. Without introducing lean, any efficiency improvements since then would likely have been relatively subtle and incremental. So we picked 1970 as a good starting point for the lean/nonlean comparison. The 1970 prices were obtained primarily from the 1997 Annual Report of the Federal Reserve Bank of Dallas, entitled "Time Well Spent: The Declining Real Cost of Living in America," by Richard Alm and W. Michael Cox. This report was still available as of November 23, 2004 at http://www.dallasfed.org/fed/annual/1999p/ar97.pdf. The 1970 prices were extrapolated to the present using the U.S. Department of Labor Bureau of Labor Statistics inflation-calculator, found at http://www.bls.gov/bls/inflation.htm. The only additional allowance made has been made for the overwhelming growth in the features and capabilities of automobiles in 2005 compared to 1970; a well-appointed 1970 model was assumed as the baseline for comparison to the plain 2005 one. Ranges and TVs have remained much more similar across the years, so their comparisons have been made without any additional adjustments. Actual current prices were obtained from various retailers' advertisements.

2. These are big claims, of course, and for the sake of brevity, we don't provide any backup data here. However, the body of this book contains many statistics that support these assertions.

ACKNOWLEDGMENTS

I WOULD LIKE TO THANK QUEEN'S UNIVERSITY, Belfast for the opportunity to carry out research. The support of Professor Danny Crookes and Dr. Pat Corr of the School of Computer Science, for and during my 2003–2004 sabbatical is much appreciated. Dr. Brian Webb of the School of Management has been a wise friend over the years.

The book *Japanese Manufacturing Techniques* by Richard Schonberger (1982) triggered my original interest in 'lean' thinking, which I then applied to software development. My thanks are due to Professor Schonberger for his work.

Professor McArthur Sayers, Imperial College, London asked the hardest questions in the kindest way.

IBM's Thomas Watson Research Center hosted visits to New York and Bangalore, India. This enabled research work on the use of lean thinking in virtual cells.

Dr. Ed Miller of the Software Research Institute, San Francisco encouraged the ideas at an early stage, which was important.

The funding and applied research enabled by the Teaching Company Scheme has been invaluable. The intelligence and efficiency of Professor Raymond Murphy and Dr. Mary Flynn is much appreciated. This has facilitated my software process research work with many companies including: Kainos Software Ltd., CEM Systems Ltd., Andor Technology Ltd., Relay Business Systems Ltd., GCAS Design Ltd., and Apion Telecommunications Software Ltd.

My time as The State University of Ohio as Visiting Professor was made most useful by Dr. Shahrukh Irani, Professor Ho Woo Lee, and Dr. Rajiv Ramnath.

Timberline Software Corporation, Oregon graciously hosted my research visit, and many thanks are due to Curtis Peltz, Amy Flaxel, and Matt Lange for their pioneering work on implementing lean software.

Proworks Corporation, Corvallis, Oregon allowed me to study them for 4 weeks and provided rich insights into the reality of software development. Special thanks are due to Ammon Cookson and Gary Prothero.

Michael Sinocchi, Senior Acquisitions Editor, Productivity Press Inc., has been highly professional. Gary Peurasaari, our Development Editor, has been outstanding and essential for the completion of this book.

Unfortunately, I cannot acknowledge all of the individuals who gave me an opportunity to learn more about software development, but they have my thanks.

Peter Middleton

A handful of people are more responsible than anyone else for my contributions to this book. Sudhir Shah, my manager at Lockheed Martin on several projects, has been a continuous encouragement and inspiration over several years. He is the quintessential lean software leader. Dr. David Parnas is as lean a thinker as you'll find in any industry. Many of the software techniques I've applied to lean software production have either come from or been heavily influenced by him. Our Developmental Editor, Gary Peurasaari, improved the structure and tone of the book considerably. Michael Sinocchi, our Publisher, has been very supportive over the entire (and somewhat overly long) time spent bringing this project to completion. And my wife, Debbie, has been most patient with a husband who at times looked more like a piece of the furniture than the chair upon which he sat writing this book. The chair wore out its springs and its welcome and is now long gone. Save for a woman saintly in understanding, love, and supportiveness, the same end would probably have come of the husband!

James Sutton

INTRODUCTION

FOR MANY YEARS, trends have washed through the software industry, wave upon wave bringing in new methods, techniques, and tools. Each trend has promised to radically improve the performance of software organizations. Most of them have focused on improving our execution of a production system that other industries have long since abandoned for being too limited to meet their business goals.

Industries besides software have found that radical business gains come only from migrating to a better production system. A production system is, loosely speaking, a way of looking at how people should work together to create things (a philosophy), combined with a set of principles that can be translated into actual work practices (a map for implementation). Other industries show us that improving one's production system has nothing to do with adopting new methods, techniques, or tools. It is more like raising the overall sea level to shift where the waves of change appear, how they look, and where they land on the shores of our business needs.

In recent years, the better production system adopted by the rest of the industrial world has been named lean production. As this book will show, lean production makes many of the software trends of late irrelevant. Adopting lean into software is a sea change that will make the waves of change break much closer to the issues and concerns of our industry. Such issues include the satisfaction of our customers, the cost-effectiveness of our organizations, and the humanity of our workplaces. Lean waves will spend less energy on today's sandbars of arcane technical issues that do nothing for bottom-line business results. And here, as in other industries, the beneficiaries will be stakeholders of all sorts—workers, managers, investors, customers, and the public at large.

Lean production gives the software industry a way to view itself in the same way that we view any other commercial activity. This is possible because the same overarching principles that work for other industries work equally well for software. Yet, for reasons ranging from the intangibility of "1"s and "0"s, to (in a few cases) garden-variety hubris, the software industry has always thought of itself as being fundamentally different from all other industries.

Occasionally, analysts point out how badly our industry's insular and maverick attitude has served it. "The software industry produces bad products . . . Software makers have done nothing to utilize better production methods because of the mistaken belief that creating software is not a traditional manufacturing process—that it is somehow different and unique."[1] However, these constructively critical voices are few, faint, and drowned out by mainstream software writings that pepper the journals with phrases such as "unlike practically all other industries, software...."[2] Of course, the practices of the software industry must accommodate the things that are unique about it. Yet, all industries must make such adaptations, since each one has its own special issues. It is wrongheaded to think that idiosyncrasies occur only in software.

Through both project experiences and field observations, the authors have met people who have acted boldly and insightfully on the belief that the laws of industry in general apply to software in particular. These people have won for their organizations greatly improved productivity, predictability, quality, and customer satisfaction—the measures that really count. Furthermore, their gains far exceed the few percentage-point bumps (at best) that riding the waves of tool, technique, and process improvements has brought to the rest of the software world. Their example is a little like the rise of renaissance city-states in the midst of medieval kingdoms: The new thinking is releasing inherent potential that the old thinking not only doesn't think is possible, but doesn't even realize exists.

Unfortunately, the renaissance mindset is still in a small minority. While researching this book, we found few software people who were familiar with even the most basic concepts of industry in general. Furthermore, hardly anyone in the software industry was aware of the foundational ideas of lean production. When the word "lean" has been used in our field at all, it's mostly been assigned to popular approaches like object orientation, extreme programming, enterprise information management, and knowledge engineering. While many of those approaches can be useful in the right context, they have little to do with the ideas of lean production found in the rest of the industrial world.

For over two hundred years, manufacturers of all sorts of products have been sharing with each other their innovations and production improvements; indeed, practically everything short of patents and detailed technical processes. And all industries have benefited from the resulting communal pool of knowledge. When we in the software industry fail to dip into this pool, we cut ourselves off from the collected and enduring wisdom of many people in many other fields. In short, we end up reinventing the wheel, over and over again. This wastes time, money, and resources. It leads to many needless business failures. Our isolationist attitude has deprived us of many helpful and mature models for understanding and improving our own youthful field.

The biggest irony is that, without their realizing it, the overwhelming majority of today's software organizations are nevertheless using classic production systems that have been used and studied to death by other industries. Those industries long ago moved on to more effective approaches, the current leading edge being the topic of our book, lean production.

Understanding how these outdated production systems worked in the worlds of other industries helps us to recognize when we've adopted them into our own. It also reveals to us the ways these systems limit our potential, because we see how they limited others. We learn why and where to replace our less-effective approaches with the better ones now common in forerunning fields such as automobiles. Then we can put them into practice relatively easily, using in many cases the same project management skills we've worked to build up over the years. In the end, we radically improve our business effectiveness, as several software organizations have done already.

Why Should You Take the Lean Journey?

We've said that companies in other industries benefit when they switch to lean production. Software has had a few large, deliverable developments that have demonstrated how lean can give us the same results. One is a major embedded-software project[3] in which Jim helped inject several aspects of lean production. Lean production helped productivity more than double compared to industry norms, while errors and anomalies simultaneously dropped to one-tenth the typical levels for that type of software (Appendix A has more details). Firsthand Jim saw similar gains on an information-processing system on which he played a similar role, so the benefits work across different types of software. This book examines these and other examples from our personal experiences and from the software industry at large.

The universality of lean is hopeful for us in yet another way: Software techniques turn over every two or three years on average. Yet, lean production is essentially independent of specific technologies and therefore easily outlasts them. This means that a company that builds on the foundation of lean production won't be competitively pressured to completely rethink and rebuild its processes every time another "latest technological breakthrough" comes down the pike. Jim has seen this strength work out wonderfully for the Lockheed Martin Aeronautics ("LM Aero") plant in Marietta, Georgia: technology was implemented where it made senseand much less retooling was applied than most others in our industry. The principles of lean production have helped LM Aero to choose durable software technologies and to avoid technologies that don't contribute much to meaningful business goals and therefore don't last very long in the marketplace. All this has helped the lean LM projects continue to measurably increase their margins above competitors in the industry, based on productivity, schedule predictability, product quality, worker retention, and customer satisfaction (details on the LM Aero experience in this regard are also in Appendix A). If "faster, better, cheaper" and more pleasing products aren't what we're aiming for, then why are we in business?

As important as company performance is, though, it is just as important to look at the need for lean production from a higher perspective. There's more at stake than the prosperity of our individual organizations. For instance, the increasing trend to outsource first-world software jobs to second- and third-world countries, if not addressed immediately, could soon decimate the IT and telecom first-world markets.

A Reuters article[4] cited a 2003 study conducted by Gartner Inc., "the world's biggest high-tech forecasting firm," predicting that one job in ten in the fields of computer services and software development would soon move to emerging-market countries. An Associated Press article in mid-2003 noted that the software jobs that had lately moved to emerging markets were both highly technical (typical of Silicon Valley positions with five year's experience) and were saving the outsourcing corporations considerable amounts of money ($20 per hour offshore vs. comparable American positions at $65 per hour).[5] In the Dallas area alone, thousands of IT and telecom jobs from large and small companies left and moved across the Pacific, largely to India.

Outsourcing has been going on for a long time in other industries. Their history shows that the only way to keep a company's center of competitiveness, as well as its jobs, anchored in expensive labor markets is to beat the bottom-line performance of the outsourcing and offshore alternatives. *The only approach in the last thirty years that has been able to beat off-shore alternatives is true lean production.* Going lean is software's only realistic strategy for preventing a rust belt landscape spreading across many high-paying software job markets of the United States and Europe in the coming years.

For those who want to bring home the benefits of lean production to their organizations, this book provides plenty of material for getting started. If you are in either of our two target audiences, leaders or developers, you can help bring this about. Even better is for both groups to work together. For leaders, there is information here about prior lean software efforts and how to apply lean principles to current and future projects. For developers, there is help with creating lean software processes and executing genuinely lean projects. Covering both has made for a relatively large book: While not all of it will be useful or interesting to everyone, we believe everything here is necessary to do justice to both groups.

In the remainder of this introduction, we share some of our reasons for writing this book. This should help you understand our goals and biases (in the interest of full disclosure!).

The Western and Eastern Perspectives of Lean

The book *The Machine That Changed The World*[6] presented the results of the multiyear IMVP (International Motor Vehicle Program) study by the Massachusetts Institute of Technology. The IMVP catalogued and analyzed the best practices of the automotive industry of the late twentieth century. These practices had a conceptual basis that was radically different from that of the automobile industry under mass production. Most of the practices and systems were first developed in the East (specifically, Japan), though many were influenced by ideas from Western thinkers like W. Edwards Deming and Henry Ford. These new practices first began to be systematically implemented nearly 50 years ago . . . yet surprisingly, it has only been relatively recently that the automotive industry has coined a name for this distinctive approach to creating products: lean production. Since then, virtually the entire world has adopted these innovations. While progress continues in the East, many important recent developments in lean production have occurred in the West.

The Machine That Changed the World cited numerous examples of how lean production has improved business performance compared to earlier industrial approaches. These include cutting work hours in half, reducing defects by two-thirds, and tripling the skills of individual employees. Of the universally positive impact of the lean production, the book stated, "Only lean thinking has the demonstrated power to produce green shoots of growth all across this landscape within a few years."[7]

For many people, the follow-up book to *The Machine That Changed The World*, entitled *Lean Thinking*,[8] has become the Rosetta Stone of the lean revolution. *Lean Thinking* organized the automotive findings into five lean industrial principles: *value, value stream, flow, pull,* and *perfection. Lean Thinking* gave many examples of how these principals apply to industries besides automobiles. Both books are now so central to the way that Westerners think of lean production that they have essentially defined the subject for this part of the world.

On the other hand, the original masters of lean production, Messrs. Nakao, Nagamatsu, and Ohno who originated the techniques upon which the IMVP study focused, do not view lean production as primarily driven by principles. They say that lean production is about purposes and creating a culture, a culture that involves everyone in a process of continuous improvement toward lean ideals, and a culture that has no need or desire for superheroes. Culture, in the way these Japanese masters have used the word, is an environment and a philosophy within a company that promotes the achievements of its common goals. It especially is not a synonym for style.

The Japanese view is that the priorities of lean production are as follows: 1) Purpose, 2) Culture, 3) Principles, and 4) Techniques. They say that *to practice lean production you must build a culture that is based on lean purposes.* For these lean masters, the way to attain lean production is to start practicing it as an organization with the help of a lean expert or *sensei* (a Japanese term for a personal teacher with a mastery of a body of knowledge). Most Western lean books to date have implied (though probably not intentionally) that the third and fourth of these lean priorities, principles and techniques, are the most important ones. This tends to sidetrack companies from doing first things first.

We accept the priorities of the lean masters, including their position on the importance of having a *sensei*. But we also believe the Western lean experts have hit it right—at least, for those who look at the world through Western lenses—that we need an appropriate model upon which to base our understanding of lean production. Unfortunately, there aren't any pure examples of a lean culture in the software industry to use for model-building. Likewise, while a number of lean software experiments exist, we haven't found any software organizations making the top-down commitments needed to create a true lean culture. We haven't even seen any thorough models for comparing software to other industries in general.

Consequently, our field hasn't identified the parallels between ourselves and others that we will need to be able to learn from them. It is the old chicken-and-egg problem: Without valid parallels, how can one start applying the insights of other industries to one's own? Therefore, our first order of business in applying lean production to software is to provide a model for showing how software relates to other industries.

Our second order of business is to discuss the five principles of lean production and show how they apply to software production. When we talk about the principles of lean production, again, remember that the principles themselves do not represent lean culture. But, by looking at concrete examples of people practicing lean principles in software production, you should also be able to read between the lines and gain an understanding of the purpose and culture that is needed to make lean principles and techniques effective. Simply put, studying principles is one of the clearest ways to look at the entire scope of lean production. Then it is a matter of using them in the right context to improve and sustain software quality and productivity.

Our final order of business will be to show examples of how lean production has been applied to the actual projects of several companies as they've created different types of software.

To summarize, the Japanese masters have a holistic perspective on lean thinking, while the IMVP view is an analytic one that extracts principles from the whole.[9] We believe these approaches don't have to be an either/or proposition. They complement each other.

This book will take an analytic approach like that put forth in the IMVP-inspired books. We've patterned the structure of our discussion of lean software development around the principles that *Lean Thinking* used to structure the fundamental ideas of lean production. While at times the five lean principles of value, value stream, flow, pull, and perfection play out in unique ways in the software industry, the use of these principles in software is mostly parallel to that of other industries. We include a few analogies from the IMVP and other places to help relate some of the more abstract ideas about software leanness to physical examples that most people will find more concrete and intuitive.

And even though we've taken the analytic approach, if you are starting down the lean path, please find someone who can act as a *sensei* to help your organization transform itself. Implementing lean will undoubtedly change the dynamics within the company. This can be quite an adjustment for everyone involved, from the top on down. Obtaining such help is the single most valuable thing you can do to succeed and sustain the transformation to lean production.

Keeping an open and encompassing mind is just as helpful for looking within the software industry as it is for sorting out the broad differences between Eastern and Western thought. One of the things that's made it hard to deal with the software industry as a whole is that the number of domains where software is used has mushroomed, contributing to the growing fragmentation of the industry over the last couple of decades. Between those domains, the development methods have greatly diverged. For example, how much is there in common between developing, say, commercial B2B applications using Microsoft's .NET, and safety-critical embedded nuclear power-plant controllers? Lean thinking has shown that stranger bedfellows than these—such as elevator manufacturers, jet engine producers, restauranteurs, homebuilders, soft-drink bottlers, and warehouse managers—have learned from each other and improved their business effectiveness through the common ground of the lean paradigm. Given the proven universality of lean production, we are confident that knowing the principles of lean production can help you get started on implementing lean in your situation, whichever type of software you develop.

How a Researcher and a Practitioner Came to See Eye to Eye on Lean

In an interview a few years ago, Dr. Niklaus Wirth, a pioneer of many of today's most foundational software-engineering concepts and practices, was asked the question: "A recent IEEE survey of what lies ahead in software revealed that there is basically no intersection between the opinions of academics and practitioners. As one of the few whose work has been influential in both fields, what's your opinion (or perhaps your secret)?"[10] Wirth answered, "If there is a secret at all, then it is that of being both a programmer and a professor. The division is rather unfortunate and the source of many problems . . . the drifting apart of practice and academia is unfortunate."[11]

This book now brings together both research and practical application. The practical principles and the academic research referred to in this book have all passed through live-fire testing in the software marketplace. There have been some shining successes and some spectacular failures. This book draws upon all these experiences. We the authors have done both research and practical large-scale software developments. We began writing this book shortly after crossing paths and discovering that we agreed upon three major points that are now at the foundation of this book.

1. The software industry is well suited to, and will benefit greatly from, lean production.
2. The lean paradigm has at best only superficially affected the software industry. Worse, the industry's present course is leading away from, rather than toward, lean production.
3. Everything needed to allow lean development of all sorts of software is now available.

The researcher's voice in this book is from Dr. Peter Middleton, an academic at Queen's University Belfast, Northern Ireland, once the home of Dr. C. A. R. "Tony" Hoare, Fellow of the Royal Society (FRS) and Distinguished Fellow of the British Computer Society.[12] For several years, Dr. Middleton's academic research has focused on the investigation of various implementations of lean principles by software organizations. Peter has also been a practitioner on real programs in various software industries, so his research is rooted in practice and by no means locked in an ivory tower.

The practitioner's voice is from Jim Sutton. Jim has led in many different managing and technical roles, such as lead software architect of the central integrating software of a fielded billion-dollar Lockheed-Martin aircraft program. Implementing lean principles in software has also been part of several other large embedded and information-processing systems on which he's worked over the last 20+ years. He has recently been sharing his time between consulting with the U.K. National Air Transportation System on how to implement a more lean approach in their project to update the London Air Traffic Control System, and leading a team that is integrating and verifying the cockpit software for the Lockheed-Martin Joint Strike Fighter (F-35). His industry, aerospace, has aspects of both a hard manufacturing industry (e.g., vehicle manufacture) where lean production is already well understood and systematically practiced, and the rather looser characteristics of the software industry. This combination has helped uncover many ways that lean production can be applied to software development.

Our regional differences also broaden the scope of this book. Peter is a European with a focus on commercial software development, while Jim is an American who's focused on software development for governments as well as commercial customers. Each of us draws from different schools of software thought and education. That these different perspectives have led us to essentially the same lean conclusions has, for us, further confirmed the universality and helpfulness of lean production for software development.

The structure of this book draws on both the practical and research backgrounds of its authors. Specifically,

- Part I: Chapters 1 through 7 provide an overview of the three industrial paradigms, largely from the practitioner's view. We discuss the general principles of craft, mass, and lean production and compare these principles with some of the most influential current software practices. This section is presented from the practitioner's perspective; Jim Sutton is the dominant voice.

- Part II: Chapters 8 through 14 address how to apply lean to the front end of the lifecycle so we can build a strong partnership with our customers. This section is also presented from the practitioner's perspective.

- Part III: Chapters 15 through 21 address how to apply lean to the back end of the lifecycle, where we work to find the best combination of lean techniques and software technologies to create products that delight our customers and build our businesses. This section is also presented from the practitioner's perspective.

- Part IV: Chapters 22 through 26 include several case studies of organizations that have applied lean concepts to software development, and ideas extracted "bottom up" from their experiences. Most of their lean implementations are compatible with the discussions in Parts I through III. However, there are some contrasting ideas as well. We haven't tried to conform their views to our own: Lean software is far too early in its evolution to begin narrowing it down to an orthodoxy yet. The alternative ideas may help you—if nothing else—better define to your own satisfaction what lean software is and what it is not. This section is presented from the researcher's perspective; Peter Middleton is the the dominant voice.

- Conclusion: This chapter presents a process with methods and strategies for getting lean actually implemented in your organization. It summarizes lessons learned from all lean software production efforts to date. And it also gives answers to some common objections to lean. As with the Introduction, the material in this chapter is intended for both practitioners and researchers.

- Appendix A: The body of this book refers repeatedly to one of the most lean software projects to date, the 382J aircraft Mission Computer software development. To avoid slowing down the flow of the earlier chapters, most of the details of this project have been placed here. The even more productive C-27J project, reusing and expanding upon many artifacts and processes from the 382J, is also discussed.

Though there are two distinct author voices in this book, our philosophies and conclusions are largely consistent and compatible. Being human, we do occasionally differ . . . but applying lean is not an exact science; differences between organizations and situations should sometimes lead to different courses (besides, neither of us claims to have cornered the market on understanding!). Please look at our few disparities as a broader base upon which you can start forming your own lean approach.

The viewpoints and explanations we present throughout this volume are designed to make the ideas behind lean production more useful to you, whether you are a leader or developer in the many fields of the software-engineering community. It is our fervent hope that this book will help you go a little further in leveraging your available resources to achieve great personal, business, and societal goals.

ENDNOTES

1. "Building Solid Software," Adam Kolawa, *CIO Magazine*, August 15, 2002.
2. P. McBreen, *Software Craftsmanship: The New Imperative*, Reading, MA: Addison Wesley, 2001; and an almost identical statement in "NO ePATENTS: A Petition to Save Software Innovation in Europe," http://petition.eurolinux.org/pr/pr1.html.
3. Lockheed-Martin 382J Mission Computer software; 250,000 flight source lines of code. There will be more on this project throughout Parts I to III, and especially in Appendix A.
4. "Report: 1 in 10 tech jobs may go overseas," Reuters, July 30, 2003.
5. "Tech jobs leave U.S. for India, Russia: Job exports may imperil U.S. programmers," AP, July 14, 2003.
6. J. Womack, D. Jones, D. Roos, *The Machine That Changed The World*, New York, NY: Harper Perennial, 1991.
7. James P. Womack, Daniel T. Jones, *Lean Thinking*, New York, NY: Simon & Schuster, 1996, pg. 28.
8. James P. Womack, Daniel T. Jones, *Lean Thinking*, New York, NY: Simon & Schuster, 1996.
9. For a holistic perspective on lean thinking, see Jeffrey K. Liker, *The Toyota Way*, New York, NY: McGraw-Hill, 2004. The book covers 14 Toyota management principles that also include Womack's five lean principles.
10. Dr. Carlo Pescio, "A Few Words with Niklaus Wirth," *Software Development*, Vol. 5 No. 6, June 1997.
11. Ibid.
12. At a lecture at the University, Dr. Hoare said, "There are two ways of constructing a software design: One way is to make it so simple that there are obviously no deficiencies, and the other way is to make it so complicated that there are no obvious deficiencies. The first method is far more difficult." The simplicity that comes with developing software under the lean paradigm fits right into the values that Dr. Hoare commends.

PART ONE

What Kind of Industry is Software?

There's Three Kinds
of Industries

O VER THE COURSE OF ITS EVENTFUL HISTORY, industry has evolved through three paradigms. It began in an embryonic stage now often called *craft production*. Later, it metamorphosed into something quite different, which we now call *mass production*. In recent years, it has moved on to yet another incarnation, called *lean production*.

At any given point in time, the majority of enterprises in any particular industry will be operating under one of these three paradigms. Joel Arthur Barker states, "A Paradigm is a set of rules and regulations (written or unwritten) that does two things: 1) it establishes or defines boundaries; and 2) it tells you how to behave inside the boundaries in order to be successful."[1] We'll discuss how the main paradigm at work in an industry largely determines its business effectiveness. The force that drives industries to evolve through these stages is that each subsequent paradigm is more effective for achieving a company's business goals than the previous one.

Craft production relies almost totally on the skill of individuals. There is little or no standardization or process definition. Craft production's major practices are driven almost totally by the interests of the owners, with little thought for the concerns of the workers or the needs of the customers (though in a craft-production business, the workers are often also the owners, so in that case and sense, are considered).

Mass production places its greatest reliance on standardization and process rather than individual skill. Yet, its interests still lie almost exclusively with the owners . . . who, by the time a business has entered this paradigm, have usually gained possession through their investment of funds rather than by hands-on involvement in day-to-day operations.

Lean production shares some characteristics of each of the previous stages but compensates for their weaknesses and adds new strengths of its own. It greatly broadens the focus to include all stakeholders; owners and investors to be sure, but also customers (often even more strongly than owners), employees, and public concerns. More importantly, unlike craft and mass production, lean production removes waste from—and continuously improves industrial processes by—effectively utilizing employees, equipment, and capital to produce and deliver products that satisfy each customer.

In any given business, you may see aspects of more than one paradigm at work. Nevertheless, one paradigm will be dominant, and the characteristics of any others present will be muted in comparison.

Beware of How and What You Measure—A Sad Tale

In the last few years, all sorts of people have become very interested in measuring the condition of software organizations. The measurers include customers, academics, regulators, and governmental bodies. Though we are speculating on this, it seems likely that one of the reasons the measurers come from these groups, rather than from the software businesses themselves, is because *the measurers are also the people who have been the most left out and poorly served by the software industry to date.* They have a legitimate interest in finding out what's going on.

Most types of software assessments today look for process maturity. A few evaluate technological sophistication. Unfortunately for both the businesses and the measurers, as we shall see, such criteria are practically useless for answering the questions that are most important to either the measurers—such as "Will the software organizations serve our true needs?"—or the software organizations—such as "Will our organization meet its financial goals?" "Will it satisfy our customers?" and "Will it be able to attract and retain the workers we need?"

What all sorts of industries other than software have discovered is that performance on these important questions correlates much more closely to industrial paradigms than to process maturity or technological sophistication. Once a company identifies its industrial paradigm, it develops a better predictive insight into how well the industry (or individual enterprise) will perform and what its major weaknesses will be. It stands to reason that this applies to software as well.

This brings us to a sad tale that demonstrates the old maxim that measuring the wrong things leads one to the wrong conclusions. In the mid-1980s, Jim Sutton watched at a slight distance (knowing some of the people involved) as an industry project broke all sorts of new ground in processes and technologies.[2] Even by today's standards, you could consider this project advanced. The project's product was an information-processing system. The scope was twenty developers for two years. Because of its size, the project institutionalized all its practices. Project management collected metrics and analyzed them to help them improve their decision making. The project used strong, tool-based configuration management that not only protected files but also had procedures for enforcing developer roles. It used a CASE (Computer-Aided Software Engineering) environment with a graphical interface: Unlike many early CASE environments, this one did its job as advertised.

The project trained everyone consistently and sufficiently. It enforced common methodologies, and applied consistent standards and structured peer reviews to ensure the quality of the products. It used structured data flow analysis to develop its requirements. As you probably know, this type of analysis is still in use as part of several object-oriented methodologies; and when employed in the proper context, is still considered an appropriate choice for this type of system.

In today's terms, we'd say the project was "repeatable," "defined," and even in many respects "managed" (using the terms of the SEI CMM[3]). If an entire company followed these practices, it would be at the very doorstep of a CMM level 4 out of a possible 5. And all this happened long before the earliest widespread CMM industry assessments showed that most software organizations were only at SEI level 1, i.e., that their processes were usually almost completely undefined.

From the beginning, the project personnel made trips to the customer's site to discuss the customer's needs. The first major design review occurred a year and a half into the two-year project. It was scheduled to last three days. The team was confident that the thoroughness of its work would make the review a mere formality. They were set for rapid coding and testing, to easily meet their scheduled delivery date.

A few hours into the first day of presentations, the customer interrupted the presenter: "You have decomposed my requirements in a way that cannot be allocated to the hardware architecture of my system. Come back when you have something that can possibly be implemented." The project team was thunderstruck. At first, they couldn't believe the customer knew what he was talking about ... but a little more investigation showed he was right. They could not implement the proposed system.

What followed was an astounding example of process-maturity reversion. With only six months left to go before scheduled delivery, the project let go of most of its people. It then assigned its two best developers as "superprogrammers" to "get the system out." After six months of eighty-plus hour weeks in a dark room with an unending supply of prepackaged pastries, they succeeded. The customer accepted the new system, though he was not happy since his confidence had been largely shattered at the review.

The postscript to this tale is that, over time, it became clear that the delivered system was incomplete and that the project had still overlooked several crucial (to the customer) but unstated requirements. The system was also practically unmaintainable except by the superprogrammers, who had—of course—moved on to other projects and were no longer available. Shortly after taking delivery, the customer abandoned the software. The organization lost the next contract, and the next, and never received another contract from that source. They forever lost a good customer who had given them a lot of lucrative business in the past.

The Industrial Paradigm Determines the Business Effectiveness

If having a mature process and using high technology leads to business success, as is assumed by most software-assessment approaches, the sad tale project would have been one of the major success stories of the 1980s. Instead, it was one of the major disaster stories in the history of the software profession. Why? We only need look at other industries to find the answer.

Process maturity and *high technology* as standards for measuring and assessing industrial capabilities have never assured long-term success. They are usually not even particularly good indicators of short-term success. Detroit had mature processes in the 1960s, yet it lost much of its market share to the greater value and quality of the Japanese automobiles of the 1970s and 1980s. Detroit's famous robotic-automation and other technology experiments of the latter period did nothing to help it reclaim its market or profitability. Even the German automaker Porsche's technological prowess did not shield it from a serious slump from 1989 to 1992, in which it lost 72 percent of its unit sales.

Japan's superior achievements in autos during that same period were based not on process definition nor on high technology, but on having a more powerful idea of what industry itself is all about. Indeed, from the time that Japan laid its foundations for beating Detroit (beginning in the 1950s), Japan's technologies were largely inferior to those of the U.S. manufacturers: "The war-ravaged Japanese economy was starved for capital . . . massive purchases of the latest Western production technology were quite impossible."[4] Japan could not rely on technology to gain its advantage. Detroit could not count on technology to keep it. Detroit began stabilizing its business base against the Japanese only when it started adopting their lean worldview and practices.

You win or lose the business game through your choice of industrial paradigm. Given a level playing field, a mass producer will beat a craft one, and a lean producer will beat them both. This result is practically independent of the producer's relative process maturities and technologies. "Lean production vs. mass production requires: ½ the human effort in the factory, ½ the manufacturing space, ½ the investment tools, ½ the engineering hours, ½ the time to develop new products."[5]

This leaves the legitimate question of whether the lean paradigm will produce these kinds of results for the software industry. Though many people assume that software is fundamentally different from other industries, software does share certain characteristics with all of them. A major one is being prone to waste creeping into production processes. As we alluded to earlier in this chapter, lean production puts a lot of attention into removing waste from industrial processes. The Northwest Lean Manufacturing Network (NWLEAN), an organization promoting dissemination of lean techniques and information among over

800 member companies, answers the question of whether lean production is suitable to fields like software as follows: "Every 'system' contains waste. Whether you are producing a product, processing a material, or providing a service, there are elements that are considered 'waste.' (Or, said another way, something that does not provide value to your customer.) The techniques for analyzing systems, identifying and reducing waste, and focusing on the customer are applicable in any system, and in any industry."[6] The characteristics of software that on the surface seem most likely to exempt it from comparisons to general industrial principles, turn out not to even matter—waste is waste no matter how you look at it.

In short, the standard of measure that gives the most useful answers about the business-effectiveness of any industry is the producer's industrial paradigm. Refined processes and advanced technologies can be helpful to businesses only when they are firmly placed in their proper role of supporting good business thinking. They are never legitimate goals in their own right.

If you want to improve your software enterprise, you must begin by correctly identifying which paradigm your enterprise is operating under. Then you begin dealing realistically and therefore successfully with all this implies in your world. Then you can lay a foundation for future efforts to change the causes of these problems and make things better.

Chapters 2 and 3 will examine in detail the major traits and implications of each of the three paradigms in general industrial terms. The latter chapters in Part I, i.e., 4 through 7, look at how the three industrial paradigms have affected some of the most favored practices of the software industry. These brief sketches will help us identify our industry's predominant paradigm and its implications for our industry's current condition. These examples will go a long way toward explaining the "why" of what is wrong in software. Practically everyone already knows the "what."

ENDNOTES

1. Joel Arthur Barker, *Paradigms: The Business of Discovering the Future*, New York, NY: Harper Business, 1993, pg. 32.
2. To glean what is to be learned from this project, it is unnecessary to name the project or the company involved. Indeed, it couldn't be discussed here except by omitting those details . . . and it is far too good an example to be left out. Other examples in the book will include more specifics.
3. "Software Engineering Institute Capability Maturity Model," discussed in much greater detail in Chapter 5.
4. J. Womack, D. Jones, D. Roos, *The Machine That Changed The World*, New York, NY: Harper Perennial, 1991, pg. 50.
5. Ibid., inside cover page.
6. http://www.nwlean.net/leadfaqs.htm; November 13, 2002.

Understanding Earlier Production Systems

To begin assessing the industrial state of the software business, we must be familiar with how the three types of production systems work in other industries. Then we need to look at how well suited each is to software development. In this chapter, we focus in on craft and mass production, the two industrial paradigms that preceded lean. They can still be found, albeit in shrinking pockets, in various situations worldwide.

Craft Production—The Niche Market

Craft production was civilization's only production system before the industrial revolution and the advent of division of labor. It entailed the practice of making things one at a time, by a skilled craftsperson (artisan) who was often a member of a regulated guild, and who used apprentices to assist and perpetuate a specific trade.

In most cases, even today, when a new industry starts out, it practices craft production. A craft producer is anyone who creates products using their personal expertise and skills rather than some systematic approach (such as an assembly line). A nascent industry hasn't had time to learn the unique lessons for its field, lessons that are essential for moving on to the later paradigms. These later paradigms apply guiding principles to lessons-learned to derive specific processes and practices. The few industries that skip the craft production stage are usually spun off from other well-established industries and will likely begin at or near the same industrial maturity as their parents.

Craft production is the easiest paradigm to understand because it has little theory or organization behind it. One could call it the "anything goes" paradigm. Essentially, workers convert designs into products in any manner they please. Because the only places that capture and store the business's lessons are the heads of the workers, craft businesses depend much more on the experience, knowledge, and skill of the individual workers than do the other two paradigms. (Of course, any production system requires at least some people with specialized levels of experience and skill.)

As a result, no two craft-produced items are the same. Even if created from the same design, each will still be somewhat different because of the variations in the human touch involved in making them.[1] People often consider this to be part of the craft paradigm's charm. Each buyer knows he or she is getting a one-of-a-kind item. Since some uniqueness is a given, it costs relatively little more (at least percentage-wise, compared to the base price) to customize any given unit for each customer. But the price is often still very dear. Though craft production is highly flexible and customer-responsive, it is expensive; it deals with products—as well as product defects—item by item rather than systematically by type.

The opportunity to be creative is one of the biggest attractions of being a craft producer. Every single production item has its own challenges and artistry. A worker will often stay with the same item throughout its entire development, thus participating in most of its production activities. Workers feel challenged and valued, so they tend to like their jobs and take ownership of them. Indeed, craft workers are often their business's financial owners, as well as the near totality of its workforce. There are no great benefits to having large numbers of employees in a craft shop, since the emphasis is on applying outstanding individual effort on an integrated and complex job, rather than on applying an army of workers to many repetitions of well-defined, simple tasks.

Some people view craft production as synonymous with high quality. Most of us have warm feelings when we hear that something has been "handcrafted." Nevertheless, the quality of crafted goods depends completely on the level of skills and commitment of the craftsmen. These can be low as well as high. But whether the item is well or poorly made, the expensiveness of craft products compared to their mass- or lean-produced counterparts puts severe financial pressures on even the best craft businesses.

In the operations of the Swedish truck and bus manufacturer Scania-Vabis, as it was operated until late in the 1930s, you can clearly see how using craft production affects a large, modern business. With protected niche markets and customers who demanded customized solutions, Scania-Vabis did reasonably well for a while in a world that had already largely converted to mass production. "The workshop at Scania-Vabis was manned by a highly skilled team of craftsmen and was very flexible. The engines and chassis were produced direct from the blueprints, and the design of the working methods was left to the workers. Supervisors and foremen were recruited from among the workers. The craftsmen set their own wages, and this was normally twice as high as the hourly wage rate. They were regarded as among the best-paid mechanics in Sweden. The way production was organized left much to be desired regarding discipline, order, and the principles for calculating wages."[2] By the end of the 1930s, cost pressures became more than even Scania-Vabis could ignore, and the company was forced to adopt many of the mass-production innovations already common in the rest of the world.

This phenomenon continues to the present. When enough businesses in a market switch to mass production, the remaining craft producers are put under great stress. Typically, they find their opportunities shrinking to a few exclusive niches. Craft producers may even find themselves compromising their own paradigm and incorporating elements of mass production as their only alternative to going out of business altogether. Not long ago, one of the most famous and admired of all the remaining craft-producers, Aston Martin, was forced by cost concerns to slot some assembly-line parts into their automobiles. In markets that are more cost-sensitive than luxury automobiles, mass production naturally supplants craft production altogether. In no modern markets (except perhaps "arts and crafts," where defects are sometimes part of the attraction), does craft production beat the later paradigms head to head.

Craft production still exists today in a few places in older industries. It works best for products that are small or simple, or for products that differ radically one from another. In the first case, the simplicity of the product inherently limits the unknowns and the options with which the craftsmen must deal. In the second, the strengths of mass production do not provide sufficient leverage to compete, since mass production works best for making many copies off the same pattern. Radical differences between products can easily be accommodated in craft production, because the work is always largely custom. For example, a craft builder of custom guitars can as easily mount one type or style of sound pickup as another.

There aren't many markets with such variability, however. "In activities ranging from motor vehicles to aircraft to industrial machinery to personal computers to home building, the trajectory of product technology is quite predictable. What's more, the end-use demand of customers is inherently quite stable and largely for replacement. We believe that the volatility—the perceived marketplace chaos—in these industrial activities is in fact self-induced."[3]

Is Craft Production Suited to Software?

Craft production does not work very well for software. Instead of software products becoming smaller and simpler, the trend is for them to become more and more enveloping. Business products subsume more and more functions that used to be served by individual and often independent utilities and programs. Microsoft Windows is an archetypal example, with its continual expansion into networking, multimedia, and personal organization capabilities, among others.

Industrial software also becomes more generalized and capable with time, from embedded microcontrollers to integrated avionics. This means there are ever fewer small-product niches in the software industry. The other craft stronghold, the ability to create unique products that radically differ one from another, continues to provide opportunity at the extreme technological bleeding edge. But such technologies tend to consolidate and their products turn into commodities rather quickly, ceasing to be unique products suitable for craft production. Nevertheless, software finds itself in such situations more often then products of most industries; so according to the criteria we've just discussed, craft production should beat mass production for developing such programs or systems. The remaining question is whether lean would beat craft in such situations. That it does, and does so convincingly, will become clearer as we get into the later chapters.

Five Principles of Mass Production

Eventually, most craft-level industries come to understand themselves well enough to gain a consensus position on the things that are consistently true about their operations. This understanding gives the businesses within the industries the foothold for the next logical progression in industrial maturity, mass production. That is, they apply principles of mass production to the body of knowledge built up during the industry's craft phase, and thereby improve their cost-effectiveness.

The switch to the mass production paradigm creates rules and standardizations that reduce the costliness and inefficiencies that occur from having to depend solely upon the skills of its workers. This leads to lower costs to the consumer, and in turn, puts pressure on the remaining craft businesses to evolve to mass production.

As we just mentioned, there are several recognized and recurring characteristics or principles of mass production. Five of the most important are:

1. Repeatability.
2. Large infrastructures.
3. Efficiency.
4. Organizational gigantism.
5. Technocentrism.

To the degree that a production environment exhibits these characteristics, it is implementing mass production. Some of these principles have a notably dark side (e.g., worker boredom or burnout, and separation of thinking from doing). Proponents of mass production sometimes argue that the negatives are simply the results of mass production done badly. Their argument seems a bit strained: For a hundred years, the values of the mass paradigm have relentlessly driven mass production implementations to adopt these characteristics. Let's zoom in on these principles to gain a little more insight into how mass production affects the climate of a business.

Repeatability

The first thing that pops into many people's minds when one mentions mass production is the repetitiveness of the assembly line. Some of the funniest situations ever filmed have involved the assembly line . . . such as the little tramp's mishaps at the nut-tightening station on the relentlessly moving assembly line in Charlie Chaplin's *Modern Times* (1936), or, a personal favorite of mine, Lucy Ricardo's falling behind on wrapping a conveyer belt's endless supply of chocolate candies in the "Job Switching" episode (1952) of *I Love Lucy*. The rapid and inhuman repetition that makes these situations so funny—and that makes mass production so, well, productive—is enabled by the first and most important mass-production principle: repeatability.

We usually think of repeatability as applying solely to actions. However, repeatability of actions alone is a simplistic view of the reason for creating an assembly line. "The key to mass production wasn't—as many people then and now believe—the moving, or continuous, assembly line [with its repetitive actions on consecutive parts]. *Rather it was the complete and consistent interchangeability of parts and the simplicity of attaching them to each other.*"[4] Part interchangeability depends on part repeatability. Unless one can reliably produce parts that are enough alike to take each other's place within a larger product, one cannot fully gain the benefits of interchangeability. Thus, repeatability applies to both actions and parts.

Eli Whitney pioneered the idea of interchangeable parts in the late 1700s when he created a system for manufacturing muskets. Interchangeable parts have relatively tight specifications, a key characteristic of part repeatability. The first inventor, however, to implement part repeatability consistently, accurately, and rapidly enough to drive a large-scale industry was Henry Ford. Without part repeatability, the only way to build an integrated product is to hire highly-skilled expert craftsmen who can adapt the varying parts into a working whole; in other words, to revert to craft production. The advent of part repeatability facilitated all the subsequent benefits of mass production.

Another manifestation of the repeatability goal is worker interchangeability. This has much in common philosophically with part interchangeability. If one can truly "plug and play" different workers at will, then the production line need never slow down, and product variance will be minimized when replacements occur: "Workers on the line were as replaceable as the parts on the car."[5] By this principle, Charlie and Lucy should have been able to keep up with the machinery . . . after all, *somebody* else presumably did before they came along. Mass assembly lines are hard on workers, who must precisely and rapidly perform repetitive and usually simple tasks. Tedium is inherent and institutionalized in the job description of an assembly line worker: Any kind of job change for the sake of variety would interrupt and slow down the flow of the line and work against the very purpose of the line.

Ford accomplished worker replaceability by "taking the idea of the division of labor to its ultimate extreme . . . the assembler . . . had only one task. Someone, of course, did have to think about how all the parts came together and just what each assembler should do. This was the task for . . . the industrial engineer. Similarly, someone had to arrange for the delivery of parts to the line, usually a production engineer . . . Yet another specialist checked quality. Work that was not done properly . . . called into play . . . the rework men."[6] Fragmenting worker occupations into specialized jobs like quality inspector and process engineer helped achieve worker interchangeability. As quickly as a worker left or was replaced, a new worker of the same description could be inserted into the line and production could immediately resume.

Large Infrastructures

A mass organization becomes even more cost-effective when it combines repeatable parts and replaceable workers with large infrastructures such as bigger buildings and higher-capacity equipment. This synergy addresses the craft production problem that "production costs were high and didn't drop with volume."[7] The power of large infrastructures is that organizations can use them to amortize production costs across production volume. Such amortization gives mass production its greatest competitive advantage over craft production, because it provides a greater return on its capital investments in building the processes of repeatability, processes that in turn increase production volume. Interestingly, many early industrial-revolution mills and factories, still operating under craft production, began to adopt such infrastructures in various degrees and could be considered early precursors of mass production in this regard.

Efficiency

The principle most strongly associated with mass production is efficiency. Merriam Webster's dictionary defines efficiency as "effective operation as measured by a comparison of production with cost (as in energy, time, and money)."[8] The word efficiency has such positive connotations that it seems a heresy to consider that it may have a downside. When we examine how the mass production world implements efficiency, however, its limitations become obvious.

In the context of mass production, efficiency means keeping the company's tools, machinery, and production workers continuously busy. That is, in the mass production paradigm, to be truly efficient, one must constantly keep one's infrastructures operating under full loading. Yet this approach to efficiency really has nothing to do with the true purpose of business, which is producing a product that satisfies the customer (provides value), achieves the company's goals, and makes a profit.[9]

The true purpose of business becomes lost as mass producers resort to complex and labor-intensive means to keep their infrastructures busy. For normal, planned production, mass producers utilize computerized monitoring and projection systems called Material Requirements Planning (MRP), or, on an expanded scope, Manufacturing Resource Planning (MRP II, sometimes also called closed-loop MRP). These systems track the quantities of materials at each stage of an assembly line and time their movement to and through the production equipment. Workers known as expediters deal with the unexpected events that happen while the line is running, by roving back and forth across the assembly line to try to keep the machines fully engaged. They may, for instance, obtain extra input materials for a machine whose input hopper has run dry for some unplanned reason.

Because efficiency is so important to mass production, there is little tolerance for stopping the lines to correct systemic problems that permit or cause defects in the products. Anyone who has worked in a mass production environment will recognize this mindset in the oft-repeated adage that "there's never enough time to do it right in the first place, but there's always enough time to do it over." After-the-fact defect detection and remediation are integral to the mass production paradigm, where the overarching goal is to keep a line perpetually busy. In mass production automobile making, rework can constitute up to 25 percent of the total effort.

Mass production began its single-minded pursuit of efficiency from its very onset: "Many visitors to Highland Park felt that Ford's factory was really one vast machine with each production step tightly linked to the next... The only penalty with this system was inflexibility."[10] This did not seem like much of a loss to the mass producers, however: "[In] the Western [mass production] tendency... line flexibility is not important."[11] Earlier, we saw that mass producers gained a cost advantage by using the assembly line; now we see what they gave up: the flexibility to respond to customer desires, and the flexibility to make changes because of variation in one's market or business, or to improve quality or reduce defects. "It was very important to make the right decision from the beginning. The [car] model, once chosen, must not be changed except very slowly and in gradual stages, as a sudden change... would mean an enormous outlay of capital."[12] This is one of the major weaknesses of the mass paradigm.

Organizational Gigantism

The care and feeding of big infrastructures requires big organizational structures. Mass producers are generally very centralized, and their market advantage is often considered to be roughly proportional to their size. Though Henry Ford was the first to put together all the essential parts of mass production, early industrial revolution textile mills had previously developed some elements of the mass approach. As we mentioned before, many of them picked out certain of their processes and created big infrastructures to support them. Their management needs grew in step: "... Textile mills needed power to operate, which they gained first from water wheels, and later from steam engines. Once those power sources were in place, various belts and pulleys conveyed the power to a great many individual machines. This in turn led to large concentrations of people working efficiently under one roof, as different parts of the production process required close interaction. Industrialists began to grasp the rather new concept of 'economies of scale': The larger a textile plant, the more efficient and profitable it was. In the ensuing competitive battles, the smaller enterprises were ground under by their larger rivals. Bigger became equated with better, and . . . organizational Gigantism was born."[13] Thus, we see how expanding infrastructures demand growing organizations.

Technocentrism

Technology is a powerful tool and there is nothing about it that is intrinsically related to the mass paradigm. Mass production, however, often makes technology an end rather than a means. Faster machines, for instance, in principle allow for a faster assembly line. Thus, much of mass production is enamored with the power of high technology. One manifestation of this is in the German industrial tradition called *technik*, which relies on superior technology as the means to market success.[14]

But high technology carries an implicit price, a price that is difficult to pay in most cases: "High-tech automation only works if the plant can run at 100 percent output and if the cost of the indirect technical support and high-tech tools is less than the value of the direct labor saved."[15] A Toyota experiment, conducted with one of its production plants,[16] tried to implement thorough high-tech automation in a lean context, and failed. Toyota pioneered many of the early ideas of lean production and is as capable as anyone of making a plant productive; that they couldn't make a technocentric operation pay off shows how difficult a feat it truly is. In fact, when you take a closer look at technocentrism, using technology for technology's sake appears to be just another infrastructure that mass producers adopt as a tool to maximize efficiency, once again losing sight of the true purpose of their businesses.

Is Mass Production Suited to Software?

The mass production mind thinks of industrial processes as a chaos that you can corral into order through a few strategies such as task and worker specialization, process standardization, management structure, and automation. Is this approach a good fit for software? Putting it another way, how well does the inherent nature of software lend itself to the assumptions of mass production?

The mass production paradigm was developed in a product domain that consists of mostly well-defined archetypal components that evolve slowly over time. Automobiles were a natural place for this approach to develop since every automobile needs to perform certain functions similar to those of every other auto-mobile. These functions are so alike between individual autos that supplier busi-nesses have historically been able to easily develop archetypal components—for instance, alternators, radiators, water pumps, and tires—and with little or no modification sell them to different car companies. Changes to these functions are usually optional or at least evolve very slowly over time, and then happen mainly to achieve marginally greater performance. Thus, components implementing these functions also change very slowly and in an orderly way. Many durable-goods industries have shared this characteristic, which partially explains the wide-spread adoption of the mass paradigm during the twentieth century.

Outside of a few narrow specialties, however, most software is about as dis-tant from these traits as one could imagine. The need for a new piece of software often comes about because some specific function or activity previously per-formed by people, mechanical devices, or dedicated electronic devices, now needs to be automated or upgraded to perform more effectively and with greater con-trol. The best way to address this need is often to create hardware/software systems to perform the old tasks. The automation may be direct (simple translit-eration of what was always done), or indirect (rethinking the *purposes* behind the original activity, and coming up with new and better ways of satisfying them). In either case, the resulting systems will almost always then need to be integrated with other existing hardware/software systems or industrial functions.

These intertwined factors frequently demand that the new software compo-nents substantially differ from any previous ones. While some functions and components in such a software program may be similar to those in previous pro-grams, the old ones still must be adapted to work in the context of the new func-tions and components and the new overall application. Even for relatively common functions, this often leads to unique adaptations and interfaces. Unlike the case for interchangeable parts in automobiles, most new software products are truly changed from previous generations of products, making the assumptions, principles, and tools of mass production more or less inapplicable and ineffective for software developers.

As we mentioned, inflexibility to changing market conditions is one of the major weaknesses of the mass paradigm. In an industry like software, which is known for its relatively high rate of product change compared to most industries, inflexibility is a very high price to pay indeed.

Let's look a little deeper into how software production works with three of the mass production principles: efficiency, organizational gigantism, and technocentrism.

1. *Software Production and Efficiency.* We have previously shown how the obsession with efficiency in mass production leads to dependence on after-the-fact defect detection and remediation, and how the resulting rework is

wasteful and time consuming. When mass production is injected into software development, the quest for efficiency also leads to relying on after-the-fact testing for verification and acceptance. The alternative, a "do it right the first time" approach that corresponds to the goals of the lean paradigm, would—in the context of many current software development approaches—slow down early-phase progress, stall infrastructures, and be inefficient in the classic sense of the word. So after-the-fact testing is the norm and is even institutionalized in most software verification guidelines, like the FAA's RTCA DO-178B and all major commercial and military software standards with just one exception, the U.K. MoD's forward-looking DEF STAN 00-55. This is why rework, in the form of correcting and resubmitting one's code following test failures, is endemic in the software industry. But after-the-fact testing and rework does not derive from the inherent nature of software development, and there's no reason to assume it's the most effective way to develop software.

2. *Software Production and Organizational Gigantism.* As with mass production in other industries, in the software industry, we see development organizations growing larger so they may better amortize the costs of separate software support groups for disciplines like quality assurance, process engineering, and safety. This is because the best way to reclaim these costs is to keep such groups continually busy. And the best way to keep them busy is to have lots of projects and developers over which to spread and level their services. This same dynamic happens on the production floor when an expensive machine has to be hand-fed to keep it busy to reduce its cost per unit time. Software-development organizations who follow this path simply replace the machine with the support groups. Ironically, this effectively reverses intuitive business priorities and puts the developers in the position of trying to better support the support groups, instead of the support functions existing primarily to support the software development. When a software business accepts the principles of mass production infrastructures and efficiency, the resulting financial incentives lead it down the road to organizational gigantism. Again, this does not flow from anything natural to software development, but rather, from the dynamics of mass production.

3. *Software Production and Technocentrism.* The software industry has shown itself prone to looking to bigger, faster, more comprehensive software tools as the way to meet aggressive development schedules. But if a powerhouse lean producer like Toyota couldn't make a technology-centric approach cost-effective, what are the chances that a mass production software producer can succeed at it? Yet software producers still consistently return to this dry well.

Conclusion

As we've mentioned, there is no cut-and-dried mutual exclusion between the three production paradigms. A company may conduct differing aspects of its operations under elements of different paradigms. Nevertheless, in other industries, craft and mass production systems have proven to be merely stepping stones to lean production. To take this a step further, since in the long run the lean paradigm will beat out craft and mass production, you could view these two paradigms as belonging to a bygone era. Every company evolves; smart ones consciously and intentionally choose their paradigm to maximize their competitiveness. This points toward lean, because the craft and mass paradigms ignore the issues that are most important to business success . . . issues that are at the center of lean and that are introduced in the next chapter.

ENDNOTES

1. It is true that, at a minute enough scale, no two items are the same, regardless of how they are produced (even in the best process, quantum effects guarantee that complete uniformity cannot be achieved). Nevertheless, the variations between craft-produced items of the same type are by far the largest. Uniformity is a high value in both mass and lean production; it is not a major concern in craft production.
2. N. Kinch, "The Road From Dreams of Mass Production to Flexible Specialization," 21st Fuji Conference for Business History, 1994.
3. *Lean Thinking*, pg. 87.
4. *The Machine That Changed the World*, pg. 26–27. The italic emphasis is in original quote.
5. *The Machine That Changed the World*, pg. 32.
6. *The Machine That Changed the World*, pg. 31.
7. *The Machine That Changed the World*, pg. 25.
8. Efficiency (definition), *Merriam-Webster Online Dictionary*, 2003. http://www.merriam-webster.com (August 11, 2003).
9. The reader is strongly encouraged to read more about the unintended side effects of efficiency fixation, in *The Machine That Changed The World* (cited previously), and in the form of the page-turning fiction of Eliyahu Goldratt's *The Goal* (Great Barrington, MA: North River Press Publishing Corporation, 1992). *The Goal* presents an alternative to efficiency, in the form of an approach called the "Theory of Constraints" (we have more to say on Goldratt's approach in a later chapter of this book). Of *The Goal*, the British journal *The Economist* said, "A survey of the reading habits of managers found that though they buy books by the likes of Tom Peters for display purposes, the one management book they have actually read from cover to cover is *The Goal*."

10. *The Machine That Changed the World*, pg. 36.
11. R. Schonberger, "*Japanese Manufacturing Techniques: Nine Hidden Lessons in Simplicity*," New York, NY: The Free Press, Division of Macmillan Publishing Co., Inc. 1982; pg. 134.
12. N. Kinch, *The Road From Dreams of Mass Production to Flexible Specialization*, 21st Fuji Conference for Business History, 1994.
13. W. Knoke, *Bold New World*, (Kodansha International, Bunkyo-ku, Tokyo; 1997, ch. 9).
14. *Lean Thinking*, pg. 189.
15. *Lean Thinking*, pg. 240.
16. Tahara, Japan. Womack et. al., *Lean Thinking*, pp. 249–250 describes how, long after Toyota's tour de force with the lean paradigm had made the company a major player in the global auto industry, they decided to try once more to make a tool-driven technology approach work. "In the late 1980s, after Ohno and his generation left the company, Toyota began to consider the possibility that perhaps it should adopt more automation, indeed some of the aspects of high-technology mass production" (*Lean Thinking*, pg. 239).

Toyota created a new production facility, the Tahara plant near Toyota City, Japan, so they could start over fresh and avoid problems with worker inertia or pre-existing conditions. The project involved a newly designed 1989 model. Toyota's experiment led the company to rediscover the lessons that had pushed it into lean production decades earlier: "High-tech automation only works if the plant can run at 100 percent output and if the cost of indirect technical support and high-tech tools is less than the value of the direct labor saved. Tahara flunked both tests." (*Lean Thinking*, pg. 240). In other words, the tool-based, technology-driven approach rests on the central assumption of mass production, that efficiency is the most important goal of a production line.

Lean Production—
Five Principles

MANY SOFTWARE PEOPLE HAVE NEVER heard an adequate definition given for lean production. Depending on the person's background, they may have heard "lean" used either as a synonym for "good," or as a synonym for "bad"... but in either case, usually without any real elaboration. In this chapter, we will look at the specific things that distinguish lean production from the earlier industrial paradigms, craft and mass.

Lean production takes a broader view of the product lifecycle than do the earlier paradigms. Practicing lean leads you to closely review the prior history of your business and its customers, and also to explicitly consider future business prospects and plans. Between these two horizons are all the activities of current projects: product development, production, marketing, sales, maintenance, modification, and all the other activities that producers perform.

This is one of the most distinguishing characteristics of the lean paradigm compared to its predecessors: Lean production is holistic and integrated. And it not only considers the entire product lifecycle, it optimizes projects and even the business as a whole for best overall results. Yet, somewhat counterintuitively, this nearly always leads to better performance in individual areas of concern (this happens because synergy comes into play). Earlier paradigms focused on resolving individual issues or suboptimizing individual areas like particular processes. The old approach of course led to less than hoped-for enterprise results. Surprisingly, it usually also failed to deliver significant improvements in even individual focus areas.

The "sad tale" we shared in Chapter 1 is an extreme example of this effect. While the organization was stellar at requirements analysis, they wasted their entire effort because they failed to adequately consider other essential lifecycle concerns such as system architecture and hardware partitioning. While most projects do not fail so spectacularly, every nonlean project, regardless of industry, experiences this effect to some extent. The justification for making such a strong statement will become clear as we go on, but in a nutshell, such failure is inevitable because all human endeavors are subject to entropy, also called the second law of thermodynamics. Among the many unique characteristics of the lean worldview is that its principles, techniques, and tools explicitly address the second law of thermodynamics in both systems and people. The older paradigms almost completely ignore it. Some have called entropy the "biggest, most powerful, most general idea in all of science."[1] It shouldn't be surprising that an industrial approach that builds upon such an important idea would provide important and practical benefits compared to approaches that don't.

Lean works in two different spheres. One is the individual product (or system, in the case of software). The other is building an industry body of knowledge (tools and techniques) that is a resource for projects. This latter aspect of lean leverages the first, the lessons learned collected from many lean projects in various industries.

This richness might make you think that lean production is complicated. Yes, it may take many years for a company to become expert at lean (nobody ever truly masters it, because it is a continual-learning paradigm). Nevertheless, lean production is known for its accessibility, simplicity, and adaptability to any aspect of any industry (lean works for service, R&D, and administration, just as it does for development and manufacturing). This simplicity stands out sharply against the complexity of many mass production techniques, such as MRP: "The Japanese way is to simplify the problem. . . . Among the simplifiers, Toyota is the standard-bearer. The simple but ingenious . . . [*lean*] approaches developed by Toyota and other leading manufacturers seem to travel easily."[2]

Like mass production under the Ford Motor Company and later General Motors, lean production first grew up in the hothouse of a working, profit-oriented business; the Toyota Motor Company. Both the mass and lean paradigms drew at least partially upon prior theoretical work,[3] but both were rooted most deeply in the thinking of their implementers. Mass production had its champion, Henry Ford; lean had Eiji Toyoda and Taiichi Ohno of Toyota.[4]

Mass production forces its workers to specialize; lean production simplifies its work divisions and empowers its workers: "Lean plants have replaced the 150 or so rigid job classifications of Fordist plants with one classification for production workers and one, or perhaps two, for maintenance workers. Workers are cross-trained and regularly rotated to different jobs. Unlike traditional plants, most workers in lean plants are also responsible for performing routine maintenance on their equipment. . . . There are few quality inspectors and quality control is the responsibility of the workers."[5] Every worker is a quality inspector, and everyone is encouraged to participate in quality and process improvements.

Unlike the organizational gigantism of mass production, lean producers instead knit together cooperative networks with other businesses. "Where the organizational logic of Fordism has been to internalize, the organizational logic of lean production has been to externalize. Instead of creating a giant, integrated enterprise, each lean producer has created their own cooperating network, in Japanese, *keiretsu*, of banks, sales and export companies, and several layers of quasi-independent and independent subcontractors and suppliers."[6] Lean producers also make it a point to work with suppliers to help them also learn and implement lean methods.

The lean paradigm evolved by addressing specific industrial needs and challenges for which the earlier paradigms didn't have an answer. An important part of this evolution was that "the Japanese originators of lean techniques worked from the bottom up. They talked and thought mostly about specific methods applied to specific activities."[7] Lean implementers proved the success of this approach in the marketplace, instinctively combining lean techniques into workable processes. Yet, these early adopters had little or no explanation for why it worked—no systematic method or blueprint to understand it at a higher level. As a result, lean adoption early on was largely an intuitive adventure, often making the successes haphazard, and in many cases, the benefits unsustainable. Each new industry or even company in an industry[8] had to discover the aspects of lean practices in unfamiliar settings that might or might not apply to their own situation. Most people found this process difficult. Relatively few were able to put together a coherent lean approach for their own situations. "We met many managers who had drowned in techniques."[9]

The great contribution of authors Womack and Jones in *Lean Thinking* was that they studied the various low-level lean techniques and formulated them into five product lifecycle principles: value, value stream, flow, pull, and perfection. With such well-defined high-level principles, people could now work their way through techniques that were applicable to their own industries and apply them in a way that would work in their situations. In this book, we apply these principles in a way that is based on our specific perspective and experiences in the software industry.

Value: Identifying What Really Matters to the Customer

Womack and Jones identify *value* as the highest principle and priority of lean development. "The critical starting point for lean thinking is value."[10] Value, in the lean sense, is *the set of things that really matter to a customer*. As far as the customer is concerned, the value a company creates, the product or service, is the reason it exists. Value, in other words, is about building the "right product." The other four principles are about building the "product right." If your organization is not building the right product in your customer's eyes, it doesn't matter how well it builds that product. One of the fastest ways to improve your business situation is to recognize you are building the wrong product and determine what your customer really wants. "Most firms can substantially boost sales immediately if they find a mechanism for rethinking the value of their core products to their customers."[11] Building the right product often won't even require radical product change; a change in emphasis on certain product characteristics may be all that is needed. Switching to a value orientation based on dialogue with the customer also cuts a business's costs significantly. (The reasons for this will become obvious as the rest of this book discusses how lean production works both in general industry and in software, but reduction in waste is a big part of it.)

However, there's a lot more that goes into assessing value than just the obvious functionality and usability of the product. One must also consider things like proper pricing, durability, availability, and many other issues important to customers. Even more fundamental than these concerns, however, is the need to know your customers. Organizations assume they can at least identify who their customers are, but are often wrong—or at least have only incomplete information—to their customers' (and their own) detriment. Genuinely insightful understanding of customers is very rare.

Having outlined the importance of value, it turns out that determining value is not the most intuitive activity in the world . . . at least, not for a manufacturing culture steeped in mass production. The manufacturing industry has been using the word "value" for a long time, but not in a lean sense at all. Nonlean businesses tend to think of value in terms of what they can offer to the market given their own current products and resources, rather than in terms of what their customers really want or need. Even using an exploratory tool like a market survey, which most people assume will reveal the customer's needs (and which *can* be used effectively in a lean process), does not necessarily capture value.

In Jim's industry, aerospace, certain assumptions are common about who our customers are and what they want to hear. For instance, in a major aircraft design review, it is often assumed that the important customer is the military buyer . . . the officers who are standing in on behalf of the government. And it is assumed that their main interests are schedules, budgets, and technical performance measures (TPMs). These are assumptions, of course, about customer identity and values.

On the 382J program in the 1990s, going into a major review, the software team decided to apply lean techniques to identify who the project's customers actually were and what they actually cared about hearing in a review. The team then deployed that information into the development of the review presentations. The lean techniques used were common in other industries but almost unheard of in software. They included hard numeric ones like QFD (quality function deployment) and the AHP (analytic hierarchy process), as well as soft techniques such as brainstorming with customer surrogates (many such techniques are discussed in Part II).

To nobody's surprise, these analyses confirmed that the military customer was indeed the most important. But they also discovered several other customers who would prove to be critical to the success of the software portion of the project. These included certain company managers, certain government regulators, and one or two support vendors. Building upon that knowledge, the software team used other techniques to discover the actual values of these parties. In addition to the values we expected them to have were values that sometimes turned out to be of even greater importance, like maintaining project stability, avoiding political landmines, and easing certification processes. The team's final step was to take the predominant messages, in their order of importance, and mold the presentation around them.

The result on presentation day run-through? A standing ovation from the audience! And this in a situation where the project leaders were tough on almost everyone else. Lean works. We will say more about this incident when we go into the details of the lean techniques that were used (and many others), in Part II.[12]

Mass production companies often offer customers products that the companies already have but that are not necessarily what the customers want. This organizational reality collides with the reality of the marketplace, where customers, more than ever before, expect to get the opportunity to express their viewpoints to businesses . . . and be listened to. Instead, the mass paradigm marketplace has created an approach to "public relations [that] does not relate to the public. [Where] companies are deeply afraid of their markets . . . the community of discourse is the market. Companies that do not belong to a community of discourse will die."[13]

Ultimately, value begins and ends with understanding the customer . . . not just identifying that which the customer does not currently have available (which is relatively easy to determine), nor which new products one's own business can easily create by reworking its current line of products. Value requires that you know your customer, what they want and need, and a fair amount about your own business realities in fulfilling this need.

To achieve this, you have to take the time to understand your customers' customers, and sometimes even *their* customers' customers. Going to such depths clarifies what value means to your immediate customers and makes it much more likely that they will be delighted with what you give them. You truly become partners with them in discourse. So it is useful to think of all your customers when looking at value, not just the customer purchasing your product or service. Look at management, shareholders, government regulators, and downstream organizations in the product-development flow, as customers. Though determining value is not always an intuitive activity, you can do an analysis of value in your organization more easily, quickly, and thoroughly than you might think. In Part II, we will explain how to use lean techniques such as the AHP (analytical hierarchy process), simulation/emulation, and the 7MP (management and planning) tools to define value.

Value Stream: Ensuring Every Activity Adds Customer Value

The second lean principle is that of the value stream. This principle demands that everything the business does should add customer value to its products. James Martin, the IT consultant, offers that a value stream is "an end-to-end collection of activities that creates a result for a 'customer,' who may be the ultimate customer or an internal 'end user.'"[14] Furthermore, the value stream is composed of two largely orthogonal substreams, the *design stream*, "from concept to launch,"[15] and the *production stream*, "from raw material into the arms of the customer."[16]

The design stream matures the concept of a product from its initial definition through its production launch. For software, this would be the product's fundamental engineering. This stream is also called *technical problem solving*.

The production stream further decomposes into two branches, material and information. The material branch is the set of activities that construct the product that comes down the production line. This is also sometimes called physical transformation. This is what people normally think of most when they think of a production line—people busily working on the product, building it up, and bringing it closer and closer to completion as it goes down the line. See Figure 3-1.

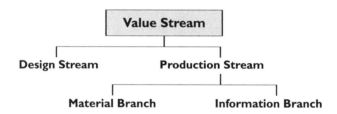

Figure 3-1. Elements of the Value Stream

The information branch is the set of activities that coordinate and control the production activities, from order-taking through product delivery. This is also sometimes called *information management* or *production controls*. Information management and production controls are important because poor information flow often derails programs, such as when people working on different parts of the project can't find out what they need to know to do their job, or when management doesn't know what's happening and therefore cannot manage.

The parts of the value stream are easy to understand for physical products in the manufacturing world. In software development, the applicability is less obvious, especially of the parts in the value stream (e.g., how do you distinguish between the design stream and the production stream when there's only one product?). There is, however, a way of looking at software development that makes all the parts of the value stream fall in place naturally. It is a variation on the idea of "product families"; however, unlike the way that product families have sometimes been implemented in software, this approach allows for cost-effective development even when there will only be one program in the family. We will explore this further in Chapter 15.

All the activities of all the parts of the value stream are designed to ensure that everything done during production imparts "the value, the whole value, and nothing but the value," so to speak. An effective value stream is like the coherent light of a laser. If you think of the laser's photons as the activities the business does while making a product, an effective value stream ensures that all its activities illuminate their target, which is to create the right product for the customer while satisfying the business goals of the company. *There is little, and ideally no, wasted work.* Traditional craft or mass production, on the other hand, is like the light from the incandescent lamp on a jeweler's bench: Some of the photons will land on the project at hand, but most will land elsewhere to no useful benefit or added value to the task performed.

This brings us back to an important point. Many of the actions of nonlean businesses have nothing to do with adding value or characteristics that the customer wants. Many activities simply feed and care for company organizational and production infrastructures, or are random activities that accomplish nothing for either customer or infrastructure. A software example is where programmers tinker with a working, acceptable code to "improve" it. Such activities are a waste of a business's money and resources. The value stream and its parts remedy this by working on two major goals at the same time:

1. Adding value to the product without wasted effort.
2. Identifying waste in existing processes and removing it.

Adding Value: Domain Orientation, QFD, and *Hoshin Kanri*

Focusing all your development efforts on adding value will help in any situation, but gives an especially high payoff for businesses that are starting a new endeavor (e.g., line of business) and thus have more leeway to rewrite their way of doing things. The three main methods for adding value are domain orientation, the value-driven action of QFD (Quality Function Deployment), and *hoshin kanri*.

A *domain* is a set of things that are closely related in function or purpose. *Domain-oriented* development is based on the similarities between related things, so that products need only minimal modification to be useful in every context. Domain orientation means that universal value (i.e., value that is true for all customers of similar products) is at the heart of the first generation of products and of all those that follow in that domain.

This is in contrast to *product orientation*, in which the needs of just the most immediate specific customer and project become the main needs the producer considers during development. You can tell when product orientation has been practiced in the past: New product developments that attempt to build upon an existing product so they can address other customers in the same market, or often even extended needs of the same customer, must either retain the first product's idiosyncratic features that add no value for the new situation, or else first go through a significant and expensive reengineering effort to make them more universally appealing and useful to all the customers and uses in the market. This is because the original product-oriented development made the unique aspects of the original product too prominent to be able to accommodate the new needs.

On the other hand, domain orientation eliminates this unnecessary work— i.e., waste—and allows the producers to put effort only into adding new value to each subsequent product. Domain orientation goes beyond object orientation (OO): In traditional OO, the producer can conceivably (and often does) use OO techniques without examining the commonalities between multiple uses and without having to base the design upon the shared characteristics. Thus, OO by itself omits the most important concern of domain orientation; identifying and building upon universal values. However, some of the concepts of OO are very useful for true domain-based design, such as classes, objects, methods, and various forms of inheritance and polymorphism.

QFD is a conceptual matrix-math technique (also sometimes called the house of quality) for focusing all cross-functional planning and communication on value-driven product development. It is a process for transforming customer wants and needs (i.e., the voice of the customer) into quantitative, engineering terms and specifications of the product (i.e., the voice of the company). We will say more about QFD in Part II.

Hoshin kanri is Japanese for "shining metal" or "pointing direction," or as it is sometimes also translated, "policy deployment" or "policy planning." It focuses on setting value-driven strategic business goals and using them to direct tactical project management. *Hoshin kanri* aligns the company's activities to these overarching strategic goals using clearly measurable targets against which the company can measure progress toward key goals. *Hoshin kanri* has been perhaps most descriptively translated as "target and means management,"[17] and sometimes is called "management by policy" to distinguish it from the still prevalent and nonlean United States approach called "management by objectives." Using *hoshin kanri* is much like applying QFD to the business instead of to the product. An excellent and very practical reference for applying *hoshin* in any business situation is *Beyond Strategic Vision; Effective Corporate Action with Hoshin Planning.*[18]

Removing Waste via Incremental Improvement: *Kaizen* and ToC

The second approach to developing and improving a value stream is to look for instances of waste in an existing production line, and then remove them. One of the most commonly heard words in lean circles is *muda*. *Muda* is the Japanese equivalent to the English word "waste." In terms of the value stream, *muda* is "any activity which absorbs resources but creates no value."[19] Toyota originally identified seven kinds of *muda*:

1. Overproduction (i.e., excess, early, or misdirected production).
2. Waiting (i.e., employees waiting for the next processing step or for a part).
3. Unnecessary transportation (moving a product in work between stages is generally non-value added).
4. Overprocessing or incorrect processing (i.e., poor process design).
5. Excess inventory (i.e., raw material, work-in-progress, finished goods).
6. Unnecessary movement (i.e., wasted motion or inefficient performance of a process).
7. Producing defective products (i.e., rework, inspection, repair, correction).
8. Later lean practitioners have identified two additional kinds of waste:
   – Dangerous working practices.
   – Not using employees' ideas or creativity.

How much waste is there in a typical manufacturing process? In a public presentation to its suppliers, Lockheed Martin's LM21 lean-implementation project answered the question as follows: "A typical analysis shows value is being added around 1 percent of the time."[20] The other 99 percent (of time, not cost) on a nonlean project is waste. In any company's current processes, some of this waste is necessary. This "type 1 waste" is removable only through major process modifications or changing to a different process, which may not be practical under certain situations. However, the remaining waste, other than type 1, is completely unnecessary. This "type 2 waste" is removable without substantial changes to the company's current processes. The Lockheed Martin presentation cites (without naming it) a project that had a "before waste reduction" total duration of 187 days (see Figure 3-2). 1.83 days of this was analyzed to be value-added work and 6.54 days non-value-added work. The rest of the duration was idle product-waiting time (sometimes called "white space").

The same project's after waste-reduction duration was reduced to 20 days total work, still with 1.83 days of value-added work, but with non-value-added work reduced to 5.17 days. White space was reduced the most substantially, from 179 days beforehand to 13 days afterward. As important as time-to-market is in most industries (especially software), a 93 percent reduction is likely to noticeably improve almost anyone's competitiveness! Such reductions are central to the value stream.

There is now at least one standards document from a technical society (the SAE[21]) focused on evaluating the ability of an organization to remove *muda* from its processes; SAE J4000, "Identification and Measurement of Best Practice in

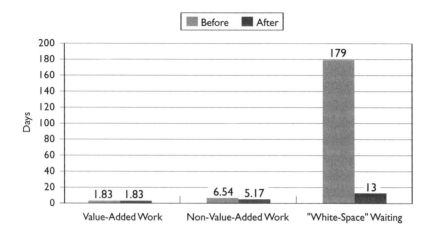

Figure 3-2. Waste-Reduction Effects

Implementation of Lean Operation." SAE J4000 defines the implementing of lean operations as "the process of eliminating waste exhibited in an organization's value stream;" a pretty strong endorsement for the importance in a lean value stream of finding and removing *muda*.

There are two main approaches to removing *muda*: incremental improvement of existing processes (*kaizen*) and radical improvement that fundamentally changes existing processes (*kaikaku*). We'll consider *kaizen* through the rest of this section and *kaikaku* in the next.

Kaizen is the Japanese word for "continuous incremental improvement." People also use the word *kaizen* to describe a short event, typically of three days up to a week long, conducted by a small team of people. The *kaizen* event begins with following a product through its lifecycle to find out what is actually done with and to it. This exercise produces a *value stream map* (to be discussed in more detail in Chapter 15). What the team discovers is usually somewhat different from what everyone expected. With the help of the value stream map, the *kaizen* then identifies all the waste in the activities and flows, and uses "root cause analysis" to determine the cause or causes of each waste. Root cause analysis often uses techniques of the 7MP tools, such as the interrelationship digraph, and the 7QC (quality control) tools, such as the pareto chart. Finally, the *kaizen* may suggest ways to remove the waste (e.g., by replacing, removing or modifying work activities) so that resulting activities add value. Even if the *kaizen* participants do not suggest ways to remove the identified wastes, the users of the *kaizen* output can do so.

As with most lean techniques, top management must drive and support *kaizen* throughout the organization. "The most crucial element in the *kaizen* process is the commitment and involvement of top management. It must be demonstrated immediately and consistently to assure success in the *kaizen* process."[22]

Goldratt's Theory of Constraints[23] (ToC) is a method for continuously removing waste from processes and production tools. In that sense, the ToC is also a *kaizen* (incremental improvement) activity, though it is not linked in any way to *kaizen* events. ToC is a management philosophy that focuses on removing the impediments ("constraints") that hinder organizations from achieving their goals. We will discuss ToC in more detail in Part III.

Incremental improvement methods are helpful even to those who have recently started up in a new product area. Even though businesses may start with a "blank sheet of paper" and do a great job creating a value stream process, inevitably there will be imperfections. Before long, these imperfections, or *muda*, will surface and will require some sort of waste analysis and remediation for removal.

Finally, lean companies have used quality circles and work teams to encourage workers to make self-initiated suggestions for improvements. Quality circles are small groups of workers (typically six to ten) from the same production area, who meet every other week or so for an hour or two with a facilitator. Work teams are more broadly composed and more continuously focused on generating suggestions. Toyota receives thousands of such suggestions a year. Ninety-five percent of the suggestions are eventually implemented, because Toyota authorizes its workers to try out their suggestions (though not on live product) before officially passing them along.

Removing Waste via Radical Improvement: *Kaikaku*

Sometimes the creeping change of incremental improvement can't meet pressing business goals or demands. Perhaps the business is currently far from being lean; perhaps there have been recent major changes in the marketplace or in customer needs. In either case, radical improvement is needed. The Japanese lean word for such improvement is *kaikaku*. *Kaikaku* is sometimes referred to as the revolution that contrasts to *kaizen*'s evolution. *Kaikaku* demands major change to one or more (usually more) of one's products, processes, organizational structures, and management strategies. Organizations that would be lean must strive to be more adaptable to significant change.

Why is radical change so important to a lean organization? Many lean practices are radical departures from the existing way of doing business. For example, changing to a flow emphasis (discussed in the following section of this chapter) requires a revolution in business practices. "It [flow] changes everything: how we work together, the kinds of tools we devise to help with our work, the organizations we create to facilitate the flow, the kinds of careers we pursue, the nature of business firms . . . and their linkages to each other and society."[24] No revolutionary change, no flow emphasis. Other aspects of lean production can similarly reward radical change.

Mass producers have a real problem with *kaikaku*. Indeed, it's hard to imagine anything more opposite to the nature of mass production. A large mass production infrastructure is expensive and time-consuming to create, and nearly as expensive and time-consuming to change. It is only natural, given the time and money involved, that once a mass producer sets up a mass production process, it will stick with it as long as possible . . . often, unfortunately, for too long. That is exactly what Ford did with his Model T: "In 1923, the peak year of Model T production, Ford produced 2.1 million Model T chassis, a figure that would prove to be the high-water mark for standardized mass production. At the end of its run in 1927, however, Ford was facing falling demand for the Model T and was undoubtedly selling below cost. (Demand fell because General Motors was offering a more modern product for only a little more money.)"[25] Given the expense of retooling a mass production line and with Ford making good profits on his existing line, why change? In the end, however, all these good and proper reasons caused Ford to wait too long to respond to market pressures. As a result, he handed over to his competitor, GM, his dominance in the mass market industry he had created practically single-handedly.

When performed correctly, the six sigma process-improvement and waste-reduction approach addresses the lean issue of *kaikaku*. The marketing introduction to the textbook *The Six Sigma Guidebook*[26] sums up very nicely the necessity of being flexible enough to support such change:

> *"The goals of Six Sigma are so ambitious—a 100✕ quality improvement every two to three years—as to constitute a completely different way of running the business . . . It is difficult to abandon a comfortable routine or an investment in existing technology just because a better way has been discovered. However, this is precisely what Six Sigma demands. Understanding what it takes to allow "creative destruction" to flourish is a primary responsibility of Six Sigma leaders. The . . . 'Six Sigma Organizational Paradox' [is] the need to encourage variation, slack, and redundancy within the organization while simultaneously working to eliminate these same things in processes."*

Six sigma has become so well established on its own merits that companies often implement it as a stand-alone program rather than as part of an overall lean initiative. In a lean context, however, it belongs with either the value stream or flow principle (we place it under the detailed discussion of the flow principle in Part III).

In short, flexibility is a prerequisite for an effective value stream. In durable-goods manufacturing, the integrated approach to achieving flexibility is known as a flexible manufacturing system or FMS. An FMS is defined as "an integrated manufacturing capability to produce small numbers of a great variety of items at low unit cost; an FMS is also characterized by low changeover time and rapid response time."[27] One would expect to see these characteristics in a lean software value stream as well. This kind of flexibility does not mean a lack of organization, process definition, or information management, however. To the contrary, essential to an FMS is "an inherent paradox of the system that activities, connections, and process flows . . . are rigidly scripted, yet at the same time . . . operations are enormously flexible and adaptable."[28]

Even after a company has successfully conducted an instance of *kaikaku*, they should continue *kaizen*, QFD, or the other incremental techniques on the resulting processes. Lean gains are easily lost unless a company nurtures and builds on them. The value-stream building methods—QFD, *kaizen*, ToC, etc.—are never either/or. They are complementary and belong together on a lean producer's tool belt. To do otherwise risks jeopardizing all of your efforts. "Anyone who has been involved with lean manufacturing for any period of time has probably concluded three things:

1. Once demonstrated, lean concepts are relatively easy to understand.
2. With support, lean concepts and tools are relatively easy to apply.
3. No matter what, lean concepts and tools are difficult to sustain and expand once implemented."[29]

Lean practitioners cannot emphasize this third point strongly enough. "If management fails to lead and the workforce feels that no reciprocal obligations are in force, it is quite predictable that lean production will revert to mass production."[30] Jim saw this happen on a project on which he implemented several lean software processes. Despite institutionalizing those processes in written form, after he left, some of the processes reverted to mass methods. One of the causes of the downfall was that people who came on the program afterward were not trained in lean thinking. Like other industries, software developers will have to exercise active effort to avoid the tendency to backtrack to mass production thinking or even more primitive practices.

Flow: Eliminating Discontinuities in the Value Stream

Flow refers to the idea that "tasks can almost always be accomplished much more efficiently and accurately when the product is worked on continuously from raw material to finished good."[31] One way to understand *lean flow* is to contrast it with its mass paradigm counterpart, *mass efficiency*, since both address the same industrial concerns, though in different ways.

Mass paradigm efficiency creates batches of work. Batching allows many individual and identical pieces to be run through a machine one after another, which "keeps the members of the department busy, all the equipment running hard, and justifies dedicated, high-speed equipment."[32] So why isn't having continuously-running equipment considered continuous work as stated in the goal of lean flow? Primarily because in the real world, there are no all-in-one tools that can produce finished products directly from raw materials (if this were possible, there would be "ACME" tools like in the cartoons, like the machine you feed a piece of wood at one end, and which ejects a completed army tank at the other! What such images reveal about our subconscious expectations on technological mass production is another interesting question . . .).

Since there are no such all-in-one tools, workers (regardless of the paradigm) must work in stages. In mass production, companies must create a separate batch for each of these stages. This forces the defining and creating of intermediate products so there is something to store up to create the batches that feed the stages. In most cases, such batches of products, called inventory, have nothing to do with the nature of the final product. If a company didn't depend on the batch tactic, its workers wouldn't have to perform the work associated with inventory at all . . . in other words, such batch-creating work is pure *muda*. Creating unnecessary intermediate products lengthens overall end-to-end production time and takes workers away from doing truly productive, value-adding tasks. Ironically, by depending on batching, the mass approach keeps the workers busy but fails to build a product in the minimum possible time or for the minimum practical cost; thereby damaging its performance on achieving its own stated more important business goals.

Compounding this problem, the additional stages with their stops and starts create extra opportunities for defects to occur and cause even more delays (waste) in finding the defects. These defects also require rework and backflows to return the corrected products to the production line, with yet more waste.

Mass production managers are as smart as anyone and understand the numerous problems that can occur with this scenario. They know that the extra work wastes a lot of time and money. One way to reduce this waste is to absolutely minimize the number of stages of production. This pushes the mass producer toward using ever larger and more comprehensive tools and environments. This is yet another reason for the inflexibility and large infrastructures that we discussed previously under mass production.

Lean flow, on the other hand, does not rely on batching, cutting the number of stages, using large tool environments, or making great investments. To make lean flow happen, the product must be developed with unbroken forward progress and ideally with no backflows (which come from rework). Such a methodology takes the main emphasis off the stages in a production line and puts it on each individual instance of product. "In a continuous-flow layout, the production steps are arranged in a sequence . . . and the product moves from one step to the next, one . . . [*product piece*] . . . at a time, with no buffer of work-in-process in between, using a range of techniques generically labeled 'single-piece flow.'"[33] The emphasis is on ordering and arranging all work so as to remove waste of all kinds, including unnecessary movements or actions, idle times during production, and accumulations of products at a given stage of production (i.e., batches). Back in 1982, this was distilled into the statement, "the Japanese success formula . . . is inventory control . . . Of course, I overstated my case."[34] As R. Schonberger, the author of that comment, recognized in his statement, he pushes matters a little too far. Nevertheless, even if you put into play other aspects of the lean principles, he was correct in saying that without inventory control, you do not have flow, and without flow, you do not have lean production.

Using Stage-Graduation Criteria for Continuous Flow

One key to achieving continuous flow is to determine the precise criteria for what constitutes success at the end of each stage of production. There must be a mechanism for dealing with the cause of defects immediately when they are discovered as they come out of a stage. To deal with defects, they must first be detected. This requires defining a standard for success in that stage (e.g., a set of measurements with allowable tolerances) and a means of measuring the work piece against the standard. Without such criteria and remediation, defective work can move on into the next stage, leading to rework and backflows when another stage discovers the defect further downstream. The lack of such criteria and mechanisms is a characteristic of mass production, which allows defective product to move down the line as people adopt the attitude that "someone else will deal with it later". . . . that "someone else" often being at the very end of the production line.

Using Self-Adapted Tools for Speed and Flexibility

Self-adapted or self-developed tools are common in lean production and help provide the needed flexibility in creating a production line with lean flow: "Self-developed machines and tools may be special-purpose, lightweight, easily move-able, and low-cost. Furthermore, setup time may be cut essentially to zero . . . even in small-scale Japanese industries, self-developed machines and tools were being used."[35] Bigger tools and environments have nothing to do with good flow. In a lean production line, "It is also essential that many traditionally massive machines . . . be 'right-sized' to fit directly into the production process. This, in turn, often means using machines that are simpler, less automated, and slower . . . This approach seems completely backward to traditional managers who have been told all their lives that competitive advantage . . . is obtained from automating, linking, and speeding up massive machinery to increase throughput and remove direct labor."[36]

"[Toyota's] Ohno and his associates achieved continuous flow in low-volume production, in most cases without assembly lines, by learning to quickly change over tools from one product to the next and by 'right-sizing' (miniaturizing) machines so that processing steps of different types . . . could be conducted immediately adjacent to each other."[37]

Instead of depending on tools that can handle many copies of identical parts rapidly, the lean producer uses reconfigurable tools or tool suites that can handle different variants of the product one after the other. "To achieve single-piece flow in the normal situation when each product family includes many product variants . . . it is essential that each [*production*] machine can be converted almost instantly from one product specification to the next."[38] This means that those who practice lean flow will develop tools in such a way as to eliminate the need to stop the entire production line. Of course, this will likely require some local tool design or customization. Surprising to some, converting from larger equipment to these smaller, more adaptable tools to achieve one-piece flow is not expensive—in fact, it removes waste and hence, it saves the company time and money. These ideas directly apply to lean software tools (we will say more about this subject later in the book).

Nevertheless, some tool procurement or development is generally required when starting a lean process: "We have come across many companies that wish to short-cut the critical addition of equipment," says Richard Ligus, president of Rockford Consulting Group (Rockford, IL) . . . "capital equipment plays an extremely important role in the success of a lean manufacturing implementation. I haven't seen a project where equipment wasn't needed."[39] This need generally applies to software development as well as to durable-goods manufacturing. But while tools are important to lean software production, they won't be the "mega-tools" so common in the past.

Pull: Production Is Initiated by Demand

Producers before the days of the lean paradigm operated much like a spec builder of homes. The producer anticipates a demand and produces products ahead of time to meet it. Pull turns this upside down. With pull, nothing is made until a customer requests it. In software, this means you don't develop programs (or capabilities in programs) without real customer interest being shown. In a dynamic field like many software disciplines, you don't, of course, passively wait for customers to come to your doorstep or you would never be first to market. You go to the customers, preferably ahead of your competitors, to assess the customers' needs. What you don't want to do, and what has been a recipe for failure for many software companies in the early 2000s, is to produce products in a speculative vacuum *with no end customer in sight.*

JIT: Right Items at the Right Time in the Right Amounts

The essence of pull is the well-known production and management system called *Just-in-time* (JIT). JIT usually refers to the system of producing and delivering the right items at the right time in the right amounts. This means that each stage of production operates only when the stage of production that follows it needs an input. JIT is one of the few lean terms that just about everyone has heard about. Some people even say JIT and lean are synonymous, though from what we've already seen in the first three principles, it should now be clear that lean production goes much further than JIT.

In a pure JIT environment, the final stage (the customer purchase) initiates all stages leading up to it. The customer's order launches the final stage of production of the product, which requires an input from production, and therefore triggers the next-to-final stage of production, and so forth, all the way back to the procurement of the original raw materials. This lean principle is aptly called "pull" because products and services are pulled into action by customer need. Each need, like a link in a chain, is attached to another need (or demand) and so on, until you finally see that the person pulling the beginning of the chain is the customer.

JIT is possible only when batch sizes drop to an absolute minimum size. Ideally, there is a continuous flow of products through various operations—design, order-taking, and production—one unit or one piece at a time (referred to as *single* or *one-piece flow*), though occasionally the absolute minimum is something greater than one. (One of the many detriments to having a larger batch size is that it reduces the number of batches making up the final product, thereby minimizing the benefits of having a repeatable process.) In software development, there are lean techniques you can use to divide a software program into pieces that are sufficiently independent of one another so each piece becomes a candidate for JIT. Setting up for this is essential if one is to obtain the benefits of JIT on a software project.[40]

One-Piece Flow: Keeping Quality Visible at All Times

From product design to product launch, one-piece flow opens up several ways to attack waste. Waste occurs in the use of batches, because they conceal the causes of defects until the company has created many defective parts. In a multiple-piece batch, companies typically sample and evaluate parts for their quality and extrapolate the results to provide a statistical estimate of the quality of all the pieces. The quality of any one piece that is not sampled is unknown. The company can create many defective pieces before sampling reveals a trend and a need to provide countermeasures. This means the company must rework and reintroduce the "defectives," as they are sometimes called, to production via backflows. The rework adds no value, so it is extra work or *muda*.

In contrast to batch production, one-piece flow keeps quality visible at all times because the company produces only what the customer requests. As a result, the piece pulled through production is either tested, or if the lean principle of perfection is at work, is produced in such a way that it is assured to be correct. In either case, the company knows the quality of the piece rather than depending on a projected statistical estimate for a lot of pieces. It has been said that "JIT . . . prescribes elimination of lots altogether (ideally) so that there can be no lots to sample from and no chance of a certain percentage of defectives per lot."[41] In pull terms, one company found that the quality of its products improved significantly after implementing one-piece flow, which is usually the case when flow and pull are combined.

Batches and inventory also hide inconsistencies in the development process. Single-piece development makes visible any variations in the output of a production stage: Either the following stage ends up waiting for incoming product that is taking too long to produce—thus wasting time—or receives products of varying quality—causing rework. The combination of removing inventories and pulling production makes the unevenness visible so the company can implement countermeasures to correct it.

Kanban: Triggering the Flow of Materials

To connect the stages of production, there must be a way for each stage to signal its upstream stage when it needs another input (i.e., when it needs an output from the upstream stage). This signal is called a *kanban*, a Japanese word that literally means "visual record." Traditionally, a *kanban* was a physical card. A *kanban*-based system is one type of "visual control" or "transparency" feedback system. It is a simple and direct form of communication located at the point where the communication is needed. With *kanban*, the production stage needing an input sends the card, along with a container or holder of some sort to carry the product itself, to the upstream production stage. The upstream stage makes the product, puts it into the container, and returns the container to its sender, the downstream stage. Using *kanban* gives the producer the ability to react immediately to changes in customer demand. This in turn eliminates the *muda* that would result if the producer continued meeting a prior level of market demand using batch production. The use of a *kanban* approach has six rules:

1. Never withdraw parts without a *kanban.*
2. The subsequent process should only withdraw what is needed from the previous process.
3. Never send a defective part to the subsequent process.
4. The preceding process should only produce the exact quantity of parts withdrawn by the subsequent process (ensures minimum inventory).

5. Maintain smoothing (or leveling) of production.
6. Fine-tune the production schedule using *kanban*.[42]

Kanban will work effectively only if you've already implemented some of the lean principles and eliminated the waste in processes, such as excess WIP (work in progress), walking, conveyance, downtime, lead times, and defects.

Takt Time: Linking Pace to Demand

Another important idea in the lean pull system is the amount of time spent producing each "piece." *Takt* time is the tool that links production to the customer by matching the pace of production to the pace of actual final sales. If a lean producer must produce 160 pieces (products) a week to meet current customer demand and has available two 8-hour shifts, five days a week, for a total of 80 hours, each piece must be produced in 80/160 or .5 hour (30 minutes). This per piece time is called *takt* time; *takt* is a German word meaning "beat," "meter," or "step," as in "to dance in step" (German industry began using this concept in the 1930s, and the Japanese lean producers took it up, along with the term, later). The lean producer measures the pace and smoothness of flow of pieces against the target *takt* time. Determining the appropriate *takt* time is the final piece in developing JIT and is the heartbeat of any lean system. Without it, a company cannot build a *leveled* or *smooth* production schedule.

Andon: Empowering Employees to Handle Problems

Andon is the Japanese word for "light." *Andon* boards, lights, and audible alarms, or a combination thereof, are visual management tools that alert employees to defects, equipment abnormalities, or other problems (Figure 3-3). The worker can see at a glance how the actual line is performing, if the workplace is running properly, or if there are any emerging problems. *Andon* indicators also measure real time processes using, for instance, quality slogans and quality indicator graphs displayed throughout the factory.

Level Scheduling: Smoothing Out Variations

Level scheduling is a technique developed by Toyota to sequence customer orders in a repetitive pattern. This smoothes the day-to-day variations in the orders so production corresponds better to the averaged ebb and flow of short-term demand.

Level scheduling takes the number of product units required in some medium-length period of time, perhaps a month, and divides them into a consistent daily quantity. The daily quantity then drives production and the issuing of *kanban*, which smoothes out extreme short-term fluctuations in the demand. This occurs when a customer presents the lean supplier with large but infrequent orders (batch production).

(Figure obtained with permission from American LED-gible Inc.)[43]

Figure 3-3. *Andon* Board

Without some kind of leveling, the lean producer would have to pass the peaks and valleys in demand through its own production chain, which would lead to waste by requiring oversized machines and high but short-duration work staffing to accommodate the peaks. Level scheduling averages the peaks and valleys so an organization can "right size" machines and work crews.

Nevertheless, lean producers must base leveling on very accurate customer knowledge to avoid building up a significant inventory and to stay reasonably consistent with the basic idea of "pull." While level scheduling seems to contradict JIT's single-piece pull and flow, it is actually based on the customer knowledge provided by JIT. Level scheduling merely "averages out" over some reasonably short timescale the variations in the known demand revealed by some amount of prior JIT experience, or perhaps, based on a "best guess" that is quickly adjusted based on subsequent JIT-like recording of actual customer demand.

As we've discussed earlier, a lean production line can accommodate a variety of products in quick succession. The *kanban* approach only works well in conjunction with the quickly reconfigurable tools of the flow principle, so that each stage can react quickly to demands from the subsequent stage for products that differ from those worked on most recently. Together, these elements enable producing products as needed—the essence of pull. You could sum up the pull principle as, "don't make anything until it is needed; then make it very quickly."[44]

The benefits of pull for software architectures are very exciting. Everything in a build should be there because a customer wanted that capability (in a domain-based system, a capability may be there because a customer other than the current one wants it, but it will be there because *some* customer wants it . . . though it may be suppressed or removed for any given customer). Capabilities should be inserted into the build as near as possible to when the customer requests or needs it. Processes should be set up to enable the developer to add, delete, or modify capabilities quickly in response to changing customer desires. Once again, flexibility is a key lean quality. The knowledge the developers need about customer desires, of course, comes through the techniques of the value principle.

Perfection: Retaining Integrity via *Jidoka* and *Poka-Yoke*

The final lean principle, perfection, is the simplest to understand and the hardest to achieve. Lean perfection is the ideal that one should eliminate all *muda*. As we discussed under the lean value stream principle, you can approach this incrementally, for instance via *kaizen*, or radically, via *kaikaku*. Both approaches are necessary, but it is important that you apply *kaikaku* first, because if you apply *kaizen* first, you may expend a lot of effort incrementally improving processes that you will end up needing to replace.

The case of Freudenberg-NOK General Partnership (FNGP) of Plymouth, Michigan (discussed in *Lean Thinking*[45]), shows the benefits of *kaizen*. FNGP chose the incremental path to perfection. In 1989, FNGP consolidated numerous American and Japanese seal and gasket plants. They found that the more *kaizen* events they conducted, the more opportunities they discovered for reducing *muda*. Rather than experiencing the "law of diminishing returns," their improvements accelerated over time: "An initial *kaizen* event achieved a 56 percent increase in labor productivity and a 13 percent reduction in the amount of factory space needed. However, in revisiting this activity in five additional three-day *kaizen* events over the next three years, it was gradually possible to boost productivity by 991 percent while reducing the amount of space needed by 48 percent."[46]

A very important concept in lean production is *jidoka*, also sometimes called "autonomation" (a combination of the words "autonomous" and "operation"). In *jidoka*, the machine detects the defect and notifies the operator. This method was invented by an earlier Toyoda, Sakichi. In 1902, he designed a mechanism by which power looms could detect a broken thread and shut themselves down. *Jidoka* frees an operator to manage several machines at the same time, while being assured of the quality of the product. *Jidoka* will not prevent defects from occurring in the first place, but it does facilitate their elimination as soon as possible once they occur.

Once the abnormality occurs, a four-step process is set in motion:

1. Detect the abnormality.
2. Stop.
3. Fix or correct the immediate condition.
4. Investigate the root cause and install a countermeasure.[47]

Manufacturers use *jidoka* on the production line to have either an operator or a machine stop the line when a defect or potential defect is detected. The operator then does whatever is necessary to correct the *cause* of the defect and restarts the line. When it is primarily the worker's responsibility to find the defect, there are often *andon*-stop cords that are pulled to stop the line. A light goes on to alert others and indicates the location of the problem. When the responsibility for finding defects primarily rests with the machine, the machine will be equipped with some visual or auditory mechanism to notify the operators. But whether the operator or machine is engaged in monitoring the line, the operator is encouraged to keep a vigilant eye out for defects. The cooperation of human and machine to identify defects is a powerful after-the-fact tool in seeking perfection.

An even more powerful approach to perfection is to prevent defects from ever occurring. This is done by choosing constructive practices that make whole classes of defects impossible. Such practices are often called *poka-yoke*, which means "mistake-proofing" or "error-proofing." Mistake-proofing devices include electronic sensors as well as other physical devices such as counters, timers, and information-transmitting devices using sensors. A few players in one sector of the software industry (high-integrity systems) already have a mistake-proofing philosophy in place, known as correctness by construction (CbC).[48] CbC means that the method of production should prevent defects from ever being introduced.

The Synergy of the Five Lean Principles

In the manufacturing industries, many lean gurus advance one or another of the lean principles over the remaining ones, as being the essence of the lean. For instance, the QFD Institute views lean through the prism of the value stream: "Quality Function Deployment is a unique system for developing new products which aims to assure that the initial quality of the product or service will satisfy the customer ... QFD is the only comprehensive quality system aimed specifically at satisfying our customer."[49] The Flow Alliance company promotes flow as the most important principle: "Implementation of flow manufacturing is usually the best investment that a company can make. There are few other opportunities that offer this kind of payback."[50] Still, others promote pull, referring to it by its lean near-synonym of just-in-time, believing that JIT is the heart of the lean paradigm. There are even a few who advocate perfection as the essential goal, especially those who dogmatically belong to the "formal methods" camp as well as those who see *jidoka* as the absolute key to lean: "The Toyota Production System is frequently modeled as a house with two pillars. One pillar represents just-in-time (JIT), and the other pillar the concept of *jidoka* ... *jidoka* is key to making the entire system stick."[51] We've already noted that many people view the value principle as the most important one: It is a small step from there to make it the only essential one.

All of these proponents have their point: Every one of the five principles is important. However, in a sense these viewpoints all neglect the bigger picture: The synergy among these five principles is more powerful than any one principle by itself. This is especially true in the software development industry, where the techniques associated with each principle only begin to have an effect when used together in an integrated development lifecycle. Indeed, lean techniques that come under the banner of a particular lean principle often have weaknesses that can only be addressed by the strengths of another lean principle. If a novice needs a simple one-liner to sum up the lean paradigm, it would be accurate to say that lean is all about using a synergistic, synthetic approach for eliminating waste and adding value for the customer.

A Way to Reunify the Software Disciplines

The reasons for wanting to unify projects within a company are obvious—such as saving on expenses like personnel transfers and retraining, the sharing of knowledge, and new program startup costs. In Chapter 1, we briefly touched on how software professionals have chosen process maturity and technological capability as standards for measuring the most effective software businesses and organizations. These standards have not been particularly dependable in the long or short term. Significantly, the current measures not only fail to assess organizational effectiveness, but also place a lid on the amount of project unification that is possible. They fail because, to date, these measures drive companies to create standard processes as their chosen means to unify their software programs.

It's hard to say how the software industry came to expect standard processes to unify distinct software projects. Reading and listening to others in the field suggests that for some, the reasoning goes a little like this: All computer programs are made of the same thing—bits—and developed on the same types of platforms—computers . . . so, naturally, they all can be built using substantially the same processes. But if we applied this logic to auto manufacturers, we could say that all auto parts are made of the same thing—atoms—and are developed on tools that are all essentially mechanical, meaning you should be able to build all auto parts using the same processes! The absurdity of the idea becomes obvious when we think about it in terms of real products instead of virtual ones.[52] Even similar products often have differences that are significant enough to warrant changing the detailed constructive processes.

If software professionals will step back from these two currently favored measures of processes and technology for a moment, and use the industrial paradigm as the standard measure, they will not only understand their industry better, they will also discover that lean is a nearly ideal basis for unifying projects throughout a company. By using lean production as the ideal, and the techniques of its five principles as the mechanism, the software industry can remove waste or *muda* across all the projects in the business.

In the relatively unusual situation where literally sharing processes among projects would be a potentially effective business tactic, lean techniques like *kaizen* events will reveal these opportunities. More important, a *kaizen* event will immediately reveal process sharing that increases rather than decreases *muda*. Process sharing then becomes not an ultimate goal, but merely one of many potential tools to achieving the real goal, which is building a healthier and more competitive business.

The five principles of lean development introduced in this chapter provide a powerful basis for software companies to unify themselves and to optimize their overall business performance. In Part II, we will demonstrate their application and you may judge for yourself what they could do for you. However, before we can set out, we need to determine what the software industry's dominant industrial paradigm actually is. We will do this by looking objectively at three of the software industry's most-favored current practices: reuse, the SEI CMM, and the Agile Method called XP or Extreme Programming. These are the subjects of the next three chapters.

ENDNOTES

1. http://www.secondlaw.com/two.htm, as viewed on December 1, 2004.

2. R. Schonberger, *Japanese Manufacturing Techniques: Nine Hidden Lessons in Simplicity*, New York, NY: The Free Press (A Division of Macmillan Publishing Co., Inc.), 1982, from the Preface, pg. vii.

3. In the mind-bending, controversial, and somewhat revisionist point of view of *Henry Ford's Lean Vision* (New York, NY: Productivity Press, October 2002), author William A. Levinson presents the view that Henry Ford himself was the philosophical father of lean production, and in some ways, went beyond what the Japanese have done. Other and less-disputed originators of concepts that have been incorporated into lean production include W. Edwards Deming and Joseph M. Juran.

4. For a clear insight on how Taichi Ohno evolved a new production system, see Ohno, Taichi, *The Toyota Production System: Beyond Large Scale Production*, Portland, OR: Productivity Press, 1988.

5. C. Dassbach, "Where is North American Automobile Production Headed?," *Electronic Journal of Sociology*, 1994. This article is a wonderful exploration of the sociological implications of lean production.

6. C. Dassbach, "Where is North American Automobile Production Headed?," *Electronic Journal of Sociology*, 1994.

7. J. Womack, D. Jones, *Lean Thinking*, Simon & Schuster, 1996, Preface

8. Automakers in the United States initially had difficulty applying lean concepts. This led to the idea discussed briefly in the 1980s that lean production was native to the Japanese culture, and would not work with Americans. This was later disproved when Ford Motor Company and other U.S. automakers succeeded in implementing lean production techniques such as QFD (Quality Function Deployment), and to a lesser extent, *hoshin kanri*.

9. *Lean Thinking*, Preface.

10. *Lean Thinking*, pg. 16.

11. *Lean Thinking*, pg. 32.

13. Another instructive example, really worth your time to read, is described in *Lean Thinking* concerning the Wiremold Company. In a nutshell, Wiremold was certain it knew what its customers valued. After all, it had been around them for years, and its products were reasonably simple. The company thought its customers wanted rugged, low-cost wireguides that were highly safe. Sales were disappointing, however. A company initiative to apply lean techniques followed. What it discovered was that its customers really wanted products that looked good and were easy to install. Needless to say, changes resulted in the product lines. Customers were happier, and so too (soon) was Wiremold. (*Lean Thinking*, pg. 31).

13. C. Locke, R. Levine, D. Searls, D. Weinberger, *The Cluetrain Manifesto: The End of Business As Usual*, New York, NY: Perseus Publishing, 1999.

14. J. Martin, "The Great Transition: Using the Seven Disciplines of Enterprise Engineering to Align People, Technology and Strategy," AMACOM, New York. September 1995.

15. M. Rother, J. Shook, *Learning To See*, Brookline, MA: The Lean Enterprise Institute, Inc., 1998.

16. M. Rother, J. Shook, *Learning To See*, The Lean Enterprise Institute, Inc., 1998.

17. Bob King, "*Hoshin Planning: The Developmental Approach*," GOAL/QPC 1989, pg. 1–3.

18. Michael Cowley and Ellen Domb; *Beyond Strategic Vision; Effective Corporate Action with Hoshin Planning*, Burlington, MA: Butterworth Heinemann, 1997.

19. *Lean Thinking*, pg. 15.

20. M. Joyce, "LM21 Operating Excellence," Lockheed Martin Aeronautics Company Supplier Conference, Nov. 2000; "Lean Supply Chain of the Future: A Competitive Advantage TODAY," https://suppliernet.external.lmco.com/suppliernet/main/supplier_programs/conf_2000_docs/OperExcel_Joyce.pdf.

21. The letters "SAE" originally meant the 'Society of Automobile Engineers.' Later this was changed to the 'Society of Automotive Engineers.' Now the charter has been further broadened and the SAE refers to itself as 'The Engineering Society for Advancing Mobility in Land, Sea, Air, and Space.' The SAE is responsible for creating more aerospace and ground-vehicle standards than any other body.

22. From the "CPP Leadership Forum" (Comprehensive Performance Partnership) notes, on the National Labor Management Association (NLMA) website (http://www.nlma.org/gemba.htm), about the M. Imai book, *GEMBA KAIZEN:*

A Commonsense, Low-cost Approach to Management, New York, NY: McGraw-Hill, 1997.

23. Goldratt, Eliyahu M., *Theory of Constraints*, Great Barrington, MA: North River Press Publishing Corporation; December 1999.

24. *Lean Thinking*, pg. 52.

25. *The Machine That Changed the World*, pg. 37.

26. http://commerce.netsetgo.com/cgi-bin/qsoft.storefront/EN/product/BKS200; Thomas Pyzdek, *The Six Sigma Handbook* New York, NY: McGraw Hill; 2003

27. http://www.nwlean.net/leanfaqs.htm.

28. S. Spear, H. K. Bowan, "Harvard Business Review," September–October 1999

29. Wm. Roper, "The Missing Link of Lean Success," SAE International; see http://www.sae.org/topics/leanmay02.htm.

30. *Lean Thinking*, pg. 103.

31. *Lean Thinking*, pg. 22.

32. *Lean Thinking*, pg. 22.

33. *Lean Thinking*, pg. 60.

34. R. Schonberger, *Japanese Manufacturing Techniques: Nine Hidden Lessons in Simplicity*, New York, NY: The Free Press, Division of Macmillan Publishing Co., Inc. 1982; pg. 1.

35. Ibid., pg. 21.

36. *Lean Thinking*, pg. 60.

37. *Lean Thinking*, pg. 23.

38. *Lean Thinking*, pg. 60.

39. A. Weber, "Lean Machines," *Assembly Magazine*, March 2002.

40. Once such "pieces" have been identified, then you can apply other lean techniques, such as using customer value to determine the order in which in you should produce the pieces for maximum customer satisfaction. There will be more on this later, especially in Chapter 19.

41. R. Schonberger, "*Japanese Manufacturing Techniques: Nine Hidden Lessons in Simplicity*," New York, NY: The Free Press, Division of Macmillan Publishing Co., Inc. 1982; pg. 44.

42. Singh, N. (1995) "*Systems Approach to Computer-Integrated Design and Manufacturing*," Indianapolis, IN: John Wiley & Sons, Inc., 1995, pp, 630–631.

43. This board is a product of American LED-gible Inc. The picture was obtained from American LED-gible's website, and is used with their permission.

44. *Lean Thinking*, pg. 71.

45. *Lean Thinking*, pg. ??.

46. *Lean Thinking*, pg. 90.

47. M. Rosenthal, "The Essence of Jidoka," *Lean Directions*, the e-Newsletter of Lean Manufacturing, a publication of the SME (Society of Manufacturing Engineers), 2002.

48. Two papers on the subject are James Sutton's and Bernard Carré's "Achieving High Integrity at Low Cost: A Constructive Approach," 1995 Avionics Conference and Exhibition, *Low-Cost Avionics—Can We Afford It?*—Conference Proceedings,

London November 29–30, 1995; and Peter Amey's "Correctness by Construction: Better Can Also Be Cheaper," Crosstalk Journal of Defense Software Engineering, March 2002.

49. A. Bolt, G. Mazur, "Jurassic QFD," The Eleventh Symposium on Quality Function Deployment, Michigan, June 1999.

50. Richard D. Rahn, President of the Flow Alliance, quoted on the Flow Alliance website home page, www.allliance.com, September 28, 2004. To be precise, the company recognizes other principles such as value stream, but subordinates them to the flow principle.

51. M. Rosenthal, "The Essence of Jidoka," *Lean Directions*, the e-Newsletter of Lean Manufacturing, a publication of the SME (Society of Manufacturing Engineers), 2002.

52. Another industry that provides an interesting analogy is that of integrated-chip manufacture. A given company in this business typically makes many different chips, often using different processes (X-Ray, E-beam, and so on). Each process has unique requirements. They couldn't do this if they had to maintain utter process-level uniformity.

4

Determining Software's Industrial Paradigm—Reuse Practice

O N THE BASIS OF WHAT WE'VE SAID about the three industrial paradigms—craft, mass, and lean—we can now begin determining the predominant paradigm of the software industry. We need a plan of attack, because
this is a very big industry and we want to get to an answer reasonably quickly.
One way is to use the principles of the science of measurement, which requires
that any measurement be validated or calibrated against something known. Let's
take as an example how NASA measures the earth from a satellite.

To validate the data from a new satellite, it is compared against data known
as "ground truth." Ground truth is the data obtained by direct (i.e., on the ground
or by air) observation of a small area within the larger area being observed by the
satellite. Once the satellite's data concerning these areas matches that of the
ground truth data, the satellite is considered calibrated and its measurements are
trusted in areas for which ground data are not available.[1] The satellite's inherent
advantage, its ability to measure larger areas than can be economically observed
up close, then becomes fully available.

Trying to measure the software industry directly as a whole is as impractical
as trying to measure the entire earth from the ground. We need to find the
ground truth of how a few parts of the software industry fit into the existing
industrial paradigms. With those comparisons in hand, we can then move our
gaze to the higher viewing level of applying industrial principles to the software
industry as a whole, without having to repeatedly examine the detailed "ground
truth" of everything about the world of software . . . an impossibly large job. Our
initial ground truth will keep our broader observations calibrated to reality.

Which measurements shall we take for our ground truth? It is important to
choose these wisely. If they are not representative, then all our other observations
will be incorrectly calibrated and not trustworthy. The best ground truth we have
is our first-hand knowledge of some of software's most highly regarded and well-
understood processes and practices. There are three major practices that each
have their avid supporters in different sectors of the industry. These practices and
their main areas of influence are:

1. *Reuse.* Mainstream commercial practice (discussed in this chapter).
2. *SEI CMM.* Government or institutionally-contracted or -regulated development, though currently expanding its influence to other sectors (discussed in Chapter 5).
3. *Extreme Programming.* Leading-edge commercial practice (discussed in Chapter 6).

Previously we talked about how industries begin as craft producers, move on to mass production, and then on to lean. Wherever the above software best practices end up on this scale will tell us a lot about the upper limit to how far the software industry as a whole has come. And even if any of these three practices doesn't directly affect your part of the software industry, you will probably see similarities between their characteristics and the practices your sector has adopted.

The Craft Approach to Software Reuse

Every company would like to take advantage of its previous product development expenditures. In its most general sense, this is what reuse is all about . . . leveraging prior investments. Reuse in its various forms has leveraged everything that producers create: code, design, requirements, processes, tools, environments, procedures, and even human knowledge and experience.

Broadly speaking, the software industry has tried four major reuse approaches in the order of increasing power and widespread usefulness: *opportunistic, library, domain inventory,* and *domain-on-demand.* The first and last of these correspond to craft and lean production, respectively. The middle two are mass production approaches.

Craft producers of software, like their counterparts in other industries, believe that their products are so unique that only highly skilled artisans can produce them. In software, this means developing each system using wide-open approaches such as ad hoc coding or rapid prototyping. Craft-paradigm software reuse therefore focuses on reusing the knowledge of programmers as well as pieces of existing systems, verbatim or nearly so. This is called opportunistic reuse, because there is little or no forethought given to making your current work reusable in the future.

When software developers look to the past to find reusable assets, they find things opportunistically. As two of Merriam-Webster's definitions revealingly put it, being opportunistic is "feeding on whatever food is available <opportunistic feeders>," and (getting to the root of the problem with this kind of reuse) "exploiting with little regard to principle or consequences <a politician considered opportunistic>."[2] This kind of reuse is opportunity-driven, not principle-driven. In truth, it reuses whatever it finds available, often regardless of the quality thereof.

Opportunistic reuse is useful only in limited situations. Once craft producers decide that a new system will take on functionality that is more than a little different from previous systems, they revert from reuse into new development. Furthermore, the rapid employment turnover commonly seen among software professionals also means that *craft producers often lose even the opportunity to reuse programmer knowledge, and therefore gain little from reuse.*

Therefore, opportunistic reuse is significant mainly in companies that have specialized in systems that evolve gradually over many years, with relatively slow changes to their foundational functions (such as usually happens with computer operating systems or banking software). In such cases, verbatim reuse of many of the previous generation's code modules is often practical. Because this accounts for a fairly small portion of the software industry, craft reuse is a minor factor in the larger world of software production.

Mass Approaches to Software Reuse

Perhaps because the most important principle of mass production is efficiency, mass software producers look first for reuse approaches that improve efficiency. This puts their focus in reuse mainly on components and processes. The perfect example of mass reuse outside of software is standardized component reuse used in mass production automobile manufacturing since the 1920s, as epitomized by Alfred P. Sloan's General Motors.

In software, we would expect component-based reuse to work well to the degree that the software enterprise resembles early GM. GM produced five lines of cars, from the common to the extravagant, Chevrolet to Cadillac. To cut the costs of all these varieties, Sloan built these cars by drawing from the same set of lower-level building blocks: alternators, carburetors, and so on. "Sloan's innovative thinking also seemed to resolve the conflict between the need for standardization to cut manufacturing costs and the model diversity required by the huge range of consumer demand. He achieved both goals by standardizing many mechanical items, such as pumps and generators, across the company's entire product range."[3]

Standardized components are the essence of mass paradigm reuse in any industry. These components can be at any level of sophistication, from individual parts (in software terms, code modules, or low-level processes) to entire architectures and development processes (such a wide range of complexity is also seen in cars, for example, from steering wheels to complete engines).

Mass production software development takes one of two broad approaches to software component reuse: the *library approach* and the *domain-inventory approach.*

Library Reuse

In the library approach, software components are collected and placed into libraries, often by mining the components directly from previous software programs. Each component is catalogued by its attributes in a sort of Dewey Decimal System of software components.[4,5]

The developer of a new piece of software accesses the library and looks for components that might match the functions and other criteria (called *facets*) needed for the new system. Specific needs covered by facets include such criteria as interface data, underlying algorithms, delivered output precision, and quality/integrity level, among many, many others. If the developer finds the right component with just the right set of attributes (which doesn't happen very often, given the number of facets that a nontrivial piece of software will likely have), the developer incorporates that component into his or her part of the system and writes the custom bits around the reused parts.

The library approach has had limited success in the 20+ years of its existence. Like craft reuse, it has been most effective in software systems that have had many consecutive releases that have drawn upon previous releases, such as operating systems, in common software tools like word processing systems and spreadsheets, and in financial software, such as for banking and payroll. Since most software doesn't fit in any of these molds, library reuse has been less fruitful for most software development than experts originally projected.

More recently, efforts have been made to extend library reuse to architectural patterns.[6,7] While these patterns are more generic than simple library components and therefore at least more conceptually useful, the excitement over and claims for them are strangely reminiscent of the enthusiasm over component libraries in the early 1980s. People have taken many tacks on generalizing the library approach to achieve a breakthrough level of software reuse, but none have achieved this goal to date. Why? Because library approaches are rooted in the precepts of the mass paradigm. That is, these reuse approaches still focus on improving efficiency, by utilizing the existing infrastructure of code and designs to the fullest. No attention to speak of is paid to either waste or flexibility, dominant lean concerns. Architectural patterns are at a high enough level conceptually that they can provide useful ideas for mid-level designs, without compromising on the lean principles, but only if they are subordinated to a lean lifecycle like that discussed in Parts II and III.

Domain Inventory Reuse

You can practice domain reuse in either a mass way or a lean way. Both are improvements on library reuse. However, mass-paradigm domain reuse is not usually practical, and therefore, people talk about it more than they practice it.

Software systems are considered to be within the same domain if they perform roughly the same kind of overall mission in meeting the needs of real customers. To understand such a domain, a developer can study the needs behind each individual but related system, to see what is common or repeated in all or most of them. Other techniques for understanding a domain are discussed in Part II.

Knowing the shared aspects of the domain is the starting point for developing a domain design that incorporates the elements common to all such systems. This nearly eliminates one of the main problems with the library approach; i.e., seldom being able to find a part that really fits your needs. If you are working in the same domain, a previously developed domain system will very likely be a good starting point for future development.

Unlike in the library approach, no one expects that components—even general purpose ones like sorts—written for a given domain will work for any other domain. Thus, the domain reuse approach works for a greater number of domains than does the supposedly general-purpose library approach. That is because, while the components in a given domain can't usually be used in other domains, the *approach* of developing domain-specific components for a given domain can.

Thus far, everything said about domain reuse can be applied to either mass or lean production. In mass production, however, domain artifacts are created ahead of time—outside of a specific project—and they are put on the shelf to be used in future programs in that domain. That maximizes efficiency by getting the most use out of each resource, i.e., each domain component. However, such working ahead is a kind of inventory. Inventory is *muda* according to the precepts of lean JIT.

Let's examine some of the sources of waste in building up an inventory of domain components. First, the developers of the domain design will do their work long before any system in the domain is developed or sold. Since no revenue will come any time soon, the work of the domain designers is usually underfunded compared to paying projects. The predictable result is that their products are less polished than they would be in a direct revenue-producing system.

Second, because no actual purchasing and paying customer is involved in the development, the resulting design will not be as deep or insightful as it would have been with a real customer. For both reasons, there usually (in our experience, always) will be some mismatching between a domain design done this way and the actual situation (the real customers and needs) in the domain.

Worse, markets change over time. A company using this approach may be faced with fundamental domain change before it has developed enough systems in the domain to recover the costs of developing the domain design. All of this is *muda*, and much of it is risk, as managers are quick to discern.

Adding insult to injury, in mass production domain development, the people who develop the domain design, called domain engineers, are not the people who develop the product based on the domain inventory, called product engineers or something similar. This is another application of Henry Ford's mass production approach to separating the work of engineering the production line from the work of engineering the automobile itself. It is a classic example of division of labor with the accompanying wastes that we discussed in Chapter 2.

In the late 1980s, an organization called the Software Productivity Consortium (SPC), funded by some of the world's largest software companies, constructed a mathematical model[8] for estimating the effects of reuse on software productivity and schedule performance. The model focused on the most sophisticated mass production reuse approach, the domain-inventory approach we've just discussed.

Based on well-documented industry experience, the model showed that domain-inventory reuse typically pays off in the third project an organization conducts using its repository of domain parts. This, of course, means that such reuse costs a company extra money and time for the first two projects after creating the repository! Since few companies can afford to give up a competitive advantage for their first two deliverable systems in a domain, domain-inventory reuse has proven a hard sell to industry.

Lean Approaches to Software Reuse

Lean reuse is also domain-based, but with important differences. It makes no distinction between domain engineers and development engineers: The same people do both jobs. Furthermore, lean domain reuse generally begins identifying domain commonalties as part of an organization's first paying project in a domain, rather than as part of an up-front speculation (the exception would be if an organization already has products in the domain and then converts to lean production: In that case, work on the first lean project would probably do some mining from the prior systems in addition to doing fresh domain analysis).

Thus, lean production looks forward rather than backward. It can practice reuse without having any pre-existing or off-the-shelf assets available. Such reuse, however, can also take advantage of previous assets. In either case, the lean reuser identifies the elements or patterns of the current project that are frequently repeated.

I like to call this domain-on-demand reuse, to echo the lean phrase just-in-time. Domain-on-demand means the lean software producer will create robust archetypal artifacts of all sorts (including but not limited to: values, requirements, design, knowledge, documentation, verification, or code) the first time the producer encounters the need for such an artifact. From then on, the producer will reuse those artifacts. Using the techniques described in Part III, even the initial creation will be done cost effectively.

Each new project in a domain creates more such artifacts, enriching the vocabulary available for future related projects. As a result, over time, the amount of off-the-shelf reuse climbs … but never at the expense of present profitability, because the organization is also directing its efforts at reducing present and future waste.

Lean's domain-on-demand contrasts with mass domain-inventory reuse. Domain inventory reuse in the name of efficiency attempts to use all available resources and infrastructures as completely as possible, as if they were machines on the factory floor. Mass producers work to get the most out of what they have accumulated from the past: past project artifacts, past investments, and past processes. However, in the lean view, sometimes the highest-payoff action is to abandon the past altogether and start with a fresh sheet of paper, discovering the reuse possible within just the confines of a project. This would never be acceptable to a mass producer charged with leveraging the reuse of its existing assets (i.e., with maximizing efficiency).

Thus, lean domain reuse requires that the developer take the time to consider other systems (real or potential) in the domain while developing its first paying system in the domain. This goes beyond what is normally done in the early stages of single-system development. However, the robustness of a lean domain design quickly repays the extra effort, including by reducing rework later in the same development cycle. It continues to reduce costs for maintenance and modification after the organization fields the system. Taken as a whole, even the first project in a domain cuts time, money, and risk compared to traditional projects. The following project illustrates these gains.

How a Lean Domain-Reuse Project Redefined the Reuse Model

In the late 1980s, Jim joined an information processing project as the lead software architect and technical-process developer. The project was called GPSSUP, an acronym for the Ground Processing System Software Update Program.

GPSSUP came about because the Air Force had recently released into service a new version of the C-5 airlifter, the C-5B. Compared to the C-5A version the company had built in the 1960s and 1970s, the C-5B design had greatly expanded the variety and amount of telemetry data collected on each mission from sensors throughout the aircraft. A new postprocessing, ground-based system had to be developed to extract information from those data to support maintenance and performance decisions.

For instance, engine maintenance in the C-5A had always been rigidly scheduled so that failures would almost never occur in the field. The customer had found rigid scheduling to be wasteful, because most engines were still in good shape at the time of their overhauls. Nevertheless, since nobody could tell which engines might have imminent problems, all engines had to adhere to the schedule. With the new onboard data-recording system, the critical parameters for each engine were available to allow maintenance to be scheduled only when it was truly needed. This and numerous other analyses promised to save the customer many work hours (they had the engine shop) and much money.

The software team had to do something out of the ordinary on the project, because it came with challenging cost and schedule goals that could not be met using traditional development approaches.[9] Even the most popular cutting-edge development practices of the time didn't seem to hold enough promise for helping the team do well enough on the key business metrics. Library reuse was too generic for this project's domain: There wasn't any hope of finding enough off-the-shelf components that we could rework for our purposes quickly and cheaply enough to put the project ahead. A mass domain inventory reuse wasn't an option because GPSSUP didn't have two reuse projects behind it to set it up to be competitive.

Working in the project's favor was its unique contract structure. GPSSUP would be conducted in four phases, with each phase being a complete lifecycle. This provided an almost ideal low-risk laboratory for trying innovative approaches to improving development processes. We decided to try out one or two potentially high-payoff innovations in each cycle, starting with the second phase (Phase 1 was in most ways traditional). We kept fallback positions for each innovation in case we saw it wasn't working out, and we were watching to discover such problems early, before much damage could be done. If an innovation worked out, we would take it into the next phase and add more innovations. In a couple of cases, we replaced a working innovation with a more advanced and even higher leverage one. Then the previous innovation became the fallback position. Most of the adopted innovations were overtly lean; a couple were stepping stones towards lean.

By the time Jim joined the program, skillful software engineers had already nearly completed Phase 1. This phase did include a small amount of craft-type utilities reuse. In the second phase, we pushed reuse into design, taking a more mass production approach (systematic instead of opportunistic, but still very primitive) . . . a stepping stone towards true lean reuse. By the third phase, we had gained a little ground on our challenging schedule and so added two more elements that were starting to be truly lean: generalization and in-project waste reduction.

1. *Generalization.* Instead of using the mass production division of labor technique and dividing software engineers by specializing them into sepa-

rate categories, the project broadened the scope of the development engineers so they also performed domain analysis. Having the same people do both types of activities gave a greater air of reality to the domain analysis, while also ensuring that development would be more domain savvy. This made each engineer conscious of both the characteristics of the domain as a whole and also the system at hand. It also helped engineers recognize when proposed design decisions would work well for the current system, but not work well for likely future changes to the system … a frequent problem with non-domain-based development, and one that leads to increased rework and costs later in a project.

2. *In-Project Waste Reduction.* The domain analysis included a search for both functional and object commonalities within the project as well as across projected similar projects or projected future variants of the same system. This provided additional immediate opportunities for reuse (dubbed "internal reuse" by the staff). We used object-oriented analysis,[10] but by looking both within the system and across the domain, the mindset was wider than is usual in OOA. This was the beginning point for domain-on-demand reuse, upon which we would expand tremendously in later projects.

In the fourth and final project phase, we removed the artificial wall between software analysis and system analysis. Applying the same methods used in Phase 3 on the software, we analyzed the hardware/software/user/world system as a whole and found many additional commonalties and reuse candidates. GPSSUP software engineers worked hand-in-hand with the systems engineers and developed a much more thorough and insightful understanding of how the software needed to perform in the context of its larger system.

All four project phases were in the same problem domain and were performed under reasonably similar circumstances. This allowed the company to compare the effectiveness of the different approaches used in each phase, much more directly than is normally possible in the software production world. The project became, in effect, a real time laboratory for making and evaluating lean process improvements. Lest you think this approach irresponsible, remember that the cost and schedule goals for this project had already been determined to be unattainable using traditional means. Thus, the lowest-risk alternative available to the project was to innovate in a controlled fashion, with low-risk fallback positions for each innovation, as described earlier.

GPSSUP was close to a double-blind experiment for comparing mass and lean reuse approaches. The results were startling: Lean paradigm reuse more than paid for itself on the project. Unlike mass reuse, it did so without having to take credit for future projects that would benefit from the reuse of the original project's artifacts. In other words, lean reuse paid for itself on the first project. By the end of the GPSSUP program, the productivity rate had nearly doubled from industry norms of the time, and quality had improved to the point of essentially eliminating fielded defects (see Figure 4-1).

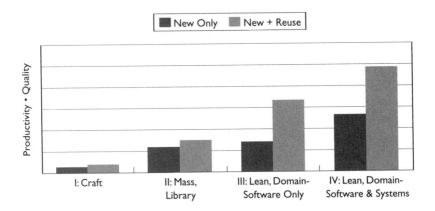

Figure 4-1. Impact of Industrial Paradigm on Reuse Effectiveness

In Figure 4-1, the vertical axis is the multiplicative product of productivity and quality gains. We'll call this 'productive quality' for convenience. To gain Lockheed Martin's permission to publish the chart, we have omitted the numbers from the axis. Nevertheless, the ratios shown graphically are proportionally correct. There are two columns for each of the four project phases. The first column represents the productive quality for just the nonreused (i.e., first-of-kind) items developed of each type—taking no credit for the second (and beyond) items of a given type. Note that as development practices move closer to the lean end of the spectrum, the productive quality goes up even without receiving credit for reused modules.

The second column in each phase accounts for all of the software developed in that phase, including modules that are reused. Here, the productive quality goes up even more rapidly. Note also that the spread between nonreuse productive quality and reuse productive quality (i.e., between the first column and the second) grows in later phases, with the adoption of more and more lean techniques. *This means that lean techniques increase the leverage of reuse: The more lean the development, the greater the benefit from practicing reuse.*

Customer relations improved at least as much as quality. The customer, who had a reputation for demanding the highest-quality product and who was always going back to its vendors for system fixes, reported that it never found a failure in the GPSSUP software during its approximately five year fielded life. Indeed, the customer's lead manager was so delighted with the system that she nicknamed the development team "the new Lockheed breed."

When the Software Productivity Consortium reviewed GPSSUP results (the actual numbers were available to them because of proprietary agreements with Lockheed), they updated their reuse model that had previously shown it taking three projects for reuse to break even. The new model showed it was possible to have a net productivity gain from reuse on a first project, as long as the project in question uses the lean elements of generalization and in-project waste reduction via immediate, internal, noninventoried reuse.[11]

The GPSSUP program demonstrated that you can greatly improve the business performance of a software organization even with a relatively primitive implementation of lean reuse. Still, at present and despite the success of GPSSUP and other projects that we will discuss in Parts II through IV, mass production approaches to software reuse remain dominant in the software industry. In other words, software is a mass production industry when it comes to reuse.

In the next chapter, we will address the second of our benchmark software practices, the SEI CMM. This software practice will speak even more loudly than did reuse of how an industrial paradigm drives software processes and business effectiveness. You may be surprised to find out which paradigm is driving the CMM and how clearly that paradigm has influenced the mandates that the CMM places on the portions of the software industry that are subject to it.

ENDNOTES

1. http://asd-www.larc.nasa.gov/SCOOL/groundtruth.html.
2. "opportunistic" (definition), *Merriam-Webster Online Dictionary*, 2004 http://www.merriam-webster.com (24 April, 2004).
3. *The Machine That Changed the World*, pp. 41–42.
4. R. Prieto-Diaz and P. Freeman, "Classifying software for reusability," *IEEE Software*, 18(1), January, 1987.
5. Amir Michail. "Data Mining Library Reuse Patterns Using Generalized Association Rules," ICSE, 2000.
6. Mark Klein, Rick Kazman, "Attribute-Based Architectural Styles" (CMU/SEI-99-TR-022).
7. Erich Gamma, Richard Helm, Ralph Johnson, John Vlissides, *Design Patterns*, Addison-Wesley, 1995; based on the pioneering idea of architectural patterns in Christopher Alexander's landmark architectural work, "*A Pattern Language*," New York, NY: Oxford University Press, 1977.
8. Not everything on this model was made available to the general public, but the best published reference to it is J. Gaffney, J. R. Cruickshank, "A General Economics Model of Software Reuse," IEEE 14th International Conference on Software Engineering, Melbourne, Australia, 19??.

9. Project management issued the challenge to better our productivity/schedule estimates by 10%, . . . and our estimates had already been submitted at 25% beneath industry norms.
10. The Paul Ward method, closely related to the better-known Schlaer-Mellor method.
11. GPSSUP used the OO concept of classes to capture domain similarity. However, there is nothing inherently lean about classes; as this chapter discussed earlier, domain similarity can be utilized in either a mass or a lean fashion. It was how GPSSUP utilized classes that made the reuse lean, not the fact of using a particular OO technique.

5

Determining Software's Industrial Paradigm—SEI CMM Practice

F ROM ITS BEGINNINGS, THE SOFTWARE INDUSTRY has been quite the problem child, with defect densities that would not be tolerated in any other
type of product, frequent cost overruns, and late or even nondeliveries. By 1982,
these difficulties had become so serious that the U.S. federal government, the
largest customer of software systems, began a serious review of possible solutions. The results of this study led to the creation in 1984 of an organization
called the Software Engineering Institute (SEI), under the umbrella of Carnegie
Mellon University.

The SEI founding mission statement said: "The U.S. Department of Defense
established the Software Engineering Institute to advance the practice of software
engineering because quality software that is produced on schedule and within
budget is a critical component of U.S. defense systems. The SEI mission is to provide leadership in advancing the state of the practice of software engineering to
improve the quality of systems that depend on software. The SEI accomplishes
this mission by promoting the evolution of software engineering from an ad hoc,
labor-intensive activity to a discipline that is well managed and supported by
technology."[1]

The SEI is a very competent and diligent organization, and has always
based its work on sound research. Watts Humphrey, one of the IBM software
practitioner–researchers who came into prominence in the 1970s and 1980s (this
cadre included Ed Yourdon and Frederick Brooks, among other luminaries), was
hired by the SEI in 1986. Humphrey had earlier observed that different organizations with similar business traits varied in their project performance by more
than tenfold. Accordingly, he set out to identify what it was in those organizations that might account for the variation.

Based on the results of this investigation, Humphrey and others working
with him at the SEI developed a framework[2,3] of criteria for evaluating the capability of software developers to conduct successful projects. These criteria were
based on practices common among most of the better-performing software
organizations. It's important to note here that such practices were (and are) not

guaranteed to be the best possible ways to produce software . . . any more than the best practices of craft producers in the nineteenth century would be better than those of the best mass producers of the mid-twentieth century. The SEI comparisons were made wholly within the context of the late-twentieth century software industry, which we have maintained all along is not the be-all and end-all of what is possible for software organizations. However, it's undeniable that the shared practices of software organizations who performed well were better than the practices of those who performed poorly.

The SEI researchers formalized these practices and expanded them into a process-centered assessment system focusing on a set of key process areas (KPAs). They distributed the KPAs among graded levels of increasing capability. The framework thus evolved into the model known as the Capability Maturity Model for Software,[4] or CMM. It continues its influence through its successors.[5]

In contrast to the minimal industry adoption of the reuse practices discussed in the previous chapter, the SEI CMM has revolutionized the way that broad sectors of the software business work. Many organizations doing business with government agencies have adopted it under mandate. For a variety of reasons, numbers of commercial developers have adopted it as well (for instance, some are suppliers to government vendors, who trickle down the CMM requirement to them; others have resorted to the CMM to try to solve development problems they haven't been able to solve any other way).

With the ever-increasing role government is playing in regulating commercial software and the sheer amount of money and encouragement government is pouring into the CMM, the CMM has become arguably the most influential trend in the entire software industry. For this reason, it is crucial that we in the industry clearly recognize the predominant industrial paradigm of the CMM.

The Five Organizational Maturity Levels of the CMM

The KPAs have been assigned to Levels 2 through 5 of the CMM. Level 1, the initial level of organizational maturity, is the condition of organizations having chaotic or ad hoc development processes. This level essentially corresponds to traditional craft production: It gets the job done by relying on the capabilities of team experts (sometimes called, with some irony but no disrespect, "heroes"), rather than on any strength of process. The second or *repeatable* level is the first stage of improvements (and KPAs). It is followed by Level 3, *defined*; Level 4, *managed*; and finally, Level 5, *optimizing* (see Figure 5-1).[6]

Since the KPAs reflect field observations of processes that have helped software developers in the past, they are of interest to virtually all software developers.

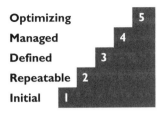

Figure 5-1. Levels of CMM

A Level 2 repeatable organization's primary traits are that it plans and tracks its work. A repeatable organization stores its products in a consistent way and knows when and how it is changing those products (e.g., by configuration control of requirements, design, and code). Such an organization also performs some sort of independent double-check to ensure that it is completing the work in the way it was planned (i.e., using quality assurance). This set of traits is the focus of the Level 2 KPAs.

A Level 3 defined organization adds to the Level 2 traits a written description of the processes it follows for doing all the steps of software development. This recording process applies to all of the organization's individual software development programs and includes a written approach to tailoring existing processes for specific situations. A Level 3 organization also extends quality assurance to verifying that it is following its own written processes. Training is another big requirement since people can have difficulty understanding the organization's written processes or how they should be implemented. Yet another requirement is to gather data (i.e., metrics) about how well it performs on its standardized processes. At Level 3, the CMM also begins to dictate the organizational structure of a company by requiring that there be a software engineering process group. It further affects the way an organization executes production by mandating peer reviews and making stipulations on the lifecycle phase activities of requirements analysis, design, coding, testing, documentation, and maintenance. The CMM does not say exactly *how* an organization must do these specific things (at least, not usually in terms of which technical approaches to use), but it does say that they must be done, and often specifies the degree to which they must be done.

A Level 4 managed organization extends the number and type of metrics gathered and requires that it use the data from these metrics to control and improve process performance.

While the Level 4 organization uses data to help itself do better at executing its existing processes, the Level 5 optimizing organization uses the same data to find ways to improve the processes themselves. At this level, an organization must have a mechanism for evaluating new technologies for their applicability and benefit to the existing processes. It must also have a special process for incorporating the new technologies in an orderly way.

Successes and Caveats for the CMM—Raytheon and Boeing

The SEI has pointed to several projects to show the value of the CMM. It often refers to the Raytheon Equipment Division as a notable success story. After flunking their initial CMM assessment, the Equipment Division improved its level twice and went from consistently poor schedule and budget performances to performing most projects ahead of schedule and under budget.[7] There is no doubt that applying the key practices of the CMM improved the condition of the Equipment Division's software operation. Since they began at Level 1, they started out as craft developers. Climbing the CMM ladder moved them out of craft production, with measurably positive results.

Perhaps the most famous example cited in favor of the CMM is the Boeing Space Transport System (STS) software team. The STS team was one of the first organizations to attain Level 5. To be fair, however, we should place the role of the CMM in STS project performance in some context. Boeing had implemented most of the practices that qualified them for Level 5 before the CMM was ever considered: "In the past two years, [i.e., 1996–1997] ... Much of the [software process] activity has been to correlate the existing STS processes to the CMM framework, though most of the practices at Levels 2 through 5 were already institutionalized in STS."[8] So STS's performance was not due to the CMM; instead, the CMM simply revealed that the STS team was already performing the practices the CMM encouraged.

The STS was unusually well suited to the strictures of the CMM. The measures promoted by the CMM called for the software team to have total control over the software process and its outcome. This was natural for the STS team, because it was developing one of the most safety-critical systems on earth, with the lives of the astronauts literally at stake. Nevertheless, whether other software organizations with similarly stringent software quality demands would find the CMM the most effective way to achieve the needed integrity is a very different question. In other words, the high CMM level of the STS team, while interesting to know, doesn't in itself tell us much about the usefulness of the CMM in other situations than the STS and especially about its helpfulness as a before-the-fact approach to improving the performance of software developers in general (even safety-critical ones).

Those who have worked with the CMM differ in their assessments of how much benefit it has provided. To get better answers to those questions, we will have to look deeper into the CMM itself. We will attempt to make the discussion more objective by correlating the characteristics of the CMM Levels 2 through 5 to the principles of the mass and lean industrial paradigms. The craft paradigm is not included in our evaluation because craft production directly corresponds to CMM Level 1 but not to the higher levels, and the higher levels are the objective of anyone seeking to adhere to the CMM.

Comparing the CMM to Mass Principles

In Chapter 2, we introduced five major principles of the mass production paradigm: repeatability, large infrastructures, efficiency, organizational gigantism, and technocentrism. Here we will compare the CMM to a few aspects of these principles and note, where appropriate, how the lean approach would handle the mass production issue being discussed.

Repeatability and the CMM

One of the first goals of implementing the CMM is to achieve repeatability. The SEI states "software process maturity implies that the productivity and quality resulting from an organization's software process can be improved over time through consistent gains in the discipline achieved by applying its software process."[9] Consistent discipline produces repeatability.

CMM repeatability is process repeatability. The CMM does not explicitly address part repeatability, perhaps because software organizations have been unable to produce repeatable software parts on any significant scale. As we discussed in Chapter 2, Henry Ford's greatest accomplishment was to be the first to achieve part repeatability on a large scale. As we saw then, process repeatability is normally built on the shoulders of part repeatability. Part repeatability is what cuts the tie of dependence on skilled craft artisans. One cannot expect the software industry to fully reap the benefits of repeatability until all its elements have been mastered. This is not so much a deficiency of the CMM as it is a reflection of the realities of our industry. Nevertheless, the CMM is not moving the industry past those realities, so the CMM only implements a part of the mass production principle of repeatability.

Efficiency and the CMM

The CMM also places a high value on efficiency: "Higher [CMM] maturity level organizations have increased process efficiency."[10] An efficiency-driven approach focuses on optimizing activities.[11] Efficiency also holds to the "commonsense conviction that activities ought to be grouped by type."[12] The CMM does this by measuring process performance at the level of the individual process area or "cluster of related activities."[13] "Key practices . . . provide guidance for improving an organization's performance in a key process area."[14] This is an example of how the worldview of the SEI researchers influenced what they said others should do to implement the effective practices they'd seen in the field. There's nothing about measuring performance that is inherently linked to activities, yet the CMM has added that linkage. *The CMM's focus on activities contrasts sharply with the lean focus on* "the real challenge ... continuous flow in small-lot production."[15] (Software qualifies as much as any business at being an industry of small lots!) Like orthogonal axes in a graph, the two approaches to optimization—the CMM's activities-first and lean's flows-first—are mutually exclusive.

The SEI's efficiency emphasis is similar to that of the reengineering movement that was prevalent in the 1980s and 1990s. "The reengineering movement has recognized that departmentalized thinking is suboptimal ... The problem is that the reengineers haven't gone far enough conceptually—they are still dealing with disconnected and aggregated processes ... rather than the entire flow of value-creating activities for specific products."[16] Like reengineering, the CMM hasn't gone far enough: It seeks efficiency as a primary goal, rather than emphasizing goals like flow and reduction of waste that are the corresponding and more business-oriented goals of lean production. In the principle of efficiency, the CMM has aligned itself solidly with mass production.

Division of Labor and the CMM

Division of labor is a natural result of the quest for efficiency (see the discussion of the mass paradigm in Chapter 2). In mass production, workers are specialized into categories like assemblers, industrial engineers, quality inspectors, and "rework men."[17] This is akin to the CMM's practice of differentiating workers by organizations. The CMM goes as far as to name what these organizations should be, for example:

- The software engineering group.
- The software engineering process group.
- The training group.
- The system engineering group.
- The software configuration management group.
- The software quality assurance group.
- The system test group.[18]

CMM statements like "at the defined level [Level 3] ... *there is a group* that is responsible for the organization's software process activities, e.g., a ... SEPG."[19] make it clear that organizations are expected to literally implement this division of labor rather than use it as a conceptual guide.

Following the CMM guidelines, organizations ensure worker interchangeability by limiting the scope of what each worker must know (via the division of labor) and by training each worker in an assigned role (via training processes and a dedicated training organization).

In the lean paradigm, such labor division is overkill—classic *muda*. "The Japanese seem to be able to let the simple system work—and resist the Western impulse to turn productivity and quality improvement over to armies of staff specialists."[20] However, the mass paradigm makes such division of labor a central goal. This characteristic of the CMM is distinctly driven by mass production.

Pressing this goal even further, the CMM uses division of labor to set up an adversarial approach to accountability. This is similar to classic mass production reengineering, which treats "departments and employees as the enemy, using outside SWAT teams to blast both aside. The frequent result is a collapse of morale . . . ."[21] The SWAT teams of reengineering correspond to the CMM's internal process groups and external assessors. The people in these two groups are often among the best in an organization, but the artificially imposed separation between them and the developers hinders everyone's effectiveness. The process people may not get the same opportunities as the developers to remain current on the latest development approaches, and conversely, the developers typically have little input into how the process people are planning to implement and enforce the CMM. Oftentimes, organizations merely inform developers of which tools and procedures they will use, without asking for their valuable on-the-ground perspective on what they need to do their job. This sad state of affairs is not by any means completely dictated by the CMM, but in our observations throughout industry it nevertheless happens more often than not. There is certainly nothing in the CMM to inhibit it, and it is the path of least resistance to implementing what the CMM *does* dictate.

Organizational splintering directly conflicts with the lean ideal that growth and change should come from within the organization. In lean production, the team itself owns and evolves the process. In the world of lean auto manufacturing, "The teams were . . . told to work together on how best to perform the necessary operation . . . after the teams were running smoothly . . . the teams [were asked] to suggest ways [to] collectively to improve the process."[22] Though it is theoretically possible to accept process-improvement suggestions from the developers under the CMM, this is far different than placing developers at the center of the decision-making process. But even such minimal idea gathering doesn't happen very often . . . and then it's almost never systematic.

Technocentrism and the CMM

The CMM states that it leaves the details of implementing process and technology up to the implementers. In practice, its mandates often force organizations into technology-dependent implementations even though these may not always be the best-adapted ones for the product or situation. Organizations under the CMM often adopt a limited selection of mass production-like mega-tools, -methods, and -techniques that they impose on all their projects in all their domains. This behavior is analogous to achieving uniformity on the mass production assembly line, where workers perform a function exactly the same way from one line to another because it is more efficient (in the mass production definition of the word) to do so.

Software companies explain that this is one of the advantages of using the CMM, because this approach limits the retraining costs needed when they move employees from one project to another (thereby keeping their employees and tools more highly loaded in the same sense that mass production works to keep its resources loaded). However, this behavior leads to *muda* in the same way as when other industries subordinate their production needs to achieve a full loading of their technologically oriented assets.

Ironically, in some areas, the technocentrism of the CMM works against adopting superior technology. For instance, in the mid-1980s when the SEI was conducting its best practices surveys, the technique of peer reviews was considered an unbending characteristic of good software development (it was shared by virtually all the good developers surveyed). It was therefore enshrined in the CMM as a requirement to be levied upon every mature software process. This effectively made implementing the technique and technology of peer reviews a prerequisite for advancing up the CMM-Level ladder.

However, there have been successful software projects since then (like Praxis' SHOLIS helicopter landing system and Lockheed-Martin's 382J Mission Computer Operational Flight Program software developments) that have used more recently developed superior technology (i.e., practical types of formal methods) in place of peer reviews. The newer technology not only produced higher quality software, it lowered the costs of accomplishing the same goals.

The conflict for CMM-assessed organizations in such a situation is obvious. Do you improve the technology, or do you remain CMM compliant (or both, at unnecessary added cost)? The best current way out of the conflict is to find forward-thinking assessors who creatively interpret the CMM, allowing for the breaking of its laws in order to better implement its highest intentions (i.e., better software development).

However, it is a large business risk for an organization to proceed with a new technology when it will not know until later whether its technology change will be accepted during the next SEI assessment, or whether it will lead to a catastrophic downgrade in the organization's CMM rating. Most organizations we have seen have not been willing to take that risk. But the only other option is to do everything the CMM wants, in the way that it asks for it, accepting substantial waste. This was the only course left to the 382J project (which went ahead and implemented redundant, superfluous peer reviews on top of its improved approach). The CMM level was indispensable to the company's ability to gain new business. The one saving grace was that the reviews went relatively quickly when they didn't find any problems of note.

Mass production tends to ossify its previous best practices until forced to change by traumatic events. It happened with the dramatic downturn of U.S. manufacturers' auto sales when the lean-manufactured Japanese automobiles swarmed the American market in the 1980s. It will eventually happen in the software industry. This is an irony of technocentrism. When technology becomes an end in itself, one becomes fixated on particular technologies rather than on the reason for using those technologies. This can make one blind to later and better alternatives. The CMM has frozen many of the best practices of the 1980s into its KPAs, and thereby frozen much of the software industry there as well. The CMM has aligned itself firmly with mass production in the principle of technocentrism.

Large-Scale Infrastructures and the CMM

Implementing the catholic infrastructures of the CMM incurs similar overhead to the infrastructures of any durable-goods mass producer. It takes both time and money to define and develop all the required procedures, roles, groups, and activities for CMM-style production. There is a limit to how much you can reduce such overhead in a small organization. However, in a larger organization, you can amortize overhead costs over more products. As in classic mass production, the CMM rewards ever-increasing economies of scale with decreasing net overhead costs per production unit (e.g., per software program developed).

One dynamic of infrastructures is that they are ever-growing. While the CMM encourages large infrastructures in an organization, it is itself a growing infrastructure. According to the SEI, "The CMM framework is designed to accommodate additional disciplines, and it is the intent to add disciplines as needed by our user community."[23] There is now a CMM for the systems-engineering discipline. More CMMs now exist or are planned for other business types and areas. The CMM is heavily oriented around large infrastructures and fits well with mass production in this regard.

Comparing the CMM to Lean Principles

In Chapter 3, we introduced the five principles of the lean paradigm: value, value stream, flow, pull, and perfection. Let's compare the CMM to them now.

Value and the CMM

As discussed earlier, the most important emphasis in lean production is value. Value is providing those things that really matter to a customer: a product, service, or capability, at a specific price, quality, and point in time. How does the CMM view value? If the CMM supports the lean paradigm, we would expect to find some orientation towards emphasizing value in one or more KPAs at Level 2 where the first and most important process improvements occur. What do we find there?

The Level 2 KPAs are concerned with laying the foundations for sound development. They cover requirements management, project planning, project tracking, subcontract management, quality assurance, and configuration management. Of these, requirements management would be the logical place to find a value emphasis. The associated KPA promisingly states, "Requirements Management involves establishing and maintaining an agreement with the customer on the requirements for the software project," and again, "The software engineering group takes appropriate steps to ensure that the system requirements allocated to software . . . are documented and controlled."[24]

However, these statements address the ability to conduct convincing audits of allocations, rather than on the lean idea of truly understanding the customer's underlying need. That is, the producer/customer agreement spoken of in the KPA is ensured through the steps of recording, allocating, and tracing requirements. The KPA never addresses whether or not these activities have determined the "right" requirements. The clear impression contained in the KPA is that the CMM views controlling requirements as sufficient. This is a common viewpoint in the mass paradigm. Since the idea of getting to know the customer is never touched upon in Level 2 or in any higher levels, it is fair to say that the CMM does not promote the primary lean principle of value.

Value Stream and the CMM

If you recall, the value stream is the step-by-step process of creating and delivering a specific product or product family that centers on customer value. In lean, once you map the value stream, you improve it by using *kaizen* (incrementally) and *kaikaku* (radically).

For the incremental-improvement part, the CMM is compatible with one aspect of the *kaizen* approach. The CMM Level 5 "Defect Prevention" KPA states: "Defect Prevention involves analyzing defects that were encountered in the past and taking specific actions to prevent the occurrence of those types of defects in the future."[25] However, this KPA focuses only on analyzing one result of *muda*, i.e., defects, rather than on identifying the root cause of *muda* itself as in true *kaizen*. Nevertheless, it is *kaizen*-like in identifying defects and removing them. The CMM's defect prevention is philosophically compatible with the principle of incrementally removing waste. *This is the first instance we've seen where the CMM is compatible with a major goal of the lean paradigm.*

Nevertheless, the KPA ignores the types of waste that occur when producing a <u>non</u>defective product. In lean, you work to remove all types of non-value-adding activities from the value stream. Unfortunately, under the CMM, a company could replace a wasteful process that produces defects with a wasteful process that does not produce defects and still satisfy the KPA.

For the radical-improvement part of the value stream, the CMM raises barriers. Only flexible organizations can accomplish *kaikaku* (radical improvement), one of the most powerful lean concepts. "The best [lean] manufacturers . . . look for flexibility first."[26] As we explored earlier, inflexibility is a natural consequence of large-scale infrastructures. And we have already seen that the CMM steers organizations toward establishing heavy infrastructures of directive procedures, labor classes, organizational groupings, personnel programs, software tools, and so forth.

Does the CMM therefore inhibit its adherents from adopting radical improvements? This question really has two parts: 1) How severe is the inflexibility encouraged by the CMM, and 2) Does whatever inflexibility there is still allow an organization enough room to practice *kaikaku*?

A large infrastructure is also expensive and time-consuming to change. The tendency is to keep the infrastructure and defer the improvements even if the organization critically needs them for its long-term health (recall our discussion of Ford's permanent loss of leadership in the automobile market to his rival, Sloan, for this very reason).

For software organizations under the CMM, it is well nigh impossible to abandon investments in existing technologies just because a new or better process is available. The CMM impels a business to encase its every software practice in an exacting written record subject to a self-imposed bureaucracy. Such process-encrusting clashes with the lean mindset. Back in 1982, when Japanese lean concepts were in full-scale collision with mass manufacturing thinking in the automobile industry, Richard Schonberger said it this way, "Japanese manufacturers have rejected our complex management prescriptions—our obsession with programs, with controls, with computers and information processing, with behavioral interventions, and with mathematical modeling."[27] Management prescriptions all aimed, then as well as now, primarily at achieving greater efficiency through large infrastructures.

Process encrustation under the CMM extends even to requiring an organization to define how it will change its processes when such change is needed. The CMM's written rules in this regard are so stringent that the whole thing begins to resemble the old Soviet idea of a "5-Year Plan." In each 5-year plan, the USSR attempted to prescribe ahead of time everything that would be done economically and industrially in the State for the following five years. Unfortunately, events in the world and national economy changed a lot faster than every five years, frequently in unanticipated ways. We all know the 5-year plan was a dismal failure for the Soviet economy.

CMM Level 3 is where this type of inflexible, prescriptive mandate begins to conflict directly with the goals of the lean paradigm and prevent any possibility of *kaikaku*. Changing processes, controls, and so forth, at anything beyond a glacial pace, leaves an organization out of sync with its extensive CMM artifacts and mechanisms. Such inconsistency in turn reduces one's CMM level (if it is detected by the assessors). The conflict only intensifies during the remaining two levels, where the overhead of change explodes. At Level 3, an organization has so strongly institutionalized its ways for developing software that making a radical change would almost certainly require the organization to reduce its CMM level. At higher CMM levels, even modest incremental improvement—simply reducing *muda*—can put one's CMM level at risk.

The problem goes deeper than the CMM simply making change difficult, however. The current CMM-based government/industrial/academic axis forces the drive of software businesses to ever-higher CMM levels. Some of the largest markets for software products are giving carrot-and-stick incentives to software organizations to climb the CMM staircase. There is no bigger stick than making an organization's eligibility to win contracts dependent on their CMM level. The SEI states, "The CMM can be used for software capability evaluations, in which a trained team of professionals identifies contractors who are qualified to perform . . . software work."[28] The 1994 *Scientific American* article "Software's Chronic Crisis" stated, "The U.S. Air Force has mandated that all its software developers must reach Level 3 of the CMM by 1998. NASA is reportedly considering a similar policy."[29] This trend has only strengthened since that time, and the focus has now moved to requiring Level 4. Prime contractors pass the same requirements along to their subs, and so on down the line, completing the net.

In a market this dynamic, to do anything that lowers one's CMM level in the short run cuts one's own throat competitively. However, failing to make a radical change can cut one's throat in the long run, too. Regrettably, long-term goals aren't a consideration when the organization's existence for the next year or two is at stake. As a consequence of this Catch-22, software developers do not have the option of pursuing radical change in how they develop much of today's most challenging and technically advanced software. Thus, the CMM works against the most basic characteristics of a lean value stream.

Flow and the CMM

In Chapter 3, we discussed the lean principle of flow and contrasted it with the mass-paradigm emphasis on efficiency and on individual activities. Lean flow looks at continuity of work on a given product; mass efficiency looks at continuity of usage of a given resource or infrastructure. Since the CMM is efficiency-focused and flow and efficiency are mutually exclusive goals, it is fair to say that the CMM not only does not promote the flow principle, it embraces the very characteristics in the mass paradigm that actively impede flow.

Implementing flow will lead a company away from differentiating its skills and partitioning itself a 'la the CMM. With lean, "A host of narrowly-skilled specialists are not needed because most . . . professionals actually have much broader skills than they have . . . ever been allowed to use. When a small team is given the mandate to 'just do it' . . . the professionals suddenly discover that . . . they do the job well and they enjoy it."[30]

Pull, Perfection, and the CMM

The CMM says nothing significant relating to lean pull. It neither promotes nor directly inhibits it. However, the CMM strongly promotes a certain type of perfection. After all, CMM Level 5 is called "optimizing," a word that seems to sum up the spirit of seeking perfection. Where the CMM's perfection and lean perfection differ is in what they are attempting to perfect. The CMM pushes an organization toward improving performance based on the localized and sub-optimized metric results it collected at the lower CMM levels. This means perfection for the CMM is the quest for mass production efficiency. Conversely, lean perfection is all about making every action add value and removing all *muda*. This and only this can lead to the highest conceivable business performance. Under the CMM, the quest for efficiency can easily lead to greater *muda*, rather than less, because eliminating waste is not one of its central tenets. In the end, CMM Level 5 optimizing and the lean principle of perfection have essentially nothing in common, and neither one will lead to the other.

And the CMM Paradigm Is?

The CMM primarily addresses defining and improving processes. This makes it superficially similar to lean thinking in this one regard. Nevertheless, it is clear that the CMM uses its process mandates to institutionalize mass production practices rather than lean ones. Indeed, the CMM is almost completely incompatible with the five lean principles, and almost completely compatible with the mass production ones. This places it squarely in the mass production camp.

Some experts in non-CMM sectors of the software industry have recognized how the CMM has hamstrung the sectors that are under its umbrella (though, to our knowledge, without identifying the underlying mass paradigm as the culprit). One is the renowned IT pioneer, James Bach. Bach said, "At worst, the CMM is a whitewash that obscures the true dynamics of software engineering, suppresses alternative models. If an organization follows it for its own sake . . . it may very well lead to the collapse of that company's competitive potential. For these reasons, the CMM is unpopular among many of the highly competitive and innovative companies."[31]

Businesses in the CMM-influenced parts of the software industry, then, are currently facing a tremendous barrier that they must overcome for their very survival. To stay competitive in the software marketplace, the CMM is forcing organizations to adopt a Trojan-horse process model that is actually destroying their competitiveness. Clearly, only radical changes in the attitudes of government, academia, and software businesses can fully address this handicap. Nevertheless, businesses in these fields can ameliorate their problems somewhat by pushing CMM interpretation as far as possible toward lean thinking.

If you find yourself in that position, first you need to correlate the highest-level goals of the CMM to the goals of lean production. Then you need to find assessors who will give you credit for working around the CMM strictures to apply lean practices. For example, you could partition the different aspects of your developers' job descriptions into virtual process groups (instead of separate physical groups), with mechanisms for obtaining and implementing management's strategic direction. While such workarounds won't create a true lean environment that is fully focused on eliminating *muda*, it will give you a competitive advantage over companies working under a literal interpretation of the CMM.

Perhaps if enough organizations begin pushing the CMM envelope and demand to break free from its mass-thinking constraints, the keepers of the CMM will hear the voices of the lean adopters and evolve. If they won't, the CMM will eventually be replaced by guidelines that facilitate adoption of lean production. As we said, there is hope. In the meantime, there is much education and work to be done on understanding the importance of lean and especially the significance of the lean value stream if software development is to begin loosening the grip of the CMM's mass-paradigm inflexibility.

Paradigms of Two Other Major Assessment Approaches

In Chapter 1, we asserted that process maturity and technological advancement are the wrong things to measure when assessing performance. Nevertheless, the idea of an assessment approach is a useful one when kept in a lean context. There are others besides the CMM; how well do they fit into the lean way?

ISO-9000

The most famous alternative approach for assessing businesses is of course ISO-9000. ISO-9000 emerged in 1987 from the British Standard 5750. Philosophically, it is very similar to the CMM regarding processes. The essence of ISO-9000 accreditation is that an organization must explicitly define the processes it uses to produce its products or services and maintains records to verify it followed those procedures. This is the similar to the CMM Level 3 requirements.[32]

ISO-9000 has become as ubiquitous in many industries as the CMM has in software, and largely for the same reasons. First governments and then many businesses began to specify that only ISO-9000 accredited suppliers would be eligible to bid for contracts. Assurances that this would lead to improved quality were everywhere, and it was simple to add a sentence into a contract for this mandate.

However, critical analysis has exposed some flaws in ISO-9000. Seddon (1997) notes that once an organization is required to document every aspect of its work for an audit, its focus moves to filling out forms rather than satisfying customer needs. He relates that such an internal focus of staff rapidly leads to worse performance as perceived by the customer. Furthermore, the work required to keep the paperwork in order reduces the amount of time and energy people have to perform the actual work, which slows down production and impedes quality control. In addition, organizations begin to rely on the auditor or assessor to identify defects. Seddon notes that an assessor is not a proxy for inherent quality control. In fact, the assessor does not inspect everything, and defects go unnoticed because neither the organization nor the assessor is accountable for the quality of the product.

While the CMM inhibits significant improvement for the reasons we discussed previously, ISO-9000 misses the issue of continual improvement by largely ignoring it. (Note: There is planned movement in this direction.) As with the CMM, this omission inhibits companies from responding to rapidly changing customer needs or flexible competitors.

Finally, Seddon objects that ISO-9000 relies too much on the assessors' interpretations of quality. Often the assessors have minimal training and are not experts in the industry they are assessing. Their uninformed assessment can be misleading at best or could even damage the company's performance. Similar points were made at an Institute of Electrical Engineers Symposium on ISO-9000 accredited certification (*IEE*, 1998, Digest 421). The concerns listed included:

- Recent recognition that quality systems per se do not ensure better product quality.
- The commercialization of the certification process and consequent overselling of its benefits.
- Variable assessments actual quality systems and procedures (due to the large numbers of organizations and individuals now involved in conformity assessment).
- There are at least three registration schemes for consultants, some 70 certification bodies, and 10,000+ assessors, yet no evidence to show that ISO-9000 is good for business.
- The claims made for ISO-9000 by government bodies have not been based on evidence.
- Poorly trained assessors monitoring an approach that simply could not produce quality products or services would start to explain the low regard held by many in the quality movement.

Because of its emphasis on repeatability, process, and infrastructure, and its lack of demonstrated effectiveness at producing quality products at cost-effective prices (an indication of suboptimization), as well as its philosophical similarity to the CMM, ISO-9000 appears to be a solidly mass production approach.

The Malcolm Baldrige National Quality Award (MBNQA)

The leanest among the well-accepted approaches is the Malcolm Baldrige National Quality Award (MBNQA). The MBNQA is different from most popular performance models in that it explicitly focuses on lean issues like waste reduction, value creation, productivity improvement, concern for business results, strategic planning, and customer satisfaction. As the official NIST website states, "the award is for *performance excellence* [emphasis added] and quality achievement."[33] Other sources confirm its better correlation to business performance than other, less lean models. The article "The Baldrige: Is It Worth It?" from the August 1998 issue of *Quality Digest* states, "MBNQA award recipients as a group significantly outperformed the Standard & Poor's (S&P's) 500 by nearly 2.5 to 1." More recently, the NIST cited the 2002 business results: "For the seventh year in a row, a hypothetical stock index, made up of publicly traded U.S. companies that have received the Baldrige Award, has outperformed the Standard & Poor's 500. This year, the 'Baldrige Index' outperformed the S&P 500 by 4.4 to 1."[34] Those implementing MBNQA priorities seem to be increasing their competitive advantage with time, rather than dissipating their gains as has been observed with many other quality initiatives.

An excellent comparison of competing models is found in Michael Tingey's "Comparing ISO-9000, Malcolm Baldrige and the SEI CMM for Software" (Prentice Hall, 1997). His extensive analysis uncovers the relative strengths of these models. Specifically, it points out the comparative leanness of the MBNQA compared to the CMM and its largest other competitor (in the sense that these models can be called competitors), ISO-9001 (which along with ISO 9000-3 are the members of the ISO-9000 family most used by software producers). Figure 5-2 is Tantara Inc.'s summary[35] of those results.

Notice the similarities in most cases between the SEI CMM and the ISO guidelines (as commented upon in our discussion of ISO-9000). Note also the distinct differences of the MBNQA from either of them. Of course, the MBNQA does not explicitly address software issues as do the SEI CMM and ISO-9001/9000-3/TickIT (the latter further applies ISO-9000 to software). However, the MBNQA points a way towards how the CMM and ISO-9000 could be reinterpreted or changed in a way that could support the lean paradigm. Also, the MBNQA could be tailored to assess software by adding software directives. The MBNQA would be even stronger if it incorporated additional concerns found in the Deming Prize checklist,[36] like policy deployment (e.g., *hoshin*

Comparing Standards and Models

(Comparison done by Michael O. Tingey, *ISO 9000,
Malcolm Baldrige, and the SEI CMM Software*, Prentice Hall)

Figure obtained and used with permission from Michael Tingey's "Comparing ISO-9000, Malcolm Baldrige and the SEI CMM for Software" (Prentice Hall, 1997).

Figure 5-2. Comparison of the CMM, MBNQA, and ISO 9001

kanri), maintenance, and leadership deployment, though the MBNQA is stronger in the crucial lean value principle because it makes customer focus a highlighted category. The Deming Prize embeds its customer focus in the overall process area.

Even while using the MBNQA as currently defined, several heavily software-based and highly competitive organizations have won Baldrige trophies, including such businesses as Texas Instruments, Motorola, and IBM. This is a promising sign for the future of lean applications of the MBNQA in the software industry.

ENDNOTES

1. http://www.sei.cmu.edu/about/about.html.
2. R.A. Radice, J.T. Harding, P.E. Munnis, and R.W. Phillips, "A Programming Process Study," *IBM Systems Journal* 24, 2, 1985.
3. W.S. Humphrey and W.L. Sweet, "Characterizing the Software Process: A Maturity Framework," Software Engineering Institute, CMU/SEI-87-TR-11, DTIC:ADA182895, June 1987.
4. M. Paulk et al., "Capability Maturity Model for Software," CMU/SEI-91-TR-24, August 1991.

5. This was its original name and is still the most descriptive label. Then the approach began to be applied to other areas, like system engineering (SE-CMM) and Integrated Product Development CMM (IPD-CMM), so the software version was discriminated by the expanded name "software CMM" or "SW-CMM." The next initiative was to integrate these CMM models into the CMMI, or "CMM-Integrated-Discipline" (with the discipline showing up as in the CMMI-SE). For our discussion, we will use the reasonably intuitive acronym CMM. We will not address the more recent nuances of the CMM, like the alternate staged and continuous representations of the CMMI. These variations do not change the general discussion nor its conclusions, and are therefore omitted.

6. Courtesy of SEI, http://www.sei.cmu.edu/cmm/.

7. Gibbs, W. Wayt., "Software's Chronic Crisis," *Scientific American*, September 1994.

8. http://www.stsc.hill.af.mil/crosstalk/1997/aug/seicmm5.asp.

9. "The Capability Maturity Model for Software," CMU/SEI-91-TR-24, August 1991.

10. M. Paulk et al., "Capability Maturity Model, Version 1.1," *IEEE Software*, Vol. 10, #4, pg. 23.

11. See the delightful discussion of a family's newsletter production, in *Lean Thinking*, pg. 22.

12. *Lean Thinking*, pg. 21.

13. "The Capability Maturity Model for Software," CMU/SEI-91-TR-24, section 3.3, August 1991.

14. "The Capability Maturity Model for Software," CMU/SEI-91-TR-24, section 3.4, August 1991.

15. *Lean Thinking*, pg. 23.

16. *Lean Thinking*, pg. 24.

17. *The Machine That Changed the World*, pg. 31.

18. M.C. Paulk, C.V. Weber, S.M. Garcia, M.B. Chrissis, M. Bush, "Key Practices of the Capability Maturity Model, Version 1.1," Technical Report, CMU/SEI-93-TR-025 ESC-TR-93-178, pgs. O-71 through O-73.

19. Ibid., pg. O-15.

20. R. Schonberger, "*Japanese Manufacturing Techniques: Nine Hidden Lessons in Simplicity*," New York, NY: The Free Press, Division of Macmillan Publishing Co., Inc. 1982; from the Preface, pg. 43.

21. *Lean Thinking*, pg. 24.

22. *The Machine That Changed the World*, pg. 56.

23. http://www.sei.cmu.edu/cmmi/comm/cmmi-faq.html.

24. "Key Practices of the Capability Maturity Model, Version 1.1," pg. L2-1.

25. "Key Practices of the Capability Maturity Model," pg. L5-1.

26. *Japanese Manufacturing Techniques*, pg. 133.

27. *Japanese Manufacturing Techniques*, pg. vii.

28. M.C. Paulk, C.V. Weber, S.M. Garcia, M.B. Chrissis, M. Bush, "Key Practices of the Capability Maturity Model, Version 1.1," Technical Report, CMU/SEI-93-TR-025 ESC-TR-93-178, pg. O-1 and O-2.

29. Gibbs, W. Wayt, "Software's Chronic Crisis," *Scientific American*, September 1994.

30. *Lean Thinking*, pg. 54.
31. Bach, James, "The Immaturity of the CMM," *American Programmer*, September 1994.
32. ISO-9001 mixes up the order in which it takes similar matters compared to that taken by the CMM, however, "The ISO-9001 standard puts its highest emphasis on *managing* and then on *implementing*. The SEI SW-CMM model ... emphasis is on *implementing* then *managing*," http://www.tantara.ab.ca/a_mbnqa.htm on October 5, 2004.
33. http://www.quality.nist.gov/Guidelines.htm.
34. http://www.nist.gov/public_affairs/factsheet/mbnqa.htm.
35. http://www.tantara.ab.ca/a_mbnqa.htm, as of October 27, 2004.
36. The Deming Prize is a Japanese award for innovative quality practices. It is administered yearly by the Union of Japanese Scientists and Engineers (JUSE), and honors the work and memory of W. Edwards Deming through its title.

6

Determining Software's Industrial Paradigm— XP: Extreme Programming

Around only since the mid-1990s, Extreme Programming and other Agile software approaches like Scrum, Crystal, and Adaptive Software Development have provided some of the most creative rethinking of software development in the last twenty years. Since Extreme Programming is the most well-known and widely-implemented Agile approach, it will be our focus. Whereas mass production approaches like library reuse and the CMM are almost completely top-down and prescriptive (i.e., regulatory), Extreme Programming—or XP, as it is often called—is bottom-up and based on a phenomenon called *emergent behavior*.

Emergent behavior occurs when several people work together on different aspects of the same goal. *Flocking* is one example of emergent behavior: The actions of an individual bird give little clue as to what a group of them will do together. The group's behavior emerges only when they are together. XP depends on the emergent behavior of many software developers working independently bottom up on their parts of a software system, which when brought together, produce a good overall system, something that no one isolated developer is thinking about or trying to achieve. It is clear that, "XP is different. It is a lot like a jigsaw puzzle. There are many small pieces. Individually the pieces make no sense, but when combined together a complete picture can be seen."[1]

But whether XP achieves the goal of emergent behavior to produce a good system depends upon one's definition of a good system. There have certainly been many good results from XP, at least when organizations have used XP on suitable projects (more on that shortly). Nevertheless, mass production approaches like the CMM can also have good effects depending on one's definition of good. So how does XP align with the three industrial paradigms? One way to determine this is to look at XP in terms of a number of project characteristics whose implementation looks very different depending upon the industrial paradigm used.

Worker Independence: XP Aligns with Craft

One obvious characteristic that differs across paradigms is the level of worker independence allowed. This spectrum ranges from the extreme of total prescription of worker actions under mass production, to the extreme of total worker autonomy under craft production (see Figure 6-1). Lean production lies somewhere between, encouraging a great deal of worker sovereignty to interrupt and change production practices, but also incorporating top-down strategic planning and policy deployment (e.g., *hoshin kanri*).

Figure 6-1. Spectrum of Worker Independence

On worker independence, XP aligns with craft production because in most XP writings to date, there is no recognition of a need for top-down direction or strategic intervention. In a way, this independent behavior appears to be a natural outcome of the pendulum swinging the other way, rather than an inherent characteristic of XP. XP appears to be a gathering place for those innovators who have a strong reaction against overly regulated mass production approaches like the CMM.

Customer Responsiveness: XP Aligns with Craft and Lean

Another telling difference between industrial paradigms is how each of them handles customer responsiveness (see Figure 6-2). The spectrum runs from mass production's "any color you want, as long as it is black" unresponsiveness to craft and lean production's customer-drivenness at the other. It is arguable which of the latter two are the more customer-driven, since lean producers have to account for business goals as well as customer concerns, while craft producers, because they have so much artistic leeway, may incorporate what they want in a product without much attention to customer needs. For argument's sake, we will simply show craft and lean as coequals at the opposite extreme.

Figure 6-2. Spectrum of Customer Responsiveness

Under XP, the customer gets involved by writing "user stories," which then serve as system requirements for the developers. User stories are generally short (around three sentences) descriptions of what the customer wants the system to do. User stories are something like UMLs use cases, except that user stories are not centered on user interfaces like in UML. The customer writes the stories in his or her own words, not in the developer's software jargon. Each three-sentence description is at an intermediate level of detail, targeted at the level of something the development team could implement in one to three weeks.

Before the developers commence with code development, a top-level, black-box acceptance test is written for each user story. The test will be targeted to demonstrate to the customer the fulfillment of the corresponding user story. There is some room for flexibility here: A single test could cover more than one user story, and multiple tests might also be used to complete coverage of a single user story. The customer reviews each acceptance test to make sure it completely verifies the user story that it is designed to cover. The customer also helps the developers assign priorities (and completion order) to the various user stories. Finally, the customer is supposed to make sure that the sum total of all its user stories completely covers the functionality needed in the system.

Because XP makes the customer a part of the development team, we can squarely fix XP as fully customer-driven. This is consistent with the lean principle of value and is a desirable situation no matter which type of development approach you use. Though XP aligns with craft and lean production on the customer responsiveness spectrum, it can be argued that XP, by omitting a top-down strategic element, goes further than either craft and lean in this direction. That's not necessarily a good thing: It may leave itself vulnerable to listening to the needs of customers a little too uncritically.

For example, Jim participated in a non-XP project that nearly self-destructed because of out-of-control customer requirements changes that led to six times the typical number of system releases found in a typical, similar program. In this project, the biggest problem was a lack of top-down strategic direction from the managers to enable the program to deliver a product to meet the most important customer needs (though inadequate customer knowledge was also a problem). The company learned from this experience and added more strategic direction on a later project that greatly reduced requirements thrashing.

Domain Orientation: XP Aligns with Craft

Yet another revealing characteristic that shows the wide difference between paradigms is domain orientation (see Figure 6-3). Recall that a domain is a set of things that are closely related in function or purpose. Domain-orientation is development that is primarily based on the similarities between the related things, so that the products are useful with minimal modification in every context. Craft production is not at all domain-oriented since it targets each individual product to a particular customer and situation, rather than too many types of customers and situations. At one end is craft, which typically doesn't even consider reusability. Mass production falls somewhere to the left of middle because it doesn't strongly consider domain similarities and differences. Lean production, on the opposite end of the spectrum, is fully domain-oriented. As discussed in the lean section on archetypal artifacts, lean intends every bit of work to be reusable in other projects at least in some sense because this reduces *muda* on future projects by not having to repeat work done on the original product. Also, by planning in reusability in the original project, it is anticipating the needs of similar projects in the future.

Figure 6-3. Spectrum of Domain Orientation

As a bottom-up technique, XP takes no notice of domain, especially since no one is really looking at the domain processes as a whole. The XP solution, which works quite well for one-customer, one-time developments, fails to account for the needs of other customers. For example, since XP is completely dependent on the customer's feedback about requirements, it cannot design in possible solutions for future customers.

XP advocates imply that XP produces domain-oriented products as the natural result of its emergent behavior. However, we haven't seen evidence that XP developers of low-level software parts automatically arrive at domain-oriented and fully reusable designs any more than have developers working with other approaches. XP advocates also claim that domain orientation is irrelevant because XP is flexible enough to allow developers to make changes easily in a system domain to meet new customer requirements. Nevertheless, changes cause *muda* if they must undo decisions embedded in earlier versions of a product, which accounted only for the customer of the moment and not for the more general needs of the market being addressed. All these issues align XP with craft production.

Worker Expertise Dependency: XP Aligns with Craft

Figure 6-4 shows the spectrum for dependency on worker expertise. Clearly one of mass production's highest objectives is to minimize this dependence. Craft production is completely dependent on the expertise of its workers (this is the distinguishing trait of craft production). Lean production is less expertise-dependent than craft production because lean philosophy accommodates the training and utilization of less-skilled workers than are required in craft settings. However, lean workers are also trained to understand lean-paradigm concepts, which take their minimal required expertise beyond that required in mass production. The need for domain understanding among the lean developers raises the needed expertise level yet again, though not nearly to the level required of craft developers.

Figure 6-4. Spectrum of Dependency on Worker Expertise

XP advocates claim their approach makes minimal demands on the expertise of its developers, which is no doubt true when it comes to merely producing a piece of software that runs in accordance with the user stories. In this sense, XP aligns more closely with mass production. However, if XP were to produce a system more comparable to that produced through lean production, a system that minimized waste and incorporated domain savvy, reusability, and ease of modifiability (which depends on architectural compatibility with all possible future changes, a kind of domain concern), such a product would require that at least some of the XP developers be domain knowledgeable. If the XP team used the practice called *pair programming*, more than one of every two developers would have to possess this more extended knowledge. In pair programming, two people, one of whom has more experience, work at one computer. The two workers trade off on individual tasks, but each is always there to participate in the work-in-progress. In this case, one of the two would need domain expertise. Developing a run-of-the-mill system doesn't require such high worker expertise as this, but an excellent system in the lean sense does. Added on to the expert in each pair are whatever leaders there are on the team (there's fewer of these in XP than in mass production). Finally, XP lacks the process supports that lean production provides to inexperienced workers . . . again raising XP's dependence on worker expertise. We rate the dependence of XP on such expertise, if it is to produce systems as good as those coming out of lean production, to be near that needed for craft production.

Stage Verification: XP Aligns with Lean

An additional common characteristic we can look at is the degree of verification that each industrial paradigm requires at the end of each stage of production (see

Figure 6-5). As discussed under lean flow in Chapter 3, lean production requires that you define strict criteria for success at the end of each production stage, and apply them to the products coming out of the stage. Craft production doesn't attempt to do this, since expert artisans can at any given point simply adapt the product's variances. Lean production does this fully. Mass production sometimes does this, but is under no obligation to do so. Indeed, doing so usually works against its prime principle of efficiency. Mass software developers often defer serious verification until quite late in the development cycle.

XP aligns most closely with craft production on the stage-verification spectrum. One of XP's most foundational principles is *test before programming*. This means that one is to write the test for code before writing the code itself. The software test becomes a precise criterion for success at the end of the stage, when the developer has produced the code module (procedure, method, or whatever form it is in). While a priori test cases are not the only way to ensure verification of product at the end of each stage, it does fully satisfy this concern.

Figure 6-5. Spectrum of Verification at Stage-End

Scalability: XP Aligns with Craft

Finally, the various paradigms have differing scalability, that is, the ability to scale up to handle large projects (see Figure 6-6). Craft production is the least scaleable because it is the least repeatable. Mass production is much more repeatable and therefore more scaleable. Lean production is the most scaleable of all because there's nothing about lean production that makes it less scaleable than mass, and lean's domain orientation allows it to even cross multiple systems in a domain.

Figure 6-6. Spectrum of Scalability Limits

Even XP's most ardent supporters admit that the most appropriate arena for XP is small systems: "You cannot use XP on a project with a huge staff."[2] The team size is normally limited to 15 or so developers, which is similar to craft-production behavior. The big difference is that XP teams are moderately more productive than are teams under most traditional software approaches.

Assessing XP's Dominant Paradigm and Lean Future

There are many other aspects of XP that deserve a closer look, such as its abilities to handle difficult customers, respond to rapidly changing requirements, and deal with difficult risk-management concerns. XP's approach to handling these issues is not nearly as waste-free as a lean domain approach using the AHP (covered in Part II). Nevertheless, XP's insistence on building the product in small incremental steps with many releases minimizes the need for inventory and promotes flow in the lean sense of the word.

We've compared and evaluated the industrial paradigms to XP and it appears that XP falls predominantly into a craft production paradigm, with some elements of lean production. In five out of six cases, XP is closely aligned with the craft, and in two out of six cases, XP is aligned with lean (one case was shared between craft and lean). Along with craft production, XP works best on products that are small and/or simple, or that are unique and will never be repeated. For such systems, there would be little point in using the domain-analysis activities inherent to the lean paradigm in performing XP-style development.

There is room for growth in the XP approach, however. If XP incorporates more principles of lean production, it could become attractive for larger-scale systems and businesses. To achieve this, it would need to take on some of the characteristics of more traditional development approaches that use a certain degree of strategic direction. More specifically, it would need to add some top-down elements and domain orientation.

Some people are already pushing XP to address the need for large-scale applications. A good example is the Extreme Modeling (XM) movement. XM applies the main characteristics of XP, such as test-driven development, to architectural modeling using UML. The extreme modeling website (there are, as of the writing of this section, no books available on the subject[3]) states, "Extreme Modeling . . . [is] applying the tenets of XP to the modeling phase. For this to be successful, two requirements have to be met: Models need to be executable and they must be testable. While traditional [software development] only requires a good drawing tool and XP a compiler and a simple test framework, Extreme Modeling requires intensive support by an integrated tool that is able to execute UML models, test models, support the transition from model to code and keep code and model in sync."[4] XM is moving in the right direction, as we shall see in the analysis of UML in Part III. UML, as it is currently formulated, lacks some characteristics needed to achieve full lean development. A combination of XP and XM also does not address many other aspects of the principles of lean development, as Parts II and III will make clearer, though the two approaches certainly do not preclude them.

Since the purpose of this book is to assess the software industry and to describe proven lean software development approaches rather than discuss ways to extend less-lean approaches into more-lean ones, we will leave the topic of XP with a final set of thoughts. Whereas mass-production reuse and the CMM are dead-end approaches with no lean potential, XP is an open-ended model with a future lean promise. It is not inherently superior to alternative lean software approaches (despite some very glowing rhetoric on the part of its supporters). XP has even stronger lean competition from the *test not at all* school of static verifiability and assured correctness, elaborated under the *Perfection Principle* in Part III, Chapter 21. Indeed, it is our belief that the latter school will ultimately prove the most powerful because of its scalability and its elimination of whole classes of errors before they are ever introduced. Nevertheless, many XP projects have already been more successful by most business and lean criteria than previous mass production projects.

It's easy to understand the enthusiasm of XP advocates. We hope XP supporters will avoid the trap of making their approach into a religion "writ large in stone," a mistake often made by software developers. XP needs space to live and grow into a full lean lifecycle approach. Once it incorporates additional lean principles and consciously works to remove major sources of *muda*, XP, with XM or something like it, could become a strong lean process for certain niches of the software industry.

ENDNOTES

1. http://www.extremeprogramming.org/what.html.
2. http://www.extremeprogramming.org/when.html.
3. A good paper, though, is M. Boger, T. Baier, F. Wienberg, W. Lamersdorf, "Extreme Modeling," *XP'2000* conference, available from www.extrememodeling.org/docs.php.
4. http://www.extrememodeling.org/whatisxm.php.

7

The Way Out of the
Software Crisis

People who have labored to produce software in chaotic development environments appreciate anything that brings more order and predictability to their work. Just as early twentieth-century mass production
improved upon nineteenth-century craft production, post-craft software
approaches like library reuse, the CMM, and XP have decreased the worries of
software managers and made life less stressful for many developers. It's no won-
der that they have become popular, given what they replaced. But most of these
approaches operate at or around a mass level, and herein lies the challenge.

As we have discussed, mass production has a darker side: It hinders achieving business goals because it limits ultimate productivity, quality, and stability . . .
and just as important, makes it difficult and expensive for software organizations
to change processes radically, even when such change is imperative.

We need a better way of producing software; better than craft, better than
traditional reuse, better than the CMM, better even than XP. We need an
approach to development that obtains for our industry the lean benefits already
being enjoyed by so many others.

Time to Recognize the Real Problem

Where do we start? People often say that the first step toward change is to recognize one's present condition. We've established that the best mainstream software
production today follows mass production. Where have these innovations left us?

Bruce Webster captured a fairly common sentiment in the software world
when he said in *Byte Magazine* in 1996: "More and more software will be behind
schedule, over budget, underpowered, and of poor quality—and there's nothing
we can do about it."[1] This statement reveals some of the desperation software professionals feel . . . that the best that can be hoped for is to keep adopting the
improvement trends, methods, and techniques that periodically perturb the software industry by promising major breakthroughs. A study performed by the IBM
Consulting Group in June of 1994 found that 55 percent of the software system

developments surveyed at that time still cost more than expected, 68 percent still exceeded schedule, and 88 percent were found so unacceptable that they had to undergo major redesign.[2] The productivity of U.S. programmers improved for a while, then declined below even previous levels, as seen in the following chart from the 1980s and 1990s[3] (see Figure 7-1).

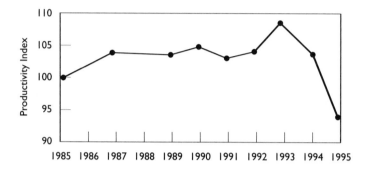

Figure 7-1. Productivity of U.S. Workers

Today, the confusion and dismay over the gap between the improvements expected from mass production and the pittance experienced only seem to be increasing. An MIT Enterprise *Technology Review* article of June 17, 2002, titled "Why Software Is So Bad," stated, "What's surprising—astonishing, in fact—is that many software engineers believe that software quality is not improving. If anything, they say, it's getting worse. It's as if the cars Detroit produced in 2002 were less reliable than those built in 1982."[4] And again, "According to a study by the Standish Group, a consulting firm in West Yarmouth, MA, U.S. commercial software projects are so poorly planned and managed that in 2000, almost a quarter were canceled outright, creating no final product. The canceled projects cost firms $67 billion; overruns on other projects racked up another $21 billion . . . Incredibly, *software projects often devote 80 percent of their budgets to repairing flaws they themselves produced*"[5] [our emphasis]. As we've discussed repeatedly in the previous chapters, having to rely on such after-the-fact error remediation is typical of mass production. It's still shocking how much we spend to undo the problems we've created.

In all camps, regrettably, the stories of software-development business failures far outnumber the success stories (and we all know that a technical triumph can also be a business failure, as companies from Apple to Xerox have amply demonstrated). In many ways, the software crisis of the craft-production 1960s and '70s continues into the present era of software mass production, as evidenced by systems that are never delivered, are delivered but never used, are used but leave customers disappointed, or fail to produce profits for their businesses.

It's not that software professionals haven't recognized the problem or have ignored these downward trends. To the contrary, these problems have been vigorously addressed with a number of expensive initiatives. To date there have been two decades—and still counting—of massively reconstructing the infrastructures of software development practice. Many innovations have been embraced. We've discussed a few of them in the previous chapters. Many others exist, such as high-efficiency lifecycle models like component-based reuse and RAD, and safety and integrity guidelines like RTCA-DO178B, U.K. DEF-STAN 0055, and the DOD's "Orange Book."

These new practices have been adopted in response to many legitimate problems for both developers and customers. They have at least sometimes (though by no means always, as noted above) led to improvements in error rates, productivity, and development predictability. Yet most of the changes have also imposed extraordinary expenses of every kind on their implementers, such as 1) increased costs in work hours to implement, 2) major organizational restructurings and turmoil, 3) direct monetary costs, and 4) an entropic loss of flexibility and therefore business opportunity to adapt one's own software process to market and technology changes. In the 30+ years since the term "software crisis" was first coined, and despite these massive investments, quality hasn't even doubled from its intolerable previous lows, while the dispersion in quality increased from 10:1 in 1990 to 100:1 by 1995.[6]

More specifically, these statistics are united in their indictment of the mass paradigm that lies at the heart of contemporary software development. The prescription to date has been that, if a little of the medicine doesn't make the patient better, surely more of it will. If more doesn't do the trick, then up the dosage until it does. There's been no evidence that this medicine will ever do more than temporarily relieve some symptoms while worsening others. We recognize the problem; it's just that we are too paralyzed by the restrictions and directives of mass production to see the lean path forward.

Time to Stop Solving the Wrong Problem

The software crisis has become so severe and so harmful to our national interests that it is receiving the direct attention of the highest office in the land. The President's Information Technology Advisory Committee (PITAC) "Report to the President" of February 24, 1999, stated, "The demand for software has grown far faster than our ability to produce it. Furthermore, the Nation needs software that is far more usable, reliable, and powerful than what is being produced today. We have become dangerously dependent on large software systems whose behavior is not well understood and which often fail in unpredicted ways. Therefore, increases in research on software should be given a high priority. Special emphasis should be placed on developing software for managing large amounts of information, for making computers easier to use, for making software easier to create and maintain, and for improving the ways humans interact with computers. Specifically, the Federal program should . . . fund fundamental research in software development methods and component technologies."

The release of this report led to increasing national funding for software research. Yet, previous decades of government funding have left the software world substantially where it was in the 1960s—in a software crisis. The report's prime research target was to look into "software development methods and component technologies." This is misdirected. What is causing the crisis is software's paradigm, not the lower-level concerns of methods and technologies (which are mass production preoccupations, as we saw earlier). What rational reason is there to think that the solution to the software crisis is to pour more government money into improving the tools and processes of an obsolete paradigm?

Time to Abandon What Has Failed

There are many business-oriented people who are troubled by both the costs and limited results of the types of government solutions discussed above. They rightly question if the right solutions are being applied to the problem, or more poignantly, if the problem itself has even been correctly identified. This has driven many of them to continue looking for better operational approaches. But to date, these attempts have been unfruitful. Why?

While software professionals may not consciously think they are adopting mass production techniques, the examples from other mass producing industries do influence their thinking. It seems reasonable to think that when software developers create new and advanced concepts from scratch, they are actually drawing upon the old commonsensical mass-paradigm worldview. This would explain why there is a mass production flavor not only in the reuse and process approaches, but in most of the industry standards and initiatives.

The Q/P Management Group, a quality and SEI CMM consultancy, states on its website, "The quality of a software product is only as good as the process used to develop and maintain it."[7] While this is undeniably true, it is not true that a rigid application of mass production is necessary to obtain a good process. As we've acknowledged, even an ill-fitted implementation of the mass paradigm will improve on chaotic craft development. Yet, many software authorities, even those who promote mass-paradigm measures like library-based reuse and the CMM, freely state that the gains resulting from these mass software process changes have been disappointing to industry and customers alike. Why don't they find these outcomes troubling? Toyota and Honda have proven that even industries suited to the mass paradigm perform better using the lean paradigm. Yet, the software industry continues down its mass production road.

It is important to remind the reader that one of the main reasons Toyota originally developed lean production was to support small production runs. Moreover, this was for an industry where only large production runs had previously been economic. Though software only has small production runs (often a run of just one product), you still hear very little talk about lean production. The software industry is missing out on lean-related techniques such as QFD, the Analytic Hierarchy Process, the 7 Management and Planning Tools (MP Tools), the 7 Quality Control tools (QC tools), *kaizen*, and so forth.

Instead, software, the linchpin of so many complex products, is being produced with exquisite technological sophistication on an obsolete foundation of mass production at best, and craft production at worst. These are paradigms that benchmark organizations in virtually all other industries long ago abandoned. Because of our repeated failures, the software industry has resigned itself to the destructive delusion that it is nearly impossible to pull ourselves out of our quagmire.

Time to Seriously Consider What Can Really Work

You would think that with so many software professionals rubbing shoulders with people from other industries there would be some cross fertilization of lean thinking into the software industry. But, as discussed in earlier chapters, the surface differences between the software industry and other industries make the classic terminology of lean seem foreign and irrelevant. In many ways, software is perhaps the most abstract of all products, ultimately being just electronic charges retained in memory devices. Furthermore, as a result of producing software more or less from scratch, the industry has developed concepts and terminology that are foreign to industries that produce physical products.

Yes, old habits die hard, and the software industry is now mature in many of its habits. Change is painful, especially since it is easier and more natural to stick with what is familiar. But the only way to clear the cobwebs of old habits is to "just do it" and take on lean production.

Lean is the only paradigm that has been able to solve the intractable problems of other mass production industries. It is reasonable to investigate whether it could also solve software's intractable problems. But even if it can, we understand that this doesn't make it any easier to embrace, especially when there is a price for leaving behind what is known and comfortable. We also know that the transition to lean isn't always easy. "Lean thinking is counterintuitive and a bit difficult to grasp on first encounter (but then blindingly obvious once 'the light comes on')."[8] Few people in the software field have looked at lean long enough for the light to come on. We believe this is one of the main reasons why lean hasn't been widely adopted in software. Yet other industries have faced and overcome this hurdle.

Time to Accept the Challenge of Change

Something the MIT lean researchers said about automobiles is also true about software, so true it almost stings: "Whenever a fully developed set of institutions is firmly in place—as is the case with mass production—and a new set of ideas arises to challenge the existing order, the transition from one way of doing things to another is likely to prove quite painful. This is particularly true if the new ideas . . . threaten the existence of major institutions . . . So we are not certain that lean production will prevail. We are convinced that the chances of lean production prevailing depends critically on . . . prudent actions by old-fashioned mass producers, by the ascendant lean producers, and by governments everywhere."[9] With the troika of government, academia, and industry united in promoting mass production practices, as they are in software development, we know that we have a lot more work to do before lean development becomes the norm.

Fortunately, the sacrifices managers and developers must make are not nearly as great as one might think. Many existing software techniques and technologies are perfectly suitable for lean production. The most important transformations are in how you think about the software lifecycle and how you manage it. Then, you can add other techniques as necessary to make the lean production line flow more smoothly and with less waste. Furthermore, a small but growing body of successful lean software projects is demonstrating that you can make software into dependably profitable and customer-pleasing businesses. These few lean software projects are also successfully bucking the negative statistical trends and proving that the industry can overcome the 40-year software crisis. As Parts II through IV of this book will show, organizations can do this with much less effort and cost than previously thought, because *software is arguably the best-suited of all industries to convert to lean production.*

Indeed, everything we discussed from this point forward strengthens the point that the time to accept the challenge of change is already here. More specifically, the challenge is for us to overcome our industry's maverick culture and its natural resistance to paradigm change, and use lean principles to create a better software-production lifecycle.

ENDNOTES

1. Webster, Bruce F., "The Real Software Crisis," *Byte Magazine*, January 1996.
2. Gibbs, W. Wayt, "Software's Chronic Crisis," *Scientific American*, September 1994.
3. Yourdon, Edward, *Rise & Resurrection of the American Programmer*. Upper Saddle River, NJ: Yourdon Press/Prentice Hall, 1996, as referenced in a web-published article "The Odd Success of the US Software Industry," Robert A. Heavener, November 4, 1996 at http://www.apl.jhu.edu/Classes/605401/hausler/cybrbob.html.

4. "Why Software Is So Bad," June 17, 2002, *Technology Review, Inc.*

5. Ibid.

6. Yourdon, Edward. *Rise & Resurrection of the American Programmer.* Upper Saddle River, NJ: Yourdon Press/Prentice Hall, 1996.

7. http://www.qpmg.com/seicmm.htm

8. *Lean Thinking,* pg. 28.

9. *The Machine That Changed the World,* pg. 225.

PART TWO

Building Lean Software— Customer Space, Early Lifecycle

Lean Value—Finding the
Gold Hidden Within
Your Customer

Jim's best family vacation came during the high summer of 1982. It began when his expectant wife, two-year-old daughter, and he rolled away from the brick-oven heat of the Silicon Valley and headed for the high, cool placer-mining towns of the Sierra Nevada. First stop: the restored settlement of Jamestown, backdrop for films like *High Noon* and *Butch Cassidy and the Sundance Kid.*

They followed it up with a side trip to pan for gold. The stream, we were told, had suffered similar assaults more or less continuously since the Sutter's Mill rush reached the area around 1850.

On its muddy banks that day they uncovered about as much gold as any other tourist . . . a couple of flecks, worth only a few cents on the open market. But the treasure captured their imaginations as they watched the sunlight glint off the chips. It didn't even blunt the excitement when the teenage staffers seemed more than a little bored with the whole exercise. *Veni, vidi, vici*—we came, we saw, and we left with gold!

The precious metals of the Sierra Nevada are a lot like the insights customers hold within themselves about their own values. As we said earlier, values are the most important element in the lean lifecycle; they are the pure gold. Sometimes you can easily get at tiny pieces that have worked their way to the surface, but the bulk of values remain hidden deep within the customer.

The wide-eyed tourists and droopy-lidded guides of the expedition resemble the two reactions we have seen the most among software developers responding to the need to understand the customer perspective. Some people, acting in the tourist role, peer excitedly into a wide, shallow prospecting pan for little flecks of gold, i.e., for a few meager insights gleaned from the surface of their customer relationships. For most software people, it takes hardly any "finds" to satisfy them to the point they are ready to showcase their gains, pack their bags, and return with their treasures to their comfortable and traditional home environment of product creation. Their motives are good, but the trip profits them pennies compared to the potential riches they could have had but left behind!

Others play the part of the prematurely jaded and world-weary guides. Uninterested in the whole experience of dealing with customers, they bide their time until the most minimal requirements job possible is somehow completed, then get on ASAP with what they really want to do, software design and coding. These people come home without even the small hoard of a tourist.

There's a third group, however. During the original gold rush, who made the big money . . . who were the real professionals? Certainly not the ones with the pans; they, on average, went broke and died at age twenty-three. No, the winners were the mine operators who used discipline, techniques, and tools to break through the surface and reach the real mother lode beneath. (Those who sold tools and food to the miners also made out pretty well, but we're not talking right now about how to make a fortune as a software tool vendor or a snack-cake baker!)

Perhaps you've had a hard time believing there is a mother lode hidden within your customers. You've seen so little "color" (value) lying around on the stream bank of customer relations that it's hard to imagine it's worth pouring a lot of time and effort into what looks like a losing stake. Project funds are tight enough already, why divert some of them away from more seemingly responsible tasks?

We advise you to make the commitment anyway. It doesn't require a lot of faith: Lean producers of all types have found that there is a 100 percent chance of a big strike. Determining customer values always pays off. As you will see in the rest of Part II, you can scale your mining operation anywhere from small-time with minimal costs, but still a multiplied profit, to a full excavation with a proportionately impressive payback. It all depends on the size of your project and the funds you're willing to allocate.

So let's get on with how to mine customer's values! Along the way, we will relate our discussion to example projects. These include a series of semi-lean software projects at Lockheed Martin Aerospace Company (hereafter called "LM Aero"). Over a period of fifteen years, the LM projects described here have implemented most of these principles, some more successfully than others. Both the successes and failures are instructive. We are grateful to LM Aero and the others for sharing their lean journeys and hope the reader benefits from their experiences.

The techniques we will describe are not exhaustive. We will not attempt to give a complete tutorial on the use of these techniques. Rather, we will give enough information to demonstrate how these and related techniques can contribute to a lean software development lifecycle. In-depth references are also given in case you'd like to go further.

The Customer Space—The Early Product Lifecycle

A project's work begins and ends with what its customers want (though business concerns are factored in all along, as we shall see). The realm of work in which organizations try to understand customer needs is appropriately called the customer space. The initial phases of the product lifecycle, when organizations explore the customer space, is sometimes called *analysis*. In practice, companies often call the customer space the *problem space* or *problem domain*. This is in no doubt unintentional irony, since producers often do view customers as problems rather than resources, and their perspectives as intrusions rather than opportunities.

The other major realm of software work, where producers labor to satisfy customer needs, we call *the producer space*. This is synonymous with *solution space, solution domain,* and *design space*. The corresponding phases of the lifecycle are called *synthesis* or *implementation*. We will discuss the producer space in Part III.

Whether businesses are lean or not, they must deal with the customer space throughout their projects. The difference is that lean organizations commit a large amount of conscious attention to this work early in the product's lifecycle. During the analysis phase, lean companies work to understand the customer space before even attempting to develop new products or services. The goal of analyzing the customer space is to identify what is important to the customer; that is, customer value.

The Weakest Link—Understanding Customer Value

Strangely, though value is the highest priority of lean production in general, the thing that is most neglected even in many lean companies is customer knowledge (there can be varying degrees of leanness). "Understanding customer requirements appears to be one of the weakest links in product and service design. In a survey of 203 projects at 123 industrial companies, 13 typical new product development processes were rated by managers in terms of the percentage of project they actually did the activity, and on a ten-point scale, how well they performed the activity. Least performed (25.4% of the projects) was a detailed market study of customer requirements, and when it was done, the quality of work was graded a 5.74 out of 10."[1] When the most important business activity is also the most neglected one, someone willing to improve in that area can quickly enhance their position against their competitors and for better business performance.

Value is the collection of all the wants and needs of your customer. It can be discovered from the customer statements about the conditions in their environments that they want to change or avoid having changed. A change of conditions is a transformation of the customer's environment from one state to another; an avoidance of change is the prevention of an unwanted transformation.

What kinds of techniques can a software business use to discover its customers' values? Value is value, whether customers are buying software or any other product. In most cases, the same techniques used in any other industry work for software (though format and content of the values themselves varies considerably from industry to industry). There are a few techniques from the software world, however, that provide very useful additional capabilities when applied to lean value capture. We'll see techniques of both types as we go along through Part II.

In this chapter, we will investigate different ways of looking at value resolution, the steps in performing it, and compare it to traditional requirements analysis.

But first, we look at how customers can communicate value.

How Customers Communicate Value

Perhaps the most common way customers express their values, at least initially, is with a casual phrase or sentence; for instance, "I need to move text around within a document." It's repetitive to say "I need . . ." or "I want . . ." in every statement, so for value-gathering purposes, this could be shortened to something like "move text within a document." Manipulating documents and text is something that many customers need to do, and thus is part of the customer space. Such manipulation would be a change in the customer's environment, so it is a value in that sense as well. The short statement defining a customer value or requirement can also be helpful, though not necessary, in creating shorthand labels for planning matrices such as those used in the QFD approach (QFD is addressed in several places throughout this book).

Normally, some sort of quantified or objective goal (i.e., numerical target) should be associated with each statement. Otherwise, you will never be able to tell if you have succeeded in implementing the solution as the customer intended. For instance, you might measure the success of a solution for moving text around by the speed at which trained people to do the operation or how easy the solution is for a user to learn or remember.

On the other hand, a phrase like "combine a mouse swipe with a left-button press to highlight a block of text, and a right-button click followed by a selection from a drop-down menu to cut it into a memory buffer" is a producer space, not value, statement. Interestingly, software requirements (as opposed to values) are often written from the latter perspective. We'll say more about the distinctions between requirements and values shortly. For now, just consider that in lean product development, it is very important to keep the customer space and the producer space clearly defined and separated. In Part III we'll continue this train of thought by presenting steps for translating customer-space values into producer-space solutions.

Other ways to record customer values include tables, mathematical formulae, and graphics. The language and format that a project will adopt to record a value depends on the nature and needs of its customers. The values of astrophysicists (as customers) will have a very different native language than the values of grocery store cashiers.

The important thing is that you record all customer values in terms of customer environment, purposes, and vocabulary. This will improve the communication between developer and customer and make it easier for the customer to participate actively in the company's product development. Developers benefit from this exchange at least as much as the customers. It is OK to use a value representation that requires the customer to receive a little training to be able to read it, as long as in the end, the added utility of the value representation is worth the training and the customer agrees to participate. We will discuss a few techniques for capturing value representations as we progress through this chapter.

Using Value Resolution in Lean Product Development

Value resolution is the process of developing a rich, composite picture of what motivates our customers. It takes into account what they want products to do for them, as well as intangibles like how they react emotionally to different features, and how much they *like* us. We can use this information to give us strategic advantage in the marketplace.

Value resolution occurs in several stages, with each stage considerably increasing the richness of the information we've gathered to that point, and the leverage it provides. Once a company completes these stages, it can define and design products based on the values most important to the customer, in the best-possible order for the benefit of the customer and the business, for least risk, with the least waste of company money and other resources, and leading to the best financial performance. None of these things are possible without having done a good value resolution.

Values include not only customer desires for the functionality of the product or service, but also for other product attributes such as installability, maintainability, usability, and availability, as well as additional traits like low cost, vendor support, independent verification, certification, and so on. Functional values usually address desired transformations in the customer's environment, where they directly experience the product. Nonfunctional values are not so obvious in the customer's environment, but they still transform it. For instance, saving money on the product cost transforms the customer's available funds upwards. This allows them to be more competitive with a service or product that builds upon the service or product you provide them, or gives them other options for action in their realm.

Sometimes value is about avoiding transformations. For example, a value for bank tellers might be to avoid needing too much specialized training to do a particular job. This value statement might read something like "the bank teller should be able to process transactions with no more than one day's training." In this customer's environment, job training is a means of transformation, one that this particular customer wants to minimize.

The Three "Lenses" of Value Resolution

Value resolution looks at the customer space through three different perspectives, or "lenses":

1. *Domain:* Universal to all customers of a given customer type, i.e., "what all similar customers want."
2. *Recognized Specific:* Specific to a particular customer, i.e., "what a specific customer knows it wants." (This is the only lens that requirements analysis uses, and it does so very incompletely and haphazardly.)
3. *Unrecognized Specific:* Specific to a particular customer, i.e., "what a specific customer doesn't know it wants."

Just as an ultraviolet lens reveals different things than does an infrared lens, so each of these perspectives reveals different things about the same customer values, as well as identifies different customer values. Looking at the same set of customers through all three lenses and combining what has been learned from each perspective gives the lean producer a broader and deeper understanding of its customer's values. After creating the composite picture, the lean producer weighs and orders each value according to the customer's priorities.

Comparing Value Resolution to Requirements Analysis

Craft and mass software developers do requirements analysis. Like value resolution, requirements analysis develops a list of the characteristics that the developers must address in the final product. Beyond this superficial similarity, however, value resolution and requirements analysis could hardly be more different (see Figure 8-1).

Lean's value resolution focuses on the priorities of the customer; requirements analysis emphasizes the functionality of a particular product.

Value resolution says that *values are more important than the individual product.* In lean thinking, knowledge of values is both the foundation for a product and its success, as well as a resource for future products, marketing efforts, and relationship building. In the end, lean producers will almost certainly not incorporate into any given product all the values identified by the value resolution process. Indeed, it would be wasteful to implement values that mean very little to the customer . . . and lean removes waste. But you'll never know which values are important and which aren't, until you collect and prioritize them using value res-

	Value Resolution	*Requirements Analysis*
Focus	Customer priorities	Product functionality
Expansiveness	Product line/ Future oriented	Single product/ Present or past oriented
Main Concerns	Customer delight, business	Organization "realities"
Detail Level	"What" and "When"	"What," "When," "How"
Other Concerns	Systematic	Sporadic
Customer Involvement	Central	Peripheral
Responsible Parties	Developers	"Higher-level group"
"Richness" of Results	Domain, recognized, unrecognized, prioritized	Usually only "recognized"

Figure 8-1. Value Resolution vs. Requirements Analysis

olution. Gaining the broad understanding that comes through a thorough value-resolution process is never wasted effort; it helps producers make better choices about their products, as well as their entire businesses.

Conversely, requirements analysis says that requirements are just a means to get to the real goal, which is the product. Requirement analysis does not have an equivalent process for understanding customers, and therefore, almost never gains much insight into them. Each product takes on a life of its own, broken off from any real tether to its customer, floating wherever the currents of the project carries it, steered only by the brittle and incomplete rudder of product-oriented requirements. Such requirements also tend to include hidden design decisions and thus limit future design options that the producer might have badly needed later on to cope with late-breaking discoveries.

Value resolution takes a big-picture view because it begins by looking at the general kinds of activities all customers within a particular customer type are performing, rather than just how a particular product affects a particular customer. This is an open-ended, product line viewpoint that looks to the future and anticipates future needs, as opposed to the single product viewpoint of requirements analysis that looks primarily to the present—at the current needs for a new product—or at best, backward to previous similar systems.

Value resolution is also primarily concerned with pleasing the customer. The main concern of requirements analysis, however, is to account for the realities of the producer organization. One common type of organizational reality is top-down directives, such as a demand to reuse previous products in the category, practically regardless of their applicability to the current situation. Another common type of reality is political concerns, such has having to involve certain groups and people in requirements analysis even if they have little or no insight into the customer's values or a business perspective. In a traditional development environment, such realities are given top priority even if they lead to practices and products that directly contradict the customer's values. This happens because most reality issues boil down to fulfilling mass production-type efficiency, where the overriding goal—as we saw earlier in the book—is to keep producer resources busy, and not to maximize the value of the product to the customer or even to the producer.

The level of detail that value resolution seeks in value statements is *what* the customer wants, *when* the customer wants it, (i.e., under what conditions), and even *why* the customer wants it (their deeper motivations), rather than *how* to bring about what the customer wants. The latter is the legitimate focus of a follow-on stage of requirements analysis, which is a useful activity when built on the foundation of value resolution. Delving into *how* too early obscures the picture of what a producer should develop or try to accomplish. When the proper time comes to address the *how*, it becomes a natural transition from *what, when,* and *why* into the producer space.

Customers have many types of concerns besides just what a product will do. We have already mentioned cost, schedule, verification, and maintenance concerns. Value resolution actively searches out these kinds of concerns with the same determination it shows in looking for functional needs, making the customer an integral part of the team. Requirements analysis, on the other hand, only ventures beyond functional concerns in a limited and sporadic way, involving the customer in peripheral ways or maybe not at all (as in going to in-house company experts to represent customer concerns).

In value resolution, the development team is involved in collecting the values. This allows a two-way flow of information and relationship between the customer and the people who will be actually serving the customer. In requirements analysis, a separate group in the organization, like market analysis, systems engineering, or hardware engineering, is delegated the task of collecting requirements. Using a separate group is, of course, using division of labor as in mass production and has the effect of further distancing the customer from the people working to meet the customer's needs.

As we said, value resolution looks at customer needs through three lenses, all within the customer space. Requirements analysis mixes together the customer space (customer-environment changes) and producer space (product characteristics) and then looks at them both through a single lens: that of individual recognized needs (the second lens of values resolution).

The list of requirements found in this way is then prioritized in a very haphazard way, based largely upon considerations from the producer space (like, "what have we been doing in our products that we can continue doing on this project?") and individual whim. All these deficiencies combine to limit the richness and cripple the usefulness of the information most important for directing a project.

Though we do not show it in Figure 8-1, a commonality between value resolution and requirements analysis is that it's common for either one to analyze associated risks.

The Seven Steps of a Value Resolution

There are many ways to conduct a value resolution.[2] The first and most important decision is to just pick a way and start doing it. It is often better (though not necessarily essential) to bring in outside help at least the first time with the lean techniques and practices. Below are seven steps for conducting value resolution. The chapters detailing each step are given in parentheses.

1. *Choosing the project.* Above all, choose a project that serves your business well. This means you need to do some strategic planning, and not just be driven by coincidences, such as having another system you've already developed that you can reuse. (Chapter 9)
2. *Identifying the customers.* Once you have picked the right project, you must identify your customers. If you do this poorly you will, at best, miss opportunities; at worst, you will develop the wrong product altogether. (Chapter 9)
3. *Finding gemba* (the customer's home turf). This is where the developer connects with the customer. If one is to connect and communicate with someone, one must know where he or she is and where these do what these do. (Chapter 9)
4. *Identifying values.* With the project selected and customers identified and located, create the list of customer values that will be used to direct the rest of the project. (Chapters 10, 11, and 12)
5. *Predicting customer reaction.* Predict how the customer will react emotionally to having each value implemented. Knowing this will help you plan and order your development. (Chapter 13)
6. *Prioritizing values.* Determine the relative importance of the values to your customer. This is different than item 5 above and also will help you plan the development. (Chapter 14)
7. *Choosing the implementation order.* The previous value-resolution steps give you the basis to decide what should go into your product, and when,

for best business success. We cover how to do that planning in a way that decreases risks and improves predictability. (Chapter 14)

These steps will be covered in much more detail in the following chapters. How you conduct each step depends on the scale of the project. You should use discretion and not be too set on which of these techniques you use or how you use them, since it's easy to get caught in "paralysis by analysis." You may also need to modify the steps to match the needs of a project: You may want to take more of a smorgasbord approach, picking your own dishes rather than sitting down to a preplanned seven-course banquet. Every project is different, and selecting accordingly has never hurt any project in which we've been involved.

A last note on value resolution: Though it is the organization's most consuming activity at the beginning of a project, especially during the preanalysis and analysis phases, it should not be limited to just the early lifecycle phase. It continues to yield great dividends when it is kept up throughout all the project's phases (though a much lower effort is needed later). This both ensures that you stay in touch with your customer and any changes they may be going through. It also keeps your customer actively involved with you, thereby preventing many of those very changes.

ENDNOTES

1. A. Bolt, G. Mazur, "Jurassic QFD," The Eleventh Symposium on Quality Function Deployment, Nov, Michigan, June 1999.
2. Two alternatives that differ in varying degrees from the approach in this book are: H. Beyer's and K. Holtzblatt's "A Customer-Centered Approach to Systems Designs," San Francisco, CA: Morgan Kaufmann Publishers, March 2002; and A. Cooper's and P. Saffo's "The Inmates Are Running the Asylum: Why High Tech Products Drive Us Crazy and How To Restore The Sanity," Indianapolis, IN: SAMS, April, 1999.

9

Choosing the Right Project

IN CHAPTER 8, WE INTRODUCED THE SEVEN STEPS of value resolution. We pointed out how crucial the first three of them are: choosing the project, identifying the customer, and finding *gemba*. There is a subtle but important difference between choosing the project (step one) and choosing the *right* project, which encompasses all of the first three steps and is discussed as a unified activity in this chapter. The distinction comes because it is possible to choose a project that makes business sense, but be mistaken about who the customers for your project should be (not just who you assume they are), or about where you should go to learn about their values. In that case, you will collect the wrong set of values and actually perform the wrong project. Thus, you really need all three steps together to choose the right project, the topic of this chapter.

Choosing the Project

This first step in the value resolution is an enterprise-level activity. If a company doesn't plan its business using lean techniques such as *hoshin kanri*, then its lean production lacks a lean directive and the company will not do as well on its enterprise business goals as it could have. That is, a business may do individual projects well but not be growing to its full potential or benefiting from synergies among its projects that would give it a major competitive advantage in the marketplace.

Good business planning is neither difficult nor mysterious. Doing it well identifies the criteria for choosing the best projects to advance the cause of the business as a whole. It also helps the business to become consistent at its lean execution across all its projects. It leads to long-term business success. For example, "In the early 1970s, Yokagawa Hewlett-Packard (YHP) was one of the least successful of Hewlett-Packard's divisions. YHP's quality was poor, the sales were low, and the profit was low. The people at YHP . . . used *hoshin* planning to orchestrate the transformation involved. By the late 1970s . . . YHP had high quality, good market penetration, and good profit."[1]

Hoshin kanri and business planning are each a world of topics on their own, and a book like this cannot cover them in depth. We will, however, expand here a little on what we said in Chapter 3.

Hoshin kanri evolved in the same industrial environment as lean production. It produces and deploys business planning rather than saleable products. It does so through both incremental and radical improvements (a 'la *kaizen* and *kaikaku*). Some of the techniques described in the remainder of Part II are useful in *hoshin kanri* planning, for instance, the affinity diagram and the rest of the 7MP (seven management and planning) tools, as well as the analytic hierarchy process (AHP). For more information on this broad subject, We again highly recommend the excellent reference mentioned in Chapter 3, "*Beyond Strategic Planning*."[2] Two other well-known references on the subject are "*Hoshin Planning: The Developmental Approach*,"[3] and "*Hoshin Handbook*."[4] Of course, companies may have other means for developing strategic planning, but if you are pursuing lean production, whatever means you use needs to be compatible with lean goals and principles.

Identifying the Customers

People often think of their customer as being the one who takes final delivery of or uses your product or service. Womack and Jones take this idea to its logical limit: "Value can only be defined by the ultimate customer."[5] In many, perhaps most situations, such simplicity helps focus on who is most important to your business. But, there is a major downside to assuming that the only customer is the product user.

In the broader sense, a customer is anyone who can hinder or enhance the saleability or (even more importantly) business benefit of your product. Such people are involved in all stages of the project, including oversight, development, production, and delivery. Company management, government regulators, and the general public are all examples of types or groups of people who exemplify the diversity of customers. Because these customers are usually important to your success, sometimes even more so than your delivery customer, you cannot just depend on your ultimate customer to define value.

From personal experience, we can say that it is critically important to understand just who these people are and what values they hold. Once a project suitable to the business has been selected, the worst mistake an organization can make in the value principle and in lean production is to misidentify its customers, or their relative importance to each other.

A further twist is that sometimes, upon closer examination, you will discover to your surprise that gaining a useful understanding of your delivery customer takes more detective work than you anticipated. You may need to consider your customer's customers. For instance, if you are developing ATM transaction-handling software for a bank, you may find it profitable to learn something about the people who use the bank and what they value in banking services. In most cases, this information can improve what you offer. You will delight the bank, who is your "ultimate customer," when you delight the bank's customers and they become more loyal to the bank because of your product.

Before you can begin prioritizing customers, however, you need a raw list of candidate customers to work with. Some customers are more obvious than others, but it is easy to overlook candidates who may turn out to be important. Brainstorming is one structured way to create a thorough candidate customer list.

Brainstorming

In 1939, the advertising field pioneered a formal technique that could generate a raw list of candidate items for virtually any purpose. They called it brainstorming.

The steps of brainstorming are:

1. Ensure that everyone agrees about the main question to be answered (in our context, probably "who are the customers?").
2. Give everyone a little time, but not too much time, to write a list of possible answers: Stay "right-brained" rather than "left-brained."
3. Keep cycling through the group so each person, in turn, can share possible answers. Make several cycles until ideas slow down.
   a. Have somebody write these down on a whiteboard that everyone can see. Record each idea verbatim and don't try to clarify anything until you stop (someone's misunderstanding may lead to a unique idea).
   b. Suspend all judgment of proposed ideas; often the craziest sounding ones lead to the best insights when everyone has had a chance to process them.
   c. Encourage outside-the-box responses and piggybacking on previous ideas.
4. Clarify items as needed on the completed list. Allow late additions to the list as they arise.
   a. Remove duplicate ideas.
   b. Remove ideas that truly don't belong on the list, but be careful not to remove unconventional ideas that may bear fruit.

Other than writing supplies, an open mind is the only equipment you must bring to a brainstorming session. The idea is to encourage nonanalytical, intuitive thinking. After the session, there will be plenty of time to sift through the results.

For software companies, a brainstormed list of potential customers will obviously include the direct users of the system. Once you identify the actual users, you then identify those with the authority to make the purchasing decisions. Still, others will be outside parties who can encourage or forbid the purchase or use of the product, such as governmental agencies, regulatory bodies, or test laboratories. In embedded system development, one must also account for hardware or systems groups. There are also corporate and political groups to consider, and so on and so forth, until you have a list that includes both the obvious and the obscure. Once you have this raw list of customer candidates you are ready to quantify and order them.

The Analytic Hierarchy Process (AHP)

The Analytic Hierarchy Process or AHP is one of the best ways to analyze the relative importance of items on a list.[6] The AHP is a matrix-algebra technique used in operations research and management science. These fields are not often on the minds of software developers. Nevertheless, the concepts involved are highly practical, immensely powerful, and reasonably simple. The AHP is almost magical in its ability to use simple A–B–binary comparisons to sort out the relative importance of all the members of any set of similar things. It works best for sets that are reasonably small, since the effort involved is proportional to the square of the number of elements in the set. With a little automation and sufficient motivation, the AHP can handle medium-sized sets: Jim has used it (with a team) very profitably with around 100 elements. We wouldn't recommend using it for anything much larger.

The AHP is especially good at turning people's qualitative feelings or impressions into quantitative results. This makes it highly useful for ordering the importance of customers, since you start out with disorganized opinions about the players on your raw list and want to end up with an objectively ordered final list.

Some of the candidates on the raw list will turn out to be so unimportant to the software project that, essentially, they can be ignored. Others will be of secondary importance, but significant enough to keep in mind when analyzing the value that will be placed into the product. You may be surprised at who shows up where on your list. The AHP, properly done, will tell you where everyone should be.

Example of the AHP at Work

Imagine that you are the software lead of a project developing the software that controls a new model of pacemakers. Besides yourself, your company's software manager, a representative of your marketing group, and a consultant from the pacemaker industry have brainstormed the following list of candidate customers:

- *User.* The patient receiving the pacemaker.
- *Purchaser.* The physician prescribing your company's pacemaker.

- *Authorizes Purchase.* The HMO that authorizes the purchase and use of your company's pacemaker. The HMO may even have a product short list that your product must be on before it can be prescribed by the physician.
- *The Systems Group.* The group that integrates the pacemaker hardware with your software. They may have the right to accept or reject your software.
- *The FDA.* The FDA's approval will make or break your company's product and potentially your company (go/no-go agent).
- *The Engineering VP of your company.* The person who favors microcoded controllers (like he or she grew up on) over the maintainable high-level language code on generic/upgradable microprocessors you prefer to use for schedule, budget, and maintainability reasons. This person can reduce your design authority and your ability to work effectively if he or she doesn't like what your group's doing.

What emphasis should you put on each of these customers? Is the patient or the physician the ultimate customer? Can you confidently ignore any of these customers and their values? How much of your limited budget and schedule should you allocate to each of your customer's concerns? It's time for the AHP.

The heart of the AHP takes each one of several alternatives in a set of items, pairs it with each other alternative, and compares the two items in each pair. If the first item in a pair is equally, or more, important than the second, you will give it a value from 1 to 9, as follows:

1 Equally important
3 Weakly more important
5 Strongly more important
7 Very strongly more important
9 Absolutely more important

If needed, you can use even-numbered values for more intermediate or subtle values, but this is not required. If the second item in your pair is more important than the first, treat the second item as if it were the first and select the appropriate importance number. Then take the reciprocal of the number (e.g., if B of an A/B pair is strongly more important than A, the comparison number is 1/5 instead of 5).

Let's say your group compared all these customers and came up with the (see Figure 9-1). If a choice is subtle or controversial, it doesn't hurt to record your rationales and thoughts so you can later revisit the context in which you made your choices, though this isn't absolutely necessary.

Note that there can be seeming contradictions in your comparisons: Since we said the physician is weakly more important than the patient and that the physician and the HMO were equally important to our business, you'd assume we'd

Comparisons	Value	Observations
Patient–Physician	1/3	If the physician doesn't prescribe it, we have no business.
Patient–HMO	1	The HMO is disconnected from the patient's needs and situation, de-emphasizing the HMO somewhat and making their importance equal.
Patient–Systems Group	5	All "Systems" needs is software that runs in processor constraints.
Patient–FDA	1/3	If FDA doesn't approve it, again no business.
Patient–VP	7	We just don't want to irritate the VP.
Physician–HMO	1	If HMO doesn't approve it, again no business.
Physician–Systems Group	5	Must get functionality the physician wants to see, or he or she won't prescribe it.
Physician–FDA	3	Physician still rules, but can't prescribe it if not FDA-approved.
Physician–VP	9	Just need to keep VP on the radar screen.
HMO–Systems Group	7	No rationale; "gut feel."
HMO–FDA	1/3	Both essentially approval agancies, but there are other HMOs; just one FDA.
HMO–VP	5	No rationale; "gut feel."
Systems Group–FDA	1/7	Same idea as in "Patient–Systems Group."
Systems Group–VP	3	Must deliver to Systems; must only avoid irritating VP (try for goodwill).
FDA–VP	7	Would be "9", but VP has been somewhat critical lately; keep him or her in view.

Figure 9-1. Initial Customer-Customer Comparisons

say the HMO is weakly more important than the patient as well. You'd even be tempted to take a shortcut and just fill in that comparison based on this assumption. Don't give in to the temptation. There are subtleties in the way we compare things that we miss out on if we just make a few comparisons and fill in the blanks of the others accordingly. Approach every comparison with a fresh view, and the AHP will work out the contradictions.

The next step is to build an N×N matrix (for the N items being compared), for instance in a spreadsheet tool. Label the rows and the columns with the names of the alternatives (the customer candidates). Each cell in the body of the matrix represents the result of comparing the intersecting alternatives. The row name is the reference alternative (the first one in the pair), and the column name is the alternative being compared to the reference. Put "1s" on the diagonal, where each alternative is compared to itself. Above the diagonal, this order corresponds to the order we took in our table above. Below the diagonal, the comparisons are in reverse order, so the value must be the inverse of the original order comparison. Said mathematically, for matrix A, the value in A[i,j] represents the comparison of the alternative on row i with the alternative on column j.

Filling in the comparison values on the diagonal and above it (the "forward comparisons"), this appears as in Figure 9-2:

	Patient	Physician	HMO	Systems	FDA	VP
Patient	1	1/3	1	5	1/3	7
Physician		1	1	5	3	9
HMO			1	7	1/3	5
Systems				1	1/7	3
FDA					1	7
VP						1

Figure 9-2. Placing the Comparison Results Into the Matrix

With the inverses (reverse comparisons) below the diagonal, the matrix appears in Figure. 9-3.

A little matrix math now allows us to turn these comparisons into numerical rankings. First, we want the sum of all the rankings or weights of all the comparisons to a given alternative to equal 1. We do this by adding up the weights in a column; then we divide each weight by its column sum. For instance, the sum of the weights in the VP column is 7+9+5+3+7+1 = 32. Then we divide each weight in the VP column by 32, so the weight for "Systems vs. VP" is 3/32 or

	Patient	Physician	HMO	Systems	FDA	VP
Patient	1	1/3	1	5	1/3	7
Physician	3	1	1	5	3	9
HMO	1	1	1	7	1/3	5
Systems	1/5	1/5	1/7	1	1/7	3
FDA	3	1/3	3	7	1	7
VP	1/7	1/9	1/5	1/3	1/7	1

Figure 9-3. Inverse Comparisons Filled in Below the Diagonal

.09375. We'll round that to 3 places, or .094. This normalizes all weights to a common reference. The column yields are in Figure 9-4.

	Patient	Physician	HMO	Systems	FDA	VP
Patient	**1.000**	0.333	1.000	5.000	0.333	7.000
Physician	3.000	**1.000**	1.000	5.000	3.000	9.000
HMO	1.000	1.000	**1.000**	7.000	0.333	5.000
Systems	0.200	0.200	0.143	**1.000**	0.143	3.000
FDA	3.000	0.333	3.000	7.000	**1.000**	7.000
VP	0.143	0.111	0.200	0.333	0.143	**1.000**
Total Wt.	*8.343*	*2.976*	*6.343*	*25.333*	*4.952*	*32.000*

Figure 9-4. Comparisons with Column Sums

Normalizing the weights to achieve a weight sum of 1 (dividing each weight in a column by the column total weight) leads to Figure 9-5.

	Patient	Physician	HMO	Systems	FDA	VP
Patient	0.120	0.112	0.158	0.197	0.067	0.219
Physician	0.360	0.336	0.158	0.197	0.606	0.281
HMO	0.120	0.336	0.158	0.276	0.067	0.156
Systems	0.024	0.067	0.023	0.039	0.029	0.094
FDA	0.360	0.112	0.473	0.276	0.202	0.219
VP	0.017	0.037	0.032	0.013	0.029	0.031
Wt. Sum	1.000	1.000	1.000	1.000	1.000	1.000

Figure 9-5. Normalizing Column to Weighted Sum of "1"

The next step is to sum up all the normalized weights of each alternative to obtain its complete net weight. We do this by summing each row as in Figure 9-6.

	Patient	Physician	HMO	Systems	FDA	VP	Net Wt.
Patient	0.120	0.112	0.158	0.197	0.067	0.219	0.873
Physician	0.360	0.336	0.158	0.197	0.606	0.281	1.937
HMO	0.120	0.336	0.158	0.276	0.067	.0156	1.113
Systems	0.024	0.067	0.023	0.039	0.029	0.094	0.276
FDA	0.360	0.112	0.473	0.276	0.202	0.219	1.641
VP	0.017	0.037	0.032	0.013	0.029	0.031	0.159
Wt. Sum	1.000	1.000	1.000	1.000	1.000	1.000	6.000

Figure 9-6. Summing Across Rows

As you can see, the sum of the net weights (the rightmost column) is 6, since there are 6 alternatives. To complete the analysis, we normalize the net weights, as before, by summing the weights in this column and then dividing each weight by the weight sum. This converts the net weight of each alternative to simply a portion of 1 (or, times 100, a percentage). Another way to say this is that you average all the weights across each row, as in Figure 9-7.

	Patient	Physician	HMO	Systems	FDA	VP	Norm Wt.
Patient	0.120	0.112	0.158	0.197	0.067	0.219	0.145
Physician	0.360	0.336	0.158	0.197	0.606	0.281	0.323
HMO	0.120	0.336	0.158	0.276	0.067	0.156	0.186
Systems	0.024	0.067	0.023	0.039	0.029	0.094	0.046
FDA	0.360	0.112	0.473	0.276	0.202	0.219	0.274
VP	0.017	0.037	0.032	0.013	0.029	0.031	0.027
Wt. Sum	1.000	1.000	1.000	1.000	1.000	1.000	1.000

Figure 9-7. Normalized New Weights

There is always a real thrill when you use the AHP on any significant problem. It is a hunting expedition of sorts, and you never quite know what game you'll find until you're finished. There are often surprises, like discovering that the physician, at a 32 percent weight, is nearly twice as important as the HMO, at 18 percent. This is despite our pairwise direct comparison that they were equally important (a "1" value).

Most importantly, the AHP has revealed that the physician is clearly the one and only ultimate customer. Without the AHP, might we have assumed that the ultimate customer was the patient? The AHP has told us who the user is of our product. Surely we can all identify with the poor patient, who finds himself fourth in priority on a list of six—and he's the one whose body is going to carry the pacemaker! But then again, this ranking reflects the understanding that the business has of the realities of the health market in which it will be selling its product.

Finally, who would have guessed, going into the analysis, that we would find the FDA so much more important than everyone but the physician? Yet without highlighting this, we might have put too little attention on satisfying the FDA. This might have led to nasty surprises late in the development lifecycle, when the FDA delayed the company's product release because it was uncomfortable with the product or process. This sort of catastrophe happens all the time in the marketplace and is usually avoidable by doing your homework up front.

The Genius of the AHP

In such ways as this, the AHP flushes out critical knowledge that may be hidden and makes it available for important decision making. If you find contradictions and surprises in your analysis, your paired comparisons are narrow in scope, but the AHP accounts for all your concerns from all your perspectives. The genius of the AHP is that it starts with something human beings do well—paired comparison—and extracts from it something we otherwise do poorly—weighting multiple, competing concerns.

One slight caution is in order about the AHP process. If, in your pairwise comparisons, you overemphasize political concerns, such as those within your company or concerning the government, you may falsely promote these types of candidates in their customer ranking. You may even lose sight of the identity of your true, ultimate customer. While such distortions might help your group's cause within your own company or regulatory environment, in the end, it will work against your product's success in the marketplace. Going for political answers is not a lean practice and will not lead to the business performance you seek. The high ranking of the FDA in the above example might reflect a little too much deference to them in your original pairwise comparisons. It's worth revisiting those comparisons and making sure your perspective was right (the rationales and thoughts that you recorded in the process can help here), but if you do end up revisiting the comparisons, you must be careful to resist any temptation to finesse the original data to reach a predesired conclusion. Keeping a business orientation throughout this process and all lean activities will help you stay focused on finding the lean answers to the questions asked by the AHP and other techniques we use.

After brainstorming and performing the AHP, you know who your customers are and how important each one of them is to your project's success. How could any software project set off without this knowledge? Customer savvy should drive virtually every planning decision and help you to allocate resources to the things that matter most in making the project a success. This reduces waste, which is, of course, a prime lean directive. It also acts as a virtuous leaven in the project while the project is still pliable, when what you do has the greatest impact on how well the project will rise in the end. Yet, most projects make do without this knowledge. They either ignore the question altogether, relying on someone else to tell them who the customer is, or they make obvious and often mistaken assumptions. Lean production starts with identifying the customer and this is one step that you cannot scrimp on. On smaller projects, the AHP will take just a day or so; on larger ones, not much longer. Even if you use lean techniques throughout the rest of the product lifecycle, your success will always be less than it could have been if only you had identified your customers correctly.

Finding *Gemba*: The Customer Home Turf

Once you know who your customers are and how important each one is relative to the others, you need to proceed to step three before you can begin studying what they value. You must somehow connect with them. For various reasons, software developers often shortchange this step. Sometimes they create their software in isolation. Sometimes, with a typical mass production attitude, they just assume they already know what's best for the marketplace. In addition, sometimes they go to the wrong sources to learn about their customers. The results are the same. Their list of product requirements are inconsistent with the customer's values and their product ends up being less useful and less successful than it could have been.

Masaaki Imai, an expert whom many acknowledge to be the father of *kaizen*, pointed out the futility of managers meeting in a conference room to solve a problem in the plant, on the assembly line, or in the R&D lab. Lean producers learned many years ago that, by far, the best place to go to connect with the customer is the customer's own environment. "To understand a problem in *gemba*, you must go to *gemba*."[7] In Japanese, *gemba* means "on location." In lean terms, gemba is where the value is, or will be added, or is to be added.

At least five distinct ways are used to connect with the customer. The first three help you understand *gemba*. From the most desirable to the least, they are:

1. Make the customer a part of your development team; go to the customer's workplace as needed.
2. Meet with the customer, who is not on your team, in his or her workplace as needed.
3. Have the customer come to your workplace and meet with you there.
4. Find a surrogate to represent the customer to your development team.
5. Have someone in your company represent the customer's interests.

The first level is full involvement and access to the customer. It requires a large commitment on the part of your customer to get this kind of access. Extreme Programming, discussed in Chapter 6, emphasizes having the customer on the development team. It is very desirable, though not always attainable: Not all customers are interested in being directly involved in the development of a product; or perhaps your business does not want them to know exactly how the product is being made for fear they might become a competitor (a fairly rare situation, fortunately).

Levels 2 and 3 involve the real customer, though at varying distances from the customer's working environment or *gemba*. Level 4 occurs when you hire someone to represent the customer to your team and your product development group. A surrogate is someone who has previously worked for the customer, now works for a similar customer, or knows the customer's industry very well (e.g., a qualified consultant). For instance, military systems developers often hire retired military personnel for just this reason. Their information is a bit second hand and may be dated, but is much better than no contact at all. It would be hard to justify calling it *gemba*, however.

Level 5 is used when it would be difficult, expensive, or politically disadvantageous (within or outside the company) to obtain true customer representation. The information provided this way is frequently little better than having no customer contact at all.

Finding the best available *gemba* level is sometimes not as obvious in software development as it is in other industries. Desktop software, for instance, is used by many different customers in a multitude of ways, at varying locations (homes, businesses, schools, and so on). It will take creativity and extra work and money to connect with customers in the most native environment possible, that is, the environment that gives you the best opportunity to experience, discover, and understand your customer's values. Perhaps finding *gemba* means building a composite customer by working with people from different industries. In the end, finding *gemba* empowers both you and your customer. It allows you to create a product that embodies your customer's values and that will please your customer. Because it promotes the customer's involvement in the production process, it will give him or her a feeling of ownership in the product.

ENDNOTES

1. B. King, "*Hoshin Planning, The Developmental Approach*," Methuen, MA: GOAL/QPC, 1989, pg. I.
2. Michael Cowley and Ellen Domb, "*Beyond Strategic Vision: Effective Corporate Action With Hoshin Planning*," Burlington, MA: Butterworth Heinemann, 1997.
3. B. King, "*Hoshin Planning: The Developmental Approach*," GOAL/QPC, 1989.
4. P. Babich, *Hoshin Handbook*, Second Edition, Poway, CA: Total Quality Engineering, Inc., 1996.
5. *Lean Thinking*, pg. 16.
6. Thomas L. Saaty, "*Decision Making for Leaders: The Analytic Hierarchy Process for Making Decisions in a Complex World*," Pittsburgh, PA: RWS Publications, December 1999.
7. G. McClure, "Is Kaizen the Answer?" *IEEE-USA Policy Perspectives*, January 2001.

10

Choosing a
Value Representation

COMING UP WITH A LIST OF CANDIDATE VALUES is step four of value resolution. We will discuss methods for doing this in Chapters 11 and 12. Before we can compile such a list, however, we must have a way to record the values that will be placed on that list. Values are substantial things that capture significant information. It is best, therefore, to have a systematic and disciplined way to record values. We call such a recording mechanism a *representation*. Beyond providing a way for capturing information, a representation also provides a way to examine it.

Many representations have been developed to capture requirements. Some can be adapted for use with values, though none of them are perfect for the purpose. We can, however, identify the traits of an ideal value representation. We will then choose one of the better requirements representations from the software industry to adapt for values capture and show how a well-chosen value representation can help you conduct effective value resolution. We'll make this real by looking at what happened when a major lean software project used that representation. Finally, we'll close with a short discussion of how your organization can apply this or other value representations for its own benefit.

Ways of Representing Value

There are many ways to represent customer values. One of the less effective ways is the simple statement format mentioned in Chapter 8. A better way is using the Unified Modeling Language (UML).

The UML is a combination of graphics and text with a syntax that defines how the pieces go together. UML is currently the most popular software analysis and design representation. However, even though the UML is popular, other representations are even better for values. One is a very powerful tabular representation associated with the Software Cost Reduction method (SCR), to which we will return shortly. While there are too many existing representations to discuss them all in detail here, we can easily list nine ideal characteristics for a value representation:

Nine Ideal Characteristics
for Any Value Representation

1. Is customer-oriented, using the customer's accustomed terminology and concepts, and being easily understood by customers.

2. Includes criteria for verification of each value statement; e.g., by quantifying the desired outcome in the customer environment.

3. Enforces independence so that individual values (and changes thereto) have little or no overlap.

4. Supports easily changing a value and then seeing what other values are affected (the latter only applies if values are not fully independent, but full independence is even better).

5. Separates *what* from *how*, so that one can quickly identify what must be done, then later fill in necessary ways of interacting with the environment.

6. Has evident completeness, so one can see when and where there are gaps within and between currently stated values.

7. Is unambiguous, thus heading off wrong interpretations by implementers.

8. Captures constraints on how the value's transformation in the customer environment is to be done or to be avoided.

9. Distinguishes between the conditions in the customer environment and the actions of the agent doing the transforming.

There is no one ideal value representation that works for every type of software. You should choose one that is well suited to your market and that has as many of the above characteristics as is practical. The first characteristic, however, is absolutely essential: You must record lean value statements in a form that is customer centered and stated completely in terms of the customer space. The more an organization can include the other of the above characteristics in its chosen form of value representation, the more completely it can implement lean production throughout the rest of the product lifecycle. In particular, the remaining ideal characteristics give great paybacks when it comes time to build up a value stream, facilitate lean flow and pull, and pursue perfection. In lean, it always comes back to this: *Everything starts with the value principle.*

Because achieving the goals of lean production are so dependent on having well-formed value statements, we will take a closer look at what it means to keep the customer perspective and to work in the customer space.

Keeping the Customer Perspective

One way to explain what it means to "define values in the customer's environment" is to design and build a value representation that demonstrates what such values could look like. To do this, we will adapt to values the requirements representation called REQ tables, which are associated with the SCR method mentioned above.

This begins an extended example. If you don't want to put in the time this will take, you can still learn much about values from the next several chapters. However, if you take the time to follow this reasoning, you will gain a much deeper understanding of values. Since values are the key to lean production, and indeed to business success, this will be time well spent.

REQ tables are very powerful yet friendly ways of representing transformations in the customer's environment. More than any other representation approach, REQ tables express the ideal characteristics of good value capture. In some cases, they even enforce them. One of the representation's greatest virtues is that it is readable, with minimal training, by everyone from the customer to senior management. Yet, it is fully useful to developers through all stages of development. Without readability, REQ tables would not be suitable for value capture because they could not communicate with most customers, who are by far the most important people in value resolution. Without remaining useful through all stages of development, a wasteful step would have to be introduced to transform the information in the REQ tables into a form the developers could use for their tasks. So readability and lifecycle-applicability are important advantages of this representation.

A potential disadvantage to basing value representation on SCR is that the method also includes means to capture lower-level information that is needed in software requirements. While it is completely appropriate to capture such details later in the lifecycle, you want to stay at a higher conceptual level during value resolution. What you want to gather are the concerns with which customers have the most direct contact, such as fields in forms, parts of documents, functions of physical devices, and so forth. At this point, you don't need to model lower-level and subtle customer concerns such as unusual error-handling situations, I/O mechanisms, or BIT (Built-In Tests).

SCR: A Method Adaptable to Value Representation

SCR was created in the late 1970s, when a team of researchers at the U.S. Naval Research Laboratory (NRL) started work on a project designed to prove the practicality of developing real-world software using some of the powerful software engineering ideas that had been proposed in the previous decade. Examples of such ideas are information hiding and abstract interfaces.

Dr. David Parnas, one of the fathers of modern software engineering, led the extremely capable team: Other team members have moved on to distinguish themselves in industry and academia, including Dr. John Shore (a founder of speech recognition), Dr. David Weiss (since then, a researcher in software product lines), Dr. Stuart Faulk (now director of Oregon Software Engineering Research Center), Dr. Paul Clements (now on senior technical staff at CMU SEI in software architectures), and Ms. Katherine Heninger Britton (now on senior technical staff in IBM for networking and mobile computing).

The NRL picked for its experiment a very demanding application, the redevelopment of the flight software for the A-7E attack aircraft. This software had hard timing and sizing constraints imposed by the capacity of the onboard computer. It also had a working benchmark—the existing flight software—against which to compare its success. The method used for requirements capture only began to be called SCR after the A-7E project.

The method itself has proven quite durable, having been applied many times since the A-7E project, including as the base for a blending of SCR with OOA (the SPC's CoRE or Consortium Requirements Engineering method; mentioned in more detail again later in this chapter), in Jim's work integrating CoRE with pattern-based design for the central control software on the Lockheed-Martin 382J airlifter,[1] in Jim Kirby's (of NRL) work in 2002 on other aspects of extending the method through the full range of design activities,[2] and of course, for its use in value capture we are describing here. The SCR method is still evolving, with automation and other extensions in the 2000s, and continues to be used with great benefit on both small and large projects.

Another reason that SCR is so good to study for lean software development is that it is almost uniquely strong on the particular fundamentals of good software engineering that especially facilitate lean production. These include such essentials as information hiding and abstract interfaces. Unfortunately, in most cases, mainstream software development continues to neglect many of these decades-old advances. The May 1999 issue of the *ACM's Software Engineering Notes* profiled Dr. David Parnas, who was, by that time, an ACM Fellow. The interviewer asked him, "What was your greatest influence?" He answered, "I suppose that my early work on 'Information Hiding' has had the most influence, but I look around and don't see it being used enough. I see it mentioned in papers and explained (very briefly) in many textbooks, but when I look at real systems, I see that it is not being used in most systems. Too many people get into programmer positions without learning how to use such basic (and frequently reinvented) ideas. As Steve McConnell has pointed out, good object-oriented design requires that objects hide something. Unfortunately, most of the OO code that I have seen hides nothing. The programs look like COBOL programs with a new syntax."[3] Dr. Parnas' answer points to how shallow the adoption has been of many of the software-engineering concepts that are the most useful for lean production. This has greatly reduced the likelihood that any lean benefits would be gained from using even the most valid current development approaches (such as OO). Studying SCR highlights things that are underplayed in our present understanding and practice and must be restored if we are to make the jump to lean.

The Four-Variable Model—CONs and MONs

REQ tables are based on an abstraction of the user's environment called the *Parnas-Madey Four-Variable Model* (FVM).[4] The FVM conceives of the user's environment (*user* and *customer* are synonymous here, since they all describe people who work in the customer space) as a collection of physical or logical quantities expressed as mathematical variables. The environmental quantities that the user wants to change are called *controlled variables*, or "*CONs*" for short. For example, the user or owner of a home might want to have an outside light come on automatically when it starts getting dark outside, if a switch inside is in the auto position. The lamp's state of illumination would be the CON in this case.

In customer values, it does not matter who or what changes the quantities in the environment (CONs)—a person, machine, or computer running a program could do the job as far as the customer cares—all that matters is that the state of the environment is changed.

To effect the change of a CON, whatever is doing the changing must usually know something about the current condition of the environment. If you don't know the conditions from which you begin, you cannot in general make a change that ends up in a known condition. For instance, if you want to take a trip to Tucson, Arizona, your end condition, but you don't know where you are starting from, your *current condition*, you can't define a route or *translation* that gets you there from here. The quantities that represent the current condition of the environment are called *monitored variables*, or *MONs*. Returning to our example, to illuminate a lamp after dark, one must recognize when it gets dark; i.e., one must know the ambient light intensity. Ambient light intensity is a monitored variable. So is the state of the interior switch.

CONs and MONs (controlled variables and monitored variables) are the only two of the four variables in the FVM that are relevant to value capture. The other two, input variables (INs) and output variables (OUTs), model the details of physical interfaces in the user's environment, a concern that is addressed only after conducting a value resolution. You can read more about the rest of the FVM in Parnas' and Madey's "Function Documents for Computer Systems."[5]

Let's look at the relationship between CONs and MONs and the before-and-after condition of the customer's environment (Figure 10-1).

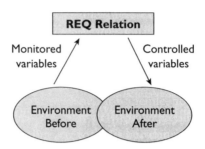

Figure 10-1. Transformations of the Customer Environment

In SCR, the before/after translation is called a *REQ relation.* If we treat the REQ relation, for a moment, as if it were a function (it is not, strictly speaking, because there can be an allowable tolerance in the resulting CON value, whereas a true function will specify exactly one possible result value), we can state a REQ as:

$$CON = f(MONs)$$

In other words, for each CON the customer desires to be changed, there is a function (roughly speaking) that specifies the mathematical relationship between the desired CON condition and the set of MON conditions. In algebraic terms, the MONs are the independent variables, and the CON is the dependent variable.

The details of a REQ relation are recorded in a REQ table. For our simple example of the outside light, the REQ table might appear as follows in Figure 10-2:

MON_Auto_Light_Switch	MON_Ambient_Light_Level	CON_Lamp_Illumination
Auto	<= twilight_threshold	ON
Auto	> twilight_threshold	OFF
Off	"Don't care"	OFF

Figure 10-2. "Outside Light" SCR Tablet

There will also need to be a data dictionary to define the possible ranges of the MONs and CONs, and the meaning of symbolic terms like twilight_threshold. For instance:

MON_Auto_Light_Switch ::= Auto | Off

This notation defines the automatic light switch MON as having only the two listed enumerated values.

Each column in an SCR REQ table represents a single MON or CON. We are using the convention that the CON is in the rightmost column. Each row in the table represents a set of conditions in the environment and the resulting transformation of the CON. That is, the rightmost cell in a row is the function (loosely speaking) applied to the CON when the MON values are in the sub-ranges stated in their cells in the row. For example, the first row (below the MON and CON label row) says that if the automatic light switch is in the auto position, and the ambient light level is less than or equal to the predefined twilight_ threshold value, the lamp is to be illuminated.

The other two variables of the four-variable model, INs and OUTs, are important because systems do not directly work with MONs and CONs; they work with devices that interface with the environment. Those devices deal with data that is encoded to best meet the device's needs. The encoded data on the input side (representing what an input device sees when looking at monitored quantities in the environment) are called IN variables. The encoded data on the output side (representing what an output device needs to be told before it can affect controlled quantities in the environment) are called OUT variables.

IN variables and MON variables are related by what the SCR method calls the IN relation. An IN relation defines how an IN interface variable is derived from one or more MON variables in the environment:

IN relation: IN = f(MONs)

OUT variables and CON variables are related by what the SCR method calls the OUT relation. An OUT relation defines how a CON variable is driven by one or more OUT interface variables:

OUT relation: CON = g(OUTs)

For now, we will focus on REQ relations and their basic components of MONs and CONs. Later in this book, the subject of INs and OUTs will become important again, especially concerning verification.

Benefits of Mathematics in Representations

There are several things that make SCR REQ tables more suitable for use in value resolution than are standard requirements tables. Of course, the first major difference is the customer environment perspective. With SCR, everything is stated in terms of the environment and tasks of the customer, not the company's products (their physical interfaces, the hardware within them, etc.). This makes SCR truly design-independent; that is, nothing is said to this point about how the product is going to do or perform the translation in the customer's environment. SCR is one of the few analysis methods that enforce such separation between the customer space and the producer space.

The second major difference is that REQ tables are based on mathematical rules, not just the use of mathematical symbols, to express relationships among variables. Software people who have run into mathematical representations or methods in the past tend to close down and stop listening whenever they hear about one now. That's because most mathematically-based methods have been so complicated and so unreadable that only a PhD could work with them. Nobody's going to hire a full team of PhD's to develop their software. SCR isn't like that at all; it's very readable and usable by regular software people, as you may have gleaned from the above examples (full SCR doesn't get much more complicated than the above; Jim has even used it to communicate with untrained customers).

SCR's underlying mathematical rules allow you to analyze and reform the contents of the REQ tables in ways that unruly representations do not allow. This in turns enables a company to do many useful things with their tables beyond what it can do with traditional requirements.

For instance, the NRL has developed software simulation tools to execute REQ tables. By associating MONs and CONs with graphical objects, one can see environmental items like switches and display screens, and operate the items in the environment according to the relations in the REQ tables. This is an excellent approach and one that enables customers to see the results of what they are requesting, to refine their desires, and to modify their REQ tables accordingly. As a pilot project, the NRL simulated a submarine weapons-control console that proved very useful for clarifying user intentions and assumptions about the tables.

Another benefit of having underlying mathematical rules at work in REQ tables is that a company can generate other products directly from the tables, such as test scripts for execution in an automated test environment. The FAA's RTCA DO-178B guidelines for certifying flight software requires extensive testing of completed code against requirements. Lockheed-Martin Aeronautical Company's flight software for the C-27J airlifter used the same REQ tables for both requirements and test cases. One of the project's subcontractors, SAIC, even created a tool that automatically generated test scripts from the requirements (the resulting scripts usually needed at least some additional hand expansion, but still required much less work than generating test scripts the traditional way).

Yet another benefit of using mathematics is that you get assured completeness. Notice in the preceding example (Figure 10-2) that all possible values in the mathematical sense of both MONs are exhausted, as well as all possible *com-*

binations of values among the MONs. The customer value in the lean sense is to effect changes to the CON based upon the current values of the MONs, without regard to any other variables in the environment. This ensures that a system satisfying the customer's needs will have a defined effect on every controlled variable in the user environment for every possible set of current conditions in the user environment. In other words, the system will never do something unexpected or undesired.

Saying that individual tables are complete is still different, of course, than saying that you have identified all possible customer values (and tables). A customer is always free to identify another want or need; value discovery is a soft science, not a hard one. True completeness ensures that any future implemented product will never encounter an unexpected set of conditions in the environment that leaves the value of a CON undefined (assuming, of course, that the software code has remained true to the assertions of the REQ table). Most other types of representations provide an incomplete picture at this initial stage, assuring surprises in the functioning of the final product. So long as the team has verified the table itself for completeness and the remainder of the development and production process has not permitted the code to diverge from the behavior shown in the REQ table, the system will not behave in unexpected ways. Such a development process actually implements three lean principles: value, the value stream, and perfection.

To verify that the implemented code retains the completeness found in the REQ table, a company can program in a mathematically unambiguous and complete (i.e., truly verifiable) language, such as the high-integrity Ada subset called SPARK[6], and add an embedded specification with the code to represent the software requirements (e.g., the value statements plus additional "how to" information). Then the company can automatically verify the continuing correctness of the software throughout all stages of its development by automated "static analysis" or comparison of the product and its embedded specification. Another approach, usable with a lower-integrity language like the C dialects, is to embed executable pre- and postconditions in the software so that the software itself verifies its own continued completeness and even, to some extent, correctness. Of course, the latter adds a considerable execution overhead. If your project allows you to use a language with higher inherent integrity, it will always provide a better overall system solution in the lean sense (i.e., balancing competing concerns like performance, quality, and cost to achieve an optimal result for your business).

People have used tools and representations like Simulink or SCADE to capture requirements so they can be simulated in a similar way to SCR, and to allow automatic extraction of test cases as with SCR. We haven't worked with these tools or their representations. From what we have seen of them, they differ from SCR in that they do not inherently assure completeness (especially Simulink), nor inherently separate analysis from design. However, these tools have undeniable benefits, and we believe they can be made consistent with lean production if they are placed in the right context (e.g., as the first part of a design process that follows a value resolution that has, in other ways, already assured completeness and design independence).

SCR and the FVM have yet another important thing to teach us: a concrete idea of the differences between values and requirements, as well as how to transition from the first to the second. Companies convert the values they record in the REQ tables into software requirements by adding:

- The details of the INs and OUTs.
- The INs and OUTs associations to the MONs and CONs through relations that are analogous to REQs.
- Information about modes in the environment (modes can be relevant to values, but that is beyond the scope of this discussion).
- Aspects of the SCR method that are not discussed in this chapter.

These additions describe the physical constraints of the environment (e.g., equipment you must use), and how to implement what the value describes. It is a big advantage to software developers to have precise definitions of values as opposed to requirements, and of the transition between them. SCR has this advantage, which, as far as we know, no other off-the-shelf value representation possesses. Regardless of which representation you choose, you should define what information you want to go into a value, what to go into a requirement, and the path to migrate between them. The SCR method and the Four-Variable Model give a good example upon which to pattern this decision.

A Lean Software Project that Used SCR

In the 1990s, Lockheed Martin developed the 382J airlifter, which was a complete modernization of the C-130 airlifter, including all-new avionics and electronics and modern high-performance engines. The central integrating software for the new aircraft was the MC OFP (Mission Computer Operational Flight Program).

During MC OFP development, Lockheed Martin recorded software requirements in REQ tables. Code for safety-critical functions was programmed in SPARK Ada,[7] a simple subset of the full Ada language that is object-oriented and somewhat Java-like, though more restrictive. SPARK Ada is based on a well-defined and closed mathematical model that, unlike full Ada, removes all the semantic (interpretation) ambiguities allowed in the definition of the full language. This makes it possible for a tool to analyze the code automatically with complete certainty about the results. The embedded specification language (which essentially restated the REQ table contents with added detail) was called SPARK annotation. The tool to compare the code to the annotations was called SPARK Examiner.[8] Using these complementary technologies allowed Lockheed Martin to immediate close-the-loop verification at each stage of production.

Recall that one of the benefits of lean production is to move from a reliance on after-the-fact defect detection and remediation, to in-process verification. REQ tables provide a strong foundation for in-process verification, as the 382J program has borne out. Combining SCR, SPARK, and other lean software engineering techniques (some covered in Appendix A) gave the program distinct quality and productivity advantages.

At the insistence of the launch customer, the U.K. MoD (Ministry of Defense), the quality of the MC OFP and all other safety-critical software was verified and validated by an independent company. The U.K. MoD is one of the world's pickiest customers: Satisfying the MoD's software-safety specification, DEF STAN 00-55, is viewed by most people in the industry as lying somewhere between extraordinarily difficult and impossible. The firm chosen for independence was Aerosystems International (AeI) of the United Kingdom. Its results showed that the Lockheed-Martin safety-critical software had only 1/10 the anomalies (errors and inconsistencies) of the other safety-critical software on the aircraft—the latter software being in the normal and acceptable safety-critical range. All the pieces of safety-critical software on the aircraft were developed to the same rigorous standard, the FAA-mandated RTCA DO-178B, so the quality differences were due to the dissimilarities between the individual suppliers' development processes. This result led the leader of the U.K. MoD certification agency to declare, during the final acceptance meeting, that the 382J MC OFP development process was "the most nearly perfect we've seen." Having a delighted customer is one of the main goals of lean production; this experience demonstrated how choosing value-driven development practices can help you get there.

Productivity on the 382J MC OFP development was also high. The project more than doubled the productivity that the team had observed among other industry safety-critical vendors, which at that time averaged 3.4 hours per SLOC (none under 3; some 4). The MC OFP development required just 1.6 hours per SLOC. This is a dramatic example of Philip Crosby's famous contention that "Quality is Free," at least in the context of a lean production process. The follow-on project to the 382J, the C-27J, reused portions of the 382J software and further reduced the time per SLOC to 0.8 hours. After climbing the initial learning curve of how to conduct a reuse project, productivity improved to a consistent 0.6 hours per SLOC. Identified improvements were estimated to be capable of reducing this time to 0.4 hours or less, still safety qualified, should another project be attempted using the same architecture in the domain. We discuss many of the techniques that could make this happen in Part III.

Safety-critical certification guidelines like RTCA DO-178B insist on using testing for verification. Because of the mathematical foundations of the 382J process, the products were largely verified long before testing began, through a combination of assured correctness (using techniques like SCR to prevent errors from being introduced) and static analysis. Subsequent testing found that very few nontrivial errors (less than 10) had slipped through the process out of 175KSLOCs, and none of the errors were safety-critical. Had the same process been used on a non-safety-critical project that could have tolerated a handful of small errors, dynamic testing could have been dispensed with. This would have further and significantly decreased costs, a virtuous and self-reinforcing cycle. Such cycles frequently happen when multiple lean techniques are applied together.

Moving SCR into Your Organization's Practice

There is much more substance to the SCR method and the Four-Variable Model than what we have discussed. The method has ways of accounting for important issues such as:

- Differing modes (collections of simultaneous states) in the customer's environment.
- Transformations that must happen only at the transition of a MON value from one of its subranges to another.
- Extended definitions of physical interfaces that are "givens" in the customer's environment.

There are other important issues; for instance, CONs and MONs don't have to be physical quantities, such as a lamp's illumination state or the ambient light level. You can make them more conceptual, like information on a display, data in a database, or any number of other abstractions. The important thing is that the quantities in the REQ tables are natural items in the environment in which the customer is working. If, for example, software producers are developing software-development tools for other software developers, your customers will be working with very different kinds of quantities than, say, bank tellers.

For a more complete description of the SCR method and Four-Variable Model, look into the *Consortium Requirements Engineering Guidebook,*[9] which presents SCR in the context of an object-oriented, class-structuring approach to organizing one's model of the customer's environment (this packaging is called "CoRE," for "Consortium Requirements Engineering," and is a product of the Software Productivity Consortium of Herndon, Virginia). In Jim's experience, the method that CoRE presents needs to be adapted to the nature of the problem domain and the rest of the development process, but it is a good starting point. Nothing is particularly complicated about it, and regular (non-PhD or -specialist) software developers use it every day at Lockheed Martin to communicate with customers, managers, and each other in the later phases of software development.

Concluding Thoughts

In this chapter, our main intention has been to use a real value representation to illustrate in a specific way what the customer's perspective means. Along the way, we have also illustrated how having a sufficiently rigorous value representation can prevent whole classes of errors from occurring. It can also facilitate automation and save projects much time and money while improving quality.

It takes a very powerful value representation to embody and demonstrate such central concepts. If nothing else, the SCR method's representations provide a standard that you can compare other value representations against when choosing one for your own business.

ENDNOTES

1. J. Sutton, B. Carré, "Achieving High Integrity at Low Cost: A Constructive Approach," 1995 Avionics Conference and Exhibition, *Low-Cost Avionics—Can We Afford It?—Conference Proceedings*, London, 29-30–November 1995.
2. J. Kirby, "Rewriting Requirements For Design," *Proceedings, IASTED International Conference on Software Engineering and Applications (SEA)*, November 2002.
3. "ACM Fellow Profile: David Lorge Parnas," *ACM Software Engineering Notes*, May 1999.
4. Described in D. L. Parnas, J. Madey, "Function Documents for Computer Systems," *Science of Computer Programming, 25(1)*, October 1995.
5. D. L. Parnas, J. Madey, "Function Documents for Computer Systems," *Science of Computer Programming, 25(1)*, October 1995.
6. The specification of the SPARK language is a product of Praxis Critical Systems Limited, Bath, England.
7. J. Barnes, *High Integrity Software: The SPARK Approach to Safety and Security*, Boston, MA: Addison Wesley Professional, April 2003.
8. The SPARK Examiner is a product of Praxis Critical Systems Limited, Bath, England.
9. *Consortium Requirements Engineering Guidebook*, Software Productivity Consortium Services Corporation. This guidebook is available from the NTIS (National Technical Information Service) of the U.S. Department of Commerce, as document number ada274691 (but neither the method nor the guidebook has any connection with the Ada programming language). 1-800-553-NTIS.

11

Values—When Customers Know What They Want

EVERYBODY LIKES TO THINK THEY KNOW WHAT THEY WANT. And customers usually do consciously know at least most of what they want . . . though even then you have to work at it a bit to get it out of them. In this chapter, we explore ways for us to get in on what customers *already know* about their wants, so we make sure we don't make the inexcusable mistake of delivering something that doesn't do even what they wanted it for in the first place.

If you have performed the first three steps of Value Resolution, as discussed in Chapter 9, and selected a value representation, as explained in Chapter 10, you are ready to begin gathering the list of values needed throughout the remaining steps.

As we said in Chapter 8, you can look at value through three lenses. To review, these lenses are:

1. Universal: "What all similar customers want" (*domain*)
2. Recognized: "What a specific customer knows he or she wants" (*recognized specific*)
3. Unrecognized: "What a specific customer doesn't know he or she wants" (*unrecognized*)

Each lens has its own unique way of looking at and capturing customer value, and leads to its own list values. Actually, the first glance through a given lens will give a telescopic look at what the customers want or need. Once you've looked this way through all three lenses, you should combine the resulting three lists into a single master list. You can then turn the initial value statements in this master list into full statements of value by adding information about each item in the final step of value resolution. We delve into techniques for doing this beginning in Chapter 13.

The first two lenses apply to the values that the customers realize they hold. This chapter will discuss those two lenses. The last lens is like the view given by a cat scan: It looks beyond what is seen on the surface and reveals what lies beneath. That is, it uncovers what the customers don't know they want (but nevertheless want anyway). We'll cover that subject in Chapter 12.

Domain: What All Similar Customers Want

Certain needs, wants, or demands are common to all users of a given type of product. For instance, virtually everyone who works with words needs to move text—literary authors, technical writers, poets, and so on—manipulating words, therefore, is a common need for a broad market of people of these types. Narrower markets refine this need to suit their needs. For instance, technical writers might want text movement to be accompanied by updating of indices, tables of content, and so on. Short-story authors wouldn't care about these specifics, but might care more about consistent literary formatting and a better thesaurus.

A closely related question to commonality is "how likely is any given need to change over time?" Needs that seldom change tend to be common needs ... but only as long as they have been expressed in terms of the customer space and not the producer space. (Producer-space statements are phrased as solutions rather than needs and often reflect how the customer "has been doing things and plans to keep doing them" ... without leaving flexibility for new and innovative alternatives.)

Chapter 8 spoke of values as being defined in terms of how the customer needs to transform his or her environment. Here, we are not talking about that specific kind of transformation change, but a change in the transformation itself, when a needed transformation in the environment is replaced by another transformation. For instance, if technology changed so that people stopped working with the written word and began working with the spoken word alone, say through some incredible improvement in voice recognition, then the need to move text around within written documents would change to a need to manipulate the order and organization of collections of spoken words. The needed transformation itself would change.

Developers must understand universal and stable customer needs and design product features that correlate strongly to these common or unchanging needs. These customer needs are more stable across product versions as companies expand their markets to include additional customers. By making the commonalities and slow-changers the backbone of their market analyses and product designs, companies will develop product lines instead of single products, and position themselves to extend or maintain their products with flexibility and less expense.

The amount of time and effort a company should spend on identifying such needs depends on scale factors, like the number of similar systems it might build for a given market, the amount of maintenance needed over a product's lifetime, and the product's size and scope. As these factors increase, the payoff from commonality and changeability analyses also increases.

In the following sections, we will provide you with several techniques to help you determine what all similar customers want (i.e., common to the domain).

You should choose techniques based on the size and number of your projects and on what is feasible and appropriate for your business situation. Some of these techniques may not be practical for one-off, small, throwaway products, though even then paying at least a little attention to this question will reward the lean software producer. We start with three of the best approaches for constructing a big picture of your market and customer:

1. Canvassing techniques
2. Domain analysis
3. Affinity diagramming

Four Canvassing Techniques

Canvassing gathers information from a cross-section of the customers in a market. The goal is to learn about their shared needs and wants. The four canvassing techniques require that you progressively increase your customer's commitment and involvement. The first technique, literature searches, is the easiest, because someone else has already done most of the work and all of the customer contact. The second technique, market surveys, concentrates more directly on your specific customers and can add high-level detail to the literature searches. Both techniques provide a predigested and high-level perspective that complements the more unrefined but closer-range customer engagement of the third and fourth techniques: focus groups and customer brainstorming. These last two powerful techniques, in particular, will make your customers an intimate part of your development team . . . an ideal for lean producers.

Literature Searches

In most target markets, there will be articles and books you can use to glean customer information. Such writings tend to focus on universal values rather than on unique customer needs and wants. If the literature is broad, you can sometimes compile a decent list of common needs from it. Beware of sampling too narrowly as your results will tend to reflect the biases of just a few authors. Beware also of writers who are too theoretical or detached from real customers. One good place to begin is with periodicals specific to customer industries. Another approach is to survey products and reverse engineer the customer needs from them. One danger in surveying products in the marketplace is that it is easy to confuse the form of a solution with a need. To avoid this misstep and ensure good results, make sure that the people doing your analysis understand your market and your customers well.

Market Surveys

A market survey is a list of questions that organizations use to sample a broad spectrum of customers in the market. Companies can conduct the surveys in many ways—in person, by mail, or over the telephone. Market surveys are typically used to collect general and high-level information about a market, such as the demographics of customers within it, the existing demand for a given type of product, the aggregate ability of the market to purchase new products, and the intensity of competition there. This tends to focus the survey questions more on the customer's present and past behavior than on their future expectations. Questions about the past are easy to create and to answer. If written creatively enough, however, they can yield clues about market values. For instance, questions about what customers like or don't like about existing products in the market can suggest hidden values, especially if several customers feel the same way. Alternatively, learning about what customers are willing to pay for certain capabilities can suggest underlying values that could apply to other capabilities. Such clues can feed development of future products, as well as be useful for higher-level business planning.

Survey questions are usually designed to stimulate one of four types of answers: boolean, multiple choice, numeric, or short text. For the first three countable questions, the answers are collected and combined, and the relative importance of their concerns is inferred from the total counts. The keys to getting good results (answers) from a market survey are:

1. An engaging cover letter
2. Covering many customers
3. Choosing customers by random sampling
4. Choosing the right questions to ask

The last is the stickiest. Asking specific questions about known customer values gives information about how important these values are to its marketplace; however, you won't discover new values. On the other hand, asking open-ended questions designed to discover new values will expand your understanding of what the customer wants or needs, but the results will be more difficult to combine to form the big-picture emphasis of the marketplace. Of course, one solution is to ask both specific and open-ended questions, then identify those answers to the open-ended questions that are similar to each other. The results might suggest a new general market value.

If an organization can contact and gain the cooperation of a number of customers in their target market, and the questions in its market survey can yield clues about market values, the market survey is a good way to learn more about the universal values of its customers. It is by no means a sufficient technique to provide a complete picture of your customer.

Focus Groups

Focus groups are a way for organizations to interview six to eight people. Conducting the focus group interview is part science and part art. A reasonably good introduction to them is *Focus Groups: A Practical Guide for Applied Research*, by Richard Krueger and Mary Anne Casey.[1] Another, available for free, is *Customers in Focus: A Guide to Conducting and Planning Focus Groups*.[2]

To begin, the organization's representatives in the interview process should consist of a moderator or facilitator, and a few members from the development team, so that they are directly exposed to the market for which they are designing. However, if you have too many people from the development team participating, you will intimidate the customers and inhibit their participation.

Since software developers are typically interested in universal needs, they will want to interview those unique customers in the marketplace that they want to understand more deeply. The team will also want interviewees that can relate to each other as individuals, not as a collective group drawn from one particular area of a market or industry. Developers will find that customers often appreciate being asked to participate in focus groups because they will feel their viewpoints are being taken seriously. You are not only gathering information, but also sending your customers the message that you value them and are responsive to their needs. If you can make your company's marketing department aware of the marketing benefits of your focus group, they may be able to help with funding the exercise.

Identifying the objective of the meeting is the most important step in planning a focus group meeting. For the lean producer, the objective is of course to discover the unchanging or slowly changing needs the customers share in their respective work environments. For this, you want to develop a limited number of questions. Some experts recommend five or six questions at most, while others recommend covering one to three major issues, with very few subissues. Even with these few questions, you'll be spending considerable time recording their answers.

The second most important step is to use the right moderator with some basic skills for running a meeting. "The truth is that it is pretty easy to run a group discussion: to get people started, to keep them on the subject, to keep the discussion moving, to bring out the people who are not participating, to inhibit the dominators, to bring people back to the subject when they stray, and to move them along to the next subject when they run out of steam."[3] However, an experienced and skillful moderator can improve the focus group results considerably: "Focus group moderators . . . know how to sort out what is important, to understand implications, to decode symbolism, to unravel complex situations, to interpret ambiguous behavior, to develop strategies, to generate and develop new ideas, to design persuasion, to predict behavior. They not only have to be superb psychologists, sociologists, anthropologists (disciplines from which most of the best moderators come), they also must be superb marketers."[4] It's clear that the quality of the information coming out of the focus group will depend on the capability of the moderator. This is not to discourage the use of focus groups without professional moderators, but if you can get an experienced moderator, you should do it. Your marketing group may again be a good resource for finding one.

Once you have the right objective, questions, and moderator, you are ready to start interviewing. The meeting should last an hour or an hour and a half at most. It's important to keep the meeting positive. Sharing refreshments at the beginning is a good icebreaker, as is thanking them for attending and making the tone of the first questions strictly positive.

Make sure you record all your meetings so you won't overlook any of the participants' answers. More importantly, you'll have an accurate customer record to examine later on. Of course, you need to get the participants agreement to be recorded. (You should have no problem with this if you assure them that the sessions are private and confidential.) Once you start interviewing, keep the questions relatively open ended, but keep the answers relatively short (answers with lists are good). Here are few ideas:

- What are the most important things you do in your business?
- What are the main things you do in a typical workday?
- Has what you're doing or the way you're doing it changed significantly recently, or is something about to change?
- What are your main challenges, e.g., the tough things to do or difficult situations to handle?

When you ask a question, give each participant time to write down their answers so they can think and capture their unique perspective. Then, open the floor for sharing individual viewpoints to reveal the commonalities and differences. Make sure some of your questions and dialogue delve into the customers' reasoning and motivations behind their answers. Such a dialogue can bring up values the customers didn't realize they had. "You can get a lot more from focus groups than top-of-mind beliefs, knowledge, attitudes and practices of respondents. Focus groups are a laboratory in which you can get to much deeper feelings, implicit beliefs, hidden attitudes and secret practices. But more importantly, focus groups are a laboratory in which you can experiment with going beyond the present to what can be, beyond this to the . . . ought to be."[5] This means a skilled moderator will do well to have fewer questions, be a great listener, allow the conversation to range further, and recognize the pearls in the field (i.e., value implications) as they come up.

It is important not to debate with the participants about their answers. The purpose of the focus group is strictly to gather customer perspectives, not to alter their opinions. It is appropriate to steer them towards stating their needs in terms of their environments (i.e., talking in terms of their customer space), but they might also offer information about existing products in their workplaces that will give you clues to their underlying needs. Finally, you want to be careful not to have too many focus group meetings. Though having many meetings allows you to explore fewer questions in more depth, it also demands greater time and commitment by all participants.

The last step, and the whole reason for the focus group exercise, is for the development team to analyze the group discussions, identify the universal or unchanging values revealed, and write them down in a succinct needs statement (like those discussed in Chapter 8) with accompanying detailed information if necessary.

Customer Brainstorming

The fourth technique for canvassing is to have a customer focus session that uses the same brainstorming technique discussed for identifying customers. In this case, however, the customers are the participants and the product is a list of candidate common values. Each customer proposes values that he or she thinks are probably common to all similar customers.

This technique, like focus groups, involves the customer working with the team to add to the raw list of candidate values. However, customer brainstorming doesn't need the skilled facilitation of focus groups, though you must still have a moderator to conduct the session. Though customer brainstorming may fail to identify some of the hidden values that can arise from the synergistic discussion of a focus group, the controlled chaos of brainstorming may lead to discovering other values that more controlled techniques may overlook.

A somewhat less effective version of the customer brainstorming technique would be to use customer surrogates or company personnel who have some experience with the customers. The difficulties here would be in ferreting out high-quality candidate values and in confirming whether the candidate values are truly common. Customers can authoritatively verify this because, unlike surrogates and company personnel, they tend to speak from the heart rather than from bias or an agenda.

Domain Analysis—Identifying Common Values (XP, UML)

After canvassing, domain analysis is the second of three best approaches for looking through the domain lens to find what all similar customers want. Domain analysis is also the first phase in domain development (sometimes called domain engineering, though the word "engineering" narrows its focus too much). Domain development is product development that is based, first, on the natural and recurring characteristics of the customer space, and only second, on the natural and recurring characteristics of the producer space. It is always a good idea for an organization to go through domain development.

The variation from product to product determines how much effort an organization should give to identifying what is natural and recurring in its products. Naturalness and recurrence are characteristics of values different customers hold in common (customer space) and/or characteristic values of different products (producer space). In the customer space, your analysis identifies the natural groupings of things related to the customer's work, like obvious classes of objects (using the object-oriented terminology) and necessary transformations of current environment conditions into future conditions. In the producer space, you will focus on things related to the designs of related products, like data structures, state machines, or functions. Value resolution is concerned only with understanding the customers, while activities like design and coding are about developing the products.

The basis that developers use for creating natural groupings is primarily based on the likelihood of change in the products. The developer would group those things that are likely to change as a result of the same alteration to the customer's world with any model the developer makes of the customer's domain. This will limit any change within the model from any given change stimulus. An example of this is how the arrival of handheld web appliances requires modifications to web browsers (to display larger web pages on smaller displays), wireless networks, web programming languages and tools, and so on. In this case, one basic alteration in the environment caused ripple changes to many other elements of the environment. Good changeability-driven natural groupings will highlight associated things like these and help you minimize the need to chase the implications of change blindly through diverse parts of your model of the domain. You will also localize the implications in the same part of the model.

Domain analysis helps developers deal with the problem of freezing the requirements spec too early. (This is one of the major objections that XP advocates have to a front-loaded lifecycle.) If the values being identified and the resulting requirements are structured based on what is common to virtually every customer in a field, then the developer can set the structure of the values and resulting requirements early on. Values unique to a customer have a natural place to go in the domain model. Even when customer-specific values change later on, as they always do, the effects of the changes will not propagate very far through the system because of the domain orientation. The changes will also be easy to accommodate because the structure of the requirements model will remain stable.

XP addresses the problem of requirements instability differently, by essentially spreading the definition of requirements throughout the lifecycle stages. But spreading the definition precludes finding domain-recurrence patterns until late in the project, if the developers in fact ever notice them at all. (It is an act of faith that XP's emergent behavior will lead them here without intentionality on their part.) This in turn reduces the possibilities for internal reuse during the early stages of a project, which otherwise can provide dramatic cost and schedule savings, as well as strongly mitigate risk. The more lean approach is to use intentional domain analysis based on value resolution.

As we mentioned earlier, the amount of time and effort an organization should spend on identifying common values depends on scale factors in four major areas.

1. Potential number of future products in this market
2. Potential number of product variants currently being developed
3. Potential number of maintenance releases of this product
4. Product size and scope

For a project that has medium- to large-scale factors, a more rigorous approach to domain analysis is definitely worth the effort, though it is also worthwhile on smaller projects. Figure 4-1 shows how dramatic these benefits can be and is repeated here for convenience as Figure 11-1.

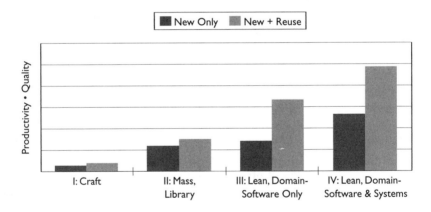

Figure 11-1. Impact of Domain Analysis on Productivity and Quality

Domain analysis requires using a person who knows quite a bit about multiple customers in the organization's specific marketplace. This will help ensure that the results of the analysis will apply well to almost any customer in the market. It also often helps, even during value resolution, to have a person who has knowledge about multiple products in the marketplace since this may provide further insights about common customer traits.

How can we record the results of a domain analysis? The UML is an extremely popular analysis and design representation language that includes graphical and textual syntaxes for recording the results of many of the important software development activities, and can be adapted to record domain analysis.

In the mid- to late-1990s, the UML's developers, Grady Booch, Ivar Jacobson, and James Rumbaugh (whimsically nicknamed the "Three Amigos") did a great service to the software industry by consolidating a welter of representation languages, whose syntaxes were mostly similar to one another, but which were often wedded to incompatible methodologies, into one overarching syntax covering most of their concerns. Through standardization and readability, the UML has since then facilitated better communications between software engineers and their customers or with other software engineers and involved parties. Such communication is, of course, a high priority in lean development.

The UML provides representations suitable for recording the results of domain analysis. Its use case provides a way to record candidate values. By focusing on the actors, use case also forces you to pay attention to the stakeholders (at least, some of them), which is a good way to keep this aspect of a lean mindset front and center. UML's *Class Diagrams* provide a way to record the natural and recurring divisions within the customer's world.

Unfortunately, in contrast to representations like SCR tables, to date there is no solid mathematical underpinning to the UML. Reportedly, there are ongoing efforts to produce such an underpinning, which would make the UML much more powerful at supporting lean principles throughout the lifecycle. In particular, a stronger mathematical base would enable developers to deploy customer values recorded in the UML more easily throughout the remainder of the lifecycle stages and products, e.g., by using automated tools.

Automation based on the UML has been done. Lockheed Martin has developed a tool for generating flight software for the F-16 directly from a UML domain model, though without rock-solid math beneath the UML. One cannot guarantee that the result of any automatic transformation is both correct and complete. You must still test or otherwise verify the product. This step would be unnecessary if the UML was mathematically rigorous. The extra step constitutes a source of waste or *muda* in any process using the UML. Said another way, because the UML allows errors, there will be errors, and where there are errors, developers must take the extra time to deal with them.

Another UML limitation is that it does not distinguish what you need from what is currently happening in the customer's environment (e.g., CONs from MONs, in Four-Variable terms). It also does not maintain a strong distinction between customer space and producer space (as does the Four-Variable Model in its distinction of INs and OUTs from MONs and CONs). These shortcomings strongly constrain the lean benefits you may attain by using the UML.

The reader can find an excellent introduction and tutorial to use cases, class models, and the many other elements of UML, as well as general ideas on using UML for domain analysis, in Martin Fowler's and Kendall Scott's "*UML Distilled: A Brief Guide To The Standard Object Modeling Language.*"[6] A detailed book on how to write good use cases is Alistair Cockburn's "*Writing Effective Use Cases.*"[7] Many people feel that Cockburn's ideas on use-case modeling work the best of anyone's to date. Part III returns to the UML for its implications to the implementation phase.

Another choice for representing domain analyses is to adapt existing methods like the UML, CoRE (OO SCR variant), and older design notations like Buhr's original diagrams and later MachineCharts,[8] to add representational ideas not available off the shelf. This is what the 382J project did: See Appendix A for more details.

Affinity Diagramming—Identifying Shared Values from Unique Ones

Affinity diagramming is the third of three approaches to find what all similar customers want. Affinity diagramming (AD) is one of the Seven Management and Planning Tools (7 MP tools) that was developed to deal with soft problems—situations in which you need to solve problems, but have only soft data available such as opinions, issues, and so forth. The 7 MP tools were developed from the findings of Operations Research after World War II. They came along after the famous 7 QC (Quality Control) tools such as the Pareto Chart and the Cause and Effect Diagram. (The 7 QC tools are typically used by front-line workers to analyze numerical data, or hard data, and to help control production processes.) The goal of the 7 MP tools is to move from chaos and lack of understanding into a level of insight that empowers you to act. The 7 MP tools' ability to deal with soft problems has made it useful to people in a wide variety of roles, from front-line workers to senior management.

Affinity diagramming (AD) is usually the first technique employed when you begin applying the 7 MP tools to a particular problem. It is a powerful, general technique you can use to find new patterns in old data, or to work with more data than you can grasp at once. "We have yet to find an issue for which an Affinity [diagram] has not proven helpful."[9] By identifying the larger issues that correlate the details, AD brings out a hidden and underlying order that makes sense of the clutter of soft details.

This nicely matches the needs of an organization when it begins with a collection of value statements, but doesn't know enough about its market to distinguish a unique customer need from one that is shared with many other customers. Sometimes detailed value statements that, at first, are not obviously common to an organization's market will turn out to relate to a higher-level customer need that is a common concern. The AD process helps to discover these higher-level customer values by relying on gut-level instincts rather than intellectual reasoning. This taps a completely different type of creativity than do most software-engineering techniques. It produces different and valuable insights.

The steps in AD are simple:[10]

The Seven Steps of Affinity Diagramming

1. *Pick the team.* Choose five to six people, maximum, who are knowledgeable about the subject of the AD exercise.

2. *State what you want to accomplish.* Broadly state it, with few details, to leave room for creativity.

3. *Collect or create the low-level data* (e.g., customer values). Record the data using individual cards such as 3M Post-Its or similar sticky notes. Optimally, use five to seven words for each card.

4. *Shuffle the cards randomly and spread them out on an open surface.* Use a bare table, or flip-chart paper. Make sure everyone has a good view and easy access to the surface

5. *Group the cards.* When anyone sees a grouping between two cards, put them together to the side, but clearly visible. Everyone works at once, silently, moving and regrouping the cards. Grouping is based on gut reaction, not reasoning. Speed and energy are key. It's OK to move anyone else's cards. Things eventually settle down.

6. *Create header cards for the resulting groups.* It may be one of the cards in the group, but usually isn't. For new headers, target three to five words. Capture the essence of what is shared between the cards. Choose a broad title that umbrellas the details. Gather the group cards into a stack, as in Solitaire, and place the header card on top.

7. *Finish the affinity diagram.* Place related groups next to each other. Circle each group with a line. Connect related groups with lines. Connected groups may warrant a super header card; if so, create it and place it above (not over) the groups; draw lines from the super-header to the related groups.

There are a couple more points to make about step 5. Groups are different than categories, and everyone should avoid thinking in the latter term. Especially avoid grouping cards into predefined categories that are already familiar to the team. In addition, don't force-fit cards into groupings; let them find their natural place, even if that means they form a group of one card.

When your list of values is too large and detailed, it hides the customer from you. AD brings to the surface the values that are really important to the customer. It can take one or more low-level unique values (even from different customers) and construct from them a smaller number of more-generalized shared values. It can make sense out of a confusing welter of individualized values, bringing out the recurring themes among them. If your customers have provided you with overly detailed values statements, AD can help identify a smaller set of higher-level values that will give you more insight into what makes that customer tick. Understanding the customer is, of course, one of the main goals of value resolution.

Recognized: What a Specific Customer Knows It Wants

Looking at the unique values a customer clearly recognizes as his or her own is our second lens. All customers have unique situations that may bring out a need for unique transformations in their particular environment. For instance, a business that has been in its field for a long time and has a lot of old technological equipment will need some transformations in its work environment that a new business in the field, with all new technology equipment, will not. We've seen this in libraries over the last decade or so; some have continued using physical card catalogs while others have quickly adopted online search tools. Additionally, different libraries have incorporated the Internet at different times. Interdependencies between old and new systems—some customized and some standardized—have changed frequently. Such an environment gives rise to values that are different and may even conflict among various customers. However, even in more stable fields, any given customer will have some values that differ from those of most other similar customers.

This is why the techniques discussed here for identifying unique values, extracting values from requirements specifications, and visits and interviews, are so different than the techniques for discovering universal or common market values. You can learn about the unique values of a single customer only by understanding his or her perspective, whereas you can learn universal values only by correlating the values of multiple customers. Additionally, these techniques are suited for customers who know what they want and are aware of their needs, making it much easier to collect value statements.

Finding the Customer Perspective in Requirements Specifications

Most projects make requirements specifications their sole source for software requirements. A customer drafts its requirements for a new software system and places them in a deliverable document. Alternatively, a software developer goes to the customer, asks for its requirements, places the requirements in a document for them, and has the customer validate the result. In both scenarios, the end result is specific to the particular customer, and also, by definition, the customer is aware of the requirements. Thus, requirements documents apply to our current focus, specific customers who know what they want.

This is where the challenges begin. In Chapter 8, we compared the differences between requirements and values. It follows that a requirements specification is a source for requirements, not customer values. Though requirements specification can provide clues to customer values, it falls far short of extracting true values, because requirements almost always mix the customer space and producer space. Any given requirement states a need in terms of the details of a particular hardware interface or I/O device and seldom states whether it is unique or universal to a customer's market.

As a result, extracting the requirements in a requirements specification and applying them to customer values is a very indirect process. This means developers must go through unnecessary work to incorporate all the non-value-oriented information of the specifications and the unnecessary work to remove it to uncover the value. This is all *muda*. Nevertheless, if receiving a requirements specification is a given, as it is in many sectors of the software industry, it can still be a valuable resource to examine for what a specific customer knows it wants.

The key to uncovering the hidden values in the requirements specification is to identify the customer's perspective. This means the developer must recognize when a requirement is referring to a solution or a design, rather than a user need. The developer should pull out the user needs, in terms of the customer's environment, and communicate with the customer to fill any resulting gaps in understanding the customer space. The resulting value list can even take on a domain perspective if you can communicate with someone besides the customer—perhaps another customer in the field (be careful of proprietary concerns, however). Or, you could use a domain expert that can provide feedback on which values are unique to the customer, known to be common in the field, or are unlikely to change over time. See the previous discussion of domain analysis for the necessary characteristics.

The long and short of the matter is that producers must be willing to dig out the actual wants hidden in the customer's stated requirements, convert them into values, and communicate them back to the customer in a way that makes the customer feel appreciated and understood, not foolish or exposed by the developer's interpretation. About 90 percent of this is caring enough about the customers to bother, and 10 percent is tact in the way you mirror the customer's values back to them.

Nevertheless, even with a set of requirement-driven values, the developer may find customers expressing the most passion about some requirements that they care least about when the company delivers the product. This is why it is imperative to go back to the customer for information to help you prioritize these values later. We discuss this under step 5 of the value resolution process, characterizing values, in Chapter 13.

Interviews—Getting Up Close and Personal with the Customer

Another effective way to identify what a specific customer knows he or she wants is by taking at least some of the development team to where the customer does their work and will be using your product. Open-ended questions are the order of the day: Let the customer tell you what is important to them. This gives the development team a first-hand understanding of the customer's *gemba* and perspective, which the development team couldn't get in any other way. Interviews, on the other hand, are more controlled and focused, and occur away from *gemba* (though meeting at the customer's facility still helps make the customer more comfortable and forthcoming).

Here are six angles of attack for questions at visits or interviews:[11]

Six Angles of Attack for Visits or Interview Questions

1. *Behaviors*—about what a person has done or is doing
2. *Opinions/values*—about what a person thinks about a topic
3. *Feelings*—note that respondents sometimes respond with "I think..." so be careful to note that you're looking for feelings
4. *Knowledge*—to get facts about a topic
5. *Sensory*—about what people have seen, touched, heard, tasted, or smelled
6. *Background/demographics*—standard background questions, such as age, education, etc.

You should put together a mix of these angles that will keep the customer focused on specific needs and environment, rather than on the specific products currently being used. (Some information about current products may provide insights into needs, especially when purely customer-space questions aren't leading to useful answers.) Start with unthreatening knowledge or fact-based questions to get the customer engaged, then move towards opinions and feelings when the customer is comfortable. Avoid leading questions that imply an answer you want or expect. Be careful about asking questions that make the customer feel a need to justify him or herself, or defend the status quo. Finally, avoid biasing customer answers: Try not to show strong emotional reactions to their responses. Act as if you've heard it all before.[12] Here are a few additional suggestions from ABB Automation, a company that uses interviews at the customer's site to collect customer requirements from a value perspective:[13]

How to Collect Customer Requirements from a Value Perspective

- Visiting team is cross-functional, but specifically excludes sales people.
- Visit a wide range of users, including users of competitors' equipment.

- Don't talk about competitors.

- Each member of the visiting team has a role, such as moderator, listener, observer, note-taker, etc.

- Concentrate on needs. "Why do you need this feature?" Avoid talking about the feature itself.

- The final report is not sent to participants (too valuable). They do get a thank-you letter.

- Process is sector-based, not product-based. (Note: Interviewers should be looking for domain or market needs.)

- Avoid price-related questions; be more interested in value than price.

The second to the last bullet point helps identify unique customer needs by eliminating common ones. The needs that a customer thinks are not marketwide are candidates to be unique to that customer. Of course, the customer could also be mistaken in his or her assessment, so you would have to confirm this through the domain analysis or other techniques for assessing common market needs.

ENDNOTES

1. R. A. Krueger, M. A. Casey, *Focus Groups: A Practical Guide for Applied Research*, Thousand Oaks, CA: Sage Publications, April 2000. This is the third edition; the second edition has additional useful appendices omitted from the third.

2. *Customers in Focus: A Guide to Conducting and Planning Focus Groups*, a "Simply Better!" publication based on materials developed by the *Technical Assistance and Training Corporation (TATC)*, under contract to the U.S. Department of Labor's Training and Development Center, http://www.workforce-excellence.net/pdf/focus.pdf.

3. Market Navigation, Inc., "How To Get More Out Of Your Focus Groups," http://www.mnav.com/getmore.htm.

4. Market Navigation, Inc., "How To Get More Out Of Your Focus Groups," http://www.mnav.com/getmore.htm.

5. Market Navigation, Inc., "How To Get More Out Of Your Focus Groups," http://www.mnav.com/getmore.htm.

6. M. Fowler, K. Scott, *UML Distilled: A Brief Guide To The Standard Object Modeling Language*, Boston, MA: Addison-Wesley, August 1999.

7. A. Cockburn, *Writing Effective Use Cases*, Boston, MA: Addison-Wesley, January 2000.

8. For more information on Buhr's methods and various ways to adapt them (though, unfortunately, not applied to domain analysis), see Jeffrey Nickerson's Ph.D. Dissertation, especially Chapter 6. J. V. Nickerson, Visual Programming. Ph.D. Dissertation, UMI# 9514409. New York University, 1994. This is also available online at http://www.stevens-tech.edu/jnickerson/.

9. M. Brassard, "The Memory Jogger Plus + Featuring the Seven Management and Planning Tools," *GOAL/QPC*, May 1996; quote is from pg. 18 of the earlier 1989 edition.

10. We are closely following Brassard's work in his "The Memory Jogger Plus" book, previously cited, for this description; please refer to it for details and an example problem.

11. C. McNamara, Ph.D., "General Guidelines for Conducting Interviews," Management Assistance Program on-line library. http://www.mapnp.org/library/evaluatn/intrview.htm.

12. C. McNamara, Ph.D., "General Guidelines for Conducting Interviews," Management Assistance Program on-line library, http://www.mapnp.org/library/evaluatn/intrview.htm.

13. From the July 18, 2001 meeting notes of the University of Cambridge Department of Engineering's New Product Introduction Club.

12

Values—When Customers Don't Know What They Want

C USTOMERS ALWAYS HAVE VALUES THEY CAN'T ARTICULATE (i.e., of which they aren't consciously aware). These are the "unrecognized values" of the third lens of value resolution, the things a specific customer really wants, but doesn't know it wants. (In the previous chapter, we covered the first two lenses, domain and recognized values.) Products that don't appeal to these types of values will leave a customer vaguely dissatisfied, though they can't quite put their finger on why. On the flip side, software that expresses those values will be perceived as going above and beyond the call of duty. Nonlean businesses (which includes almost all software developers) almost never look for these things.

Lean suppliers in other industries pay great attention to little unspoken things (e.g., Toyota, and where cupholders should be located). If their experience is any indication, i.e., if the human nature of their customers is the same as that of ours (and of course it is), the small amount of extra attention it takes to plumb this area will translate into a big competitive advantage over the nonlean software developer.

In this chapter, we will use the three techniques below to look for unrecognized values:

1. Five Whys
2. Simulation
3. TRIZ and USIT

Using the Five Whys to Uncover the Root Need

A simple way to uncover unrecognized wants is to return to a recognized one and begin asking "why?" For each answer, ask "why?" again, up to five times. Often, this will uncover a root desire or root need that is more important than the one with which the customer began. For example, suppose a customer states the value "I want to have a service automatically pay my bills on the web." Note that this value is really stating a solution, not a need. This is not what you want to end up with in your list of values. To work towards finding the underlying desire, you begin asking "why?" You'll continue until you've found a fundamental underlying need, whose statement has no flavor of a preselected solution.

Using the Five Whys with our example might go something like this:

"I want to have a service automatically pay my bills on the web." "Why?"

"Because I'm always late with mailing in my payments." "Why?"

"Because I never remember when they're due." "Why?"

"Because I forget to check my calendar." "Why?"

"Because my calendar is not handy so I don't think about it."

Once you've reached the root need, you can recast it into a corresponding (and usually unrecognized) value. In the example above, that root value might be, "I need to be actively warned when my obligations are about to come due," which is a very different value from the originally stated and conscious need to have an automated service. It is also not prescriptive of a specific solution.

You never want to tell customers that they are wrong in wanting a particular solution (such as the automated bill-pay service in our example), because that can shut down their willingness to share their thoughts with you, and also because their chosen solution may indeed be the best thing for them.

However, by using the Five Whys to uncover their root reason for their stated need, and turning that into a root value, you have learned something important about the customer. This new information might lead you to offer a different capability than they originally requested, but which better addresses their root need. Perhaps, in the case of our example that might be a computer-desktop pop-up calendar.

The Five Whys are guidelines, not commandments. The "five" in the name Five Whys simply emphasizes that it may take a lot of repetition to reach the value.

Using Simulation to Help Customers Discover Their Values

Following the Supreme Court's Jacobellis v. Ohio decision of 1964, Justice Potter Stewart famously said of pornography, "I know it when I see it." Many customers cannot describe their values, but they know them when they see them. Simulation can help customers become aware of these values by giving them a means to see their values through a concrete implementation.

A simulation is a low-cost analog of what a developed system would do for a customer in some area of need. You build a simulated product based on what the customer is able to tell you. As the customer interacts with the simulation, he or she becomes aware of other needs to express. The customer uses both the customer space and producer space to express these needs. After all, the customer is interacting with a producer-space tool, an implemented system. However, once the customer's preferences have been identified, it is relatively easy to turn that into statements of values in customer-space terms (e.g., using the Five Whys).

Simulation has been one of the major tools used by Sudhir Shah, the manager of the 382J program discussed previously. Earlier in his career, Mr. Shah worked in the R&D department of General Electric's Simulation Control Systems Company, which produced flight-training simulators. The charter of the department was to invent new technologies that improved graphics performance and to validate them in small proof-of-concept demonstration projects. When Mr. Shah joined the department, the demonstrations were merely establishing the performance of the technologies. No one knew whether real customers would find any value in any particular technology they invented. Furthermore, no one had integrated the new technologies into existing product lines, so there remained a compatibility question.

Mr. Shah proposed that they develop a special simulator; not a flight simulator itself, but one that modeled the new technologies into something that looked like a flight simulator. By using slower mainframe computers and software they wrote to do the work of the new technology, but much more slowly than an actual flight simulator would, Mr. Shah's tool would produce a visual frame for every 30 minutes of processing time. The simulation job was done when enough visuals (say, 30 seconds of frames, at 16 frames per second) had been accumulated.

Then the customer was asked to view the resulting display. One of the first of the group's new technologies subjected to this treatment was a new way of generating cloud graphics. When the cloud technology was simulated and shown in a 30-second clip to the company's main customer, the customer responded that it looked cartoonish, that the clouds had the wrong texture. This revealed a value held by the customer about cloud textures. This stimulated new technology development to meet the newly stated value. Another simulation revealed the customer held a value for fogging, or the fading away of detail with an increase in distance from the viewer. The company then invested in developing their technology and putting it into deliverable hardware and software.

G. E. estimated that these simulations saved the company millions of dollars that would have been invested in technologies that wouldn't have satisfied their customers' needs or wants. It also allowed them to more fully explore technologies and flush out additional customer needs that otherwise would have been too expensive to try with prototyped graphics hardware, i.e., in a real flight simulator system.

There are two keys to using simulation to discover customer values:

1. Construct the simulation cheaply and quickly.
2. Make the interface to the simulation as similar to the customer's environment as possible.

Pragmatic measures like Mr. Shah's use of existing mainframes and simple programs in place of dedicated graphics hardware, made it practical for G. E. to explore its customers' values deeply. The realism of the simulation display made it possible for the customer to recognize its values. The combination of cheapness, quickness, and user-orientation gave the company an advantage in the flight-simulator market that has kept it highly competitive in that market over the years.

Properly done, simulations communicate with the customer in terms of their customer space. When you show a customer an inexpensive analog for some aspect(s) of a product you might make, based on your current understanding of their needs, their reactions will tell you much more about their actual needs. Furthermore, the customer never has to learn your technical terminology; so they can use their own (which makes them much more comfortable and cooperative). This strength contrasts with the great shortcomings of older techniques like requirements engineering, which force customers to meet us—the producers—on our terms, and leads us to make products that do not reflect their values. When we do things the old way, customers may choose not to buy the product, or may buy it but be dissatisfied and do less business with us in the future, without our ever even knowing what we lost or why.

Simulations remain a useful technique throughout the implementation stage of the development lifecycle. As you refine a product's design, you are free to simulate specific implementations to see if the customer is satisfied with design attributes, such as response time, state behavior, and menu or screen organization. Small and incremental releases of actual product can accomplish much the same thing. A combination of these techniques will minimize risk, lessen *muda*, and maximize customer satisfaction throughout lean product development.

TRIZ and USIT—Systems for Generating Creative Ideas (AFD, DE)

TRIZ (pronounced "trees") is a breakthrough approach for understanding the customer space as well as for and satisfying customers in the producer space (the larger topic of Part III). What is so unique about TRIZ is that it uses patterns of problem solving and innovation that, together, form a pattern language of sorts, discovered in the same way as were Christopher Alexander's architectural patterns,[1] by observing what has consistently worked for others. In particular, parts of this breakthrough approach can help you identify user needs that no other method currently has the capacity to recognize, and which few companies are using.

In 1946, a 20-year-old Soviet patent clerk in Russia named Genrich Altshuller began noticing similarities between the breakthroughs reflected in a large number and variety of the patents he was filing. He speculated that a systematic study of many patents from different specialties and eras might reveal a manageable set of general, technology-independent problem-solving techniques. Perhaps, he reasoned, these techniques could even be taught to others to help them create yet more inventions or solve other problems.

Altshuller conducted this study over many years and through many hardships. When he proposed this idea to Joseph Stalin's representatives, he was convicted of treason and sentenced to five years in a gulag. Rather than making him quit, though, he continued his studies in prison interviewing scientists and other problem solvers who had also been imprisoned.

For decades, Soviet authorities resisted his work at every turn, but Altshuller pressed through. Eventually, with the help of others, he analyzed two and a half million patents. He taught his discoveries to a cadre of gifted technologists. However, there was only one period, between 1970 and 1974, in which he was allowed to teach his method publicly.

The result of Altshuller's work is an all-encompassing method for technical problem solving. It is a system for how to think and how to make decisions. Altshuller's method enabled people to actually teach creativity in the sciences, something that most experts had previously assumed was impossible. Altshuller called the method the "Theory of Solving Inventive Problems," a phrase whose acronym in Russian is "TRIZ." Despite the word "theory" in its name, however, there is little that is theoretical about it. It is firmly rooted in how real people have created real inventions or solved real problems in the past. TRIZ simply identifies the common patterns of thinking that led to these inventions and makes them visible and repeatable. Distinguishing itself in another way from most other problem-solving approaches, TRIZ focuses on breakthroughs rather than tradeoffs.

TRIZ includes principles and techniques for accessing available knowledge, for breaking out of nonproductive thinking molds, for understanding problems, and for finding solutions. It does the latter especially by reformulating unsolvable problems into problems that can be solved, using a process called *contradiction solving*. TRIZ also includes procedures for using these concepts together, called "Algorithms of Inventive Problem Solving." Altshuller and others verified the method by trying it out on problems in many fields. Since then, TRIZ has proven itself by being used to create many inventions and solve many industrial and practical problems. (See the TRIZ model for problem solving, in Figure 12-1.)

Though TRIZ remained largely inside the borders of the USSR for its first 40 years, it began seriously penetrating the world outside the old USSR during the 1990s. This breakthrough approach had remained isolated within the USSR for so long for a number of reasons. One is that Russia's closed society provided

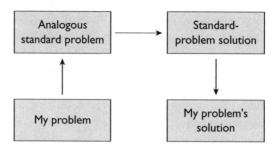

Figure 12-1. TRIZ Problem-Solving Model

no incentive to translate the work into other languages. Another is that fully mastering TRIZ's 40 Principles of Invention, 76 Standards of Inventive Solutions, its large knowledge bases, and its matrices for correlating types of problems with solution methods requires two years of intensive schooling for even highly educated technologists. This does not mean, however, that it takes two years of full-time study to get anything out of looking into TRIZ; in a much shorter time, the interested reader can glean useful techniques and insights for use in software and other fields (especially by following some of the TRIZ derivatives, discussed a couple of sections down). And, in a telling endorsement of the legitimacy and worth of TRIZ, despite the large learning curve, many Israeli, Japanese, European, and American companies (including very large ones like Ford) have adopted it. Its use is currently proliferating.

Applying the TRIZ techniques to the customer space is fairly simple. We will briefly discuss a couple of them, which address two main groups of values; those concerning failures in the customer's environment, and those concerning future customer values that you can predict based upon current customer values. If you can anticipate future customer values and serve them now at a reasonable cost, the customer will be delighted and the organization will gain a great advantage over its competitors. Respectively, the techniques for discovering these two kinds of values are: Anticipatory Failure Determination (AFD) and Directed Evolution (DE).

While AFD is related to TRIZ, it has been developed more recently than Altshuller's work.[2] AFD explores possible failures in the customer's environment. As we discussed in Chapter 8, values are about transformations in the customer's environment; either desired ones, or ones to be avoided. Failures are undesired transitions in the customer environment, so they reveal values. These values are essential ones (must-be values, in the language of the Kano Model we shall study in the next chapter), because if the customer didn't care deeply about avoiding these transitions, they wouldn't consider them failures. But customers often haven't thought through all the failures that might happen in their environments, so coming at it from this perspective may reveal the existence of values they haven't recognized. And once a producer has identified the failures significant to the customer, the producer can ask the customer intelligent questions about their preferences on how to avoid or mitigate the failures, potentially identifying yet more new values (these are not necessarily essential or must-be ones).

AFD is much more thorough at identifying unrecognized values through failures than are traditional failure analysis methods like FMEA (Failure Mode & Effects Analysis), FTA (Fault Tree Analysis), and HAZOP (Hazards and Operations Analysis). Traditional methods ask what can go wrong with the system, then proceed with the assumption that you already understand the system you are questioning—in this case, the system of must-be failure-avoidance values of the customer's environment. But, such understanding is the developer's goal, not the starting point. AFD looks at failures in reverse: It asks, "How I can destroy the integrity of the system?" This allows the developer to explore and pick the system apart a bit at a time, leading to the eventual discovery of more failures and must-be values. For more information on AFD, see "Introduction to AFD" by Dr. Stan Kaplan.[3]

Directed Evolution (DE), another extension of TRIZ, recognizes and exploits the fact that products evolve in predictable ways. By anticipating future developments in products that are already in use by a customer, one can reverse engineer the associated future values and then meet them before the customer even knows to ask. As one TRIZ expert put it, "Directed Evolution is itself the latest derivative of Technological Forecasting. Technological Forecasting is a TRIZ capability because of Altshuller's discovery of the Laws of Technological Evolution. These eight laws represent repeatable patterns depicting the natural progression of products through Life Cycle 'S-curves.' Through the efforts of Zlotin, Zusman, and others, additional gradations to these laws have been provided called *lines of evolution*. For each major law, there are lines that refine and pinpoint the understanding of the evolutionary life cycle progression. The lines of evolution provide organizations insights into future product derivatives. These derivatives will occur naturally over time or they can be directed to appear as a part of an organization's product development strategy."[4] Note that predicted future needs are more likely to be domain-oriented values, and therefore, worth evaluating for incorporation into product-line planning. For more information on DE, see *Directed Evolution: Philosophy, Theory, and Practice*, by Boris Zlotin and Alla Zusman.[5]

Though the producer space is outside our topic in this chapter, it's worth noting here that there are also TRIZ techniques that address the producer space, that help with inventing ways to address customer needs that the producer has already identified. The quickest route to using TRIZ in the producer space is

USIT (Unified Structured Inventive Thinking), which is the result of a series of efforts to simplify TRIZ and make it more acceptable throughout industry. USIT came from SIT, or the "Structured Inventive Thinking" approach, which was developed in Israel during the 1980s. Then, in 1995, Ed Sickafus of the Ford Motor Company developed USIT from this base.

Since 1999, USIT has been picked up and further refined by Japanese advocates. Some of them explained USIT as follows: "The whole process of problem solving can be characterized by three principal phases, i.e., Problem Definition phase, Problem Analysis phase and Solution Generation phase, according to USIT. During the first two phases, we prepare in various ways only for the last phase in which we want to make some breakthroughs to actually obtain new, innovative conceptual ideas.... Comprehensive principles and rules in the Solution Generation methods in TRIZ have been reclassified into the framework of USIT. USIT has only five Solution Generation Methods: they have been found successful in accepting such a large variety of individual principles/rules in TRIZ."[6] A reader interested in applying TRIZ and USIT in the producer space will be rewarded by reading the articles of Toru Nakagawa on the subject.

To fully explore TRIZ and its techniques (translations of TRIZ publications and new works are now rapidly appearing), the reader is encouraged to check with sources like TRIZ training vendors and booksellers who keep ratings databases to find the latest and best resources. At the time of this writing, major trainers include GOAL/QPC of Methuen, Massachusetts; Ideation International Inc. of Southfield, Michigan; and Strategic Production Innovation, Inc. of Brighton, Michigan. A fine layman's introduction to the TRIZ way of problem solving is found in Altshuller's "And Suddenly the Inventor Appeared."[7] This is an English translation of writings Altshuller used in Russian schools during the brief period he was allowed to teach there.

ENDNOTES

1. C. Alexander, *A Pattern Language*, Oxford University Press, 1977.
2. AFD was created by Ideation International, Inc., one of the main TRIZ implementation firms: www.ideationtriz.com.
3. S. Kaplan, S. Visnepolschi, B. Zlotin, A. Zusman, *New Tools for Failure and Risk Analysis: An Introduction to Anticipatory Failure Determination (AFD) and the Theory of Scenario Structuring*, Southfield, MI: Ideation International, Inc., 1999.
4. S. Ungvari, "TRIZ Within the Context of The Kano Model, or Adding the Third Dimension to Quality," *TRIZ-Journal*, October 1999.
5. B. Zlotin, A. Zusman, *Directed Evolution: Philosophy, Theory, and Practice*, Southfield, MI: Ideation International Inc., 2001. Note that this text depends on

familiarity with the contents of a work published in 1999, "TRIZ In Progress," by the same authors and publisher.

6. T. Nakagawa, H. Kosha, Y. Mihara, "Reorganizing TRIZ Solution Generation Methods into Simple Five in USIT," ETRIA World Conference: TRIZ Future 2002, Strasbourg, France, November 2002.

7. G. Altshuller, "And Suddenly the Inventor Appeared," Worcester, MA: Technical Innovation Center, December 1996.

13

Predicting How Customers Will React to Having Their Values Implemented

L ET'S SUPPOSE WE ARE WORKING TOGETHER in a software company and we've been doing everything written about in this book until now. We have picked out the best project to pursue for our business's sake. We've worked creatively and analytically to identify our potential customers. We have located their *gemba*, the place where they do what they do, and the best ways to connect with them there so we can take advantage of their great wisdom about their own needs. We have selected ways to identify their values and a means to represent them. We've collected those values, both the ones they hold consciously and the ones hidden even from themselves. We know which of their values are shared by virtually all potential customers and which are unique to them in particular.

What could there be left to do with values? Two things. First, we can project how a customer will react to having a particular value implemented. It turns out that they react in one of three major ways. Having a reasonable guess of which it will be for each value will help us shape our product-development plan. Second, we can prioritize the list of values by how important each of them is to the customer. This too will help us plan.

We'll cover the first issue, projecting customer reaction, in this chapter. The second, prioritizing values, is discussed in the next chapter.

In the late 1970s, the Konica Company brought in a Japanese quality expert named Dr. Noriaki Kano to help with their development of a new line of cameras. Konica wanted these new products to increase its share of the camera market. The company's R&D department surveyed potential customers and reported that they all requested slight, incremental changes to what was already available on the market. The management knew that small improvements would never entice large numbers of customers to switch to its products. Konica needed a new way of looking at its customers to determine what could motivate buyers to switch over to buying their products. They needed to identify breakthrough product attributes that would win them market share. Such attributes would undoubtedly trace back to different customer values than the values being addressed by other cameras of the day. But, how would these values be different?

The common assumption of the time was that customers react to all attributes of a product in the same way. However, after examining the ways customers responded to product attributes, Dr. Kano realized that they were actually reacting in three different ways. He said that any given product attribute would fit into one of three categories, based on how the customer reacted to them: 1) must-be factors, 2) performance factors, and 3) attractive factors. These three categories became the starting point for developing what we now call the Kano Model. Though the model speaks in terms of product attributes and "factors," these also correspond to underlying customer values, so we can, in principal, characterize each value in one of these three types as well. Dr. Kano also created a method or procedure for determining into which category any given attribute fit. After we discuss the three categories, we will explain how to apply the Kano Method to a list of values instead of to product attributes.

Must-Be Factors

This first attribute, sometimes called a basic factor, is what any customer would expect in every product of a particular type or class. For instance, any customer buying a software package for a personal computer would assume the software uses the computer's mouse as an input device. If asked to make a list of product wants, a customer probably won't even include any must-be factors. They're too obvious. Typically, customers won't even notice if a must-be factor is included in the product: They take it for granted that it will be there. As a result, the company is never told that the customer wants them (there's no "mouse requirement") and doesn't receive credit for implementing such factors.

However, if a must-be factor is missing from a product, the customer will immediately notice and be very unhappy with the product. This may seem unfair—not to be told of an expectation being placed upon you, to be punished if you don't live up to it, and to be ignored if you do, but it is human nature. The best a company can do with must-be factors is break even. This is why must-be factors are also sometimes called *threshold factors*: If the developers execute them perfectly, they only get to the threshold of beginning to satisfy their customer. If a company doesn't meet this threshold, there is nothing else they can do to satisfy their customer(s). This is why it is imperative that companies develop a thorough list of the must-be factors for each product.

Note that the must-be factor in our example, the desire for a mouse, is a producer-space issue. A mouse is a specific kind of implementation. That is typical with the classic Kano model. Other implementations of the same needs (values) relative to human inputs are possible; for instance, a trackball. That's why we will shortly discuss a way to use the Kano model with values instead of product attributes, which gets us to the root of the matter, not the symptom. It's worth saying here, however, that sometimes a particular producer-space implementation (product attribute) has become so well accepted that it becomes, in essence, a customer-space value as well. If you think you can come up with an implementation that is greatly superior to and more easily accepted than the one now in place, then work with the underlying customer-space value (e.g., "move around easily"). Otherwise, it is sometimes wise just to accept the implementation (e.g., "mouse") as a value and implement it as is in your product (i.e., with a mouse). One way or the other, however, you must find a way to get credit for addressing the customer's must-be values.

Performance Factors

Whereas customer satisfaction with must-be factors is so non-linear, it is nearly binary, that is, the customer notices little beyond their presence or absence in a product, performance factors (sometimes called *one-dimensional factors* or *linear factors*) elicit a range of satisfaction levels in direct proportion to how well the attributes are executed. A website's visual appeal will lie somewhere on a spectrum ranging from plain and utilitarian to graphically appealing. If all other attributes of the website are equal (e.g., content, organization), most people will prefer an implementation of these attributes or factors in direct proportion to its graphical finesse.

Since customer satisfaction is proportional to performance, any advantage gained over the competition on attributes of this kind is typically hard-won. Fortunately, there are breakthrough approaches to making big gains for smaller-than-expected efforts, such as some of the problem-solving TRIZ approaches (though not AFD, since it finds primarily must-be values). The conscious values a customer brings up when asked about his or her needs are typically performance factors, along with perhaps a few must-be factors.

Attractive Factors

With attractive factors, a customer is delighted when the are addressed in the product, but unconcerned and unaware when they are not. To understand how a customer can flip from being neutral to being unexpectedly delighted, see the *attractive curve* (see Figure 13-1).

An attractive factor takes a customer by surprise and pleases or excites him or her. Indeed, attractive factors are sometimes called *excitement factors* or *delight factors*. These types of product attributes strike at values a customer holds but is probably unaware of (so, your list of unrecognized values is fertile ground to look in to find them). After all, the customer has probably never seen such attributes in other products, and he or she probably wouldn't notice their absence. However,

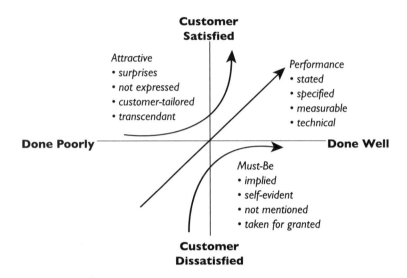

Figure 13-1. Kano Model

once the customer sees his or her value implemented in some way he or she never experienced before, and his or her life unexpectedly becomes in some way easier, more enjoyable, or more empowered, you're going to have a delighted customer.

A classic example of an attractive attribute was the introduction in January 1983 of the Apple Lisa (predecessor to the MacIntosh), which brought the Graphical User Interface (GUI) to the world. Before its introduction, few people outside the Xerox PARC labs had ever seen anything like it. We now take for granted that our computers use mice and drop-down menus, but the Apple Lisa was the first computer to offer such advanced technology. It also was the first computer to offer preemptive multitasking and the ability to copy and paste things between applications. This was the beginning of the truly practical computer for the masses, and sales soared.

Having knowledge of the customer's hidden values—plus a small amount of creativity—will help the developer design attractive factors that will reward a company well beyond any effort it expends. It's worth keeping in mind, however, that attractive factors tend to change into performance factors and finally, must-be factors over time. We only need to look at what resulted from the Apple Lisa GUI. When GUIs first hit the market, people loved them and were delighted. Not too many years later, when the cost had dropped significantly from its 1983 norm of nearly $10,000, most people refused to use a tool that didn't have a GUI. This converted GUIs into a must-be factor.

Figure 13-1 also shows the effects of producer performance upon customer satisfaction for the three Kano attributes we've just discussed (the curves are rough drawings, not exact mathematical representations).[1] Assuming that there is the same amount of work on the company's part in each case, the reward in customer satisfaction is none for must-be factors, a moderate amount for performance factors, and much for attractive factors. This would lead one to focus on attractive factors, and that is a useful bias to have. However, the company must balance the attractive factors with the necessity to cover all must-be factors and a certain competence in implementing at least the major performance factors. For example, the customer might forgive a piece of software for its slow response on a deeply buried menu, especially if the program has some highly-desired attractive factors, but they won't forgive the same slowness on a top-level menu.

Applying the Kano Method to Value Resolution

Dr. Kano's method bases its evaluations on customer inputs rather than on producer speculations. With just two questions, a company can quickly discover how the customer really feels about a given product attribute. We have adapted Kano's method to evaluate customer reaction to the implementation of particular values (a more abstract and customer-space concern), instead of their reaction to the implementation of particular product features. That is, the original Kano method asks questions about product attributes; we ask them about values.

For each value, ask the customer the following two questions:

1. How would you feel if this value were present in the product?
2. How would you feel if this value were absent from the product?

The perspective of the first question is called the *functional* form; the perspective of the second question, the *dysfunctional* form. You need to make sure these questions are stated in the customer's terms (customer-space), rather than in product terms (producer space). Provide the customer with five options for answering each question, graded from the most pleasure to the most displeasure, called the *hedonic scale*. For each question, choose one of the alternative versions provided below. There's no "one-size-fits-all" version; some versions make more sense when discussing certain values than do others.[2]

1. "I like it;" or "I enjoy it that way;" or "This would be helpful to me."
2. "It must be that way;" or "I expect it;" or "This is a basic requirement to me."
3. "I am neutral;" or "This would not affect me;" or "I don't care."
4. "I dislike it but can live with it that way;" or "This would be a minor inconvenience;" or "I can tolerate it."
5. "I dislike it that way;" or "I can't accept it;" or "This would be a major problem for me."

Keep the number of values covered by the questionnaire reasonable so the customer is not overwhelmed. The amount of effort appropriate to ask of a customer depends on many factors, such as customer patience, customer resources, and degree of customer involvement in the program. If the list with all values on it is too long or burdensome for the customer, you could condense the list using the affinity-diagramming technique discussed in Chapter 10. Then, apply the results for the condensed value back to the individual values afterwards (some interpretation may be required). Alternatively, with a list that is only moderately too long (say, up to twice what your customer could handle) you could prioritize the values as described in Chapter 14. Then, starting from the top of the list, select as many values as your customer has time for, and apply the Kano Method to those values only. But you should still try to identify any must-be values in the omitted part of the list, even if only informally (i.e., by educated guess). This strategy, though, is riskier than somehow having the customer evaluate all the values.

In both the functional form (value is present) and dysfunctional form (value is absent) questions for each value will have five answer-choices selected from the alternative versions above. You should test the questions and the choices of answer variants for clarity yourself, and refine the questionnaire, before sending it to the customer.

When answering these questionnaires, customers sometimes wrongly assume their choice of answer should reflect the importance of the attribute or value being evaluated. For instance, one of the biggest questions asked about the five answer choices is why "must" comes after "like" on the hedonic scale. If the scale was about importance, then the order would be reversed. However, the scale is about pleasure: I *like* to eat chocolate more than I like to eat greens, even though I *must* eat greens for my health. Chocolate is less important but more pleasurable; hence it gets the "1" and greens get the "2." Some people even suggest leaving the numbers off the answers on the questionnaire to avoid the problem altogether. In any event, the list measures pleasure, not importance.

For an example, let's suppose that you are a developer of automobile engine-control computer systems. A customer value is "minimize VOCs (Volatile Organic Compounds) in the exhaust of the engine at all times." (We will assume there is also a must-be value that federal emissions limits must not be exceeded, separate from this value.) This is a fairly "squishy" value that requires quantification. Kano analysis will help. We begin by asking the customer (actually, customers, in this case) the two functional and dysfunctional questions:

- If your engine's VOCs are minimized at all times, how do you feel?
  1. This would be helpful to me.
  2. This is a basic requirement to me.

3. I don't care.
4. I can tolerate it.
5. I dislike it that way.

- If your engine's VOCs are not always minimized, how do you feel?
    6. I like it that way.
    7. It must be that way.
    8. I don't care.
    9. I can live with it that way.
    10. I can't accept it.

Note that in four out of five cases, we've chosen different variations of the answer for the functional versus the dysfunctional question (only for answer number 3 do we choose the same variant—"I don't care"—for both question forms). Consider also that the answers we receive will depend on which customer we ask. An environmentalist car buyer will undoubtedly answer these questions differently than will a major automobile manufacturer. Once again, we see the importance of step 2 of the value resolution, identifying your customers and their relative importance to your company.

Suppose one customer is an automotive manufacturer. He or she answers the first question with "This would be helpful to me." To the second, "I can live with it that way." How do we use these answers to find this value's Kano category? We look it up in a table (Figure 13-2):

Functional \ Dysfunctional	Like	Must	Don't care	Can live without it	Dislike
Like	Q	A	A	A	P
Must	R	I	I	I	M
Don't care	R	I	I	I	M
Can live with it	R	I	I	I	M
Dislike	R	R	R	R	Q

Figure 13-2. Kano Characterization Matrix

For simplicity, we have chosen short versions of the five answers. To these you will map whichever versions of the answers you chose for your questionnaire. The letters in the body of the chart have the following meanings:

- M: Must-Be factor
- P: Performance factor
- A: Attractive factor
- I: Indifferent
- Q: Questionable
- R: Reversal

"I," or "indifferent," is essentially an implied fourth Kano category, so when you are assigning Kano characterizations to a value, you should put the indifferent factor on the same footing as the must-be, performance, and attractive factors. Interestingly, a developer can omit "I" values from a product and the customer would never miss them. If you drew it on the Kano Model graph, it would be a horizontal line laid upon the X-axis, implying that, no matter how well or how poorly you handle this factor, the customer will be neither pleased nor displeased. That is, implementing indifferent values gains nothing for either the company or the customer and is total *muda*. However, there is a practical concern to consider. If your company has derived the "I" value from a requirement in a customer requirements specification (described under "Requirements Specifications" later in this chapter), the contracts or company policies may demand that you implement and trace that requirement. In that case, knowing it is an indifferent requirement should trigger a request to have it removed (attaching the customer's Kano analysis results to justify the request). Some have suggested that the cell for the functional "must" and dysfunctional "can live with it" answers should be an "M," not an "I." It's worth checking if this interpretation makes sense for any value whose analysis selects this cell.

"Q," or "questionable," results show a contradiction in the customer's answers to the two questions that you should attempt to resolve and place in one of the four Kano categories.

"R," or "reversal," results show that the developers are thinking about the factor from the opposite perspective of the customer. An example would be if you receive a high displeasure answer to the functional form of the question and a high pleasure answer to the dysfunctional form of the question. One way to deal with "R" results is to reverse the two questions, calling the dysfunctional one the functional one and vice versa. Then use the table accordingly. For instance, if the original functional question received a "dislike" answer and the original dysfunctional question received a "like" answer, this earned an "R" characterization. Reversing the two question forms leads you to a "P," or performance cell in the table, something you can use. You need to make sure to update the corresponding value in your value list accordingly (reversing it as well).

In this table, the manufacturer's Kano characterization of the "VOC minimization" value is in the fourth cell from the left in the top row: an "A," or attractive factor.

An environmentalist might answer the same questions with "This is a basic requirement to me" and "I can't accept it," pointing to the 5th cell from the left in the 2nd row—a must-be factor. A government emissions inspector, whose only criteria is that VOCs are below a threshold, might answer them both "I don't care"—an indifferent response in the exact middle of the chart. An urban planner, whose region's pollution has exceeded Federal Clean Air mandates for four of the last five years, and is therefore facing massive fines, might give the same functional and dysfunctional responses as the environmentalist car buyer—another must-be factor.

The company has to determine how to serve all four customers because all of them can influence the sale of its engine-control systems.

- The automotive manufacturer influences directly by buying or not buying the engine-control computer systems.
- The environmentalist influences by buying or not buying the car, which motivates the manufacturer to buy or not buy the engine-control computer systems. They may also picket the manufacturer, or lobby Congress to pass laws against them restricting their ability to sell that model.
- The emissions inspector influences by possibly failing the cars' inspections shortly after they've been purchased, giving the cars a bad reputation that makes them sell for less (avoidance of this outcome motivates the manufacturer to buy the engine-control computer systems).
- The urban planner influences by being on the board that sets state emissions regulations (such as those in California), which also affects the manufacturer's ability to sell cars (and motivates the manufacturer to buy the engine-control computer systems).

However, these four customers have chosen three different responses to the question. How does the company identify which values to place in the product? More specifically, how does it integrate the differing opinions of more than one customer to gain an overall characterization of a value? You start by giving the same Kano questionnaire to each customer and determining each one's Kano category for each value using the above table. Next, you create a table that lists the values down one axis (say, one per row) and the customers across the other axis (in this case, at the head of all the columns). Then you record each customer's Kano characterization of a value in the cell where that customer and that value intersect.

Once you have filled the table, look across a value's row and pick out all cells that contain the same Kano characterization, for instance, all the "M"s for that value. Sum up the customer weights (from the results of doing the AHP as it was described in Chapter 9) for each "M" to gain a composite "M" score. Do the same for the other Kano characterization types on the row. The characterization type with the highest score is the predominant Kano type for the value. In the VOC example, the table would appear as follows (see Figure 13-3):

	Automobile Manufacturer	Environmentalist Car Buyer	Emmissions Inspector	City Planner
Minimize VOCs	P	M	I	M

Figure 13-3. Example Row of a Customer Characterization Matrix

To complete the example, assume you previously did an AHP weighting of these customers and assigned to them the following weights:

- Automobile manufacturer: .45
- Environmentalist car buyer: .29
- Emissions Inspector: .08
- Urban Planner: .18

So, M" receives .29 + .18 = .47. "P" gets .45. "I" gets .08. Even though the automobile manufacturer is in first place as a customer, the sum of the "M"s exceeds "P." This value is therefore, by the method, predominantly a must-be factor. However, you need to take into account the fact that these two categories are ranked so evenly. This value clearly means a lot to most people, with almost everyone—.92 of the sum of the customer weights—caring about this value in one way or another. Indeed, in many cases, you will do well to consider a value as having the characteristics of all Kano categories with a significant vote, so this value is both a must-be factor (so you have to implement it) and a performance factor (so implementing it well will bring you added approval from many customers). Knowing this will affect your strategy for how to implement the value in the actual product design.

When the weighted approach described above gives too coarse a result, there are ways to get deeper insights into what the differences imply, such as one innovated by Mike Timko of Analog Devices.[3] In many cases, however, the simple weighted approach will suffice, and in any case, is much better than no such analysis.

Organizations have embedded the Kano Method into other larger processes besides the one illustrated in this book. For example, "In Concept Engineering, the Kano questionnaire and analysis are used to confirm and categorize the customer requirements"[4] (useful to study for the senses in which requirements are similar to values). Such processes add rigor to this aspect of value resolution, and the reader is encouraged to study them further. References on the subject are available from the Center for Quality of Management (CQM).[5]

ENDNOTES

1. This chart draws elements from several other versions of the same chart, including Dr. Kano's and Dr. Asbjorn Aune's ("World Class Quality—the Role of Top Management," Norwegian Academy of Technological Sciences, Seminar Proceedings 1991), plus the author's wording.
2. These versions are adapted from "Center For Quality Of Management Journal," Volume 2, Number 4, Fall 1993, pgs. 25–26.
3. *Center For Quality Of Management Journal,* Volume 2, Number 4, Fall 1993, pg. 17.
4. *Center For Quality Of Management Journal,* Volume 2, Number 4, Fall 1993, pg. 7.
5. *Center For Quality Of Management Journal,* Volume 3, Number 2, 1994, entire issue; and G. Burchill, D. Shen, et al., *The Concept Engineering Manual,* CQM Document 7I, Center For Quality Management.

14

Planning Implementation

I N THE LAST CHAPTER, WE SAW HOW YOU CAN GAIN INSIGHT into how your customer will feel about having each of its values implemented. We also said that this reaction has nothing to do with the value's importance. Rather, it is all about the value's Kano type.

Now we move on to the sixth step in value resolution: determining the relative importance of values to the customer. This is the final major customer input we need to be able to plan what we will implement and when. Later in this chapter, we will look at how to use this information, along with the findings from all our previous analyses, to come up with an order for implementing the customer's values that serves both them and us best.

Putting every value in the complete raw value list into a product would probably cost too much and take too long to make for either a happy customer or a successful project. Fortunately, customers view some values as being more important than others. They will be highly satisfied if the company covers their most important performance values, along with all their must-be values and a few of their most important, attractive values. From the previous chapter, we know how to identify each value's Kano type. Now we will explore how to identify the importance of each of the values.

Prioritizing Values

Traditional requirements make little if any note of priority. Requirements are written as "shalls," as in "the software <u>shall</u> sort all input fields." All "shalls" are mandatory. At best, traditional projects make subjective decisions about implementation order, without any solid objective reasoning behind their choices.

Values, on the other hand, have gradations of importance. We can use these gradations to finely tune our development to best please our customers and finesse our work for the greatest benefit from the smallest expenditure at the least risk. That gets us into planning however, which is step 7, so we will save that discussion for later in this chapter.

Here we look at three ways to prioritize the values. From lowest fidelity to highest, they are:

1. *The three-pile method.* Useful for smaller projects when you do not need much detail and when not much is at stake if you don't get the values into exactly perfect order.
2. *Self-rated importance questionnaire.* Resembles the first but requires more inputs and provides better fidelity results.
3. *AHP (Analytic Hierarchy Process) and the Affinity Diagram (AD).* Our old friends help us deal with large numbers of values and make sure the ordering is precise.

The Three-Pile Method

This technique is easy and quick, but coarse. The developers simply present the compiled list of values to each customer and ask them to place each value into one of three categories or piles, based on whether the value is of low, medium, or high importance.

That's it. It may not seem like much, but it is far more useful than having no priorities from the customer. Even with these coarse priorities, you have criteria from the customers to help you choose which values to implement.

If you have several important customers, you can use their relative weights (determined as described in Chapter 9), along with a numeric weight for each pile, to come up with three piles that apply across all customers. For instance, let's say that being in the high-importance pile gives a value a weight of 1.0. Values in a medium-importance pile receive an 0.5, and a low-importance pile gets an 0.1.

Once we do this calculation across multiple customers, a value will receive a net weight somewhere between these starting amounts. Treat anything that ends up with a net weight of less than .4 as a low-importance value, anything from .4 to less than .7 as a medium-importance value, and anything from .7 up as a high-importance value.

For example, assume there are three customers (A, B, and C) with AHP *customer* weights of .6, .3, and .1, respectively. Let's suppose that A puts a particular value in the low-importance pile, B puts the same value in its high-importance pile, and C puts this value in its medium-importance pile.

The value's net weight is $[(.6 \times .1) + (.3 \times 1) + (.1 \times .5)] = .41$, a medium-importance value, though just barely. If you have only one customer, of course, you don't need such ordering across customers.

Using any method, even a simple one like this, not only prioritizes your values, it also covers your bases. If you do *not* get the customer's input on their priorities, they can challenge you later as to why a particular release didn't contain some piece of functionality corresponding to one of their values. As often as not, the value in question is minor even to the customer, but without prioritizing, you can't appeal to that line of reasoning. Knowing the customer's priorities, even coarsely, protects as well as helps both you and them.

The three-pile method suffices for projects that are small or noncritical, and when the customer is "friendly" with the company. With larger projects, this method may leave too many values in each pile to be of much help (unless you have multiple customers, each of significant weight, who can help differentiate the values better—as in the above example). Even on larger and more demanding projects, the three-pile method can be useful for getting an early feel for the customer's mindset; in that case, if possible, it should be followed up with a more rigorous method like the AHP (discussed shortly).

The Self-Rated Importance Questionnaire (SRIQ)

This technique provides more detailed insight and lies somewhere between the three-pile method and the AHP. Thus, it provides a useful midground approach. The self-rated importance questionnaire (SRIQ) simply rephrases each value and provides a scale on which the customer can evaluate the value's importance. The scale ranges from "Not at all important" to "Extremely important" (see Figure 14-1).

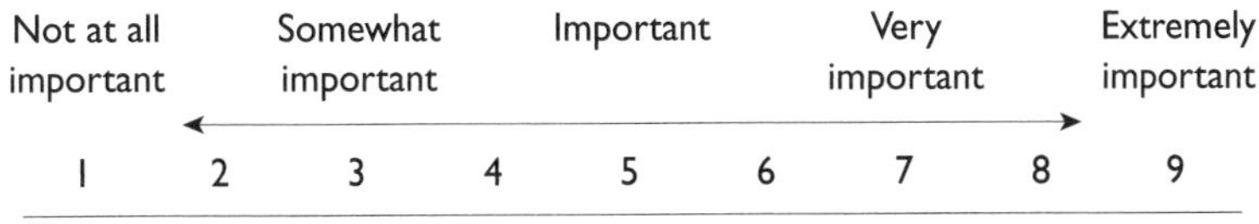

Figure originally appeared in *Center for Quality of Management Journal*, Voume 2, Number 4, Fall 1993. (Used with permission from the Center for Quality of Management.)

Figure 14-1. Self-Rated Importance Graph

The format for questions in this technique is: "How important is it or would it be if <state value here>?" Applying the SRIQ to our VOC example in the Kano Method discussion, the question would read:

- "How important is it or would it be if VOCs were minimized in the exhaust of the engine at all times?"

You then provide the customer with a line graph to mark their assessment of the importance of the value. The example in the CQM Journal appears in Figure 14-2:[1]

As with the three-pile method, if you have several significant customers, use each of their AHP-derived customer weights to combine their individual value weights into a composite value weight.

	Not at all important	Somewhat important	Important	Very important	Extremely important
How important is it or would it be if: The car has good gas mileage?	1 2 3	4 5	6 7	8 9	
How important is it or would it be if: The car has good brakes?	1 2 3	4 5	6 7	8 9	
How important is it or would it be if: The car has a long warranty period?	1 2 3	4 5	6 7	8 9	
How important is it or would it be if: The car has a small turning radius?	1 2 3	4 5	6 7	8 9	

Figure 14-2. Example from Self-Rated Importance Questionnaire

Using the AHP with Affinity Diagramming

In Chapter 9, we saw how powerful the AHP is for ordering lists. It does have a limitation however: As the number of items in your list grows, the number of comparisons you must make explodes (on the order of n^2, for n items). On small lists, this is not a problem. A list of customers, like the one we prioritized in Chapter 9, will typically be small. A list of values, like we will use the method here, will be much larger. Nevertheless, when a list gets too big for the AHP, there are ways to tame it.

You can return to affinity diagramming (AD). In Chapter 11, we used AD to group low-level values into higher-level ones; in that case, to identify market-wide domain values from a larger set of detailed customer-specific ones. Here we use AD to condense a list of values that is too big for the AHP into a reasonably sized list for that analysis. If at all possible, have the customer do all the associating and grouping. After all, you're trying to understand *their* values, not your own. At the end of the AD, you will then do the AHP on the header cards of each group of original values. You'll need to state the header card as a high-level textual value (something like an SCR table doesn't work on a header card!). You'll then use the AHP on the header-card "values." The smaller number of comparisons at this level will greatly reduce the time and effort required in using the AHP.

The AHP results are a prioritized list of the header cards for the groups of original values. As it is, this gives us tremendous and useful insight into what makes our customer tick. We must remember, however, that at this point, we still do not have priorities for each value in our original list. And it is the original values that we will implement. Our work is not done until we have a priority assigned to each original value.

One way to prioritize the original values is with the three-pile method we've already discussed in this chapter. We dive into each set of values grouped by

AD and place each value in the group into one of three piles: low, medium, or high importance. See if you can place at least half of all the values in any given group into the low-importance pile, with the other half divided between the medium- and high-importance piles (ideally, there will be more in the medium than the high).

We're not quite done yet, though. Many times, high-importance values in a group that received an overall low score in the AHP, will be more important to the customer than other low-importance values in a group that received a higher AHP score. That is, the individual values in different groups may overlap each other in importance (see Figure 14-3).

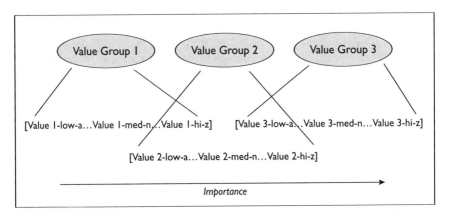

Figure 14-3. Overlapping Value Priorities Between AD Value Groups

The overlaps can be significant. One of the easiest but lowest-fidelity ways to deal with this is to combine your own and your customers' judgments to spot any obviously misplaced individual values, and move them to where they seem to belong (even if this moves them into the range of another AD group). This approach is certainly not perfect, but it is rapid and a lot better than no ordering at all. But quite a few values may need moving this way, and some may end up grossly out of place.

Another often better approach to dealing with the overlap is to take the medium-importance and high-importance piles from each AD group, put them all together in one big collection, and do the AHP on all these values. If you followed the guideline we gave earlier, of using the three-pile method to put at least half the values of each AD group into the low-importance pile, this cuts the number of values to run through AHP in half. Since the workload of the AHP is proportional to the square of the number of items being compared, this cuts your effort on the AHP to no more than a fourth of what it would have been without using AD. However, if even a fourth of the work needed for the original list is still too much, you can do the AHP on just the values from the high-importance piles of the AD groups.

The downside to this approach is that even the low-importance pile in a highly-important value group may have some relatively important values. If you do what we just suggested, none of these will end up any higher than the middle of the final weighted list (i.e., just below all the medium- and high-importance pile value priorities). If you can afford to increase the number of values you feed into the AHP on the second pass, you could choose some cutoff point in the prioritized AD value groups and use the values in all three piles for each group above the cutoff and in the medium and low piles below the cutoff. Or split the prioritized AD groups into three zones, and use all three piles in the top zone, the top two piles in the middle zone, and just the top pile in the bottom zone.

If, for some reason, the above strategies do not suit you, an alternate way to decrease the number of comparisons feeding into the AHP (either the first or second pass, per the above) is to hierarchically layer the values using a visualization called tree mapping.[2,3] Please see the references provided in the endnotes if you desire more details.

All of these approaches are compromises. They attempt to gain the best understanding of the customer that can be obtained given the limitations of project time and budget. This strategizing and analyzing will pay off extremely well in the final step of value resolution, when we put together everything we've done thus far to order our project for the greatest benefit to our customer and ourselves.

Choosing an Implementation Order

The seventh and final value-resolution step is to choose which customer values you will implement and when. There is never enough time or budget to put all of them in the product. And the order you choose to do them in matters as well. Both considerations contribute to major goals of a well-run project. Some of these goals are:

- Quickly gaining the customers' confidence and enthusiastic support.
- Keeping the customer loyal throughout the entire project.
- Minimizing what you must spend to do both the above.
- Getting a good price for the product.
- Reducing project risks as quickly as possible.

The ways these goals are pursued may look a little different depending on the type of software being developed. For instance, speculative or off-the-shelf software development doesn't see many of its customers until after it is completed. However, even in that case, there should be some customer representation during development, for the reasons we've been discussing all along. The same lean principles (value, in this discussion) and techniques apply regardless of the type of project.

Typical nonlean software development practices serve these goals poorly. Most projects that start with a traditional requirements analysis phase, for example, never find a way to do a good job on all the goals at once. The things developers do that best serve one goal often work against the things that best serve another. For instance, doing what it takes to minimize costs, in the absence of understanding customers, often conflicts with doing what it takes to keep customers loyal. This dilemma forces either/or choices near the very beginning of a project, before much is known about the basis in reality for making these choices. It sets up classic mass production win/lose scenarios from the outset: Which goal(s) will be pursued at the expense of which others?

There's no need to sacrifice important goals. With adequate knowledge of the customer we can optimize a project for good performance on all its goals. Why would a customer complain about us minimizing our costs and making a good profit, for instance, if they're happy with what we've done for them and with what we've charged them compared to their other available sources? To the contrary, if they like us, they will want to see us remain financially healthy so we'll be around later to help them again. Win/win is a viable strategy.

However, we can only achieve a win/win if we build our developments upon adequate information. That is why we have done all the preceding value analyses. Gaining the customer's early support (goal #1 above) requires that we engage their emotions early on. Recall that the Kano method reveals to us which values will give the customer the most pleasure (positive emotion) upon being implemented. Knowing the Kano classification of the values allows us to pick values for early implementation that will quickly win over our customers (later in the chapter, we'll say more about how to do this). We'll also be doing much better on this goal if we've involved the customer(s) in our team and made them feel appreciated and important during the value-resolution process. Notice how the different lean techniques are reinforcing the same business goals? That is a trait of lean production and part of what makes it a *system*.

The goal of keeping the customer loyal throughout the project (goal #2) requires that we show the customer we will always do what is in their best interests, that is, what matters the most to them. The information that allows us to do this is a prioritized list of how important their values are to them, like what we obtained using the AHP and supporting techniques. We simply work our way down the list over time.

Goals #3 and #4, minimizing our own costs and getting a good price for our products, requires that we have both types of knowledge. If our development team can implement the values the customer is most emotional about (per Kano modeling), as well as all the higher values on their priority list (per the AHP), we can skip doing the values low on their list and save the costs involved. That the values we do implement are the ones they care the most about tells them they are dealing with a software producer who is more responsive to their needs than the vast majority of software companies in existence. They won't begrudge that we didn't waste our time or money (or theirs!) implementing what they cared about only little. This should allow us to both cut the costs of our products to them, and to increase our own margins, at the same time.

To achieve goal #5 and minimize project risk as early as possible, we must introduce the activity of risk analysis.

Risk Analysis

Risk, from our perspective, is the possibility that we will lose some business positioning or project circumstance that is favorable to us.

Bad things happen on projects. Sometimes they happen because of events outside our control. Other parts of our business may execute their parts of the project badly (for instance, marketing or hardware design). Our companies may choose, despite our most persuasive arguments, to capitalize our project insufficiently (e.g., for tools and staffing). Or, they or our customers may impose practices on us that work against our business goals or our judgment of the best way to conduct the software development. We do the best we can with such problems. Risk management is a huge field, going well beyond the scope of this book. Risks that are outside our direct control are mostly addressed with techniques we will not touch upon here. For instance, with the kinds of risks we just mentioned, such seemingly unrelated skills as negotiation and relationship-building may be as important to success as are technical abilities.

Usually, however, our most serious risks are issues that *we* control. The most important of these is the risk that a value particularly important to the project's success will be more difficult or expensive to implement than we originally expected. Entire projects have been shipwrecked on this single risk. This is why *it is wise to implement the high-risk, high-importance values in early builds, when there is time to adjust the project according to the outcome.*

The overall risk level of a value is based on two things: how difficult it will be to implement, and how severe its impact on the project will be if it can't be implemented properly or completely. The latter is another way of asking how important the value is to the project. This question is, however, somewhat different than asking how important this value is to the customer, since company and business concerns are being added here to customer ones.

An interesting and reasonably simple, though somewhat controversial, approach to determining a value's risk to a project is found in the risk-assessment method used by the U.S. Air Force, called the Standard Practice for System

Safety, MIL-STD 882D.[4] We discuss it here both to illustrate the mindset of risk analysis, and as an approach that you can adapt for value analysis.

Though the Air Force uses this approach to deal with risks of injury, death, and equipment destruction in systems with safety implications to their users, with a little interpretation, we can apply it to products whose main concerns are usability or business impact—the risks found in developing customer values into executing software—rather than safety. The impact of failing to develop a value successfully (or doing so very late) won't usually be injury or property damage. It can be serious, however; anything from shaking the confidence and loyalty of your customer, to the product failing in the marketplace, to even something as severe as the destruction of your business (e.g., if you are sued and lose because of a critical software failure). This is the severity side of the analysis (see Figure 14-4 from MIL-STD 882D).

Description	Category	Environmental, Safety, and Health Result Criteria
Catastrophic	I	Could result in death, permanent total disability, loss exceeding $1M, or irreversible severe environmental damage that violates law or regulation.
Critical	II	Could result in permanent partial disability, injuries or occupational illness that may result in hospitalization of at least three personnel, loss exceeding $200K but less than $1M, or reversible environmental damage causing a violation of law or regulation.
Marginal	III	Could result in injury or occupational illness resulting in one or more lost work day(s), loss exceeding $10K but less than $200K, or mitigatible environmental damage without violation of law or regulation where restoration activities can be accomplished.
Negligible	IV	Could result in injury or illness not resulting in a lost work day, loss exceeding $2K but less than $10K, or minimal environmental damage not violating law or regulation.

Figure 14-4. Suggested Severity Categories

You select the most severe consequence you think can come from failing to successfully develop each value (e.g., catastrophic, critical, marginal, or negligible). On the side, write down exactly what worst-case consequence you foresee, in case you want to go back and reconsider your results later.

If you need to save time, you can do this assessment only for the Kano must-be and performance values, starting from the most-important one (from the AHP priority analysis) down through the level of importance you choose for a cutoff. The lower-priority performance values and the attractive values won't have nearly as severe consequences.

The probability side (see Figure 14-5 from MIL-STD 882D) of the analysis is to estimate how likely it is that you will encounter the kinds of difficulties in implementing a particular value that will lead to the worst-case consequence you identified under the severity side.

Description*	Level	Specific Individual Item	Fleet or Inventory**
Frequent	A	Likely to occur often in the life of an item, with a probability of occurrence greater than 10^{-1} in that life.	Continuously experienced.
Probable	B	Will occur several times in the life of an item, with a probability of occurrence less than 10^{-1} but greater than 10^{-2} in that life.	Will occur frequently.
Occasional	C	Likely to occur some time in the life of an item, with a probability of occurrence less that 10^{-2} but greater that 10^{-3} in that life.	Will occur several times.
Remote	D	Unlikely but possible to occur in the life of an item, with a probability of occurrence less than 10^{-3} but greater than 10^{-6} in that life.	Unlikely, but can reasonable be expected to occur.
Improbable	E	So unlikley, it can be assumed occurrence may not be experienced, with a probability of occurrence less than 10^{-6} in that life.	Unlikely to occur, but possible.

Figure 14-5. Suggested Probability Levels

To record your thoughts, adapt the numbers and the probability words from MIL-STD-882D as follows:

- Frequent means extremely likely.
- Probable means somewhat likely.
- Occasional means marginally likely.
- Remote means barely likely.
- Improbable means unlikely but possible.

For instance, extremely likely means that implementing the value in question will almost certainly be so difficult that the severity consequence (whatever that was identified to be) will happen.

We combine the results of both judgments using the following table:

Severity Probability	Catastrophic	Critical	Marginal	Negligible
Frequent	1	3	7	13
Probable	2	5	9	16
Occasional	4	6	11	18
Remote	8	10	14	19
Improbable	12	15	17	20

Figure 14-6. Example Risk Assessment Values

The lower the number, the higher the risk (and need for attention). The example in MIL–STD–882D identifies 1–5 as high risk, 6–9 as serious risk, 10–17 as medium risk, and 18–20 as low risk. The document does suggest that you use your judgment to choose ranges to correlate to risk level for your purposes.

Let's use the 882D matrices on a fairly clear-cut example. A particular must-be customer value is known to be technically difficult to develop. Further, the project must succeed for your company's survival. We therefore give it a severity of catastrophic and a probable likelihood of failure. According to the 882D tables, this value would have a risk level of 2, which is near the top of the high-risk range.

High-risk values should be implemented early in the lifecycle, with a plan to maximize the probability of successful development as well as a fall-back plan in case of failure. In these cases, there should probably be some high-level management visibility, and in some cases, even direct senior management involvement.

As we can also see from the tables, a value that has a high severity impact but a lower probability of development difficulties can still be a high risk. Some impacts are so severe that you don't want to take any chances of them happening. In the safety world, loss of human life is such a risk. Even if it's not likely in a given system, you still spend a lot of time managing the risk to *make sure* it doesn't happen. It works the same way in software development: If the result of failing to develop a particular value well would be very harmful, then even if you think you'll probably have no problems with developing it, you'll want to give the development of that value extra attention anyway.

Balancing Emotion, Priority, and Risk

We now have a set of customer values and know three important things about them. We know their:

- Emotional impact
- Priority
- Risk

An implementation order that does well on all the project goals we previously discussed must balance all these issues. To review, those project goals are:

- Quickly gaining the customers' confidence and enthusiastic support.
- Keeping the customer loyal throughout the entire project.
- Minimizing what you must spend to do both of the above.
- Getting a good price for the product.
- Reducing project risks as quickly as possible.

Before going any further, here are a couple of things to keep in mind:

1. Emotional impact divides the values cleanly into three Kano groups: must-be, performance, and attractive values. Priority and risk-level, however, apply to every value (though you may choose to not derive an exact priority or risk level for less-important values).
2. It's a good idea to create a spreadsheet with a column for the value names (one value per row), a column for the values' Kano types, a column for the values' priorities, and a column for the values' risk levels. Then you can sort the values by these criteria (e.g., by risk, or by Kano type and priority) as needed to support these planning activities.

The strategy for ordering the implementation to maximize our project goals is simple: In every build, implement a mix of values of these four types:

- Must-be values (to assure the customer you are covering the basics).
- High-risk values (to deal with risks while there's still time to adapt).
- Attractive values (to gain the customer's emotional support).
- Performance values (to address the main capabilities the customer's buying).

The earliest releases should include a few must-be values to reassure the customer of your basic competence, several of their performance values to demonstrate you are tuned into their greatest needs, and an attractive value or two to capture their enthusiasm. One or two high-risk values in each build will quickly and greatly reduce the dangers to your project. If a particular high-risk value is giving you a lot of trouble, simply drop it out of the current build, keep people working on it on the side, and continue with your planned builds; add the high-risk value back in once the problems with it have been solved. Start with the highest-priority values of each type and work down the priority list. Of course, at times, you'll have to implement a less-important value to provide the prerequisite for a more important one; that's fine.

In later builds, the relative emphasis on the value types will change. The number of performance values will go up (relatively), and the number of high-risk ones will go down (as the major risks are retired). Customer reaction to the order in previous builds should be considered when determining what will go into upcoming ones. For instance, if the customer wants to see performance values realized faster than the project can respond, sometimes mixing in an attractive value or two ahead of schedule can compensate by delighting the customer and making him or her more forgiving. It the customer expresses concern about whether all his or her basic expectations will be covered by your software, upping the percentage of must-be values implemented in the next few builds can reassure him or her. Adjusting your implementation order on-the-fly has several good effects, not the least of which is making your customer aware that you are listening to him or her and taking him or her seriously. Furthermore, he or she have fewer objections about what is and what isn't going into the product at any given time.

These criteria continue to be useful during actual implementation (discussed in Part III). An organization can use these same criteria to choose when to quit working on a particular value. For instance, once a must-be value is in place and its functionality working acceptably, little is gained by further improving its performance. Instead, resources can be redirected to improving performance values. When a high-risk but otherwise lower-priority value has been explored enough to remove the major concerns about it, it can be shelved for a while to allow more important values to be worked. And so forth.

A word of caution is due here. As we said in Part I, flexibility is a major trait of lean production. This does not mean, however, that making changes is always better than not making changes. Without contradicting anything we've just said about the benefits of changing implementation order, if we can adequately predict what factors might force future changes, we can often account for them in our initial planning and avoid the need to change. You could call this flexibility ahead of time. You could also call it proactivity. Pick the best order you can up front, so that the only order changes you need to make later are due to factors you *could not* have foreseen from the beginning. If you approach ordering in this way, you will make every change (and the time and budget overhead associated with the change) improve the state of the project beyond what it would have been, and not just compensate for needless deficiencies in planning.

The cost of changing the order of value implementation is miniscule compared to the cost of changing the values themselves (either modifying existing ones or adding to the original list). Each change of a value, or a requirement in traditional projects, causes repeated downstream development work; the later the change, the more work. This is another reason why the techniques in this book make such a point to get the customer involved in the value-resolution process and its analyses. The customers' efforts invest them in the values list. This slows their demands for change in two ways: First, more of their values are identified (and with better accuracy and detail); and second, their emotional commitment to the list will be much greater than in traditional projects, where they typically have little involvement in requirements development at all.

Customer-driven value change on lean projects corresponds to requirements creep on traditional programs. Requirements creep has mortally wounded many software projects. On one program (for obvious reasons, the project and company will remain nameless), the program manager decided to save money by canceling all analyses of the system requirements. He wasn't stupid: He was under extreme budget pressure. His plausible and optimistic argument was "we've built systems like this for years; we already understand what this one has to do."

However, the outcome did not confirm his optimism. Not only did system requirements keep evolving, but their rate of evolution continued accelerating until just before the end of major development (when emergency jake brakes were applied to requirements engineering, to allow the system to be delivered).

This situation had ripple effects. Changes to high-level requirements drove, as they always do, even more changes to software requirements. The software developers found themselves making several versions of most pieces of code, repeating each time all associated integration, verification, and acceptance tasks. Two or more of the later versions of a requirement would be revisions to earlier versions. However, the team typically could not simply resurrect an older version of the code when this happened, because even though the requirement was now the same as before, the rest of the system around the code in question would have since changed (due to the evolution of the other requirements). The code therefore still had to be redeveloped.

Hardware development and the other portions of the project suffered just as much as software—pure *muda* all around. You've probably guessed the results: exploding costs and late system delivery. Certain project officials decided that the most politically acceptable way out of the mess was to tell the world the software group had shown itself unable to keep its commitments. Unfortunately for the officials involved, higher-level corporate managers privately did not buy the explanation. After a short outside investigation, retirement announcements flooded in, ending a total of six senior careers on the project. No one in software was even reprimanded: Indeed, the software managers were privately told that their efforts had in fact turned a catastrophic situation into merely a bad one. The public cover story of software incompetence, however, was never officially retracted.

Value resolution is needed from the highest levels of a project on down. If software is part of a larger product, it cannot insulate itself from the project's deficiencies in value resolution for the system as a whole. It's still worth doing (at least software will understand the customer's values that apply to the software portion of the product), but the project as a whole will still suffer from not understanding its customer. The moral is, do what you can, but also try to persuade the larger context around the project to do better as well.

Good value resolution does more good than anything else for project success. Bad value resolution hurts everyone: the customers, the software developers, the project, and not too far down the line, the entire business.

Defining Build Scope the XP Way

XP has some excellent ideas that can be applied to almost any value-driven development. In a nutshell, XP takes its version of values, called user stories (which may include aspects of the producer space, unfortunately), and assesses how long each will take to implement. XP then chooses a fixed release cycle as its heartbeat—generally between one and three weeks per release. To each release, XP has the team allocate the number of values it believes possible to implement in that time. After a few cycles, the allocation becomes more accurate and the original estimate of the total scope of the program is verified; or discrepancies become clear which assists in re-planning. Several of the major XP references cover this topic in detail, so we will not explain it further here.

Value Resolution on a Large Aerospace Project

Early in the 1990s, while developing the 382J aircraft integrating software mentioned earlier, we used several of the techniques discussed in Part II. In the end, several customers whose interests were normally considered incompatible all said they were very satisfied with how their concerns (i.e., values) were being handled.

First, the software team used brainstorming to create a list of candidate customers. The list included purchasing customers, regulators like the FAA, hardware and systems groups on the program, and people in several managerial functions within Lockheed Martin. The team used the AHP to rank the candidates by who mattered the most to project success and by how much. This established a weighted customer list (kept private within the software group to neatly avoid the problem of having to inform some senior managers that their weights were relatively low!).

Next, the development team went directly to each customer (when possible) or their surrogate (when not), and collected a list of issues that were important to them. You could consider these issues to be values . . . though without the detail and attributes of value described in this chapter (this was an early experiment for me in using these techniques). The team weighted the values on each customer's list, again using the AHP. We combined the list into a single weighted value list by multiplying each value's weight by the weight of the customer on whose list the value appeared. If multiple customers cited a value, the products of value and customer weights were summed up for all the citing customers. This gave shared values a higher score that reflected their overall importance. The result was a single weighted value list.

The software team had already been working with the systems engineering group to turn its traditional systems requirements into a set of software requirements in the form of SCR tables. To this point neither the systems nor software requirements had an obvious order of importance. Nobody knew how much any requirement meant to the project's customers (indeed, the earlier customer analysis marked the first time anyone knew exactly who those customers were). This situation left the team with no objective criteria for implementing any requirement before any other. Risk was high and the likelihood of satisfying the customers early in development, low. The weighted value list from the previous step was the key to turning this around.

The development team compared each SCR requirement to the list of high-level (textual) values. Each requirement's contribution to each value was assessed as a value between 0 and 1. In many cases, a requirement contributed to more than one value, so every contribution was assessed independently. Next, the team assigned a weight to each requirement by multiplying its contribution to a value by the weight of the value (from the earlier weighted value list), and summing these up for all values to which the requirement contributed. The results were stored in tables and sorted. The following is a small but real sample (Figure 14-7):

See the earlier discussion of SCR to understand the naming convention. REQs are requirements. With the REQs ranked, the team had nearly everything it needed to decide which requirements to implement in which builds. The remaining consideration was risk. On an airplane program, the biggest risk is usually safety. So the safety-critical requirements were built into early builds to reduce the risk that they would be difficult to implement.

The ordered requirements list also provided criteria for making tough decisions on what to implement and when. Requirements below a predetermined

Requirement number	REQ_<Descriptor>	Numeric priority
1.2.3.1	REQ_vertical velocity	4.6
1.2.3.11	REQ_true_airspeed	4.5
1.2.4.5	REQ_air_data_validity	4.5
1.2.2.2	REQ_glideslope_status	4.3
5.1.4.7	REQ_anti-skid	4.3
8.5.1.7.1	REQ_groundspeed_indicator	4.2

Figure 14-7. Value-Weighted Software Requirements

cutoff weight limit in the list would be either moved onto an unscheduled, "someday" list, or eliminated.

Beginning the project in this way set a road map of production performance throughout the project that has served Lockheed Martin well.

Success Comes from the Early Lifecycle

Value resolution in the customer space early on is the main foundation for lean software production. Most software projects virtually ignore it. Major industry and government initiatives to improve software development are focusing on using mass production to improve later-lifecycle implementation techniques in the producer space. Though XP and its kin provide a radical alternative to such initiatives, they depend too much on the unseen hand of emergent behavior to explore business strategy or unveil customer values. To know yourself or your customer, you must make a conscious effort to collect, analyze, and understand. Both mass production and extreme approaches never gain visibility into the business and customer concerns that are thoroughly mapped by techniques common in lean industries. In software, using a methodical process to combine these techniques into a coherent approach is almost unheard of. That gives a spectacular advantage to those who are willing to make the effort.

We can take everything we've discussed in Part II and combine it to define lean production in yet another way. Lean production is an integrated approach to achieving the following goals (with where it's addressed in this book):

- Understand why you are in business and where you want to go (Part II).
- Determine who your customers are, what they want, and why (Part II).

- Build, with minimum waste, products that address all these concerns (Part III).

The first two goals are strategic; the third is tactical. You can win a battle with great tactics, but you win a war only with great strategy. Yet, what has traditionally been called "software engineering" has focused almost exclusively on the tactical aspect of a project; i.e., on building a product in the producer space.

Clearly, lean software production has a much broader scope than does traditional software development. Even applying lean techniques within only the bounds of traditional development misses out on the main benefits of lean. Incremental improvement of development processes removes waste from what you are doing: It doesn't address whether you're doing the right thing. To say it another way, you can have a successful business without *kaizens*, but not without deep insight into your own and your customers' needs and wants.

Only after a company has begun adopting the lean emphasis on business planning and customer value in the early lifecycle, will it be ready to begin designing and coding in a lean way. Lean strategy greatly improves business performance even in the absence of lean implementation.

With that perspective clearly in mind, it is true that the synergies and benefits multiply when you end a project as leanly as it began. In the endgame of projects, in the producer space, we need to leverage what we have so diligently set up for in the early stages, in the customer space. This will be our topic in Part III.

ENDNOTES

1. "Center for Quality of Management Journal," Volume 2, Number 4, Fall 1993, pg. 12.
2. Shneiderman, B. *Tree Visualization with Tree-maps: A 2-D space-filling approach,* ACM Transactions on Graphics 11, 1 (Jan. 1992), pgs. 92–99.
3. Asahi, T., Turo, D., and Shneiderman, B., *Using treemaps to visualize the Analytic Hierarchy Process,* University of Maryland Department of Computer Science Technical Report CS-TR-3293 (June 1994).
4. "Standard Practice for System Safety," MIL-STD 882D, February 2000.

PART THREE

Building Lean Software— Producer Space, Late Lifecycle

15

The Value Stream—Design

IN PART II, WE LOOKED IN THE CUSTOMER SPACE for the indispensable foundation of the lean lifecycle, understanding our customers and our own businesses. We also found that most of the techniques for understanding customers of software systems are the same as the techniques used for understanding the customers of any other industry.

In Part III, we will explore the producer space. The producer space is the set of technical means and implementation strategies that producers draw upon to satisfy customer needs. The producer space is also sometimes called the implementation space, or somewhat more loosely, the implementation phase. The work done in the producer space is often called synthesis; and contrasts with the analytical flavor of most work done in the customer space.

Software-industry work in the producer space uses both general industrial techniques and also techniques unique to software. Some of the latter apply even more narrowly to just certain types of software. For the next few pages, we will gradually work our way from industry generalities to the specifics of software. From then on, most of Part III will be focused on software issues.

Just as there is a lean way of approaching the customer space, there is also a lean way of dealing with the producer space. Lean producers take a wait-and-see attitude towards specific implementation strategies. That is, they wait until as late as practical in the value-resolution process to commit to specific implementation strategies. We will see the ultimate application of this idea in the pull principle discussed in Chapter 21, which works in the context of an established domain design (domain design is discussed later in this chapter).

Generally, understanding the customer as much as possible, as early as possible, has a bigger impact on the success of implementation than any other factor; bigger than software tools, bigger than human factors, bigger than hardware platform. The work in the producer space is best based on thorough preceding work in the customer space.

Nevertheless, the lean way does not totally ignore the producer space while working in the customer space. Some implementation strategies must be committed to relatively early. The choice of programming language, for instance, can either work with or against value-resolution techniques, as we'll see in Chapter 18. And even in the earliest talks with customers, it is wise to think about what we believe it will be possible to implement in the end. What you think can or cannot be implemented should not prevent you from gathering all possible customer values. If you think some of the values will be difficult or even impossible to satisfy, you should log this information just as you did for priority and Kano category. Use it to help decide which values to place into the product and when to do so. You never know when something you currently think is impossible may become possible because of a technical breakthrough or an inventive idea.

Part II concerned itself with the first of the five lean principles, value, which explores the customer space. The remaining four lean principles apply most strongly to the producer space and will be the focus of Part III. They are the value stream, flow, pull, and perfection.

One way to describe the roles of these principles is to compare them to the systems of the human body. Think of all the work done to create the actual product, based on the values, as the totality of systems in the body. Within that body, the techniques of the value stream principle are the skeletal structure that support everything else and position everything relative to everything else. The techniques of the flow principle make up all the major tissues, skin, muscles, and organs, in short, the flesh. They do the actual hands-on work in producing the final product(s). The techniques of the pull principle help define and create controls over the production line, forming the body's nervous system. Finally, the techniques of the perfection principle build up the production line's ability to reject and prevent defects—creating the body's immune system. This is also a logical order in which to discuss them, so we begin with the value stream.

The value stream principle focuses on two major purposes. The first to turn customer values into product attributes; i.e., the things that add value. The second, and nearly as important, is to make sure that scarce resources like money, people, and time are used to the greatest benefit of the project and the customer; in other words, to eliminate waste. This second goal is important because either waiting around doing nothing, or generating valueless work such as feeding organizational and production infrastructures is a pure loss to the project. Yet, it constitutes over half of what most nonlean businesses do (recall the example in Chapter 3 of the project in which 99 percent of its development calendar time was nonproductive waste). Value-stream techniques reduce such wastes.

In fact, creating a lean value stream is the most effective thing one can do to improve productivity quickly and inexpensively. "We've learned . . . that a specific sequence of steps and initiatives produces the best results. The trick is . . . to begin with the value stream itself, quickly creating dramatic changes in the ways routine things are done every day."[1]

Even traditional craft or mass production projects always have some approach to converting customer desires into product attributes. However, in nonlean businesses, the "values" feeding the stream may also come from other, less-beneficial (to the business) sources, such as developer bias. They are usually poorly defined and incomplete and are often arrived at from the wrong perspective (e.g., mixed with producer-space concerns). Adding insult to injury, even if a company practices requirements traceability, it almost certainly is inconsistent and unsystematic in the way it injects these requirements into its products (this is true even in houses that have tightly defined mass production processes; why we can say this will become more clear by the end of this chapter, and especially in the chapter on the perfection principle). So, the transition from values to products, as it is done traditionally, is loosely defined, wastes time and money, and yields products that bear only a loose resemblance to the customers' picture of what they originally wanted.

The lean techniques described here tighten up the value stream until customer values are truly reflected in products, and as much as possible, all work is directed solely towards adding value.

As discussed in Chapter 3, lean splits the value stream into two major substreams:

1. Design stream
2. Production stream

Generally speaking, the techniques of the design stream are more focused on the first goal of the value stream, adding value. Likewise, the techniques of the production stream are more focused on the second goal, eliminating waste. But, there are also overlaps. In this chapter, we will look at what distinguishes these two substreams in software development and then zero in on the design stream.

Product-Family Development

The division into design stream and production stream makes perfect sense with durable goods. A product is designed (design stream), and then copies of it are produced on the line (production stream).

In the traditional way of developing a single piece of software, the distinction between design stream and production stream becomes confusing. For a single piece of software, essentially all the effort in the entire project goes into designing the product. Making copies of a piece of software is trivial work; a matter of simply typing in a command-line copy statement or even just "dragging and dropping." This makes the production stream seem irrelevant to the software industry, a perception that simply isn't true.

The key is that most software producers shouldn't be thinking of their jobs in terms of developing single pieces of software. "You'll ... need to devise a practical strategy to fully utilize all of the resources being freed up by the shift to lean production. Doing this requires reorganizing your business by product families."[2] A company that applies lean production to isolated products receives smaller rewards than one that applies lean to the production of groups of related products, i.e., product families. In a moment, we'll see how this can work for even someone who is developing a one-off solitary product.

With software product families, the design stream is concerned with the overall design of the family, and the production stream is concerned with producing the individual variant programs. The distinction between the two parts of the value stream becomes clear.

Software companies often miss out on the possibility of building product families by thinking this only applies to development of many different but related programs, a situation that doesn't happen too often in the software industry. However, you can add more systems to this category if you think of future variants of the same product, such as upgrades and maintenance releases, as being additional members of the same product family. Taking it a step further, the natural sequence of enhancements that happens in almost every product's development and especially in spiral approaches can be thought of as various incarnations of the product . . . again, supporting a product-family view of many projects.

Looking at every project as belonging to a product family changes in very practical ways what we do in the producer space; i.e., in design and implementation. Many of the techniques of the value stream only make sense if there is a product family. Software businesses *can* take advantage of those techniques, even in single-item software developments that would normally write off such techniques as irrelevant. In the next section, we will see how to create a software product family even for single-product developments and obtain these benefits.

The two most important approaches in the software design stream are domain engineering and QFD. They address very different issues: Domain engineering deals with creating product-family designs that prevent waste in the production of individual software products. Domain engineering, as we know it today, originated in the software industry. QFD deals with focusing all design efforts directly on customer values. QFD comes from other industries. Both techniques are among the most effective lean approaches available. Both are among the least practiced approaches in most sectors of the software industry. We'll begin with using domain engineering to build product families.

Domain Engineering

The ideas of domain engineering are quite simple and yet very powerful. A domain is a set of customer-space tasks and resources that are related to each other by some higher-level purpose. Domain engineering is the process for developing a system for a particular domain, based on the natural and recurring characteristics of the customer space of the anticipated system. Note that this definition of domain is different than that used by UML practitioners. They tend to look at domains as a producer-space concept for a design-time abstraction: "Domains organize class specifications . . . A domain is an independent subject matter area with an independent vocabulary . . . Domains organize things that exist only at design time—i.e. classes and types."[3] In any system, there will be some classes that relate primarily to the producer space. However, there are many advantages to relating as many classes to the customer space as possible, as we shall see now and over the next several chapters.

Applying the first definition of domain and domain engineering to software development has been useful and practical to ourselves and others for many years and on many projects. Domain engineering by this definition reduces *muda* in myriad ways, from eliminating redundant work across product variants, to improving communication with the customer and thus, reducing misdirected work and non-value-adding activities.

Let's turn to the world of pharmacists to illustrate the natural and recurring characteristics of a customer space. The world of pharmacists includes classes of drugs (e.g., controlled substance vs. noncontrolled prescription vs. non-prescription), government regulations concerning pharmacies and drug distribution, the need for bookkeeping, insurance handling, and so on. Each of these is natural, that is, normal, in the world of any pharmacist. Each is also repeated, giving rise to many similar instances (e.g., dealing with multiple insurers or numerous controlled painkilling drugs).

The producer space for products serving pharmacists might include POS (Point of Sale) hardware/software systems, credit/debit technologies, specific drug-dispensing technologies, existing pharmacy software packages, the forms supplied and required by a specific insurer, specific database technologies or even database tools, middleware choices, 4GL code generators, and so on. You could structure a software system around either perspective—the pharmacist's or the pharmacy-automation developer's. However, lean domain engineering will pick the former over even the most straightforward technology-dependent implementation for several reasons. Two stand out particularly:

1. *The customer space tends to change much more slowly than the producer space*, i.e., what the users do is more long-lived than are the tools they use to do it (e.g., people have written things for thousands of years, but the technologies for writing—chalk, fountain pens, pencils, ballpoints, typewriters, word processors, and so forth—have changed much more frequently). So of course, designs that are oriented primarily around the customer space are more stable over time. Practically speaking, in a

customer-space structured system, any additions or changes you make to program functionality will more easily find a place to land in the existing system. It is usually harder to construct custom interfaces between changing pieces of technology than it is to fit a different technology into an unchanging task that customers perform. The task may be performed differently than it was in the past, but often (though not always,) its relationship to other tasks will not have changed significantly. Thus, customer-space structuring leads to smaller changes to a program's design or code as the system evolves and therefore wastes less work throughout the system's life.

2. *It's heavily in the software producer's interests to involve customers in development*; this especially helps with the value-stream goal of keeping all work focused on adding value (though it also reduces waste). It is much easier to communicate with a customer about a product under development when speaking in terms of the customer's concepts. Speaking their language also makes it easier to sell the customer on becoming involved this way.

Pharmacists may not understand a 3-tier client/server/database access model using CORBA and JDBC, but they certainly understand information flows between their pharmacies, HMOs, and the government. Indeed, it is an application of Dr. David Parnas's information-hiding concept (covered in more detail later in this chapter) that makes the classes and interfaces of a system mirror the natural structure of the customer's world. As a result, your implementation technologies become the "secrets" (in Parnas' terms) that only the most involved parties—i.e., yourselves, the producers—need to know about. Once you structure the design around the customer space, everything else about a project can be fruitfully communicated between customer and developer.

Structuring systems around the customer space has one notable disadvantage. It typically costs an extra 10–20 percent in processing speed or memory usage, and thus won't produce the absolutely fastest or smallest code. This means that systems pushing their computing resources to the limit may not be eligible for domain engineering the way we define it. This is mostly a concern in embedded hardware/software products that are produced in huge numbers for a commodity market. Then the small unit savings of going with the least capable processor may add up to large enough savings over an entire project to make sub optimizing the software seem justifiable.

However, processors continually get cheaper and more powerful. By the time you deploy a product, it may be affordable to buy enough horsepower to do a domain implementation and obtain its benefits. Furthermore, a software application that is expected to have less than 10 percent available headroom from its earliest planning stages is accepting a high level of risk from the beginning. That is, there is no ability left to deal with unexpected software growth during even initial development, much less during maintenance releases or future upgrades. If one believes that one of the fundamentals of project management is risk mitigation and control, then this strategy for saving money is arguably based on bad management. It will probably backfire and lead to higher costs or even, in the near future, to a product that is not viable or maintainable.

One other major benefit of a domain-structured design is that, like XP, it permits developers to begin work before they have a complete or finalized set of requirements. However, where XP counts on having to change the design due to future surprise discoveries in the customer's requirements, domain design anticipates evolution through analysis of the types of changes that might happen. It then structures the design so that it accommodates such changes with minimal impact. This type of proactive behavior is typical of lean production in general.

Clearly, the first step in structuring a system around the customer space is to understand the customer space itself. This means you must develop a good model of its natural and recurring characteristics. Such characteristics have three major traits:

1. Class-like, in that there are multiple instances of them in the domain
2. The most stable elements in the domain (i.e., they change the most slowly)
3. Grouped together with other elements that tend to change as a result of the same change stimuli in the customer's world

A lean producer develops a model of the customer space in the first stage of domain engineering, called domain analysis. Domain analysis focuses on the user's perspective of his or her purpose, context, and surroundings in his or her work. It considers the history of previous similar systems, as well as the values implemented by any current systems they use, and the user's reaction to those systems. It also attempts to project the "future history" of the user's work; i.e., how it is expected to evolve. (Recall that this was also the purpose of the TRIZ approach called "DE.") If the user and other people in the user's field have ideas about how the ways they do their work might change in the not-too-distant future, the modeler may be able to find higher-level ways of describing the customer's work that will work for both their current activities and also their new ones when the work changes.

For instance, it was not that long ago that service stations recorded credit card information by using physical roller machines and multilayer carbon-copy forms. A model of the customer space could have included entities for the roller machines and the multipart forms. These things were, after all, familiar to all gas-station attendants at that time. However, the roller machines and their forms were actually intrusions of the producer space into the user's world; they were technology-dependent solutions to which the user had merely become accustomed. Of course, not all technologies are so ephemeral. Some are so long-lasting that they become good customer space abstractions as well. Returning to our writing analogy, paper and pen have lasted many years, show no sign of disappearing any time soon, and provide a good analogy for other technology solutions such as the tablet computer.

However, the technologies of the credit card roller machine and multipart form have nearly disappeared, being replaced by swipe readers and custom-printed receipts. Who is to say that some other technologies might not in turn replace these? Neither the roller machine and multipart form nor their replace-ments are good customer space abstractions; they are simply short-term design-space mechanisms. What has proven stable about the world of the gas station attendant is the work of accepting credit payments and acknowledging receipt of those payments. One could build a domain model around these tasks with some higher-level entities or abstractions, like "credit payment" and "acknowledge-ment," that correspond to the tasks without naming specific technologies for doing them. A domain model at such a level would accommodate the future but still speak in terms familiar to the user. Because such a model would be more sta-ble, it would require less maintenance over time, which would reduce wasted work and make it more lean.

A domain model includes more than the raw list of customer values created using the techniques of the value principle. Customer values touch upon, but don't directly focus on, the structures of the customer's world. To do domain engi-neering, you must explicitly and thoroughly understand these structures. Such a clear model will give you natural ways to group customer values, which will help with future model expansion, modification, and system implementation. Indeed, studying these structures is one of the few positive ways to move producer-space work into earlier in the overall lifecycle (by analyzing these structures while gath-ering customer values). This puts the team well on the way to a domain-oriented product family design while value resolution is still in full swing.

There are several ways to identify the structures in the customer space. One way is to start with Grady Booch's approach of writing down a description of what your system is supposed to do. We could have taken the above discussion of gas station payments and completed it this way. The nouns in such a description correspond to either objects or classes (and we may be able to group some of the objects into classes). If we write our description in terms of the customer space, the classes will be customer space abstractions.

Another way to identify classes is to base them on the Madey-Parnas Four-Variable Model (FVM), discussed in Chapter 19. We won't preview that discus-sion here, but it's worth noting that something like the Booch approach and the

FVM approach can be combined, which is the approach Jim used on the Lockheed Martin 382J Mission Computer Operational Flight Program project described in Appendix A.

However you choose to identify your classes, their content and interfaces must then be defined. Dr. Parnas' information-hiding principle shows how this is done. The form and details are folded into what Parnas calls "abstract interfaces."

Abstract interfaces can be used for either customer-space or producer-space (e.g., software-oriented) abstractions. The concept of information hiding doesn't really care. However, our description below uses some examples from the producer space (stacks) because that allows the examples to be substantial, yet short enough to be placed within the short bullets. Customer-space classes such as credit payment and acknowledging of the payment defined similarly and are created before the producer-space ones. Producer-space classes get added to an architecture either late in the design stream, to support the customer space classes with specific software capabilities (such as a stack), or in the production stream itself, when an individual product in the family needs some additional and unique (so there's no need to add them to the domain architecture) capabilities not provided by the domain architecture.

Abstract interfaces are used for both classes and for their methods or operations. The abstract interfaces for a class include the following kinds of information:

- *Name:* A short, descriptive name for the class; e.g., purchase receipt, or data stack.
- *Abstraction:* What the class encapsulates, from the user's view. For example: if the class implements simple stacks, "a simple stack, supporting LIFO adding and removing of elements."
- *Secrets:* Types of details that are likely to change and that are visible only within the class. Example: "how the structure of the stack is represented internally." However, one would not state specifics here, like "the stack is currently kept in a linked list."
- *Invariants:* Statements about the class that must always be true. Example: "The stack will never exceed its bounds."
- *Initial State:* Predefined condition of the device's parameters. Example: "stack starts out empty." This state must also satisfy the invariants.
- *Usage Requirements:* Conditions the class will assume are true when any of its methods are invoked via its operations. Example: "Editor class assumes any text files it opens end with ASCII ^Z." Also called "preconditions."

Identifying invariants is particularly helpful, though seldom done in traditional development. As Parnas said, "Abstract interfaces . . . are less likely to change than the 'secrets' that they hide. In fact, the design of that interface is quite difficult.... We have, however, found a procedure that seems to be practical—even in real-world situations. It breaks the design of the interface into two phases: 1) The development of a list of assumptions believed unlikely to change during the lifecycle of the product, and 2) the specification of a set of interface functions whose implementability is guaranteed by those assumptions. We have found that the first phase, which is the most difficult and time-consuming because many people must be consulted, eliminates a lot of errors that were made when it is skipped."[4] The things that never change come at two levels; the things in the domain that stay the same (e.g., pen and paper), and their invariants. We have already discussed the former. Of the latter, we'll say that, if you know the invariants of the class, you have found a great clue to the most stable way to select its interface operations. Maximizing stability is at the very heart of the domain mindset, so discovering the invariants is a key difference between single-product and domain design.

The abstract interfaces for each method or operation included the following information:

- *Name:* A short, descriptive title for the method.
- *Type:* Either "Generalization" or "Specialization." Generalization is essentially a class of operations within the class, for which instances will have to be identified and defined later, such as during detailed design. Specialization is a class of operations with one and only one instance, whose nature is already known so no further work will need to be done to identify it later. There are examples of both types of operations in the 382J software architecture described in Appendix A.
- *Effects:* What the method does for its caller, in terms of the class abstractions. For a pop operation on a stack class, the effect would be "stack returns the element on the stack placed there most recently by the 'push' method."
- *Parameters:* Names, each followed by direction, i.e., input, output, or input/output.
- *Usage Requirements:* Especially of the following two types:
  - *On previous processing before method invocation.* For example, if beforehand, other operations must have been invoked.
  - *On the class's data.* For example, "class internal data must have been initialized."
- *Undesired Events/Results.* Identifying undesired things that may be attempted in using the method, and what should be done to handle them. Example: "if pop stack is attempted when stack is empty, return a status and do not change stack."

Note that the examples in the above bullets do not always represent good software engineering (particularly the dependency on other operations being invoked first): They are chosen to illustrate what kind of information goes under each item.

The remainder of Part III, combined with the project example in Appendix A, gives many ideas about ways to conduct domain-oriented product-family development. Unfortunately, there are not many good references describing lean approaches to domain engineering. The best ones come from the Software Productivity Consortium in Herndon, Virginia. One that's available to nonmembers is the *Reuse-Driven Software Processes Guidebook*.[5] If your company belongs to the Consortium, it is also worthwhile to read their documentation on their OOASIS[6] method. If you do not have access to the SPC members-only material, you can find some of the ideas upon which the creators of OOASIS drew, in *Object-Oriented Software Engineering: A Use Case Driven Approach*.[7]

The Domain-Driven Lifecycle

Domain engineering does not end with developing a domain model, of course. It carries the domain structuring to the end of the development so that the product does not lose the flexibility and expandability that you've obtained by orienting around the customer-space structures. Also, in a business environment where software development is a lower-level activity that fits into a larger system development and where the line between software and system engineering isn't drawn too sharply, software developers can help develop a domain model of the entire system. Later development of the software goes better when the system as a whole is also structured around the natural divisions of the customer domain.

We can break domain engineering into the following six phases and their subsequent tasks. We assume that there is tight interaction with real customers. In an iterative (e.g., spiral) lifecycle model, many of these phases will be happening simultaneously on different parts of the software system.

Six Phases of Domain Engineering

1. System engineering

- Identify subdomains (if applicable, and if overall domain is too large).
- Software group feeds back to system group the software implications of system-level decisions, especially those concerning how the system partitions the overall product domain.
- Facilitate concurrent engineering with hardware and systems groups.

2. Software analysis

- Create high-integrity software requirements from customer values.
- Assess the likelihood of change for each customer value and any requirements derived from it.
- Identify natural and recurring structures in problem (customer) domain.
- Assign customer values and requirements to structures in problem domain, accounting for possible change.

3. Software architectural design

- Identify generalized entities and processing structures (customer-space oriented at high levels, producer-space oriented beneath).
- Isolate functionality with high change risk.
- Separate system-specific functionality and structures from domain functionality and structures (different classes, different methods).

4. Software detailed design

- Create templates from generalized processing structures.
- Produce specialized versions of generalized processing structures for specific uses.
- Structure detailed interface data based on domain information.

5. Software coding and unit verification

- Fill out the domain-structure with the particulars of the design space (complete the secrets of the objects based on the classes).
- Verify the units based on generalization structures (test or statically analyze for conformance).

6. Integration and acceptance

- Order the implementation based on priorities developed under the value principle.
- Tightly involve the customer with acceptance through small build increments, simulation, and other strategies.

Note that halfway through the detailed design activities listed above, the transition between the design stream and the production stream begins. That is, creating templates is clearly part of creating the product-family design. However, filling out those templates for a particular product in the product family (and doing all subsequent activities) is outside the scope of the design stream, but inside the scope of the production stream. Nevertheless, planning for how the filling out, coding, verifying, integrating, and accepting will be done is still inside the design stream.

Some concrete examples of work done in these stages are found in Appendix A, which explores a major project that has used domain engineering and other lean production techniques covered in this book. That project is the software development for the Lockheed Martin 382J Airlifter's Mission Computer (MC) Operational Flight Program (OFP). The discussion of that project refers to techniques introduced throughout Part III, so it won't make complete sense until you have finished reading all the chapters here. However, you can look it over at any time to see how specific approaches like domain engineering have been used on a real project.

Model-Driven Architecture (MDA)

A relatively recent approach to development that meshes well with domain engineering is Model-Driven Architecture (MDA).

Software technologies grow more and more abstract and powerful. First, there was machine code; then assemblers, then compilers, then 4GLs, then middleware, and so forth. With more and more competitors in the technologies at any given level of abstraction, the implementation choices grow, and the clarity of the line between the customer space and the producer space blurs ever more. That's because the closer the technology gets to the work, the easier it is to confuse the technology with the natural characteristics of the customer space. People tend to assume that ATM machines are givens in the banking world, simply because they are so ubiquitous. ATMs are, however, merely a popular implementation technology. One could imagine replacing them, for instance, with reader/writers for smart cards that a customer could recharge at home (Europeans already have large pieces of this technology in place).

MDA is an approach to keeping the two spaces separate and distinct. It comes from the OMG (Object Management Group). The OMG is a consortium of hundreds of companies in the computer industry and many from other industries like aerospace, healthcare, telecommunications, and government. From its beginnings in the late 1980s, the OMG was composed mostly of the users of object-oriented technology, rather than its originators. "The OMG is responsible for providing solutions to industry problems."[8] The OMG was created because users wanted standardized approaches to their problems, and existing standards groups, like the ISO and the SAE could not react quickly enough to rapidly changing software technologies. One of the first major standards of the OMG was for a middleware layer for distributed databases, called CORBA (Common Object Request Broker: Architecture).

Developers originally conceived of middleware as a way to separate the user's needs from the changing technologies of operating systems, database servers, and so forth. However, by the late 1990s, it was becoming clear that even middleware was becoming a producer-space technology. User applications needed to be ported between different middleware environments, e.g., ONE, .NET, CORBA, or EJB. To continue to support specifying systems in customer space terms, a broader perspective and higher layer of abstraction was needed; so developers created MDA (Model-Driven Architecture).

MDA conceives of a system at two levels: PIM, or Platform-Independent Model, and as many PSMs, or Platform-Specific Models, as necessary. Each PSM defines an interface between the PIM and a platform-specific environment such as a specific type of middleware. Anything that is platform-specific belongs to the producer space, so dividing along these lines strengthens the separation between customer space and producer space, which is so important in a lean software process. "MDA divorces implementation details from business functions."[9] This also supports the idea of an abstract interface and secrets. Because MDA is a metaspecification approach, it is also being used for other abstractions, like capturing the business requirements for new standards and relating them to new technologies that implement them.

Both PIMs and PSMs are recorded in UML. MDA also draws on other abstractions and information representations like XML, XMI (XML Meta-Data Interchange), MOF (Meta-Object Facility), and the CWM (Common Warehouse MetaModel). CWM is itself recorded in UML (UML and CWM were the first and second metamodels conforming to the MOF worked on by the OMG—phew; what a string of acronyms!). The CWM is essentially an abstract representation of data schemas, "an object model with a set of Application Programming Interface (APIs), interchange formats and services for the wide range of metadata involved in the extraction, transformation, transportation, loading, integration, and analysis phases of data warehouse projects."[10] In other words, the CWM allows integrating data from all the various databases, web pages, text files, XML documents, and other types of repositories in which data are found. The CWM is at a higher level than XML: "XML does not understand the basic principals of inheritance, polymorphism, collaboration, and different types of relationships. XML understands containment, which means you can embed documents and links and you can have access across content and links, but you cannot have different types of relationships."[11]

Some vendors have tightened up UML by subsetting it and adding a semi-formal executable specification language. This is a tremendous advance because it makes it possible to also implement the lean perfection principle in the UML end of the domain-engineering world. The British have always been leaders in formal methods, and a standout vendor of semiformal UML is a British firm, Kennedy Carter Ltd. Their product, iUML, combines an MDA methodology with their xUML representation (xUML is real UML and obeys the UML metamodel). It also supports dynamic simulation of the model and automatic code generation from the PIM and a PSM. Lockheed Martin Aerospace Company used some of this technology to create a successful autocode generation environment for aircraft mission software on the F-16 MMC demonstration project. Kennedy Carter is mentioned here simply as an example of how this technology can be made increasingly lean. Other vendors are also taking MDA in the same direction.

Object Orientation

Object-oriented methods provide some useful tools for working on domain models; for instance, all object-oriented methods derive classes. This satisfies the first of the three points for developing a good domain model, being class-like—so multiple instances are allowed for the classes in the domain. You can enhance most object-oriented methods to create a domain-modeling method by adding analyses of the second and third issues, i.e., class stability, and grouping of classes, functions, and data based on change due to the same stimulus.

Whichever OO method you choose, you should incorporate these three aspects of domain analysis (they are not inherent to OO):

1. Stability over time
2. Grouping by response to change stimuli
3. Information hiding

Since this book is not a primer on object-oriented methods, it is left to the reader to select a specific method. The evolution of late has been towards layered metamethods like Kennedy Carter's iUML, discussed above. The Rational Unified Process[12] methodology is still quite popular. Sally Schlaer and Steve Mellor of Schlaer-Mellor methodology[13] fame have developed an interesting recursive methodology.[14] As mentioned earlier in the book, XP includes a methodology that is based on user stories and that you can adapt for use outside of XP. Many methodologies can be effective, and different domains call for different approaches. In most cases, the best approach is the grow-your-own method, which combines techniques, representations, and tool support from various sources. Then you can account for the unique needs of your domain, the priorities of your organization, and the respective strengths and weaknesses of each off-the-shelf method. In many cases, you can represent products using the UML symbols and diagrams, though again, with the exception of formal subsets of UML, the representation will lack the benefits and waste reductions that come with mathematical rigor.

Jim used several object-oriented methods for domain analysis and design, and found them all helpful *in the context of a lean lifecycle*. However, when the lean principles are not applied, any method—OO or otherwise—will lead to high levels of *muda* (two common side effects of nonlean development are paralysis by analysis and rampant backflows—a condition where fixing is a major part of the process, and which we will more fully explore later in this book).

It is easy to become so intoxicated with modeling, metamodeling, and extended computing metaphors that one tends to lose day-to-day sight of the point of the whole exercise, which is to deliver value to the customer and to improve one's business performance. Even among those who keep business purposes firmly in mind, there is a tendency to assume that OO naturally leads to better business outcomes. People have assumed the same thing about each of the popular technologies before OO, and each time, the assumption has proven wrong (the sad tale about the promising project discussed in Chapter 1 being a particularly stark example).

The most advanced object-oriented project Jim has ever seen—one that used the most powerful software methods, tools, and partitioning and interfacing concepts, such as domain development, XML-based techniques, and MDA-like layering—could only produce software at slightly worse than the average industry productivity rate for traditionally developed non-OO projects. This was far less productive than the C-27J project, which used fewer of these advanced OO techniques but many more lean ones, and is discussed in Appendix A along with its antecedent, the 382J. What the advanced OO project lacked was the infrastructure of a lean project. There was little value resolution, and the requirements analysis lacked the consistent integrity needed to undergird many of the lean techniques discussed in this chapter and throughout Part III. Furthermore, there was little sign of value stream or flow, and no sign of pull or perfection.

Experience in other industries has shown that the potential performance of new techniques and technologies is hampered when they are employed in antiquated production paradigms. There has been no evidence to date that software gets a pass from this rule.

Synergies

Domain engineering, as helpful as it is, is not a panacea. It has weaknesses too, particularly in its area of greatest strength: Because a domain design produces so many parts and products from so few architectural elements, if the domain design is flawed, it will seed flaws into every product.

A domain design can be flawed because its requirements are flawed, or because its development has corrupted the good that was in the requirements it received. Yet, domain engineering itself pays little attention to either the quality of its inputs (it assumes they are good), or to ways of retaining its own quality as it goes along.

Fortunately, other techniques complement domain engineering in these areas. Where domain engineering is weak on protecting itself from poor incoming requirements, value resolution (which we studied extensively in Part II) and formal methods will ensure it receives correct and complete requirements. Where domain engineering is weak on retaining quality, formal methods help protect the integrity of the evolving domain design.

Let's look at how these three strategies relate to and work with each other.

Formal Methods

Formal methods, which we've touched upon a few times already, are approaches to developing requirements, design, coding, and verification based upon rigorous mathematics (formal design and code only benefit a project that begins with formal requirements, because of the GIGO or Garbage-In, Garbage-Out principle).

As such, formal methods produce high integrity software, i.e., software that is correct, unambiguous, complete, and nonredundant. Formally produced software will function predictably and without failure under every circumstance in its targeted environment, surely a positive to most customers. Also, the rigor of the mathematics makes verification simple. All one must do is show that the rules of the mathematics have not been violated. This is much easier to demonstrate than it is to verify nonformal systems. Verification of the latter must attempt to rule out a nearly infinite universe of possible misbehaviors by the software. Mathematicians have proven that this cannot be done exhaustively for anything except trivially sized software. Doing it even reasonably well requires multitudes of test cases. So, verification is much less expensive with formal software.

However, formal methods also have tremendous weaknesses. Chief among them is that most are poor at communicating ideas with anyone except the method experts. This is because most FMs use specialized, abstract, and non-intuitive mathematical representations. Such formal methods are therefore weak at validation, i.e., at helping you get the customer's feedback on whether your requirements have correctly represented their values. This in turn undercuts your ability to cultivate good relations with your customer—one of the two top concerns for having a successful project (the other being business planning, which formal methods do not affect one way or the other). The opaqueness of formal methods also complicates personnel management, because the unusual expertise the methods require limits the labor pool available to the business and drives up costs.

Using formal methods to develop a given piece of a system takes longer than developing the same piece nonformally. This makes costs balloon quickly when there are going to be more than a trivial number of changes to the system during or after development, because the more changes there are to a given piece, the more times you redevelop that piece. This weakness is exacerbated in systems that are highly volatile, or whose architectures fail to isolate change to the minimum possible scope (allowing inherently small changes to affect larger than necessary parts of the system).

Requirements produced under most formal methods do not import easily into other lifecycle phases without significant between-phase manipulation, and such manipulations are wasteful, time-consuming, and costly. Such requirements are a form of inventory, which, as we will see in a later chapter, is a classic form of mass production waste.

Finally, formal methods do not scale-up well. That is, they work best on very small pieces of logic, but as the logic becomes more complicated or involved, the time and complexity required to use them goes up exponentially.

Most formal methods, therefore, are poor on most of the criteria for good requirements! The one formal method of which Jim is personally aware that does well on several of these areas of weaknesses (though not all of them) is SCR, which we discussed under value resolution. SCR will play a role in our discussion again shortly.

In the past, the weaknesses of most formal methods have ruled out their use on all but a few applications in which obtaining their strengths at verification are mandatory. Even with their downsides, formal methods have proven invaluable in situations where failure is not an option. One is nuclear power plant control. Others are fields like secure software, to assure it cannot be hacked, and in transportation systems where system failure could mean the destruction of a vehicle and the death of the passengers. In such cases, nothing but formal methods will do. Of course, we'd like for any system we build to be failure-free. The trick is to procure the benefits of formal methods without being dragged down by their shortcomings.

Domain Engineering

Domain engineering has strengths and weaknesses that are in many cases opposite to those of formal methods.

Domain engineering is strong on validation, at least of the natural structures in the customer space. After all, one of the main purposes of domain engineering is to identify that which is universal about a category of customers, and that which is likely to change. You must understand the customer's values, and get their agreement that you've understood them correctly, to have a true domain design.

Whereas formal methods are sensitive to change, domain engineering is focused on creating a stable design and on isolating the effects of change to the smallest possible scope, to individual modules, when possible. In a domain-engineered system, any given change will affect the smallest part of the system possible.

While formal methods do not scale-up well, domain engineering is ideal for creating an architecture composed of naturally small pieces. Not every domain architect does so. There is nothing about domain development that requires the architectural elements it produces to be small, though small pieces are more in keeping with the spirit of domain architecture which includes limiting the effects of system changes to the smallest possible part of the system.

Value Resolution

Figure 15-1 shows how combining the previous two methods with value resolution creates a complementary approach to address important customer and business needs. The parenthetic explanation in the final column should be read as, "due to a reduction in;" for example, "the <u>customer benefit</u> of <u>cost reduction</u> from <u>domain engineering</u> is due to a reduction in proliferation" (i.e., the extra costs due to the proliferation of discrete products when there is no domain-based product-line). Three dots indicate greatest strength; no dots indicate complete weakness.

Note how at least one of the three approaches solidly contributes to each important benefit. The strong approach in each case overcomes the weaknesses of the others in the area of that benefit. Some benefits, like cost and reduction of *muda*, are solidly addressed by all three approaches.

As important as these benefits are, there are many more of them when you have an integrated lifecycle. We shall see more on this when we explore the flow principle in Chapter 19.

Every approach or means (method, technique, tool, etc.) discussed in this book is potentially useful for creating an integrated lifecycle. No single project or business will need all of them. But when planning a project, you should consider how all of their strengths and weaknesses could be combined to achieve the specific goals of the business and project.

Customer Benefit

	Identifying Value	Deploying Value	Product Integrity	Cost Reduction
Formal Methods			● ● ●	● ● (rework)
Value Resolution	● ● ●			● ● ● (non-values)
Domain Engineering	●	● ● ●	●	● ● ● (proliferation)

Business Benefit

	Identifying Value	Deploying Value	Scale-up	*Muda* Reduction
Formal Methods				● ● ● (defects)
Value Resolution	● ● ●			● ● ● (wrong work)
Domain Engineering	●	● ● ●	● ● ●	● ● (redundancy)

Figure 15-1. Lean Benefits of Three Development Strategies

QFD

Quality Function Deployment (QFD) is a set of techniques that focus all efforts and all design traits at deploying a set of values into a set of product features. It was first used in the United States by Ford Motor Company around 1980, and reached software development in the United States in the late 1980s.

The concept of QFD is extremely powerful. Its original form uses matrices to map from customer values ("what's") to design characteristics ("how's") to design tradeoffs ("how much"). For larger projects, it provides a number of different matrices for deploying values through differing levels of development. An introduction to this form of QFD is Dr. Christian Madu's *House of Quality (QFD) in a Minute*.[15] QFD has been correlated to OO methods in the superb paper, "Integrating QFD with Object Oriented Software Design Methodologies."[16] The details of QFD fill many good reference books. Among them are Bob King's *Better Designs in Half the Time: Implementing QFD Quality Function Deployment in America*,[17] Louis Cohen's well-regarded *Quality Function Deployment*,[18] Herzwurm's, Schockert's, and Mellis' *Joint Requirements Engineering: QFD for Rapid User-Focused Software Development*,[19] and Guinta's and Praizler's *The QFD Book: The Team Approach to Solving Problems and Satisfying Customers Through Quality Function Deployment*.[20]

QFD Derivatives

The pure form of QFD has, on occasion, been criticized both for being too limited and too time-consuming. Various parties have both extended and simplified the original QFD methods. A U.K. company, Time To Market, promotes an alternative they call pragmatic QFD, or pQFD.[21] pQFD simplifies the processes and adds greater consideration for market segmentation, Kano modeling, risk analyses, and a few other concerns. One of the leading consultants for applying QFD to software, Richard Zultner, has created Blitz QFD.[22] Zultner says that traditional QFD is more complex than it needs to be for most purposes, especially the portion called the House of Quality. Consequently, Blitz QFD largely dispenses with the matrix math and distills the QFD process to the following steps:

1. Go to *Gemba*
2. Sort the Verbatims
3. Structure the Customer Needs
4. Analyze the Customer Needs Structure
5. Prioritize the Customer Needs
6. Deploy Prioritized Customer Needs
7. Deploy Value Throughout Project

Note the similarity of the first five steps with the value principle (value resolution) we discussed in Part II, though the steps we used were derived quite independently. In step 2, Zultner distinguishes between different types of customer statements by calling the raw inputs "verbatims" and sorting them into categories such as needs, reliability, cost, technology, usability, and portability. He then allocates those to different treatments during the lifecycle. You may or may not find this treatment useful, but it is another potential tool in the toolkit.

One other adaptation of QFD that is worth noting is Distributed QFD (DQFD), originated by Digital. It extends QFD to support development that incorporates multiple work locations, work teams, and customers.

QFD and Concurrent Engineering

One of the best uses of QFD is to facilitate Concurrent Engineering (CE). CE takes the activities of product development that are sequential in traditional development—gathering of market information, development of customer requirements, development of design requirements, and production—and works them in parallel. Parallel work demands some sort of common touch point where everyone can see what everyone else has done, and extend it for the concerns of each activity. Developing the matrices and other products of QFD provides this common touch point, and enables CE. This addresses the same lifecycle weaknesses as does XP, i.e., a *dependency* on getting everything right, up front. Additionally, it does so in a way that incorporates more of a top-down strategic approach (again, through the matrices and other QFD products). For more information on using QFD to enable CE, see Madu's *House of Quality (QFD) in a Minute*.[23]

Though QFD is primarily focused on adding value, the first goal of the value, followed stream, then following it diligently (i.e., by not allowing work outside the mandate provided by the QFD matrices except by consciously deciding to accept it as type 1 or necessary *muda*), QFD will also contribute to the second goal of eliminating non-value-adding work.

Other Ways of Defining Product Families

Additional interesting references on how to create product families include Clement's and Northrop's "*Software Product Lines: Practices and Patterns*,"[24] based on the SEI's Product-Line Framework program, and Atkinson et al.'s "*Component-Based Product Line Engineering with UML*,"[25] a UML-based approach to product-family development. Be careful how you adapt what is in these books: Too literal a reading can lead you back into mass production and the problems we noted in Part I. Hold to the principles of lean production first, and ideas like these become good resources to draw from in creating a lean production process that helps you better achieve your company's goals.

ENDNOTES

1. *Lean Thinking*, pg. 247.
2. *Lean Thinking*, pg. 255.
3. *Real-time Object Oriented Analysis & Design Using the UML V 5.2*, pg. 71, I-Logix, Inc., 2002.
4. D. L. Parnas, "Some Software Engineering Principles," pg. 263, from *Software Fundamentals: Collected Papers by David L. Parnas*, Reading, Massachusetts: Addison-Wesley, 2001.
5. *Reuse-Driven Software Processes Guidebook*, SPC-92019-CMC version 02.00.03. Software Productivity Consortium, 1993.
6. http://www.software.org/MEMBERSONLY/OOASIS/pverview.asp, as of July 12, 2004.
7. Jacobson, Christerson, Jonsson, Övergaard, *Object-Oriented Software Engineering: A Use Case Driven Approach*. Reading, Massachusetts: Addison-Wesley, 1992.
8. *The OMG Hitchhiker's Guide*, December 2002, pg. 3.
9. From the OMG website FAQs on MDA: www.omg.org/mda/faq_mda.htm, February 15 , 2003.
10. R. Seeley, "Is CWMI the Holy Grail of Meta Data Standards?," eAI Journal, February 15 , 2003.
11. R. Seeley, "Is CWMI the Holy Grail of Meta Data Standards?," eAI Journal, February 15 , 2003.
12. I. Jacobson, G. Booch, J. Rumbaugh, *The Unified Software Development Process*, Reading, Massachusetts: Addison-Wesley, February 1999.
13. S. Shlaer, S. Mellor, *Object-Oriented Systems Analysis: Modeling the World in Data*, New York, NY: Yourdon, 1988; and S. Shlaer, S. Mellor, *Object Lifecycles: Modeling the World in States*, New York, NY: Yourdon, 1991.
14. S. Shlaer, S. Mellor, *Recursive Design*, Englewood Cliffs, NJ: Prentice Hall, January 2003.
15. C. Madu, *House of Quality (QFD) in a Minute*, Fairfield, CT: Chi Publishers, November 2000.
16. W. Lamia, *Integrating QFD with Object Oriented Software Design Methodologies*, QFDi, Proceedings of 7th Symposium on QFD, 1995; article available online at time of publication at http://www.nauticom.net/www/qfdi/7thSymposium.Papers/QFD_OOD.pdf.
17. B. King, *Better Designs in Half the Time: Implementing Quality Function Deployment in America*, Methuen, MA: GOAL/QPC, December 1989.
18. L. Cohen, *Quality Function Deployment*, Englewood Cliffs, NJ: Prentice Hall, July 1995.
19. G. Herzwurm, S. Schockert, W. Mellis, *Joint Requirements Engineering*, New York, NY: Springer Verlag, 2003.
20. L. Guinta, N. Praizler, *The QFD Book: The Team Approach to Solving Problems and Satisfying Customers Through Quality Function Deployment*, AMACOM, 1993.

21. At the time of publishing, a website giving an overview of their approach was http://www.ttm.co.uk/xtspqfdpage1.htm. Any significant information on the approach would have to be obtained directly from the company.

22. Zultner teaches a course on Blitz QFD, and a couple of articles have also been published:

    R. Zultner, "Blitz QFD: Better, Faster, and Cheaper Forms of QFD;" American Programmer, October,1995, pgs. 24–36.

    And, specifically for use in Rapid Development (RAD):

    M. P. McDonald, "Achieving Software Quality in a RAD Process;" ASQC 4th International Conference on Software Quality Proceedings, McLean, VA, October 1994.

23. C. Madu, *House of Quality (QFD) in a Minute*, Fairfield, CT: Chi Publishers, November 2000, Chapter 9.

24. P. Clements, L. M. Northrop, *Software Product Lines: Practices and Patterns*, Reading, MA: Addison-Wesley, August 2001.

25. C. Atkinson, J. Bayer, C. Bunse, E. Kamsties, O. Laitenberger, R. Laqua, D. Muthig, B. Paech, J. Wust, J. Zettel, *Component-Based Product Line Engineering with UML*, Reading, MA: Addison-Wesley, November 2001.

16

The Value Stream—Production

NOW THAT WE HAVE EXPLORED HOW TO CREATE lean product families using the design stream, we can move on to the development of a final product or program based on a family. As we said in the last chapter, this part of development is called the production stream.

Chapter 3 showed that the production stream breaks down into a material branch and an information branch. Recall that the material branch is the set of activities that construct the product that comes down the production line. Material, in the software world, includes things like values, requirements, design, and code. Material passes from one stage of production to another.

On the other hand, the information branch was defined as the set of activities that coordinate and control (rather than perform) the production activities from order taking through product delivery. The information used to do this needs to be proactively shared between interdependent stages of material production, including those that strategically plan and track all of production.

One of the main things that makes a project's value stream truly lean is the explicit consideration of its two major streams, design and production, and of the branches of the production stream, material and information. Traditional mass production reengineering limits itself mostly to the information branch side of production and largely ignores both the design stream and the material branch side of the production stream. On the other hand, software management often emphasizes the material branch (the steps directly involved in producing the code), while going light on the information branch. We'll examine techniques that help with both branches of the software production stream.

Production is done by a framework of cooperating activities inside of a particular lifecycle model. The relationships between those activities, and the model in which they occur, dictate how the material branch and information branch operate. Let's begin by identifying which activities are naturally related to each other, using the representation called the V cycle.

Associating the Production Activities: The V Cycle

All major lifecycle models break a lifecycle into discrete high-level activities like specification (e.g., value resolution, requirements analysis), design, implementation (e.g., coding), and acceptance (e.g., testing). Varying models differ in how they define these activities. Maintenance and modification are usually accounted for by some variation on the main production activities.

Furthermore, the associations between activities are very similar from model to model. Such associations include both material passing and information passing. One representation of these associations is the V cycle chart (see Figure 16-1). The V cycle has been around for many years but remains current and useful today. While the V cycle is not a lean concept per se (it was invented before lean production took hold outside of Japan), its ideas help to avoid waste, a central concern of lean production. It's current for another reason: Its ideas can be implemented in any lifecycle model except the waterfall, as we shall see later. And finally, projects need, but often fail, to sufficiently define or support the material and information dependencies between their major development activities.

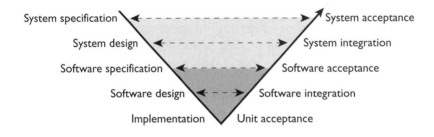

Figure 16-1. The Classic "V" Lifecycle

The V cycle chart has four quadrants: Development activities are on the left side of an imaginary vertical line splitting the middle of the V chart (i.e., everything on the chart's down arrow), release activities are on the right side of the imaginary line (on the up arrow), system activities are above an imaginary horizontal line splitting the chart at the natural transition between system and software, and software activities are on the lower half of the chart, below the same imaginary horizontal line.

By explicitly showing system-level concerns, the V chart addresses software that is placed within systems of systems. Software is, of course, often integrated with other software or hardware elements. The upper part of the V chart represents the concerns of this level of development and integration. The shading within the levels of the chart roughly represents the ideal degree of software-personnel involvement in that type of activity. As one would expect, the shading is darkest in the software part of the lifecycle, where software people are fully involved. Shading is lighter, but still present, in the system activities, because it is important for software people to be active contributors to the team that does this work as well (e.g., providing feedback to the systems engineers about how the alternatives they are considering would affect the upcoming software development).

The most important message of the V chart is that any development-stream activity is connected to other activities along two dimensions: 1) along the main (diagonal) arrow (roughly speaking, the time dimension) and 2) across horizontally (the conceptual dimension). Along the main arrow, each activity looks forward to the next activity to be performed and backward to the activity performed immediately before it. Horizontally, only one associated activity is closely related (the one at the same level on the other side of the V).

Consider the activity of software requirements specification. Looking ahead along the main arrow, the next activity is software design. The previous activity along the arrow is system design. The activity across the V, at the same conceptual level, is software acceptance. These three activities have the direct material- and information-passing interfaces with the software requirements specification activity.

Each of the high-level activities in the V is composed of lower-level tasks that are not shown on the chart. For instance, software requirements specification contains lower-level activities like value resolution (if it has not been done at the system level, or if it was done, but needs to be extended at the level of the particular software product to be created), requirements analysis, requirements validation, and so forth. Bigger projects may need to model the relationships between these tasks as well, to get a handle on the material and information flows between them. Simple techniques like data flow analysis come in useful for this. Even better is to divide the activities and their products into classes with information hiding and abstract interfaces (as we discussed doing with the domain architecture in Chapter 15). The resulting process architecture is less sensitive to change and has fewer, simpler, and more fundamental interfaces, all of which contribute to making production more robust.

Lifecycle Models

While the V relates individual lifecycle activities to each other, a lifecycle model relates all lifecycle activities to each other and to management strategies as well. How well the techniques of the value stream work together depends, to some extent, on which lifecycle model you chose for development. We'll look at a couple of the most important ones from this perspective. Our discussion isn't intended to cover all the models that exist; only the ones most relevant to our topic of the production branch.

Waterfall

The familiar waterfall is what we get when we navigate the V one–dimensionally, that is, when we restrict ourselves to a forward traverse of the main line of the V, from system concept to final system acceptance. There are no repetitions and usually little looking ahead, such as that from software requirements to software acceptance.

It's probably no surprise by now that the waterfall model is poorly suited to lean production. After all, even without becoming lean, software businesses have largely abandoned this most venerable of the lifecycle models. The high walls between the phases of a waterfall lifecycle effectively limit both material- and information-sharing to being one-way . . . from an earlier phase to a later one.

This prevents using all of the most powerful lean production-branch techniques: They all depend on activities being repeated so they can be improved. Furthermore, lacking the opportunity to feed lessons learned from later phases to earlier ones, you cannot adapt to prevent errors from repeating; all you can do is go back and fix them afterward.

Spiral

The spiral model lifecycle is the dominant lifecycle of the software industry, especially when you consider its many incarnations, including RAD, component-based reuse, and narrow-slice anticipatory development (the latter is discussed in its own section shortly). Whether projects are capitalizing on the potential in the spiral is another question that we will consider later in this chapter, under the topic of the information branch.

The classic spiral model is illustrated in Figure 16-2. You could call it the "strategize, explore, build, and prepare" (to start again) cycle. The spiral could be applied to a monolithic project built all at once, but that is not its best or its intended use. Far better is to divide the project into a large number of similar pieces (see the discussion of "Big Parts" in Chapter 19 for how to do this). Then think of the project as a stack of spirals, each piece with its own spiral. Early pieces go through the complete spiral, while later pieces go through only the parts of the spiral that apply to them individually.

The spiral model is risk-driven, because the first thing you do after determining what you want to do (the first quadrant, on the upper left) is identify and understand the risks to your successfully doing it (the second quadrant, on the upper right). Then you try out ways to decrease those risks (the prototyping at the end of that quadrant). At a project management level, you devote the earliest

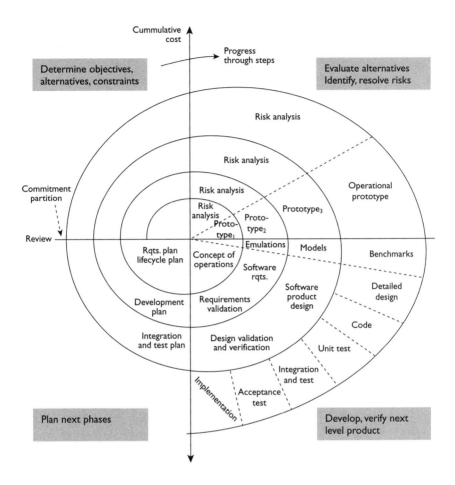

Figure 16-2. The Classic Spiral Lifecycle[1]

repetitions of the complete spiral to the highest-risk as well as highest-value parts of the system.

By building a system in small increments, in which each increment goes through its own lifecycle development, the spiral model supports production-stream techniques such as value stream mapping and *kaizen*, which analyze past iterations of work to improve future ones, and to which we will return in the material branch section of this chapter.

If the product being developed is the first one in that domain for the business, the project can also use the spiral model for the design stream . . . taking a spiral or two to lay a good foundation in value resolution, domain orientation, and value deployment (e.g., using QFD), especially if the narrow-slice approach is used (see the next section).

There have been some very interesting extensions to the fundamental spiral model. One is the Win–Win Spiral (Figure 16-3), which incorporates elements of the lean value principle:

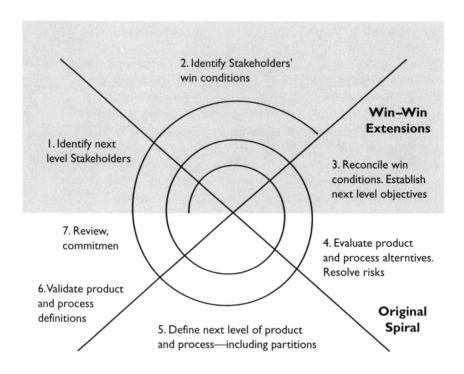

Figure 16-3. The Win–Win Spiral Lifecycle[2]

Another fascinating extension of the classic spiral model maps its phases onto the V cycle, as shown in Figure 16-4.

Each of these extensions moves the classic spiral, already a good basis for lean development, further towards the principles of lean production.

XP

XP is very friendly to the production-stream aspect of the value stream and provides a good environment for VSM and *kaizen* in particular. However, both domain engineering and QFD require strong up-front commitments. XP, in its purest form, puts little weight on or effort into such setup work. Instead, it counts on requirements and design to evolve over many generations of changes. This approach limits the benefits that XP can gain from the techniques of the design-stream aspect of the value stream. (As we've discussed before, it is highly questionable that refactoring a design repeatedly will lead to an optimal domain

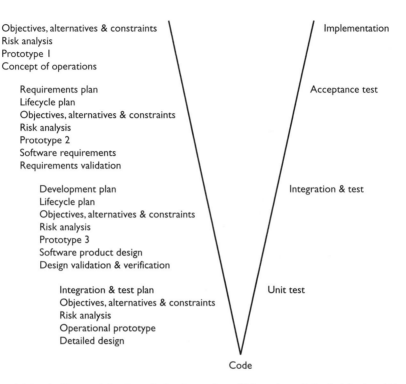

Figure obtained with permission from Cutter Consortium: 37 Broadway, Suite 1, Arlington, MA 02474; 781-648-8700)

Figure 16-4. The V Form of the Classic Spiral Lifecycle[3]

design for a product family, even though it may well lead to a good single-system design. In addition, repeatedly refactoring a design, instead of avoiding most of these changes through a domain approach, injects more *muda* into development.)

However, if you allow more up-front work in an XP project to lay a stronger-than-usual foundation through value resolution, QFD-style design allocations, and domain structuring, thus delaying the start of the wide-open extreme evolutionary part of the lifecycle, then an XP project could benefit from both major branches of the value stream. In this case, XP essentially becomes a special case of the classic spiral development lifecycle.

Narrow Slice Anticipatory Development

Lockheed Martin Aero's 382J project used a spiral lifecycle with an additional twist dubbed narrow-slice anticipatory development. This addressed some of the concerns of XP in a spiral context and proved very helpful and effective.

A narrow slice is a complete piece of the system, functional from system inputs to system outputs, though aspects of either inputs or outputs can be simulated to help with carving out a small enough piece.

The narrow-slice lifecycle depends on having initial versions of the domain (i.e., the product family) architecture and of the production development processes, already defined. A small rapid-response team then takes the intended development processes and architecture and essentially prototypes the production through a complete lifecycle iteration for the narrow slice of the system.

The members of this team are essentially the scouts for the project, moving quickly ahead of the army of developers following them. The scouts validate the domain characteristics of the design, the efficacy of the processes, the testing approach, and any other decisions made to that point. Which slice they choose depends on which part of the system is defined well enough at this early point to allow development. It also depends on which slice will give the best validation of design and processes for the amount of effort expected. There is no formula for choosing a slice, but the 382J project found that people who know their domains well could also choose a slice effectively. The C-382J narrow-slice scouts provided quick feedback on weaknesses in the domain design, identifying producer-space issues that had not been addressed well enough. The scouts also identified weaknesses in the processes, which actually hindered the work rather than helped it.

On the 382J, the domain design and the technical processes quickly evolved because of the feedback from the narrow-slice team. When the overall project lifecycle and the main body of developers reached the point where many people were developing the major parts of the system in parallel, the domain design was robust enough that it needed very few additional changes. Furthermore, the changes that came after this point tended to affect only a few isolated parts of the system and impacted few of the developers and few of their products (detailed designs or source implementations). The main-body developers also found the processes to be generally smooth and supportive, facilitating the high rates of productivity needed and reached on this program.

The Material Branch

The material branch is the set of activities and processes that construct the product. Another way of saying this is that the material-branch processes are the ones that directly add value to the product. Thus, the material branch deals with items such as requirements, designs, and code. However, it does not create (though it does use) the domain architectural design. That comes from the design stream side of the value stream.

Our focus in this section will be on removing waste from an existing production line and its activities that create this material and from the transitions between those activities. In Chapters 17–21, we will take an extended look at creating a production line and material branch, i.e., at specific techniques and tools that can be used to add value to the product.

Value Stream Mapping

Most software production is filled with *muda*. The goal of the lean technique called value-stream mapping, which we will cover in this section, and of *kaizen*, which we cover in the next, is to identify and then remove these wastes from production processes.

Production workers often don't realize when their work is not contributing to any useful results from the customer or business perspectives. The only good perch from which to view the purpose of each production activity is at a high enough elevation that which you can see all the steps and their relationships at the same time. In lean thinking, the best way to do this is to draw a map of the value stream for the entire production line. In the software industry, the map will describe the stages in software production and the information and product streams between them. Beware, however: Everybody wants to think his or her work has been important to the group's success. Some may strongly resist any analysis that could conceivably suggest otherwise. Tact is called for in creating and using a value stream map. A good way to explain this is that all the previous work was important, because it was all part of the process used to develop products. All that is in question now is what is needed in the new, lean process, not the necessity of people's work to the old one.

Value Stream Mapping (VSM) is a technique that tracks a product as it proceeds through production. VSM starts with the product's inception and goes through to its delivery. It includes all activities on the material branch, as well as on the information branch (covered later in this chapter). VSM aims to identify wasteful processes or activities that do not add value. VSM also detects "snags" where progress on building the product stops for long periods of time (so-called "white-space" time).

Using VSM makes the most sense in an iterative incremental lifecycle, such as a spiral. This is because there are many repetitions of the lifecycle as you produce each element in the overall system and you can learn from prior repetitions so you can improve future ones. What constitutes an element in the system varies depending on the particular type of lifecycle. For example, XP breaks up the product into increments based on user stories. Jim has done VSM in which the product increments were individual SCR requirements being incorporated into the product. We'll say more about building a product this way, when we get to the lean flow principle (Chapters 19 and 20).

VSM would not be useful in a traditional waterfall lifecycle: There is only one product, and by the time you've followed it through its lifecycle, it's too late to help that product's production stream. Perhaps VSM, under these conditions, could help with future developments of the same type, but the better approach would be to scrap the waterfall process and switch to an iterative process. VSM in our lean software lifecycle would start with production of an individual program from an existing product-family design.

You can do VSM in many ways. You can simply draw the map with pencil and paper, creating a picture of each work stage as an icon, with time annotations (when each stage begins and ends) and information dependencies between the stages shown as arrows. You can draw it as a timeline, with a square wave, which hits its upper bound only when productive work is being done, and with the names of the activities written above the line. You can record it as an industrial-engineering Process Flow Diagram (PFD), which explicitly shows operations, delays, storage, transport, and decisions.[4] Or, as Jim personally prefers, you can enter it into a spreadsheet as in Figure 16-5.

Regardless of how you record the VSM findings, you follow a single representative product element through its complete lifecycle (literally called "walking the process"). You do not apply the technique to every product element, just to one or, perhaps, a small sample. The level of detail with which you examine the work would take too much time (and drive the workers up the wall) if you applied it to everything.

For example, when using the spreadsheet approach, each time the product-in-work enters a new stage of production, you write this down along with the value-added time spent in the previous stage. You also record information that moves into or out of that stage to other stages. It helps to note why non-value-added time occurs. Combining all this information produces a current state map of what is actually happening during production.

You should avoid spending too much time creating any one VSM: Anywhere from 30 minutes to one day at most will do. Typically, the period of production time examined by single VSM will be longer than a day.

Each time the product transitions from one development stage or activity to another, a new row is added to the sheet. Also, each time a new productive period within the same activity occurs, a new row is added. There can be more than one row for the same activity, as when work starts and stops repeatedly on the same task. Don't explicitly record unproductive time (including idle time), but you can deduce such time at any point from the difference between total time to complete the activity minus productive or value-added time. State the reason for all unproductive time on the row recording the next productive period. Note the information dependencies between activities. Where there is *muda*, assess whether it's type 1 or type 2, as discussed in Chapter 3. A type 2

Activity/stage	Start		End		Info flow to next activity	Reason for delay since last productive	Muda type
Change control board	1/14/03	15:00	1/14/03	15:05	Approval to add to software build		
Initiate	1/15/03	10:30	1/15/03	10:31	Notification to next stage (NNS)	Software lead didn't check "incoming list"	2
Reqts. analysis	1/17/03	8:17	1/17/03	8:45		Reqts. analyst didn't check "incoming list"	2
Reqts. analysis	1/17/03	12:00	1/17/03	14:21	Updated requirement, NNS	Reqts. analyst had to wait for system engineer's reply	1
Design	1/17/03	14:30	1/17/03	14:31		Designer away from desk	?
Design	1/21/03	8:00	1/21/03	9:40		Designer busy on designs of other elements	1
Design	1/23/03	13:14	1/23/03	17:42	Updated package spec and body I/Fs, NNS	Designer given a "top priority" interrupt for another design	1
Coding	1/25/03	8:00	1/25/03	9:04	Problem Report (PR), action to reqts.	Coder didn't check "incoming list"	2
Reqts. analysis	1/26/03	11:38	1/26/03	15:18	Updated requirement, completed PR, NNS	Reqts. analyst out sick previous day	?
Design	1/27/03	9:52	1/27/03	14:40	Updated package spec and body I/Fs, NNS	Designer didn't check "incoming list"	2
Coding	1/28/03	10:12	1/28/03	11:32	Updated code, unit test results, NNS	Coder occupied with coding other elements	1
Integration	1/31/03	8:04	1/31/03	8:07		Waiting for other elements to include in the build	1
Integration	2/1/03	9:37	2/1/03	16:17	Integration test results, NNS	Last minute "add to build" request from management	?
Close development	2/1/03	18:21	2/1/03	18:22		Updating tool records to log closure	2

Figure 16-5. Form for Gathering Value Stream Map Information

activity may wait to be done until several people can discuss it and come to agreement. The type 2 *muda* items are particularly good targets for improvement, as they can be eliminated even if you continue to use the current production process.

From the spreadsheet (Figure 16-5) you can produce a graph (Figure 16-6). You do this either by hand-drawing (which is usually good enough and fairly quick) or with graphing software that uses the first three columns of the spreadsheet as inputs. One could also draw in the information transfers from the end of each work bar to the beginning of the next.

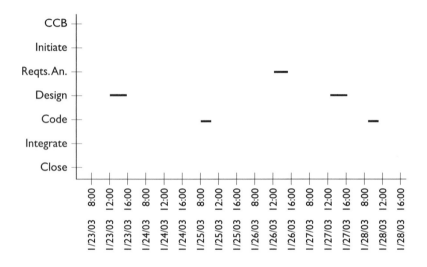

Figure 16-6. Graph of Productive Time vs. Activity

Note that the graph in Figure 16-6 shows just a portion of the calendar time covered by the spreadsheet. In an actual VSM, you would produce a full graph (omitted here so the example will fit on the page). Also, the graph ignores hours of the day when production is not occurring (this graph assumes all work occurs from 8 AM to 8 PM). Blank areas (without a horizontal bar) are unproductive times.

Such a graph makes it obvious how much, or how little available time is spent on value-adding (productive) work, as well as when inefficient backflows (like the above transition from Coding back to Requirements Analysis) occur. It is useful to go to a lower level of detail than in this example, that is, subtasks of requirements analysis or design, and in an actual VSM effort, we would do so. However, even at this high level of detail, we have learned much about the weaknesses of the existing production process.

Now you take what you have learned from making the current-state map, analyze the muda and its causes, and produce a future-state map that may change or rearrange activities and information transfers between them to eliminate waste. For instance, a consistent problem in the above current state map was that the next workers in line frequently didn't realize that new work had arrived for them to do. This added much to the white space in the process. By changing the information transfer from a passive list item to an active attention-getter and acknowledgement, you could greatly reduce or perhaps even eliminate this source of white-space delay.

Kaizen

The technique of value-stream mapping is usually the first stage of an overall *kaizen* event focused on identifying and eliminating waste from existing production processes. The typical steps in a *kaizen* event are:

1. Just-in-time (JIT) training of the participants in what to do
2. Develop the VSM current-state map
3. Identify irreducible process requirements
4. Brainstorm improvements and solutions
5. Select best improvement ideas
6. Rapidly implement improvements for immediate benefit
7. Measure results of improvements

The main idea in step 3 is to challenge anything in the process that is being treated as if it were a requirement on the process. People often assume you must do an activity simply because it has been done that way for some time, or because it is imposed as an organization policy. One of the most important goals of a *kaizen* is to challenge these and all other assumptions. In the end, the aim is to get down to an irreducible set of essential requirements on the process.

For instance, some processes will probably require assurance that the software products always be in a known and reproducible state. It will not usually be essential, however, that the means to this assurance be the GNU CVS Concurrent Version System configuration control tool (a generic, common, open-source tool), even if CVS has been the standard in the organization for some time. Of course, if CVS is imposed on a process by company edict, it isn't currently optional. However, by identifying the underlying real requirement on the process (software in a known state) and distinguishing it from the imposed implementation (CVS), and showing any waste this causes (through the VSM), you have just made the beginning of an argument for possible future improvements.

Now you are ready to begin step 4, brainstorming solutions. We discussed the basics of the brainstorming technique in Chapter 9, and we will discuss additional useful techniques under the flow principle. For our purposes here, you can use brainstorming to generate ideas to incorporate into your value-stream future-state map, to assist in its development.

The remaining *kaizen* steps are pretty self-explanatory. Choosing the right things to measure in order to assess improvements is important but relatively straightforward. Essentially, the right things to measure are the things we discuss later in Part III, especially the Industrial Cost Drivers listed in Chapter 19.

VSM is an important foundation for a *kaizen*. Without the lifecycle perspective provided by the value stream map, the *kaizen* participants may select improvements that help with a particular problem, but which make the overall process no better or even worse than before. With a value stream map, the team can avoid what has been called kamikaze *kaizen*, in which a part of the value stream is improved, but the overall value stream is not. This is *muda* because it is work, and yet provides no net benefit. It is kamikaze because after a few such events with nothing long-term or permanent to show for the effort, managers will stop any further *kaizen*.

The best way to learn how to be an effective participant in *kaizen* is by just doing it, rather than reading. Most experts agree that it is well worth the cost to bring in a *kaizen* consultant to lead you through the first event or two. An excellent reference on the techniques and feel of *kaizen*-style process improvement, strongly oriented around doing rather than theorizing, is George Robson's "*Continuous Process Improvement*."[5]

The Information Branch

The information branch concerns the set of activities that ensure each person working an activity knows what he or she needs to know about other activities with which they must interact. Related to this is the need to keep them from being inundated by irrelevant (to them) information, which would waste their time and distract them from using the information they do need. Management has a similar need to know and to inform, except that the need there is to get information from everyone, to everyone, but only the limited amount that is needed to allow managing.

For both the activity workers and the managers to accomplish these goals, we need two things. First, we need an idea of which activities are related to which. That's what the V cycle and lifecycle models provide, along with possibly a more detailed analysis (a 'la DFD or class definition using abstract interfaces), as we mentioned in the section on the V cycle. Second, we need to be proactive about selecting and moving information. In other words, we need to know who needs what information, and then put mechanisms in place to move that information automatically, without the need for somebody to remember to move it.

These ideas may sound elementary, but Jim has seen them both ignored on a very big scale, with equally large and negative results. Here are a few of these results:

- Schedule planning in disarray
- Inability to stabilize requirements
- Fluctuating interfaces
- Late on critical milestones
- Vendors slipping deliveries
- Internal project standards a moving target

Maybe you've been on a project that had these kinds of problems. While many factors can contribute to them (simply practicing mass production development will lead to a lot of them), there's a single root cause that is a bigger contributor than any other: *poor information management.* And information management is the province of the information branch.

If you've lived through this situation, you recognize the symptoms:

- Subjects are discussed in meetings, and decisions are made, without inviting or even identifying all affected parties.
- The only way to find needed information is to luck into making the right contact or happening to walk into the right meeting. Even then, one must dig out each bit of information for oneself.
- Planning meetings are filled with surprises. Organizers find that they have not invited people who turn out to be necessary to the success of the meeting. Attendees learn that other attendees have been doing things that directly affect them, without their knowledge.
- People make decisions without knowing who they will affect or how.
- Decisions made by mutually dependent groups are made independently and incompatibly. At some later point, the parties have to go back and change their decisions (with accompanying schedule delays) because the approaches they adopted unilaterally could not be made compatible with the others who depended on them.

The latter situation has interesting ripple effects. One project in which we were involved had a disagreement between two coworkers about which internal file protocol to use on major portions of the software. They each worked on different parts of the project, and each proceeded as if their decision had carried the day. The nature of the system was that only one protocol could be used, so one had to eventually win. Design of many parts of the deliverable software, and of several testing and integration tools, required knowing which protocol to use. In the absence of a decision and with both men proceeding as if their choice had won, the application and tool developers had to guess and work at risk accordingly. Many months later, the project finally forced a decision. When it went against many people's expectations, it invalidated the at-risk work and forced substantial rework of products and delay of deliveries. Note that allowing the two coworker's activities to run without information coupling ensured the waste would happen, no matter which choice won. Different people had kept working based on different assumptions.

This kind of situation leads to the uncontrolled, nonstrategic change known as fire fighting. People in this kind of environment become resistant to any kind of change at all because their experience with change is that it is mostly a pointless waste of time. General resistance to change soon becomes a business problem, however. When the information branch isn't working, changes due to poor communications can't simply be avoided. Unless those changes are made, activities in the lifecycle will not create working product. However, a far easier kind of change to resist is strategic change. This kind of change can save a project significant amounts of schedule and budget. Strategic change "merely" makes things go better. It typically doesn't have its full effect until after the next looming milestone. Change that should be the strong suit of any advanced technology organization like a software company is thus the first to go. Thus, a dysfunctional information branch hits the business where it hurts the most: in its business performance. We are not speaking hypothetically or theoretically here. Since Jim has worked for several corporations, that shouldn't tip any hands!

A properly running information branch identifies and manages all the information dependencies across a project. What is needed is an effectively coordinated, top-down analysis of information across all levels of the program, and the creation of an effective infrastructure for disseminating information and actively involving people when that is what's required.

If the project contains just one software system, the information dependencies are solely between the activities in developing that system. If the project contains multiple communicating systems, the information dependencies between the systems, at the activities level, as well as at the management level, must also be identified.

Just as there's a design stream and a production stream for creating software products, there is a sort of design stream and production stream for creating software development processes.

In a product's design stream, the domain architecture is created. It uses concepts like classes and abstract interfaces to specify hidden information (e.g., secrets) and exposed interfaces like data and control information. In a product's production stream, that architecture is adopted and then fleshed out to build a specific product.

In the process's design stream, a process architecture is also created. As with a product architecture, there should be some change analysis behind the process architecture that anchors the architecture to the things least likely to change over the course of the project. As we mentioned under the V cycle, you can even use similar abstractions as those found in production: The activities that work on the product can be treated analogously to software product classes. These classes can have their own abstract interfaces of hidden information (i.e., internal products), invariants, and exposed interfaces, like the material and information dependencies between the activities. Often the same analysis and design methods can be used to create a best process architecture that has been used to create a best product architecture.

Failing to specify activities' information dependencies and to set up the mechanisms for distributing that information is like skipping product domain design, and cutting straight to the production-stream part of software development to identify your product's classes. Actually, it's even worse; it's more like never identifying any product classes at all. You lose all the leverage of the lean metaphor when you fail to create such a process architecture.

A nonlean project not only skips creating a process architecture, it also expects each of its workers to figure out what they need to get and to know and then to go get it for themselves. A lean project creates a process architecture that identifies all its material and information dependencies and has mechanisms for passing that information when it is needed as the project proceeds. In lean terms, the mechanism for passing both material and information can be via pull (as in *kanban* or just-in-time; see Chapter 21), but as in any other pull situation, the workers requesting the inputs won't be defining what they will be getting; they will just say (in effect) that it's time for you to give me what you're supposed to give me. Note: The workers in a lean process know which production activities to request information from.

Occasionally, however, information about activities must be pushed. This happens primarily when the way that some activity of the process is done must be modified partway through production, especially when the change alters what the activity either needs as an input, or produces as an output. Then a different kind of information must be passed, unexpected information that forces (and enables) the activities around it to change how they work as well. That kind of information must, of course, be pushed rather than pulled. Even so, the project should anticipate the possibility of this happening and create mechanisms for disseminating this kind of information as well. These mechanisms will be based on knowledge of which other activities are affected by the change (e.g., as recorded in the V cycle and other activity dependency models). In a lean situation, of course, this won't happen as often, because the project will have engineered its processes as carefully as its products, and there will be fewer emergency needs to modify the processes during production.

The mechanisms for moving information between activities can be simple: We already mentioned creating meeting notification lists, which can be managed using a scheduling tool like Microsoft Outlook. They can also be sophisticated;

such as putting all needed visible information about an activity or phase into a database and creating standard queries against that database that can be invoked to pull the needed information. However it is done, the important information must both exist and be easily and quickly obtained when needed.

Three rules for constructing information interfaces between activities are especially important:

1. Have an authoritative source for all dependency information.
2. Make sure that all necessary information is transferred.
3. Prevent passing unnecessary information to the receiving activity (i.e., minimize information "coupling" between activities).

The reason for the first rule is obvious: If there's no authoritative place to go for the information, the information will be informal and undependable, which is no way to build a solid, lean process.

Let's explore the other two rules by going back to the V cycle and considering the activity of software requirements specification. Looking ahead along the main arrow, the next activity is design. Rule 3 tells us, for instance, that we want to make sure that no requirement puts design constraints on the upcoming design. Constraints are a type of information coupling. Design constraints coming out of requirements analysis are often, in effect, premature design decisions (there are, of course, constraints that are true requirements rather than premature design decisions). Design constraints force the later design to be less effective than it could have been, because the requirements-analysis activity isn't intended to—and has not—fully considered the implications of design. Design constraints are not, strictly speaking, necessary for production. Nevertheless, per rule 2, if the requirements do impose design constraints on the design, the requirements activity needs to explicitly let the people involved inthe design activity know what those constraints are.

So, how can we reduce the necessary information coupling between requirements and design in this regard? The best way is to develop implementation-free requirements, as we discussed in Chapter 10 (point 5 of the nine ideal characteristics for any value representation). Doing so keeps design options open until during the design phase, when presumably more will have been learned and people can make better design decisions. This strategy leads to less waste and thus is more lean. It decouples the two activities, lessening the information that must flow from requirements to design and eliminating any need for information to flow to requirements from design (i.e., preliminary information from design to help requirements analysis make better design decisions . . . decisions that it shouldn't be making anyway).

Looking backward along the main branch of the V, the software requirements specification activity is related to the system design activity. Those who are developing the software requirements need to understand the aspects of the system design that will constrain what can go into the software requirements. For instance, if the SCR method is being used for software requirements analysis, the system design will determine where the boundary is between the software and its environment. This is a relatively simple dependency. Other software requirements methodologies may need more detailed information about the system design in order to do their work.

Looking along the other dimension, horizontally, the V chart shows that software acceptance is also associated with software requirements specification. The chart relationship says that one should make sure software values and requirements provide a good foundation for verifying software acceptability. That requires a material flow of requirements to the acceptance task, to be used for test-case development. It may also require an information flow one or both ways.

An information flow may be needed from requirements to acceptance to confirm that the requirements are ready (good enough) for test-case creation. A common basis for such an indication is manual evaluation (e.g., walkthrough) of the testability of the requirements. However, manual evaluations can be incomplete or incorrect. Requirements that pass evaluation may still prove to be untestable or otherwise verifiable. The flaws allowed by this approach led to much waste and hurt the performance of many programs.

A way to eliminate a confirmation information flow is to simply combine the most important parts of two activities and develop test cases along with the requirements. This is the XP way. It is a big improvement over just inspecting the requirements for testability; by doing both activities at once on the same requirement, it ensures that the requirement is testable. If you find you cannot create a test case from a given requirement, it probably means there is a deficiency in the requirement. You can then immediately repair the requirement. This approach thus eliminates the need for any confirmatory information flow.

An interesting, slightly off-topic benefit of this approach is that it nearly eliminates the situation in which the acceptance team has to augment requirements with design information in order to develop useful test cases. Basing acceptance tests on the design, even partially, leads to releasing products that satisfy the developers, but not necessarily the product's customers. Note also that developing test cases from design is based on a dependency that does not appear on the V chart. That's a good indication of a bad information dependency, which is only necessitated by the insufficiency of a good one (from requirements to acceptance).

The third and best way to eliminate a confirmation information flow between requirements specification and acceptance is to select a requirements modeling method that inherently assures that the requirements are correct and testable, without any further need to confirm that fact. Some such requirements methods exist; and some of them even enable you to automatically derive acceptance test cases.

Picking a method that allows automatic creation of test cases not only eliminates an information interface, but also drastically reduces the entire activity of acceptance testing! This can be done with formal requirements methods like SCR. With such known good requirements, acceptance can be based either on testing (dynamic execution), or if the software product itself has mathematical integrity (e.g., if it is coded in a formal language like SPARK, discussed in Chapter 18), it can be based on a static tool-based comparison of the requirements with the code. Static analysis goes even faster than testing, shrinking the acceptance activity yet further.

In a note of warning, however, many formal requirements-analysis techniques that are popular today—such as writing requirements in the "Z" requirements specification language—are wasteful in other ways. For instance, requirements written in Z are practically impossible to validate, because the people you would want to validate your requirements (such as customers) can't read them! As always in lean production, you must take the broad view of what you are trying to achieve, so that what you do to help in one area does not detract from the intent of the whole.

Integrating Production and the Project

This brings us to the goal of the production stream: to execute the material branch and the information branch in a coordinated way to develop a product. The production stream, in turn, must be combined with the design stream into a lean value stream, to make sure the product fully contributes to broader project and company goals.

There is no single-point solution to achieving an effective value stream. Building a value stream that does justice to both the customer and the business requires choosing among all the process approaches, technical means, and other resources at your disposal. These include lifecycle models, lifecycle phase products and results, methods, techniques, tools, design strategies, actual designs, programming languages, verification approaches, reuse strategies, and the knowledge and wisdom of all the people involved, from management through customers.

The premise for integrating the lifecycle is that every means at your disposal has both strengths and weaknesses. You choose your means so that their combined strengths best address your most important business goals and so that individual strengths cancel out their individual weaknesses. Then, all resources complement and reinforce one another to pull off a product and a project that fulfills the values of the customer and of the business. Creating an integrated lifecycle is the most powerful way to focus all work on adding value.

The lack of an integrated lifecycle was the major downfall of the sad tale of the promising project of Chapter 1. The software requirements phase was highly optimized, but disconnected from the system design phase and its products. While most projects have less extreme lifecycle disconnects, they have many disintegrations that hamper their progress on individual tasks as well as strongly limiting their performance on major project objectives.

This point also touches on the integration of the design stream and the production stream. Indeed, it touches on every aspect of a project. To create an integrated lifecycle requires that you first understand what you are trying to achieve. This implies, of course, that in addition to knowing the customer values, you must also know the project and organization business values. Indeed, business values are the more important considerations in targeting the integrated lifecycle. If you haven't already identified business values in a form that the software developers can use, producing them need not be a major effort. The decisions in constructing an integrated lifecycle only need very high-level guidance. You identify business values in much the same way as customer values, primarily through the techniques of value resolution, though you would want to notate them more informally, say as English statements. SCR definitely wouldn't work here!

You can identify business values simply, using the AHP, or more rigorously, using the full arsenal of *hoshin*. Typically, business values will include factors like building a customer base, nurturing customer loyalty, increasing market share, improving profitability, attracting employees, retaining employees, strengthening shareholder value, and so on. You should place these values in an order, as happens with the AHP. The ordered list will help with making the tradeoffs needed among the technical means you have available for accomplishing them.

For example, suppose that your highest business goals include both maximizing profits and gaining customer trust and loyalty. These goals are usually somewhat contradictory. Maximizing profits has your own interests at heart. Cultivating the customer means having the customer's interests at heart. How can one do well on both at once? The integrated lifecycle approach would require you to pick an approach that has strengths in both areas, strengths that cancel out each other's weaknesses. You would then integrate them so they work together smoothly.

Good software projects seriously consider the best way to do individual tasks and activities. Better projects consider choosing a way of performing a given activity that sets up for effectiveness in the activity coming afterward and that minimizes the amount of information that needs to flow between them. Exceptional projects consider both these concerns, plus the effects of a given activity on other activities at the same level of abstraction (e.g., requirements and acceptance testing, or design and integration). The latter concerns are what the V lifecycle model makes visible. However, the very best lean projects do all of these, and add to them such considerations as value resolution and strategic business planning.

ENDNOTES

1. B. Boehm, "Spiral Development: Experience, Principles, and Refinements," Spiral Development Workshop, Figure 1; Carnegie Mellon Software Engineering Institute, February 9, 2000; http://www.sei.cmu.edu/cbs/spiral2000/february2000/SR08html/SR08.html as of June 12, 2004. This diagram is recreated from Dr. Boehm's original drawing in his article "A Spiral Model of Software Development and Enhancement." Computer, (May 1988), pgs. 61–72.
2. B. Boehm, "Spiral Development: Experience, Principles, and Refinements," Spiral Development Workshop, Figure 7; Carnegie Mellon Software Engineering Institute, February 9, 2000; http://www.sei.cmu.edu/cbs/spiral2000/february2000/SR08html/SR08.html as of June 12, 2004. We highly recommend you read the entire article for ideas on extending the spiral lifecycle. It is especially interesting that it incorporates the idea of "invariants," which we shall discuss more in Chapter 19.
3. Adapted from the V-spiral chart in D. Phillips, "How To Make A V-Shaped Spiral—And Vice Versa," *American Programmer*, August 1997.
4. See G. D. Robson, "Continuous Process Improvement," New York, NY: The Free Press (division of Macmillan Inc.), 1991, especially pgs. 67–77.
5. G. D. Robson, "Continuous Process Improvement," New York, NY: The Free Press (division of Macmillan Inc.), 1991.

17

The Value Stream—
Verification-Smart Development

THE NEXT TWO CHAPTERS ON THE VALUE STREAM zero in on two of the most important aspects of the production stream: verification (in this chapter) and programming languages (in the next).

Actually, verification is so important a concept and so all-encompassing in its effects on what we do that it can't be contained in any one aspect of development . . . not even one as large as the production stream. Verification spills over onto every aspect of lean software, as we shall see throughout this chapter. However, properly setting up for verification has perhaps a more positive impact on how well things will go in the production stream than it does on any other aspect of a lean project . . . which is why we have placed this topic in this part of the book.

Thorough, low-cost verification is a business necessity, not just a technical one. By verification, we mean comparison of the product to some standard of correctness or excellence. This comparison can be via testing (which is what most people think of), by some form of human inspection or demonstration, or by automated analysis. Verification has two purposes: to find defects (i.e., errors) in the software and to provide an objective basis on which people can build their confidence in the capabilities and absence of defects in the software.

Verification is necessary on most lean projects, because even if lean processes have eliminated the introduction of defects and therefore the need for the first purpose of verification, there will probably be someone important to the project who wants objective confirmation that the software is correct (e.g., a customer, regulator, or manager). Verification provides that confirmation.[1] The strategies that improve verification mostly involve integrating the lifecycle so that value isn't lost throughout production. This is the flip side of the emphasis in the previous two chapters on integrating the lifecycle to put value into the product, which is why we have included this topic under the value stream.

As much as half the cost of creating a typical piece of software today is tied up in verification. So, you'd think software businesses would be pointing their biggest guns at cutting verification costs, but in almost all cases, you'd be wrong.

Verification is a complete afterthought in nonlean software development. Now how's that for a conversation ice-breaker? PDQ[2] you hear back, "How can you say that? FYI, our verification program is CM'd, QA'd, FI'd[3], CMM'd, and thoroughly TLA'd[4]!"

Nevertheless, massive proceduralization of traditional testing approaches is not a cost-effective verification approach. What is being proceduralized in these cases is an ineffective approach to verification. The added rigor merely increases overhead costs and clogs up progress.

Shortchanging verification doesn't work either. Having less effective verification during development just pushes error detection out to a later stage, and in many cases, all the way out to the customer. Almost everyone has seen studies showing that later detection leads to greater costs and that the cost growth is exponential. If you wait until your customers find your errors, your cost could be the loss of your market.

On significantly sized craft-production projects, verification, if it is given any attention at all, is expensive, because it has little if any theoretical foundations and even less consistency from tester to tester.

On mass production projects, verification is expensive because the principles of mass production work against the principles of cost-effective verification. As we've seen before, mass production focuses on procedures for the sake of procedures, as if the very fact that a way of work has been put into a procedure means that it has been improved. Yet as we've noted, creating procedures for work done wrongly does more harm than good. And creating, training, executing, monitoring, and managing those procedures costs a lot of money and time.

There's a relatively small return on that investment because those efforts largely focus on individual defects and ignore root causes. Of course, that oversight also means that the changes that would have been needed to address those root causes are never implemented, and the flood of such defects continues largely unabated. Guidelines like the CMM speak of the need for root cause analysis, but usually focus on low-level causes such as poor training or inadequate peer review processes, whose correction often provides relatively small paybacks. The big paybacks come from identifying the high-level causes such as flaws in the overall concept of the software lifecycle or the paradigm for software production. This kind of thinking, however, is at best ignored, and often inhibited, by mass production approaches. We will talk about some of these root causes in the remainder of this chapter.

Another problem with mass production is that it accepts as a given that the development tasks will insert defects. It then counts on the verification tasks to find the defects so the products can go back to development for correction. This is just like a mass car assembly line with a big rework area at the end. It is the classic develop-then-test lifecycle. It institutionalizes backflows, whose inherent wastefulness we will study further in Chapter 20.

Finally, mass production is in tension with the fact that, to be performed adequately, development and verification both require the services of highly talented people. The nature of development concerns itself with what the program should do: The nature of verification concerns itself with those things, but also with things the program should not do but could. The former requires imagination, creativity, knowledge, and skill. The latter *well* requires at least as much of each of these qualities.

Yet, in accordance with the division of labor principle, mass production assigns different people to each of these types of tasks. Unless different top quality people in an organization have already chosen each of these jobs, this puts mass production software managers in a no-win position: Assign your best people to development, and let verification suffer; or assign them to verification, and let development suffer. Sometimes managers don't even have that much choice: People will refuse to do one job or the other because it's outside their specialty (in the mass production sense). This is an artificial and avoidable dilemma that only comes into play when you are operating under the mass production paradigm.

In contrast to the assumptions of mass production, lean production says that development and verification are two sides of the same coin, not two separate specialties. This implies that good verification is most cost-effective when it is thoroughly integrated throughout all the phases and activities of the software lifecycle. By applying the integrated lifecycle mindset we've been discussing under the lean value stream principle, every decision we make about software production will be with an eye towards making verification as rapid, easy, and inexpensive as possible.

Indeed, since verification is the single largest expense in nonlean software production and it is required even in most lean software projects, it should be the single biggest driver in choosing project lifecycle models, methods, tools, and personnel utilizations. You can call this mindset the verification-driven lifecycle or verification-driven development (VDD). The emphasis on VDD complements the emphasis of the rest of this book on using lean principles and techniques to "do the right thing." VDD completes that idea by making it easy to find defects that have slipped through our lean processes and to instill confidence in our lean processes and products among our stakeholders: customers, management, regulators, and so forth. This is also, as the title of this chapter suggests, verification-smart development.

Choosing a Verification-Friendly Lifecycle Model

We discussed lifecycle models in the last chapter. Here we add verification to the concerns related to the lifecycle model that were discussed there. Which lifecycle model you choose either prepares for effective verification, or inhibits it. The lean choice here would usually be a spiral, since the smaller increments between the beginning and ending of each cycle in the spiral certainly make it easier to verify than a waterfall. Narrow-slice anticipatory development, a specific application of the spiral, is designed to verify both design stream (domain-oriented) architectural elements, and production stream processes, as early in a project as possible. This is very verification smart. It is also an effective form of proactive risk reduction and risk management.

Reducing the Cost of Requirements-Based Testing

Following the selection of lifecycle model, there are important choices to be made concerning requirements, design, coding, and of course, testing. Requirements and testing are especially closely linked, so we will begin our detailed examination with those two concerns.

Selecting a verification methodology begins with choosing a suitable methodology for requirements. A good requirements methodology for a verification-driven lifecycle will enforce completeness or highlight incompleteness. A methodology that supports verification will also make it extremely difficult, if not impossible, to inadvertently include design information. The latter goal can be assured by expressing everything in terms of the customer space. One method we have studied with these characteristics is SCR. SCR also enforces completeness. Its support for verification is another reason this method has proven so useful as part of a suite of complementary lifecycle methods. In case you haven't noticed, Jim likes SCR, because it supports so many different aspects of lean production at once.

A mathematically-based, but readable, method like SCR or formal subsets of UML, (iUML comes close), can save a project a tremendous amount of time and money in verification. Having designers and developers use these methods to model their requirements will allow a project to get double duty from requirements. Besides the obvious purpose of driving development, the requirements also serve as the test cases for Requirements-Based Testing (RBT). This eliminates the need to create separate test cases, and the time and schedule that go with that work.

Developing test cases separately from requirements is a redundant activity and pure *muda*. The whole point of RBT is to identify where the product diverges from its requirements. The requirements must be the standard against which the software is directly compared.

The reason software organizations need a separate test-case development activity on most projects, of course, is that their requirements are too loose to be an adequate basis for verification. Requirements are often so weak that the design, coding, integration, and test phases must add requirements-related information to the official requirements they've gotten from the project, in order to make the requirements complete enough to support the rest of the lifecycle tasks.

Unless the people working the latter phases are also the people who studied the customers' values, they are probably not the right people to be updating requirements information, and thus, effectively, steering the project. When requirements-related information is added to lower-level artifacts like designs and code, people like managers cannot see it happening. This effectively conceals real changes in the direction of the project from those who are officially supposed to be making the project's strategic decisions. This is a high-level verification issue. The requirements of the project should be as open to inspection and comparison as any other aspect of the product. When the actual requirements differ from the official requirements, major trouble is already brewing and will shortly pour out on the project and business.

When requirements information is added at later stages to the project's pool of knowledge, those updates don't usually make their way back into the original requirements even if a mechanism for tracing requirements is in place. This leaves the written requirements incomplete at best and incorrect at worst. In this situation, a mechanism for tracing requirements can actually make things worse, giving a false sense of security by providing false proof that all the requirements are being fully handled, when they are not. The flip side of this problem, and equally problematic to verification, is that the requirements are often seeded with non-requirements information, especially design decisions. In this case, later design changes may invalidate the original requirements, again, often without going back and updating the requirements accordingly.

Whatever requirements methodology you choose, when requirements have the above kinds of weaknesses, the test group is forced to get current design information so it can build test cases that are close enough to reality to evaluate the software against what it is actually supposed to do. Speaking from prior personal experience on nonlean programs, sometimes, against all the rules of good testing, necessary information must be obtained by talking informally with systems engineers or software developers. Sometimes, getting necessary information even requires studying design documents or, worst of all, code. These pragmatic measures may be necessary to enable testing to be done at all, but they contaminate the purity of the standard of correctness against which the software will be compared. A contaminated standard means that confidence is compromised, which undermines the second purpose of verification, i.e., giving others an unassailable reason to trust the product.

Going a step further, if the requirements have been created in a methodology with good verification characteristics, an organization can construct mappings between the terminology of the requirements' customer space and terminology of the software's producer space (e.g., the names of the actual variables or interfaces). Once that mapping has been made, writing test scripts, the second big verification task on most projects, can be done quickly from the requirements, either manually or automatically. Of course, it costs money to create such tools for automated test-case creation. However, it doesn't take a very big project to justify the investment, and if the tools are used on subsequent projects, the payoff will multiply.

For instance, if the requirements are in the form of SCR tables, you could create test scripts for each row in an SCR table. All that is needed is a mapping of the MONs and CONs in the table and therefore the test scripts, to the corresponding IN and OUT interfaces to the software.

Let's see how this might look, using the SCR table we first saw in Figure 10-2, reproduced as Figure 17-1.

MON_Auto_Light_Switch	MON_Ambient_Light_Level	CON_Lamp_Illumination
Auto	<= twilight_threshold	ON
Auto	> twilight_threshold	OFF
Off	"Don't care"	OFF

Figure 17-1. "Outside Light" SCR Table

A straightforward translation of the three rows of the table into a test script might look something like the following:

—Requirement CON_Lamp_Illumination
—Row 1
Set MON_Auto_Light_Switch = Auto;
Set MON_Ambient_Light_Level <= twilight_threshold;
Expect CON_Lamp_ Illumination = ON delay 4 frames;
—Row 2
Set MON_Auto_Light_Switch = Auto;
Set MON_Ambient_Light_Level > twilight_threshold;
Expect CON_Lamp_ Illumination = OFF delay 4 frames;
—Row 3
Set MON_Auto_Light_Switch = OFF;
Expect CON_Lamp_ Illumination = OFF delay 4 frames;

The delay statements in the scripts allow time for the software being tested to react to the changes in the monitored variables and to update the controlled variables.

Software often fails on data-range boundaries: Additional test cases and scripts can be written for the extreme values in each range; i.e., for the lines between the rows in the table. For instance, MON_Ambient_Light_Level is set in two of the above scripts; once (in the row 1 test case) to <= twilight_threshold, and once (in the row 2 test case) to => twilight threshold. You could add additional boundary test cases for the smallest defined value of MON_Ambient_Light_Level (this still falls under row 1 of the SCR table), one for the exact value of twilight_threshold (also still under row 1 of the SCR table), and one for the largest define value of MON_Ambient_Light_Level (falling under row 2 of the table), and so forth.

If the project's selected programming language allows out-of-range values, you can add more test cases to try to force the MON accordingly. Better to avoid the need for this by selecting a language that strictly defines all variable ranges so that you cannot accidentally write code that exceeds the desired ranges. Then, out-of-bounds testing can usually be eliminated (the caveats go beyond the scope of this book, though experienced verification engineers know about the exceptions). Boundary testing remains, of course, as important as ever. In the next chapter, we'll have much more to say about selecting programming languages for lean projects.

Running these tests requires feeding input interface variables to the software being tested and observing the output interface variables coming back from that software. To use these scripts that way, we need an interpreter that translates between the MON and CON variables in the scripts and the IN and OUT variables on the real interfaces to the software under test, and feeds or reads the latter as the test progresses.

The SCR IN and OUT relations we discussed in Chapter 10 make this mapping possible. As you may recall, the IN relation defines how an IN interface variable is derived from one or more MON variables in the environment.

IN relation: $IN = f(MONs)$

The OUT relation defines how a CON variable is driven by one or more OUT interface variables:

OUT relation: $CON = g(OUTs)$

If these tables are stored in a machine-readable form, the interpreter can refer to them each time it sees a MON or a CON in the script, and convert them into the equivalent IN and OUT variables (as long as a data dictionary is available online with supporting information about the characteristics of the variables and symbolic constants. Also included should be aspects, such as range, format, accuracy, and encoding, as needed, depending on the type of item being specified.)

Finally, the interpreter also needs rules for interpreting what a construct like "> twilight threshold" means, based on the defined range of "twilight threshold." The interpreter can then automatically choose a legal value inside that range for that cell in the table (you only need one value to cover a cell on the row).

Jim specified an approach like this and wrote the requirements for such a script interpreter while working as process architect on a project a few years ago. Once the interpreter was in place, it cut verification costs and times substantially. The approach and tool have been reused on several projects since then, including one that was having difficulty getting timely regulatory approval. That project's verification approach and requirements analysis were traditional. The project converted its requirements into SCR tables, made REQ-table based scripts, and ran them using the interpreter. Even counting the additional requirements-conversion work, the project met its goal and obtained the required approval when it needed it. However, this kind of approach is much more cost-effective when it is prepared for from the beginning of the project.

Unit Testing and Structural Coverage for Free

Another advantage of creating test cases from formal requirements is that they guarantee very high structural coverage of the code. That is, running tests based directly on formal requirements, e.g., using test scripts such as those we discussed earlier in this chapter will result in a higher percentage of the statements and branches in the code being executed. Most people who are interested in the verification results also want to know that the structural coverage was high. That's because low structural coverage implies there is a lot of functionality in the software that does not come from the software's requirements. This naturally causes them to ask what all that untested code is there for and whether it contains undetected errors.

If each requirement has been placed into a single procedure, a highly recommended architectural strategy we used on the 382J MC OFP, and which we discuss in more detail in Appendix A, then running a requirements-based script test not only verifies the software against its requirements, it extensively tests a single unit. In other words, the correlation between requirements and units means that each requirements-based test is well targeted to a specific and known section of code.

With all these preconditions in place, you can take credit for three kinds of testing at once: requirements-based, structural, and unit. Nevertheless, it only makes sense to defer unit testing to this point if most errors have been precluded by a lifecycle based on extensive lean practices. This is another example of the synergism of an integrated lifecycle. The 382J's lean practices allowed unit testing to be deferred until the natural time for requirements-based testing. The project was confident that code units would be found correct and that therefore, few backflows, as discussed under the lean flow principle, would be needed to correct defects. If you expect to have many defects in your developed units, it is probably worth doing unit testing while coding. Backflows are more expensive and disruptive than redundant testing. In either case, if your requirements-based tests are built on the foundation of high-integrity formal requirements, you can still use them to gain credit for structural coverage testing.

One way such testing can be usually conducted is to create two parallel builds of the software to be tested. One build will be pure, and one will be instrumented. The instrumented build includes added code at each branch point that records whenever execution has reached that point. The test suite is run twice: once on the pure code for requirements-based credit, and again on the instrumented code to determine the structural coverage. If those who drive your choice of verification activities will allow it, you may be able to run just once, on the instrumented code. However, this would require that you have high confidence in your means of inserting instrumentation, e.g., a well-verified, automated instrumenting tool, so you know that the instrumentation does not corrupt your software in any way. Also, the instrumentation should not exceed with critical software timing (e.g., a hard-core, real-time software system might not be able to run within its time constraints if it was instrumented).

The Benefits of Using the System Simulation-Emulation Lifecycle

As we discussed in Chapter 10, simulation is a valuable technique for discovering and validating customer values and their subsequent software requirements. However, this technique is useful for more than just exploring the customer space. You can extend it downstream into the implementation space as well as upstream into overall product definition (hardware, software, and environment). When used in this fashion, simulation is no longer just a software development technique; it is a System Simulation–Emulation Lifecycle, or SSEL, covering the entire product lifecycle. This almost completely blurs the sharp division usually drawn between system and software development. In most cases, this is a very good thing because it reduces the *muda* that normally occurs at the transition between the two levels of activity.

The SSEL begins with a top-level simulation of the overall product as a whole, which helps identify customer values. As the project moves into the implementation space, you identify subsystems and their interfaces and then simulate each subsystem. Layer by layer, this continues until the system has been fully broken down. This works for low-level hardware design as well as software. For instance, if dedicated circuit boards will be created, they can be emulated to represent the actual hardware as well as the software, and even, in a system combining dedicated hardware and software, to trade off what functionality should go into each. The SSEL is practical because the simulation is a black box at each level and much faster to develop than the real product.

As development work progresses through each level of detail, developers simulate and select design tradeoffs based on the success of the resulting simulation. Thus, an SSEL helps make system design a more objective and informed process. Once the development team has fully decomposed the system design, designers of actual software and hardware modules plug their individual parts into the overall simulation, replacing the corresponding simulated parts. They then test their part of the system within a working whole. Production lines in other industries have stations for stages of production. In system/software development, the SSEL, in effect, draws the stations of the production line closer to each other and shortens the time the product assembly needs to move forward between them. This movement is rather abstract, since it proceeds on many fronts at once. It also speeds work within each station and thus improves lean flow throughout the line. The analogy to industrial production lines is explained in more detail in Chapter 19.

Not only does the SSEL help ensure that each part of the system will work properly, it also gives each developer a much better idea of what and how his or her part of the system contributes to the whole. On their first pass through this lifecycle, many of Sudhir Shah's coworkers at GE (recall our discussion in Chapter 12 of his work in system simulation/emulation) remarked that this was the first time they had really understood what their part of the design added to the system. This type of employee involvement increases morale as well as productivity and work quality.

There is a superficial resemblance between the SSEL and XP. Both allow exploration and evolution throughout their lifecycles. However, XP intentionally distributes its requirements development throughout the lifecycle. Thus, in XP, major design decisions are made long before the customer's needs have been extensively explored. The SSEL, on the other hand, lays much more foundation in the customer space up front, removing one of the major lean objections to using XP. Where applicable, the SSEL is a very powerful lean approach.

Six Sigma: Reducing Variance

Six sigma techniques reduce variance in production processes. Such variance often leads to *muda*, especially *muda* of waste of repair and correction, and waste of motion.

Six sigma does not aim for perfection, in the sense of the lean perfection principle. Indeed, "six sigma capability is decidedly not perfection."[5] Instead, it attempts to reduce the standard deviation from an ideal. Since it is harder to establish an ideal for a piece of software than it is, say, for the dimensions of a metal part, six sigma is more applicable to the production of traditional goods than to software. In addition, traditional products are subject to laws of physics that do not always apply in the digital domain, for instance, physical copies of durable products can never be perfect; however, digital copies of data files can. However, six sigma's goal of reducing the variability of work, especially in terms of introducing defects, is still often a useful concept.

That said, one should be careful about applying six sigma too literally to software processes. First, the six sigma mindset can focus too strongly on minor goals, leading one to overlook the major goals of lean. For instance, take "one of Dr. Deming's most familiar questions, 'For what purpose?' We all know the classic difference between management—doing things right—and leadership—doing the right thing. I believe that, in general, our work falls somewhere in between. I also believe that six sigma leans heavily toward the management side . . . The natural inclination is to use six sigma to drive down the cost of existing products and services. But if customers are increasingly disinclined to want these products and services, or if they are unable to purchase them because they are unemployed, these reduced costs won't help profitability much."[6]

Furthermore, if you apply six sigma slavishly, it can take too much time. "An important aspect of the six sigma program is total process characterization, which involves optimizing all manufacturing processes to a very high Cp and Cpk value . . . It usually takes a team working a few hours a week for a few months to characterize a machine or process. Characterizing all processes in a manufacturing site usually takes continuous effort for a few years . . . A five-year plan mapping the organization's progress from its present state to six sigma is necessary."[7] Needless to say, five years is an eternity in the software industry.

Six sigma then, is a useful concept in the software world so long as you keep it strictly within the overall framework of the lean principles. Given that caveat, individual lean businesses and projects can apply Six sigma techniques where they may find them helpful. Nevertheless, once an organization has mastered the techniques of the lean perfection principle, six sigma becomes irrelevant, since there is no longer a need to reduce variance if one's products have no variance. While that is not possible when producing physical goods, it is possible with software (see the discussion of the perfection principle in Chapter 21). Companies can then drop these expensive six sigma efforts for improvement and save budget while approaching lean perfection.

ENDNOTES

1. Another way to supply that confidence is to create development processes so perfect that defects cannot be introduced into the product. That kind of approach comes

under the perfection principle discussed in Chapter 21. Then the objective basis that people are looking for would be evidence that the processes were truly that good and that airtight. Even then, however, people might not accept the argument . . . simply because it is so unfamiliar in the software industry, and they might not believe it. In that case, separate verification tasks would still be needed.

2. Pretty D***ed Quick.
3. Fagan Inspected.
4. Two- or Three-Letter Acronym.
5. D. R. Schwinn, "Six Sigma and More: Continuing What Would Deming Do," Quality eLine, May 2002, Vol. 4, No. 5.
6. "Six Sigma and More: For What Purpose?," Quality eLine, October 2002, Vol. 4, No. 10.
7. M. Perez-Wilson, "Six Sigma Strategies: Creating Excellence in the Workplace," QCI International, 1997.

18

The Value Stream— Choosing Programming Languages and Tools

RECENTLY, THE MANAGEMENT TEAM of a European software project brought Jim over to recommend ways they could achieve high integrity, at low cost, on an accelerated schedule, in a politically charged environment. Most of these goals are mutually exclusive in craft or mass production, i.e., in any kind of traditional software development approach. However, the principles of lean production break this logjam and make it possible to achieve all of them at once. The first thing Jim did was ask to meet with as broad a cross-section of their leaders and workers as practical. Together, they identified and collected their concerns, which were essentially their values for their project rather than for their products. With a list of these values in hand, the could address what *they* felt was most important, rather than just what Jim might want to tell them.

The project arranged access to the most capable in the company, from company management, project management, systems engineering, software management, requirements analysis, design, programming, verification, safety, and configuration management. Together Jim and the team did the kinds of analyses described in Part II (particularly using the AHP), to determine what they wanted, who their most important customers were, and what those customers wanted. Everyone agreed that the degree to which we could identify and then satisfy those concerns would determine how successful their project would be in the end.

The AHP, as you may recall, does a bottom-up analysis. It is very hard to bias the AHP to predetermine its results, because you usually can't predict how your results will turn out while you're using the method. Therefore, when we'd completed the work and bubbled up the low-level issues they had identified and weighted, we had a high confidence that they had really identified the high-level factors that would determine their project's success. Those factors and their relative importance to their projects success appear in Figure 18-1.

What makes these results so interesting is that these are real numbers from people under tremendous business pressures. There's nothing academic about them. The leaders on the ground actually expected the single biggest determinant of project success to be the continued satisfaction of the project's various customers,

Aspect of the Project	% Contribution
Customer satisfaction (corporation, users, public)	34.0
System integrity (safety, reliability, quality)	30.1
Project management effectiveness (cost, schedule, leadership)	24.1
Technical performance	11.8

Figure 18-1. Project Success Factors

inside and outside the business! (How often is there general agreement on that point?) Closely behind was the integrity of the software. Good project management was rated a little lower, but still significant, and the technical performance of the product was, by far, the smallest area of concern.

This is the same order of emphasis as that of lean production. It also mirrors our experience of what helps a project the most.

Interestingly, this is exactly opposite to the order of priorities on many programs I've seen in industry. They make technical performance the most important issue, with project management following, then product integrity, and finally, customer satisfaction a distant fourth. Such priorities are almost certainly driven by mass production values, especially technocentrism and efficiency, which we discussed in Chapter 2.

When we look at the list of project success factors in Figure 18-1, the choice of programming language doesn't obviously belong to any of them. Therefore, the factor with which we associate programming language determines which language we should choose for any given project.

A pretty common view is that programming languages should be chosen primarily to best support development of the functionality in the software. This would place choice of programming language under the fourth row, technical performance. It leads to choosing languages primarily based on their technical hooks; features such as sophisticated ways of handling tasking, data, encapsulation, and so forth, and having back doors to circumvent the normal structures of the language so you can do whatever you might want to, however you might want to do it.

This view tends to go along with a mass production mindset that technical performance is the single most important thing on a project. It says that choosing a performance-centered language is one of the most important things you can do to ensure project success. And many people do believe and act that way. Indeed, several people on the above project confided they were worried that a language of this kind would be imposed on them by people who thought like that.

However, if the lean viewpoint is right, and if the leaders on the above project have estimated the success factors correctly, then technical performance only gets you about 1/10 of the way to having a successful project. Putting choice of programming language under that category means that picking a language based on performance considerations can only contribute trivially, at best, to project success. We'll soon look at some actual results from using various languages that back up this conclusion.

The lean worldview places choice of programming language under a different category: system integrity. There, it is much more important to project success than it was under technical performance, because system integrity is about three times as important, at least, in these leaders' view (we agree). But putting it here leads to different criteria for choosing a programming language. To understand what those criteria are, we first need to understand how a programming language can contribute to system integrity. Or to put it more precisely, how a programming language can prevent *loss* of system *integrity*.

Integrity cannot be added to a product. Every product starts out as a pure concept with complete integrity—exactly what it represents itself to be, totally consistent with its charter. Like the Platonic ideal of a chair in your mind, it is whole and perfect. However, integrity can be lost from a product as it goes through its development lifecycle. This degradation is what we must work to minimize, both so we end up with the product we originally envisioned, and so we avoid wasting budget, schedule, and customer goodwill.

Developmental processes convert the original concept into a real product that people can use. These processes include methods, tool usages, and techniques, as well as procedures and rules of production. In software, as in other types of industries, this conversion happens in stages. The processes in each stage either retain the integrity of what they have received from the prior stage, or diminish that integrity. They never add to the integrity of what they receive. That can only be done with a backflow to an earlier stage where some original integrity was compromised and can therefore be repaired. When they diminish integrity, processes are entropic, that is, they reduce the order that is inherent in the product.

Actually, integrity alone is not enough; it must be combined with visibility. Integrity is the quality of something being just what it represents itself to be; in other words, being consistent with its purpose or charter. Visibility is the condition of making important characteristics of a product easily seen. We need visibility to get the full benefits of integrity, because it's not enough for a product just to have integrity; we need for others to realize and acknowledge that integrity.

The integrity of a product can be seen through the processes that advance the product. Processes can either retain integrity or lose it. They can also either make visible what they have done to the product's integrity or they can conceal what they have done in this regard. If the processes retain product integrity and also make it clear to interested onlookers that they've done so, then the processes and the product(s) they've produced have visible integrity. Let's briefly review how the processes of the lean lifecycle affect integrity leading up to the coding phase, where the choice of programming language can either retain or lose that integrity.

In the lean lifecycle, value resolution is the first stage of development. We spent all of Part II looking at ways to retain integrity throughout the resolution of value. Integrity, in that case, is making sure that we understand everything the product has to be for it to live up to its purpose in its customers' eyes. Value resolution, done well, provides a reasonably accurate picture of what the product should and will be.

Requirements analysis builds on value resolution by adding more detail and by preparing the value information for use in the upcoming design activities. Few requirements methods rise to the standard of visible integrity. Nonformal requirement methods mostly lack integrity; formal methods mostly lack visibility. SCR, and potentially formal UML (with some voluntary constraints on how it is used), come as close to having both as anything currently available.

Lean design methods and architectural decisions again work to retain the integrity of the developing product. The development lifecycle continues in this way until we reach coding. Here, more than in any other stage of the lifecycle, projects are willing to relinquish the integrity they have previously worked so hard to keep. They do this primarily through their choice of programming language.

Before we look at what aspects of languages most contribute to integrity, and therefore, to project success, it's worth looking at some of the reasons people give for choosing lower-integrity languages. Sometimes they're simply unaware of this issue. Sometimes people are aware, but compromise anyway for reasons like "the coders like this language" (perhaps the most honest answer), "it's the only thing we could have chosen" (the answer that best dodges personal accountability), "we couldn't hire anybody if we didn't make this choice" (heard a lot during the dot com boom, but certainly not defensible since its bust), "Major Bob really likes this language," and "this one's more like the first one I used in my career." When those in authority accept such excuses, they trade away a big portion of one of their greatest assets: their product's integrity. In any event, they've certainly made their product much harder and costlier to integrate and verify, the biggest piece of most projects, even if they only need to verify to typical commercial levels of integrity.

Languages can be grouped a number of ways. Based on our interest in integrity, however, we'll divide them based on how strongly they protect their objects; i.e., whether they type them statically or dynamically.

Before we wade into this subject, let's acknowledge that there are language wars in the software world. Switching metaphors, every language has its own priests, who become illuminated with its hidden secrets and proselytize to everyone who will listen. We don't think of languages in that way. Every language has its strengths and weaknesses. Nevertheless, some languages are more supportive of lean priorities than others, especially of those improving business performance and serving customers. We will look at programming languages through those eyes, and hopefully sharpen our critical ability to evaluate any language's support of the lean lifecycle. We apologize if this discussion offends anyone who is partial to a language that does less well in this light. If it's any consolation, none of the languages we will discuss support lean production perfectly.

Statically Typed Languages: C++, Ada, SPARK, Java

Statically typed programming languages are the default choice for people who care about software integrity. This is mainly because statically typed languages have fewer possible failure modes, and because it is usually easier to verify their programs to a given level of confidence than it is with dynamically typed languages.

In Jim's part of the software industry, aerospace, there's currently a very hot debate about the merits of two relatively common statically typed programming languages. Almost every new project ends up choosing one language or the other. Both are commercially viable (that is, they both have a large selection of stable vendors of compilers and other necessary tools). Any kind of system functionality can be programmed in either language, for a reasonably similar level of effort. Both are object oriented.

So, why the controversy? These languages differ dramatically in two regards: the wow factor, and the ability to preserve the integrity of products coded in them. By looking at why people choose each of these languages, we can see mass vs. lean reasons for choosing any particular programming language on a project.

The first language we'll look at is currently very popular with coders. Full-color magazines with exciting, informal writing targeted at its users. Its underlying language specification is based entirely on pragmatic criteria, such as useful, and sometimes fascinating, abstractions and shortcuts. No one, however, can know with any confidence that a program written in this language is correct. It has no underlying solid criteria, such as mathematics, that would allow for evaluating program correctness. Indeed, some of its main constructs have the side effect of strongly concealing errors in written code.

You cannot even show that a compiler for this language is correct. The language specification allows for so much variability in implementation that no two compilers, indeed, no two versions of the same compiler, can be assured to work the same way. Time after time, it has been seen that a program that works correctly when run through one compiler will not work after it has been run through another without being significantly modified. In every way, the language lacks integrity. Building a house from bricks that have bypassed the kiln leads to a weaker house. Just as surely, writing code in a language that lacks integrity lessens the integrity of the resulting product, and therefore, its verifiability as well.

The second language is considered "uncool" by most programmers. It, too, has publications dedicated to it, but they are journals, stodgier and more serious in tone than the writings for the first language. The underlying language specification is, like the first language, not completely solid (i.e., not mathematically closed). However, it does at least pay more attention to the issue of integrity. Its specification consciously excludes constructs and concepts that the history of programming has shown lead to the highest number of defects in developed code (original development of this language was driven by a set of requirements, including one that "the language shall be designed to avoid error prone features and to maximize automatic detection of programming errors"[1]). This language also excludes constructs that present great difficulties to subsequent error detection and isolation (i.e., verification) efforts. Researchers have shown that this set of priorities has led the language closer to having a solid foundation than does any other major language.[2] Indeed, researchers have chosen this language as the basis for building other languages that do have a fully solid foundation, one of which we will cover shortly.

Finally, this language enforces a high degree of consistency between all its compilers. The language creators of C++ and Ada95 specified a detailed validation suite to be imposed on every compiler of the language. This suite of code is compiled on each would-be compiler and run. The results must match a predefined set of results that come from an ideal, correct compiler.

The functional characteristics of these languages have changed significantly from those of their ancestors, i.e., from C and Ada83 (primarily by adding support for object orientation). However, the characteristics of these languages, with regard to integrity, have not changed much at all. C++'s foundations are just as pragmatic as those of C, and its controls on compilers are equally loose. Ada95's stands against troublesome constructs and, for a strict validation suite, follow the precedents of Ada83.

Prior industry experience with C and Ada83 illustrates the difference that the integrity of a programming language makes. We'll begin with a project whose developers have been ranked amateurs, then look at one using more typical programmers, and finish with one whose people have some of the highest qualifications in industry. They all lead to the same conclusions.

Since in the early 1980s, university professor John McCormick has taught a course in real-time embedded systems software development, "the curriculum's capstone course [where] students must integrate knowledge from their previous work in computer science, electronics, English, mathematics, and physics."[3] The students break into teams and develop the software for an integrated hardware/software system, from system-concept definition through compiled and unit-tested code (integration is optional and can be done if enough time is left at the end of the term).

For the first six years that he taught the course, McCormick had students code their projects in C. The results were not encouraging. "No team successfully implemented minimum project requirements when the C language was used. To ease student and teacher frustrations, I made an increasing amount of my solutions available to the teams . . . [but] even when I provided nearly 60 percent of the project code, no team was successful in implementing the minimum requirements."[4]

After receiving additional funding that allowed him to upgrade the project lab, he decided to try a different programming language: Ada. "I expected a disaster the first year with the new equipment and new language . . . to my amazement, nearly 50 percent of the student teams had their projects working before the end of the semester . . . when I supplied some additional software components (simple Windows packages not relevant to the real-time aspect of the project), more than 75 percent of my teams routinely completed their projects."[5] He attributed much of the difference between C and Ada to the better way that Ada handles scalar quantities . . . in other words, to an improved specification underlying the Ada language, compared to C.

The next example is a more or less regular software business. A few years ago, Vision Systems Ltd. of Australia switched its main development language from C to Ada. It found this decreased its code error rate from 1 in 80 lines to 1 in 270. The company also "cut five months of testing from its newest video security system, and tabulated a savings of over 90 percent in debugging time."[6] Vision Systems attributed the improvement to the stronger typing in the Ada language. The effects really started showing up in the integration phase: "It's usually the integration phase which is the most time consuming . . . with Ada we had very few problems in this area . . . The time fixing error rates plummeted from a traditional four hours to twenty minutes."[7] Perhaps most surprising was that "writing a line of Ada did not require any more time than writing a line of C."[8] The switch also allowed the company to change "its process to one of team responsibility instead of depending on one or two individuals,"[9] in effect, switching from a craft-paradigm organizational structure to a more lean one.

The most advanced example was that of the Verdix Corporation in its compiler and associated tools development. Of the 62 people who developed these tools, 60 developed some C parts and some Ada parts, and "most have master's degrees from good computer science schools."[10] Early tools development was in C; later development was in Ada. Over time, the ratio of code in their products grew to be evenly mixed; approximately 50 percent C and 50 percent Ada. The company reported that the Ada portion was developed for 35 percent less than the C part, while the C code had twice as many bugs as the Ada. An analysis of this experience by Rational Software Corporation, after it acquired Verdix, concluded that the Ada part of the development was not quite as complex as the C part, and therefore, that the Ada advantage was not quite as great as the above figures indicate, but that the advantage was real and still very significant.

Three different types of projects with three different levels of programmers all showed that a project does better when its programming language has higher integrity. There have been many other such cases in industry (try a simple web search on "C++ Ada"). In our research, we haven't been able to find any cases where moving from Ada to C or C++ even maintained the same level of business performance, much less held or improved it. Jim has personally worked on projects using both languages and can vouch for the increased problems that both developers and verifiers have experienced with C and C++ compared to the Ada variants. Many of the problems—e.g., difficulty with isolating error locations—are considered virtually irrelevant in a mass production house. However, they are very serious issues in a lean operation.

By Murphy's Law, a program written in a language that is more error prone *will* include more errors. More errors that are more difficult to find, i.e., less visible, make it harder to gain an equal degree of confidence in a C program than an Ada one. Thus, all other things being equal, it is harder to keep a system from losing its integrity when writing in C than it is when writing in Ada.

All these examples show that a language whose charter includes a high emphasis on integrity and visibility will be a better candidate for use in lean production than a language whose charter does not. A higher-integrity language has another benefit: code written in such a language is generally easier to run through a static analysis tool to find errors. Such a tool detects classic problems, such as misuse of variables, risky program structures, and even departures of the code from its design or requirements long before its time to run tests. Static analysis can detect more errors, more completely, for less cost, and earlier in the lifecycle than testing can. This is a major advantage of high-integrity languages, though by no means the only one.

In choosing any language, consider that the coding activity generally consumes no more than 15 percent of the lifecycle, and then it's largely over. Choosing a language that slightly, or even significantly, improves some aspect of the coding activity, say for supposed better technical performance, if it also lessens the integrity of the entire product and increases the cost of the much larger (often 50 percent or more) integration and verification effort, is a tradeoff that detracts from the success of the entire project. This is an issue that projects cannot afford to cave in on, though they seem to do so more often than not. This principle applies to any language tradeoff, whether it involves C, Ada, Java, or any other option.

One way to soften the impact of using a language with less than perfect integrity is to use a subset of it; i.e., to choose not to use the most troublesome constructs and practices allowed by the language. "[There are] a number of reasons that promote the use of restricted programming models . . . :

- Increase efficiency by removing features with high overheads,
- Reduce nondeterminancy for safety-critical applications,
- Simplify the run-time kernel for high-integrity applications,
- Remove features that lack a formal underpinning, and/or
- Remove features that inhibit effective timing analysis."[11]

For instance, the C language has been subsetted by MISRA (Motor Industry Software Reliability Association).[12] MISRA C reduces or constrains the use of the most problematic or contradictory parts of C, including pointers, structures, and conversions, though it is does not enforce such restrictions the way Ada does. It is about as good as C gets: "We all need reliable software and not just in cars. . . . Given the cost and clarity of the standard there is little excuse for not using it as a guide on all embedded C. Come to that any C, embedded or not."[13]

The Ada language has also been subsetted to improve its integrity. For one, the full Ada language has many ways for implementing multitasking, so many that it isn't possible to know if a multitasking application coded in Ada is correct or not. People who were concerned about this weakness in Ada met in 1997 at the 8th International Real Time Ada Workshop in the Yorkshire village of Ravenscar. They adopted an "'official' definition [that] defines the restrictions that are needed to reduce the full tasking model [of Ada]."[14] These restrictions were named the Ravenscar Profile. Tasking in programs that follow this profile can be easily analyzed for correctness (e.g., to detect problems in order of execution). The principle of subsetting has also been applied to Ada in developing the SPARK language, discussed a little later. The Ravenscar Ada and SPARK subsets have made it "no longer axiomatic that concurrency should be forbidden or even discouraged [for high-integrity software],"[15] a great gain for the language.

Most people we've spoken with in the high-integrity world (and we've worked with a lot of them, especially in Europe, where software integrity is a much bigger issue than it currently is in the United States) believe that using Ada with its built-in restrictions leads to higher-integrity software than using C, even MISRA C with after-the-fact restrictions. Subsetting Ada as discussed above widens the gap even further in their eyes.

Java, a language that is more popular in the IT world than in embedded systems, has a mixed record on integrity. On the one hand, the language has excluded some of the more compromised features of C++, despite the fact that it borrows heavily from that language. Java has no pointers. It doesn't allow casting objects of one type into another type. It generally prohibits backdoor access to private (hidden and encapsulated) data. "Data entities are accessed by only those objects that are supposed to have access to them."[16] Code cannot use a variable until it has been initialized. Java programs run inside a "sandbox" that limits their reach into other programs and parts of the computer on which they are running. There are many other such helpful characteristics.

On the other hand, Java adds features that are hard on integrity and that aren't found in C++, such as automatic garbage collection (memory cleanup), dynamic class loading mechanisms, object serialization (which permits a kind of limited backdoor access to private data), the Java Memory Model (with semantic difficulties), and many factors leading to nondeterministic (i.e., unpredictable) execution timing. "The construction of high-integrity real-time systems requires that both the functional and the temporal behavior of applications is analyzable. This requirement . . . influences the semantics that the language of the profile has to provide."[17] These factors have seriously degraded Java's integrity: "Despite all [its] valuable features, Java has been criticized for its unpredictable performance as well as some security concerns . . . [several of its] mechanism are often considered problematic, especially under time- or performance-critical situations. Moreover, a number of security bugs in the Java virtual machine have been discovered . . . . These fears make Java and its associated technology simply unsuitable for high-integrity systems."[18]

On the whole, Java seems to lie somewhere between C++ and Ada at preserving product integrity. It compromises integrity much more than SPARK, which preserves integrity perfectly. Still, there are ongoing efforts to improve Java's integrity, both by tightening up its weakest aspects, for instance by making compilers which generate deterministic (predictable) garbage collection code,[19] and by subsetting the language through approaches like RTSJ (Real-Time Specification for Java)[20] profiles,[21] and so-called Ravenscar Java.[22] These efforts could bring Java up to a high enough level of integrity to make it the highest-integrity alternative among the languages that are well accepted for IT. The subsets could at some point make Java suitable for real-time embedded software as well.

Of course, Java interfaces well into many IT systems and situations, which can further commend its selection on a project. But integrity is still an important consideration even then, and project development processes and coding standards should work to minimize the use and impact of Java mechanisms that cause a loss of program integrity. A full discussion of the Java language or any other language is outside the scope of this book. Hopefully, the discussion of integrity here will provide the interested reader with enough leads to do your own research of the integrity issues of whatever languages you may be considering.

While one can subset an imperfect language to obtain a less imperfect language, it is better to use a language that is perfect. A perfect language, in this context, is one that can be used to turn a design into code without any loss of product integrity. Another way of saying this is that the language is nonentropic. Its use does not automatically corrupt the product. Of course, even a non-entropic language can be used to write code that has less integrity than there is in its design. In that case, however, the loss is due to avoidable problems in the work done by the coder(s), not to unavoidable deficiencies in the language itself. That is the premise behind the SPARK language.

SPARK is the most mature nonentropic language we've seen yet. SPARK is a subset of Ada and has many of the advantages of regular Ada (such as availability of commercial compilers). So, SPARK programs will compile on standard Ada compilers.

There's more to SPARK than subsetting, however. The syntax of the SPARK language has then been extended with the idea of annotations, or formal specifications of what the code is supposed to do based on its requirements and design decisions. To a standard Ada compiler, the annotations look like comments. A tool called the SPARK Examiner, however, compares the annotations to the code and highlights where the two are inconsistent or incomplete. The tool can also analyze whether the code can allow run-time errors.

The SPARK subset does not compromise integrity. The SPARK annotations add visibility to that integrity, at the cost of added effort. The annotations can also restore integrity back to the level of the product upon which the annotations are based, e.g., restoring the integrity of the code back at least most of the way to the original integrity of the requirements (the annotations do not increase the integrity of the code; as we saw before, nothing can do that).

In Jim's experience, coding in the SPARK subset is always worthwhile. Writing annotations certainly pays off when the complexity or criticality (e.g., to safety or the basic purpose of the software) of the functionality makes it especially important that integrity is fully preserved and avoids all defects. Some people believe using the annotations is always worth the effort. The jury is still out on that in: Jim has specified the use of annotations on parts of a project and not specified them on other parts. In the latter case, quite a bit was saved by giving up a small amount in integrity: Only a few, minor bugs escaped.

Annotations would have played a more important role in overall product quality however, if the rest of the project had not already been using an integrated, lean production approach. The main reason there were so few bugs for the annotations to catch was that the lean techniques of all the previous stages had retained so much of the product's initial integrity. A more traditional development lifecycle upstream would have introduced more bugs and allowed them to make it into the design stage, bugs that would have needed to be caught at this point. This would provide a stronger reason to use annotations. In either case, if annotations are to be used, the product's designer(s) should follow a few design recommendations that can be obtained from the SPARK vendor.[23] Violating those recommendations will make using the annotations much more time-consuming and less cost-effective than it should be. Most of the design recommendations we make in this book also help get you ready for successful SPARK annotation.

SPARK also has its limitations, including lack of tasking (though this is planned to change in the near future) and limited support for object orientation. It is very good, however, for real-time embedded, or high-security, or high-integrity applications that don't require too much interfacing with systems built in different languages.

If you choose a programming language based on how well it upholds the integrity of the system, you can make a big contribution to project success. If you choose a language based on its technical capabilities, you may gain a little in that area, but real-world experience to date shows that your project as a whole will lose far more than it gains overall ... such as by stretching schedule and delaying delivery of the product (if the project takes the time needed to remove the coding-seeded defects), or squandering customer goodwill (if the project does not take the time to remove the coding-seeded defects).

Dynamically Typed Languages: Perl, TCL, Python, PHP

Another class of programming languages does not fit well with the deliverable projects we have been discussing, but its languages have a legitimate, if limited, place in the broader world of lean software development.

When a project is relatively small, or when it doesn't matter if there are undetected errors or differences between the product and the customer values (such as, when you, the developer, are your own customer), then it is worthwhile to consider the category of dynamically typed programming languages, or simply, dynamic languages. These include languages like Perl, TCL, Python, and PHP.

These languages differ from statically typed languages in that they exist primarily for the sake of the developers, rather than for the sake of the business or the customers. "Dynamic languages were designed to solve the technical problems faced by their inventors, not to address specific goals identified as part of a 'strategic plan' to influence buyers of IT solutions."[24] The way they are made and extended informally, by programmers and for programmers, implies that the main customers for these languages are programmers, and that the languages themselves are the main products, evolving rapidly to satisfy programmers' constant values but shifting needs (the constant values are related to the main job of writing software; the shifting needs are the continuously changing technologies of development, e.g., the nature of the web).

Dynamic languages differ from static languages in other ways as well. They are harder to verify than statically typed languages, so they are inappropriate where software security and integrity are a concern. However, if a program isn't being written primarily to advance the business or serve its customers, and software security and integrity are not factors in the project, then dynamic languages can be useful alternatives. Situations like this include development of internal tools, building a prototype to help initially identify customer values, or providing the glue to make otherwise incompatible parts of a system work together, such as when a new development must integrate with legacy software. This kind of integrity is a design goal of many dynamic languages, and there are few other good language alternatives in such situations. These areas are important niches, and this discussion is not intended to detract from that in any way.

This discussion *is* intended, however, to analyze dynamic languages relative to the lean paradigm. One of the greatest strengths of these languages is that they provide high levels of coding productivity. In the kind of strategically directed lean lifecycle we've been discussing, as we've said, coding is only about 15 percent of the lifecycle, so coding productivity should not be the major driving force behind language choice. However, if the lifecycle is already minimizing all activities other than coding, making the coding effort a much larger portion of the overall lifecycle than its typical 15 percent (as in prototyping), then the gain in programmer productivity can make these languages the best tools for the job. This productivity extends to code modification, "if a web application changes the schema of the data being transmitted, clients written in a dynamically typed language will require fewer changes than their statically typed counterparts, all other things being equal."[25]

Even when dynamic languages are appropriate choices, the principles of lean production still hold. Other lean practices should be considered for the project, such as value resolution, changeability-driven domain orientation, and simulation/emulation. Each should be evaluated for its applicability to the specific project.

Interestingly, dynamic languages have been especially popular with members of the Agile-methods community. There is a lot of similarity between the two camps: emphasis on increased coding speed, decoupling coding from requirements analysis, and perhaps most significantly, de-emphasizing strategic planning: "To date, dynamic languages have not been driven by strategic plans . . . the pragmatic, tactical approach to fix what's broken today as opposed to anticipate the problems of tomorrow, has . . . led to a survival of the fittest for *today's* problems, rather than rewarding those with the most compelling vision for *future success*."[26] And again: "The dynamic languages' affinity for loosely-defined, rapidly changing requirements is evident . . . the ease with which people can 'hack something up' with dynamic languages makes them ideal for the frontier."[27] These shared characteristics mean the dynamic languages are also likely to be about as lean as Extreme Programming, which is, as we saw in our analysis in Chapter 6, at least in its current incarnation, much more closely related to craft production.

Dynamic languages are only lean when they are used in the niche whose description began this section. When used outside that niche, they push a project towards craft production.

Limitations of Tools and Automation

Languages come with a set of accompanying tools: compilers, linkers, loaders, and so forth. These were some of the first tools to be developed as the software field grew. And they remain the most essential to software production (who would want to hand-compile code?).

Over time, tools were introduced to cover more and more aspects of the lifecycle: upstream for requirements analysis and design; downstream for testing and integration; and through the lifecycle, for configuration management, process control, software engineering environments, and other overarching concerns.

Perhaps you've wondered why everyone seems to jump on tools as their first, best hope. Since, as we have seen, software is primarily a mass production industry, the answer goes back to the traits of mass production we discussed in Chapter 2. You may recall that this paradigm looks to technology and tools to solve business problems.

Tools are one of the main places in software production where people tend to look for magic bullets. And there are always plenty of software sales professionals standing around, pen and pad in hand to take our orders for their latest silver projectile. Homegrown tools aren't as alluring, because they don't appeal to our technocentrism. We reason that surely a million-dollar tool from a mega vendor will do us more good than writing a piddly utility for ourselves. Yet, lean production favors just such roll-your-own toolmaking. Chapter 3 explored the benefits of specifying and building local tools based on lean analysis of need. In the last chapter, we saw how Lockheed Martin has benefited over several years and through different projects from a purpose-built testing tool.

What one factor would you expect to exert the most influence on the critical production decisions of software industry projects? Most of the projects that we've followed over the years have been driven, more than anything else, by bias in tool choice. Not value, and not even processes, though in a CMM and ISO-9000 world, process of course has a large influence. It even partially determines the choice of programming language. People sometimes choose C++, for instance, at least partly because of a certain support tool they favor. There may be equivalent support available for other languages, but they are eliminated from consideration because their tools aren't *that* tool.

For reasons we will explore, making vendor tools the primary driver for process decisions leads to *muda* and away from lean production. People have come to believe that automation is a solution to development problems and that using it will greatly (and relatively easily and painlessly) improve project performance. We've already seen how flawed that idea is in other industries, such as mighty Toyota's failure to pull off a tool-centric production plant. Technocentrism doesn't work any better in software development.

Oddly, software organizations are just as credulous in believing miraculous tool claims and failing to consider the consequences of adoption, whether the projects are small and insignificant or large with high stakes. Here are three examples. We've intentionally blurred the identifying details to bring out the essential points without unduly embarrassing anyone or betraying any confidences.

- A very large project had a tool-created canyon that blocked information flow between the product engineering and software engineering functions. Both groups used the same modeling language. Each group chose a modeling tool incompatible with the other group's tool, but which was promised to ideally serve that group's needs. The only way to transfer products between the groups was to print them on paper and re-enter them in the other tool by hand. This effectively stopped real-time information flow between the two groups, and therefore, most opportunities for lean flow and cooperative work.

- Another large project existed in which the software organization's management wanted above all else to avoid having to set up its own tool environment. As a result, it subcontracted development of an all-in-one solution to a vendor that, though large and prestigious, had never done such work before. This didn't stop them from promising they could deliver, if that's what it took to get the contract. Ten years later, the solution they developed still did not support some of the most basic development tasks for which it was originally procured. Also, the vendor had long since stopped supporting its product, because it had failed to gain enough customers to make it economically viable. This stranded the project between the proverbial rock and a hard place. The project was, by now, totally dependent on the environment: The work products were all structured around the vendor's custom conventions. Ironically, the only real choice left for the organization was to invest much more heavily into the tool business so the tool would continue; this cost them much more than they would have spent had they decided to create their own environment in the first place.

- A major project existed in an industry heavily regulated by the government, which chose to greatly increase its costs, jeopardize its relations with its regulators, and even risk its ability to put its product into service, in order to pursue the seemingly promising tools it desired. It abandoned a language and tools that its highly critical regulators had officially accepted.

The organization instead chose a newer programming language and related tools that were more popular with the technical staff. The newer language lacked features that directly supported the regulations. This forced the project to reinvent or do without nearly all of the capabilities available off-the-shelf for the previous language. Even with rewritten tools, the task was taking much longer to perform than it would have previously. Some government requirements were impossible to meet with the new language, and required waivers. Amazingly, the organization made its decision knowing it was at risk, without even asking for assurances that the government would accept the new and less verifiable approach.

What is common among all these projects is that tool preference was more important to the organization than foundational lean principles like value, value stream, and flow. Indeed, tool bias determined much more than technical details: It changed everything from organizational structure (e.g., the division of the product and software engineering functions, and therefore, the separation of their respective people), to where the organization had to allocate project resources (e.g., to tool maintenance instead of product development), to the manner and tone of government liaising and customer relations. None of these changes were for the better.

As we said in Part I, adopting a tool-based, technology-driven approach is based on the central tenet of mass production: That efficiency is the most important goal of a production line. Yet we've seen repeatedly through this book that what projects really need is not efficiency, but rather flexibility and waste reduction.

So why do software professionals pin their biggest hopes on their mass-paradigm tools? When we've asked this of the people who are doing it, certain patterns have emerged in their answers. They've said that new tools and technologies:

- Shorten tasks
- Help them with hiring and retaining the best and brightest
- Make their work more interesting
- Contribute to moving the overall field forward
- Are the easiest thing to change and just maybe they will help!

Let's address the fallacies of each of these points.

Fallacy One: New Tools Shorten Tasks

The first point, shortening tasks, is a way of restating the argument for greater efficiency, the classic justification for mass production tooling. In mass production, one always wants to buy the faster tool with the shorter processing time per part. This way, you can increase the number of parts being processed per time period. As in Toyota's Tahara plant, this only helps if one can keep the tool busy all the time. If you can't do that, the extra tool speed doesn't help with the real cost driver, which is assembly span time (discussed in Chapter 19).

Additionally, faster or more powerful tools tend to be a lot more expensive. If the tool doesn't help the overall cause, but it costs more, then the tool cost per unit is actually higher than it was with the older, cheaper tooling. In other words, the improved technology has increased overhead costs. That hurts, rather than helps, profitability.

Does such waste actually happen with advanced software tools? Yes, and it's inevitable in a nonlean production line. Here's why. Recall the example software project discussed in Chapter 3: Only 1 percent of its time span was spent in productive work in the stages of its production. The other 99 percent of its time span was idle or wasted.

Most software tools address tasks that occur within the stages of production. Various modeling tools, code-generation tools, analysis tools, and so forth, are in a nonlean software production line seeking to speed up what starts out as only 1 percent of the overall time span. The project still pays its people, its light bills, and its lease for the remaining 99 percent of the time, *the part of the cycle that the new tools hardly ever affect.* Even if the new tools double the work speed, this only improves the overall flow by ½ percent! The increased cost in using the new tool must be less than the savings from this ½ percent acceleration, or else the organization's costs per unit produced will actually increase.

This isn't a Luddite argument. There is a place for new tools and technology; they just shouldn't be in the driver's seat of production line planning. Here are at least three cases in which new tools and technology are called for:

1. When the process has been so leaned that time-in-stage has become a significant portion of the assembly span time
2. When a tool cuts the time to move product between stages
3. When external constraints like safety, integrity, or tool obsolescence mandate improvement in technology

In every case, a key thing to keep in mind is whether the tool improves the overall assembly span time. (This characteristic is discussed in more detail in Chapter 19.) If it doesn't, the tool is likely suboptimizing some aspect of the work, without benefiting the overall production line or business performance.

Fallacy Two: New Tools Help in Hiring and Retaining the Best and Brightest

Our personal experience has been that better tools are not really what bright, desirable people are looking for in their careers. Most of them are looking for a project that is well managed, reasonably low in stress, respected in the company and preferably in the industry, in which they feel they can succeed and grow, and yes, one that is using at least reasonably current technology. But people's decisions to come, stay, or leave are seldom based primarily on having absolutely the most cutting-edge tools. The 382J program saw several people leave for the greener pastures of the technology *de jour*. Almost all of them returned a few months later, and nearly all said that they had forgotten how poorly most software projects were run. On the more recent C-27J project, which extended the lean approach of the 382J, there has been almost no voluntary turnover.

Fallacy Three: New Tools Make the Work More Interesting

The third reason given for putting tools first is that it makes work more interesting. Setting aside whether the main purpose of a business is to interest its workers, the experience of other lean industries is that the lean paradigm does indeed keep up worker interest. It gives people broader job descriptions, greater decision-making discretion, and more respect. Most workers in these lean industries find these broader benefits more than compensate for occasionally having to use an older or smaller machine or tool. Returning to our personal experience, worker morale and interest on lean projects like the 382J and C-27J have always been very high, even when the telecoms, dot coms, and other software producers were offering hotter technologies (many of which have since also become obsolete).

Fallacy Four: New Tools Contribute to Moving the Overall Field Forward

This fourth justification, that driving toward newer tools moves the software field forward, is meaningless. Moving forward should be driven by building systems that customers want, making them more affordable, and making our software businesses more successful. The criteria for needing new technology should be these concerns, not technology for technology's sake. Unfortunately, the technologies of most software and other industries do not address basic business needs and so the technologies die off quickly. We should not be cynical about technologies in general and thus miss out on the good gains they sometimes provide; the point is that we must simply evaluate them against our most important goals and justify them on this basis before adopting them.

Fallacy Five: Tools Are Easy to Change and Just Maybe They Will Help

The final point is perhaps the truest one. If a software process is broken, and if one doesn't understand why, there's always a new tool and someone to promote it as the answer to the problem. One of the best things about lean principles is that they give you a rational way of evaluating what is wrong with a software production line and establishing strategies (often inexpensive!) for fixing it. Then there is no need to resort to "tool craps" and "winning the big one" to get out of the bind caused by having an ineffective process.

As with Toyota in Tahara (see Chapter 2), most organizations in most industries—even lean ones—have temporarily reverted at some point to the tool-driven, technology-dependent mindset. Much of Detroit periodically takes another stab at finding an automated solution to its labor and cost challenges. So we shouldn't judge software businesses that haven't even begun the journey to lean production too harshly for expecting great things from advanced tools. But in a nonlean environment, any benefits from automation will be swamped and even, in many cases, prevented by the other kinds of waste that are left in the lifecycle.

Despite this limitation of tools, we should never discount their usefulness. Well-chosen ones can greatly help with lean production. The right tools for software, like the right tools for any other industry, will be those that improve movement between stages of production (improving flow), are flexible and can be reconfigured quickly to handle product variations, and are well adapted to the concept and execution of the overall production line. There may also be a need for tools to help with specific concerns, like evaluating products against the postconditions of a stage of production, enforcing techniques of the perfection principle, or making verification dependably repeatable.

The single most important function of tools, however, is to improve the overall flow of the line, because you spend 90 percent or more of your time in software projects in the transitions between productive stages. The most beneficial use of tools then is usually to speed product assemblies (e.g., requirements sets, portions of a design, or builds) on to the next stage of work. That is, tools that strongly address the assembly transport cost driver (also discussed in the next chapter). To do this job, tools must usually support common data formats or even shared knowledge metaconstructs (XML and the CWM can help here). As the standards in the software industry become stronger, it becomes easier all the time to find common ground among differing tools and so improve the products' flow between them. More importantly, tool cohesiveness improves work activities to develop the products.

Creating custom tools for a project's own specific needs is a lean tradition in many production industries. It is not necessary or even desirable to purchase everything off-the-shelf from commercial vendors. A simple homegrown tool, well adapted to a particular need of the production line, is often the key to making everything else work together optimally. In lean production, these tools are also usually less expensive to obtain or develop, and somewhat lower tech. Of course, before an organization even considers tools, it should identify and remove any impediments to product movement resulting from the current process architecture. This gets back to the importance of the rest of the value stream, and of techniques like *kaizen*.

ENDNOTES

1. Requirement 1B of the "Steelman" specification; published in D. A. Wheeler, "Ada, C, C++, and Java vs. The Steelman," at www.adanome.com/History/Steelman/steeltab.htm and viewed on August 7, 2004.

2. Dr. Bernard Carre' of the University of Southampton and creator of SPARK, now retired, did much of this work over a period of several years.

3. J. W. McCormick, "Software Engineering Education: On the Right Track," *CrossTalk, The Journal of Defense Software Engineering*, August 2000.

4. Ibid.

5. Ibid.

6. From online article at www.adaic.irg/atwork/hideo.html, August 7, 2004.

7. Ibid.

8. Ibid.

9. Ibid.

10. S. F. Zeigler, "Comparing Development Costs of C and Ada," Rational Software Corporation, March 30, 1995.

11. P. Puschner, A. Wellings, "A Profile for High-Integrity Real-Time Java Programs," 4th IEEE International Symposium on Object-Oriented Real-Time Distributed Computing (ISORC), 2nd–4th May 2001.

12. Published in the 1998 MISRA document, "Development Guidelines for Vehicle Based Software," and available for a small fee from the MISRA organization through its website at www.misra.org.uk.

13. Chris Mills, "A Standard for Embedded and Real-time C," http://www.phaedsys.demon.co.uk/chris/misra-c/misrac.htm as of July 22, 2004.

14. A. Burns, B. Dobbing, T. Vardanega, "Guide for the use of the Ada Ravenscar Profile in high integrity systems," University of York Technical Report YCS-2003-348, January 2003.

15. J. Kwon, A. Wellings, S. King, "Ravenscar-Java: A High-Integrity Profile for Real-Time Java," University of York Technical Report YCS 342, May 2002.

16. S. Oaks, "Java Security," O'Reilly & Associates, Inc., 1998, section 2.1.

17. P. Puschner, A. Wellings, "A Profile for High-Integrity Real-Time Java Programs," 4th IEEE International Symposium on Object-Oriented Real-Time Distributed Computing (ISORC), 2nd–4th May 2001.

18. J. Kwon, A. Wellings, S. King, "Ravenscar-Java: A High-Integrity Profile for Real-Time Java," University of York Technical Report YCS 342, May 2002.

19. J. Ventura, F. Siebert, and A. Walter in their paper "HIDOORS, A High Integrity Distributed Deterministic Java Environment," WORDS 2002, January 2002. The claim that this can be done is "based on synchronization points for constant-time exact root-scanning of stacks and registers, write-barriers and a non-fragmenting object model." Jim Sutton has had no opportunity to verify this claim.

20. G. Bollela, B. Brosgol, P. Dibble, S. Furr, J. Gosling, D. Hardin, M. Turnbull, "The Real-Time Specification for Java," Reading, MA: Addison Wesley, 2000.

21. P. Puschner, A. Wellings, "A Profile for High-Integrity Real-Time Java Programs," 4th IEEE International Symposium on Object-Oriented Real-Time Distributed Computing (ISORC), 2nd–4th May 2001.
22. J. Kwon, A. Wellings, S. King, "Ravenscar-Java: A High-Integrity Profile for Real-Time Java," University of York Technical Report YCS 342, May 2002.
23. Praxis Critical Systems; Bath, England. Actually, the lean design principles discussed in this book go a long way towards preparing for the successful use of SPARK. In other words, lean and SPARK are highly compatible.
24. D. Ascher, "Dynamic Languages – ready for the next challenges, by design," July 27, 2004 whitepaper published at http:/activestate.com/Corporate/Publications/ActiveState_Dynamic_Languages.pdf as of August 4, 2004.
25. Ibid.
26. Ibid.
27. Ibid.

19

Flow—Applying Industrial Insights to Software Production

T HE INDUSTRIES OF THE WORLD HAVE LEARNED many important things in the last two hundred years. Some of their best lessons are about ways to optimize a production line. Much of this falls under the category of the lean flow principle. Software hasn't considered itself a production line industry, so it has been relatively unaware of these ideas.

Nevertheless, as we have seen, software can and should be thought of as a production line industry. Then all the benefits of this advanced industrial thinking can be ours. All we must do is conceptualize the lifecycle as a production line with product families and products. This is the same conceptualization that other industries have had to adopt to gain the benefits of lean production: "Converting the entire organization to continuous flow [*is done by*] reorganizing by product families."[1]

Because we covered the general ideas of lean flow back in Chapter 3, we won't repeat them here (though this would be a good time to reread that section if you'd like a refresher). What we will do in this chapter is take these ideas and apply them to software development.

Good flow is at the heart of the smoothest running production lines, whether they are making software or some other product. Flow focuses on individual products, in the context of product families. As we saw under the value stream principle, lean domain engineering makes it possible to turn almost any individual software product into a member of a product family, with a net gain in productivity, even if only one product is ever created in that family. In this chapter, we will see how even one product can be divided into large numbers of similar parts, allowing flow techniques to be applied repeatedly. That's how the benefits of flow multiply.

In software development, the production process consists of value requirements analysis, detailed design, coding, and verification (domain analysis and architectural design having already been performed under the design stream). So, software production takes the product-family architecture and high-level processes provided by the value stream activities, and combines them with the specific requirements for the current product being developed, to create a real executable and usable piece of software.

The relationship between flow and the value stream goes the other way as well. Value stream activities must prepare for good flow as they are defining the product family. Industry has learned that product designs must have certain characteristics if their production is to flow well.

When you are creating a software product-family architecture, you should consider these flow-oriented design concerns along with the design concerns we've been discussing in the last two chapters. We will discuss the flow-oriented design characteristics and how they apply to software in the upcoming section about software DFMA.

However, before we see what those design characteristics are, we need to see why they are needed. For that we look to another kind of wisdom from industry; the traits of a production line that others have learned can help or hinder flow. Since good flow has been shown to drive down costs, these factors are often called "*production cost drivers.*"

Industrial Cost Drivers and Software Production

Every industry wants to decrease its costs of production; this makes its products more affordable and therefore more competitive. Many industries have discovered that flow-related issues can greatly affect the costs of production. Most of these cost drivers are not recognized at all within the software world, and therefore, have no standard names in our field. Nevertheless, they affect us as much as any other industry. Certainly, if we handle these aspects poorly, our costs go up quickly, and conversely, if we deal with them well, we drive costs down out of all proportion to the effort we expend on them. The cost drivers are:

1. Assembly span time
2. Part count
3. Part simplicity
4. Alignment
5. Verification time
6. Assembly transport

Assembly Span Time

In many industries, a product being built and moving through the production line is called an *assembly*. A software assembly is either an entire software build, or some part thereof, being constructed from a product-family design. What we mean by a software part will make more sense when we get into software

DFMA. However, that discussion isn't necessary to understand the idea behind this cost driver.

Assembly span time refers to an assembly's total time of production from beginning to end. In software terms, part span is more important than build span (because build span is largely determined by part span), but it's only useful if there are many similar parts in the design. If the parts are different, it's hard to identify the production issues that are common to them all and target them for improvement.

The longer the span time, the more opportunities there are for the work in progress to become disconnected from demand, for instance, as market conditions change while the product is being produced. And, customers could become impatient with the slow progress on the software. There are fixed overhead expenses that continue throughout development, which add to the cost of the product. Also, there's the possibility that competitors may beat you to market because they can build a product faster than you.

Part Count

Part count affects costs because fewer parts, in general, means there's less assembly work to do. This helps in two ways: fewer stages in production and fewer activities per stage. Industries making modern products from appliances to vehicles, for instance, use newer materials like plastics and composites to build using a smaller number of larger parts than was typical in the past. Production stages that in older projects would have bolted, screwed, glued, or welded together the smaller parts are no longer needed. Fewer stages of production also lead to fewer transitions between stages. Common stages in software production include requirements analysis, detailed design, coding, unit verification, integration, system verification, acceptance testing, delivery, and maintenance (various lifecycle models differ on these).

The benefits of reducing in-stage work are obvious. The benefits of reducing the number of transitions may seem less clear. Transitions, however, are where much of the non-value-adding work and time on the production line occur. Recall the example in Chapter 3 of a typical nonlean project, in which 99 percent of its assembly span time was taken up by waiting. During waiting times, you are not adding value to your software.

The goal of having fewer parts and an easier, quicker assembly is addressed by the mainline industrial technique called *Design For Assembly* (DFA). DFA applies strategies to reduce the number of parts, which tends to make each part (assembly) in the new version of the production line larger. In software, the size we're talking about is not in lines of code nor in complexity, but rather, in the amount of the end system that can be legitimately generated from a given design element (e.g., class). The Lockheed Martin 382J MC OFP architecture has a low part count, because just three classes cover well over half the entire software system. We will say more about this strategy later in this chapter.

Part Simplicity

Part simplicity is the idea that parts should be made as simply as practical. While at The Queen's University of Belfast (Dr. Middleton's institution), Dr. Tony Hoare said, "There are two ways of constructing a software design: One way is to make it so simple that there are obviously no deficiencies, and the other way is to make it so complicated that there are no obvious deficiencies. The first method is far more difficult."

Nevertheless, part simplicity needs to be considered in conjunction with reduced part count. One could make simple parts by creating a multitude of tiny parts with little functionality in each one; but that would drive up the amount of assembly (i.e., integration) work. Alternatively, one could reduce part counts by making fewer, bigger, more complex part designs, but they would be difficult to manufacture. The key is to make fewer and simpler parts. For instance, the three main classes in the Lockheed Martin 382J MC OFP's architecture are unusually simple, and the project has made no compromises on reusability, understandability, productivity, or integrity. There's more information about this project in Appendix A.

Making simple parts is addressed by the mainline industrial technique called *Design for Manufacture* (DFM). For the reasons we just discussed, DFM is usually combined with DFA. The combination is sometimes contracted to "DFMA," or "Design for Manufacturing and Assembly." DFMA applies integrated strategies to both reduce the number of parts and their complexity of manufacture.

Interestingly enough, the goals of DFM and DFA are conflicting: Reducing the number of parts, as an isolated activity, tends to make each resulting part more complicated. Conversely, making parts simpler, as an isolated activity, tends to shrink them (i.e., decrease the portion of the final system each one covers). This is where the designer's creativity is needed: It is usually possible to find a strategy that achieves both goals to a large degree, as we shall see in the discussion of software DFMA.

Alignment

Alignment influences how quickly the work is done within a given production stage. Manufacturing of durable goods often positions holes within parts so that locator pins can be inserted at particular stages of production. These pins precisely align the parts that are being joined, greatly reducing the time required to mate the parts and the overall time in the stage. Of course, this also decreases complete assembly span time. The software analogy to this is to have regular, repeated, and simple interfaces. This leads to easy and quick alignment of the instances of the product-family classes made for specific products; the famed "Lego-Block"™ construction experience. This approach is related to the DFA component of DFMA.

Verification Time

Verification time is the amount of time required for the project to gain an acceptable amount of confidence that the product coming out of all production stages is reasonably free of defects.

As we discussed in the last chapter, verification often consumes the single largest pool of time (and money). Shortchanging verification early in the lifecycle allows defects to be passed along onto later stages. These lead to more backflows later in development, costing even more to fix than if they had been detected and corrected in the stage in which they occurred. This approach also hurts assembly span time. Cutting final verification time turns the customer into the final and unpaid verification agent, seldom a good business move. Making verification quick and easy is a better move, as we discussed in Chapter 17.

The easier it is to verify an assembly within a production stage, the cheaper the verification costs will be, and the sooner the assembly can move on to the next stage (assuming that you are verifying it in the stage and not, in the mass production way, deferring it all to the end). This helps shorten assembly span time.

The most cost-effective way to cut verification time and costs is to eliminate the need for it at all. You do this by producing perfect products at each stage according to the lean-perfection principle covered in Chapter 21. Nevertheless, when this can't or won't be done completely, the best way forward is to combine as many perfection techniques as practical (even if they are done only incompletely) with verification-driven development.

Assembly Transport

Assembly transport refers to the effort and delays in transporting an assembly between stages. Earlier, we noted that the part count cost driver is also concerned with transitions between stages. However, the strategy in that case was to design with fewer parts so we can reduce the number of stages and therefore the number of transitions between the stages. We deal with the assembly transport driver by minimizing the time a product spends while it is in those transitions. We do this by determining what happens to the assembly (or software part, or software build) as it moves through its production sequence.

In performing a *kaizen* for a durable good, we would literally walk around the factory floor to see where the assembly went and how it made it between stages. We would then find ways to bring the stages closer together in distance, and in the effort and time between ending one stage and beginning the next.

With software, we take this walk more conceptually, but with just as much discipline. The mental exercise involved is to find a way to reduce the conceptual distance between software development stages and accelerate the movement of the assembly between stages. The VSM techniques we discussed in Chapter 16 show where the delays are actually occurring and often give insight into why. Sometimes simple management actions can bring about big improvements, such as in the problem we discussed where people didn't realize something was ready for them to start working on. The solution might be to implement a better notification system.

However, some delays are due to technical reasons that cannot be addressed through simple management changes. For instance, it is quite time-consuming to convert most kinds of software requirements into a form that can be used to create test cases. This is part of a transition between stages, i.e., between requirements analysis and acceptance testing.

For this kind of situation, the only way to greatly improve project performance is to improve technical practices. For instance, if SCR is used for value resolution and requirements analysis, the resulting requirements can be used as-is for test cases. This completely eliminates the transition between requirements and acceptance testing, and it also eliminates the first major activity within acceptance testing (i.e., test-case development). Likewise, SCR requirements can become the low-level requirements of the design, if the architecture assigns one SCR requirement to one software procedure. Jim has used this strategy on several projects, and discuss it further both later in this chapter and in Appendix A. This removes the transition of adapting requirements to be ready for design and so forth.

Software DFMA: Design for Manufacturing and Assembly of Computer Programs

These cost drivers are reality, not theory, and will reward being managed even on software projects. The industrial design approach called "DFMA" addresses the root causes of waste in these cost drivers. DFMA is a cornerstone of the lean production of durable goods. As we stated above, creating the fewest, biggest (most replicated), simplest parts possible reduces the number of stages of production and the costs that go with transitions between them, while speeding the work within stages.

We can apply the techniques of DFMA to software, with a tremendous potential to reduce costs and shorten assembly span time. This is both because DFMA is one of the most powerful lean techniques, and because of all the lean techniques, it has perhaps had the least impact to date on software industry thinking. "Reducing the number of parts and simplifying their fabrication can be much more effective than either automation or a fast work pace in reducing product costs."[2] We can get a relatively bigger jump on our competitors by doing well what they do especially badly.

"Big Parts"

In our previous discussion of the parts count cost driver, we saw the advantages of having fewer, bigger parts. However, in most software projects the design has a multitude of small, unique parts. Even in OO projects, most designs still have dozens, if not hundreds, of completely different classes. Most classes are instantiated into from one up to only a handful of objects. If any classes give rise to larger numbers of objects, they nevertheless account for little of the overall size of the final system.

The result of traditional development approaches is programs composed of myriads of unique small parts, the antithesis of DFMA. None of the typical strategies—not even in OO—chase after what is by far the biggest prize, the fundamental internal repetitions and similarities among the many things that any system does. If developers leveraged those similarities, they could drastically reduce the number of parts and make serious progress on DFMA.

Now, in Chapter 15, we said that good domain architecture divides a program into many small pieces. How can we say we want both small pieces and big parts? The answer is simple: What we want to keep small and what we want to make big are two different things. The code size of the individual program modules should be small; at least, as small as practical for the modules to be naturally cohesive and complete. We'll explore what that means in lean software production, presently.

However, the number of objects we instantiate from each of the main classes in the architecture should be large. Good lean architecture can easily accomplish both things. It can have small numbers of classes, which give rise to large numbers of similar objects, each of which has as few lines of code as practical. And, if the main classes are expansive enough, then adding up all the code from all the objects instantiated from these classes will account for a sizeable portion (in total lines of code) of the overall program.

How do we make this happen? Certainly not by OO alone. As we've said, traditional OO leads to too many dissimilar parts.[3] Also, not with mega classes that instantiate into large numbers of objects that require so much work by the detailed designer on each instantiation that the benefit we're looking for is lost. And certainly not by functional orientation: Any system of significant size performs so many dissimilar functions that there is no way to leverage that into large numbers of small, similar objects.

One way forward is to look backwards to an idea that was far ahead of its time. When it was first presented to the software world in the 1970s, nobody recognized its power. It was inherently lean, but it arrived before most U.S. industries even recognized there was such a thing as lean production. Needless to say, it didn't catch on in the craft software development world of the time, where the first tentative forays into software mass production were considered cutting edge.

This deceptively simple idea is a set of guidelines for software architecture called "the Parnas criteria."[4]

The Parnas Criteria

The Parnas criteria are based on Dr. Parnas' principle of information hiding. Information hiding is the concealment of any information about what a software module does, that the users of the module (e.g., other modules that call it) don't need to know about in order to use it. This concept may sound familiar: The literature of object orientation sometimes uses the phrase "information hiding." But, as Dr. Parnas points out in his comments on object orientation, which we quoted in Chapter 10, few object-oriented projects ever actually use information hiding. There is still much untapped potential in the principle and much unrealized power in the Parnas criteria.

The Parnas criteria identify three major categories of software modules:

1. Requirements-hiding (sometimes called "behavior-hiding")
2. Hardware-hiding
3. Implementation-hiding (or "software decision-hiding")

Requirements-hiding modules hide the details of the requirements. They present to the rest of the software system only a high-level interface to the logic of the requirements. One seldom finds requirements-hiding modules in software architectures.

Hardware-hiding modules conceal the details of how the hardware in the system works. They present a high-level interface to the hardware. Something like this idea is common in software development today, especially in ideas like middleware. However, it's worth noting that Dr. Parnas gave a much more restrictive (and beneficial) definition of hardware-hiding than what is commonly used: "Much of the complexity of embedded real-time software is associated with controlling special-purpose hardware devices. Many designers seek to reduce this complexity by isolating device characteristics in software device interface modules . . . While these . . . modules generally do make the rest of the software simpler, their interfaces are usually the result of an ad hoc design process, and they fail to encapsulate the device details completely. As a result, device changes lead to changes throughout the software, rather than just in the device interface module. We developed a systematic procedure based on the abstract interface principle to design the interface to . . . device interface modules."[5]

The trick is in deciding what gets hidden and what is made visible. Most current attempts at hardware-hiding apply the idea imperfectly and miss out on the biggest benefits of the approach. The article from which this quote came explains in more detail how to define hardware-hiding modules (and the other two types as well). We'll discuss a simple way to define them in our own projects, shortly.

Implementation-hiding modules deal with processing that is derived, and neither directly related to the hardware being used, nor to the system's high-level requirements. Again, there is more information on this subject in the Parnas article quoted above.

Each of the three Parnas categories is the perfect basis for a class in OO terminology. That is, you can have a class for requirements details, especially if you have a standard format for requirements, i.e., with standard inputs and outputs to the requirements themselves, which can be used to define how any user of an object of this class will interface with it. You can have a class for hardware details, especially if you have a standard way of defining hardware interfaces (as in the standard procedure Parnas has created for defining the abstract interfaces to hardware-hiding modules). And you can have a class for implementation details and intermediate processing, again as long as it has standard structure and interfaces.

If you standardize these three types of classes for your own use in software development, you now have the basis for building software-DFMA style big parts, i.e., classes that instantiate into many objects. This is because any system of significant size has many requirements. Most systems have several hardware interfaces, and most have at least some implementation issues worth hiding as well. Creating classes based on other types of similarity—functional, subsystem, or even domain structures—does not give rise to nearly as many recurrences of similar processing as when they are based on requirements or hardware items or software decisions.

Beyond the benefit of big parts, subdividing architecture according to the Parnas criteria also addresses some of the domain considerations discussed in Chapter 15. For instance, we said that a good domain design strictly limits the amount of the system that must be changed as a result of any given change to the charter of the system. Such charter changes usually consist of either modifying requirements so that the system does something differently than before, porting the system to run on different hardware (either execution platform or interfaces), or changing an algorithm or heuristic. We will focus on the first two of these for our discussion here (you can apply the idea to the third as needed, or again, refer to the Parnas article for more information).

Seldom are requirements and hardware changes coupled together. Adding functionality may expand a system, however, more often than not, the system continues to use the same hardware to do the new tasks. Or, a system may be ported to different hardware because of a change in vendor, or the desire to prepare for future functional expansion, but such porting is often not directly connected to any specific functional change. An example of a direct connection between functionality and hardware would be something like adding voice-recognition, necessitating the addition of a hardware microphone: Such direct coupling is much less common than decoupled change. In fact, good software management intentionally works to separate implementations due to different causes, a technique sometimes called separation of concerns or change isolation. Separation of concerns makes it easier to verify that changes have been made properly, or to identify the cause for failure when they have not.

Defining separate classes based on requirements-hiding and hardware-hiding keeps these two major causes of system change from being coupled within the software. In a Parnas-criteria architecture, any single requirements change will usually affect only the inner details of some single object of the requirements-hiding class, without changing the object's interfaces to the hardware-hiding or implementation-hiding objects. A single hardware change will likewise affect the inner details of some object of the hardware-hiding class, without usually changing its interfaces to the requirements-hiding or implementation-hiding objects. Using implementation-hiding decouples other concerns in a similar way, but as we said, we won't go into that further here.

We'd like these classes to have good alignment. That is, we'd like every object derived from these classes to have predictable interfaces analogous to the pre-drilled holes and locator pins of lean parts in durable-goods assembly. Software designers have long sought mechanisms for bringing about good alignment, for instance, in various schemes like software backplanes. However, the most successful of these have always worked only on a limited scale. What is different about software DFMA is that we seek a more universal approach that obtains such benefits across a much greater variety of software systems and in a larger portion of each program.

While there are doubtless other ways to make software big parts with good alignment, one way that has been proven to work particularly well is to structure Parnas-criteria classes with the parts of an SCR specification, from the Parnas-Madey Four-Variable Model. The variables, i.e., MONs, CONs, INs, and OUTs, become the interfaces to these classes,[6] and therefore the holes and locator pins of the software parts, e.g., if one type of class exports MONs and another imports them, the two will go together smoothly (and so on, for the other types of variables). The REQ, IN, and OUT tables that use these variables are hidden as secrets within the requirements-hiding and hardware-hiding classes; they become the jigs that bring the parts (objects of the classes) together at their holes and pins (SCR variables).

The reason this works is because the SCR method divides the specification of a system in terms of the environment surrounding the system. It produces specifications of requirements (MONs, CONs, and REQ relations), and also specifications of hardware interfaces (INs, OUTs, and IN or OUT relations). Requirements and hardware interfaces are, of course, the subjects of the first two categories in the Parnas criteria. Thus, if we have done our value resolution and requirements analysis in SCR, we have already identified the raw materials we need for directly creating objects derived from Parnas requirements-hiding and hardware-hiding classes.[7]

So, objects of the requirements-hiding class use software variables to represent the MONs and CONs of the REQ relation. These variables become the standardized interfaces to the objects of the requirements-hiding class. Within the objects of the requirements-hiding class are the details of the REQ relations and their constraints.

Similarly, objects of the hardware-hiding class use software variables to represent the INs and OUTs of the IN or OUT relations (the MON variables also get involved here, because MONs—or internal software variables that represent the external actual MONs—are outputs of the hardware-hiding class, as well as the inputs of the requirements-hiding class). Within the objects of the hardware-hiding class are the details of the IN and OUT relations and their constraints.

The beauty of organizing your architecture this way is that, every time an SCR requirement is added or changed, you can do a complete lifecycle development on it. That is, you can take the specific requirements-hiding object that will receive that requirement and put it through requirements analysis (of the requirement being added), detailed design, coding, and verification. Estimation is a piece of cake, because the SCR table's dimensions (rows and columns and the complexity that you estimate) tell you how long it will take to run through that lifecycle. You get better at this rather quickly after running through a few SCR requirements.

This approach leads to very short cycle times, massive parallelism in development (many SCR requirements can be worked at the same time), reduced risk (both because of improved estimation and also because of almost complete decoupling of all the work going on at once), less complexity (decoupled work is inherently much easier), and a myriad of other benefits. See the discussion in Appendix A for specific examples.

For our purposes here, as we said, we'll ignore the software decision-hiding class. However, you should read the Parnas articles to discover how they are constructed and used.

Now, compare this approach to the way that traditional architecture handles alignment. Each time a new requirement is levied on a system, the first step is to decide which objects to deploy for each of the various aspects of the requirement. Where the requirement goes is not predetermined like in the SCR/Parnas-inspired approach. If the project is conscientious, it will then have someone analyze possible side effects of the change. Nevertheless, unless the development lifecycle is completely formal, there is no objective assurance that the analysis will have detected all possible problems. Once the changes have been approved, objects are modified to implement the requirement. Tests are devised to cover not only the effects of the requirement, but also to demonstrate the absence of side effects. This testing is as uncertain as the design decisions: One never knows if the test cases are thorough enough.

Every step along this path takes longer to perform, and the quality of the results is less certain, than with big parts and good alignment as with SCR and Parnas-based architectural concepts.

Design Patterns

One fairly popular design approach that, done wrongly, will lead a designer away from DFMA is to uncritically adopt patterns like those in a design-patterns book. "The key [in DFA and DFM] is NOT to know the rules . . . but rather HOW and WHEN to use them. This requires designers to be reflective and to think not only about the design problem, but also about the environment in which they work and their own capabilities. Reflective designers will have much more success than designers who just plow through a problem assuming that there is a 'cookbook' answer available."[8]

Design patterns can be useful, but they must be subordinated to the more important lifecycle goals of customer satisfaction and business performance. Any pattern being considered for use must account for the unique needs of the domain, the priorities of the organization, the respective strengths and weaknesses of the off-the-shelf patterns, and the goals of DFMA. Given that caveat and used in that spirit, design patterns can be another useful tool in the designer's toolkit, rather than (as usually happens) a set of directives to be followed whenever possible.

Other Benefits

DFMA solves several other problems that are typical in most software lifecycles. Alignment strictly limits the amount of collateral damage that mistakes made while implementing any given change to the software system can do to the rest of the system. It decreases stress, by giving developers a reasonably well-defined job to do with a much lower risk of major unexpected difficulties (there will always still be difficulties, of course!). The Lockheed Martin 382J MC OFP developers consistently commented on how much they appreciated this characteristic of the program, as did those on its follow-on reuse program, the C-27J MC OFP development.

Finally, DFMA makes it very easy to train software engineers new to the project—even those new to software engineering—to become quickly productive. Since there are fewer architectural parts to learn about to be able to implement software and since the implemented parts integrate easily when they have been made correctly (providing quick feedback and correction of when they are not), a well-documented DFMA-oriented process helps greatly with the management- and people-challenges of software development. These are some of the most important and often difficult aspects of software projects.

ENDNOTES

1. *Lean Thinking,* pg. 95.
2. *Lean Thinking,* pg. 240.
3. Four strategies of OO do reduce part counts: static class inheritance, object composition, type parameterization, and multiple inheritance.

   Static class inheritance fixes inheritance at compile time. Static inheritance is a sound strategy that lean development uses as well. However, traditional OO static class inheritance is based on criteria that provide limited leverage (i.e., few objects, on average, can be derived from each class): things like active controller classes that coordinate the operations of customer-space objects (though many OO designers frown on having such behavior-only classes unless they are absolutely necessary), classes for storing data or information needed beyond the current execution instance, transaction classes to track actual run-time system behavior, hardware-specific classes, communications classes (e.g., for using specific buses), middleware classes, and so on. Though many of these class types can also be at home in a lean system, none of them will produce objects that cover large portions of the overall system . . . one of the main goals of DFMA. Furthermore, building classes based on some of these criteria (such as active controllers) will compromise on other important design criteria and the capabilities discussed in Chapter 8.

   Object composition is essentially dynamic inheritance. Object composition leaves it up to executing objects to form associations with other objects as needed at run time. In effect, an object can choose among operations available in other objects at run time as its own needs change. The book, *Design Patterns,* gives an example of an object called Window (in a windowing system) that can switch a window between being rectangular and circular simply by changing whether its windowing operations reference the operations of an associated Rectangle object, or those of an associated Circle object. Object composition decreases the number of classes in the design. However, again, this strategy has too little leverage to be the basis for true DFMA.

   In type parameterization, proto-classes like C++ templates or Ada generics are declared in a program along with the type(s) they handle. Compilation then completes the definition of a class based on the proto-class. This likewise reduces part count somewhat (one proto-class can give rise to multiple classes), but the natural opportunities to use this mechanism don't occur often enough, nor are the number of classes able to be produced from most proto-classes sufficient, to support DFMA. There are also verification problems with this technique, which is why safety-sensitive systems often forbid using this strategy.

Multiple inheritance abstracts out things that are common across many classes and puts them into separate higher-level classes from which lower-level classes can inherit. Again, this can reduce part count somewhat, but not generally on a large scale. Multiple inheritance has other problems, for instance with maintainability and verification, and we certainly don't want to improve one cost driver (part count) at the expense of another (verification time). Thus, none of the OO strategies for reducing part count are a suitable basis for software DFMA.

4. D. L. Parnas, "On the Criteria to be Used in Decomposing Systems into Modules," CACM, December 1972; and many other Parnas writings. An excellent collection of these—a must in every software engineer's library—is found in D. L. Parnas, D. M. Weiss, D. M. Hoffman, "Software Fundamentals: Collected Papers by David L. Parnas," Reading, MA: Addison-Wesley, April 2001.

5. K. H. Britton, R. A. Parker, D. L. Parnas, "A Procedure for Designing Abstract Interfaces for Device Interface Modules," pgs. 295–6, from "Software Fundamentals: Collected Papers by David L. Parnas," Reading, MA: Addison-Wesley, 2001.

6. Actually, the *real* MONs and CONs are "out there" in the environment. What becomes the interfaces are internal software variables that only imperfectly represent the real MONs and CONs (imperfectly, because of time delays, accuracy limitations, and so forth that come about when you try to represent reality inside of software).

7. If the requirements are to be in some form other than SCR, we can still use the three Parnas categories as the foundation for our software architecture, but we then need to understand the Parnas criteria more deeply so we can translate whatever analysis information we have into this kind of design structure. However, increasing the translation of a product after it comes out of one stage of work and before it goes into another causes growth in the "assembly transport" cost driver; the translation activity may be waste. Non-SCR requirements should be carefully evaluated against this issue. SCR is superb in this area; however, it is not ideal for every kind of software . . . for instance, it is very weak for systems where there will be a lot of algorithms in the software; the SCR approach leads to an "explosion" in the number and size of its tables (speaking from personal experience!). Another approach should be considered for this kind of specification. In some cases, SCR can be combined with aspects of other methods to offset its weaknesses (e.g., using SCR to specify the relationship of the algorithms to the environment, leaving the algorithms themselves to be specified another way, be it formally (Z, equations) or informally (pseudocode, UML).

8. F. A. Salustri, "Contradictions between Design for Manufacturability and Design for Assemblability," Ryerson University, located on http://deed.ryerson.ca/~fil/T/cs/dfma-contradiction.html as of February 16, 2003.

20

Flow—Through Stage Transitions

THE MOST CHALLENGING PLACE TO MAINTAIN GOOD FLOW is at the transitions between stages. Transitions occur when work that has been going along suddenly changes in kind, typically stopping, sometimes even changing hands. When there is significant change in what is being done, there is extra opportunity for things to break down or to fall between the cracks.

Shortening Forward Transitions

By far, most of the time consumed in typical production occurs between stages, as we saw from Figure 16-6 in the section on the results of a VSM of a hypothetical process that showed lots of white space, and from the Lockheed Martin example in Figure 3-2, where 95 percent of the time in production was spent in just waiting around (another 4 percent was wasted in other ways). In well-executed traditional software production, most of this white-space time happens in forward flow, which is the normal and definitely most effective direction of product development through the production line.

Even good traditional production, however, institutionalizes delays by creating intentional buffers (inventory) between stages. Buffering holds an assembly (piece, part, etc.) from a previous stage in a state of limbo, until the next stage is ready to work on it. Buffering is a consequence of adopting the mass production efficiency principle. It allows full loading of the resource (whether a machine or a person) that will be working on the assembly. However, you pay a big price for using buffering, especially in increased assembly span time. Clearly, all the concerns other industries have about buffering are just as applicable to software. The techniques we'll discuss here will at least reduce, and can eliminate, the need for buffering (local inventory of work artifacts for an upcoming activity).

Shortening Through *Kaizen*

The VSM produced in *kaizen* events usually shows that the first place to improve forward flow and shorten assembly span time is in the transition areas. In the

VSM, these are the white-space areas of the chart where there are no horizontal bands and no productive work being done. VSM maps both forward and backward transitions, which are differentiated by the vertical placement of the consecutive bands (a band that is higher than the band to its left, shows a backflow; see Figure 16-6). Wider white-space areas and white-space areas in the middle of backflows should receive special attention, as they are the worst offenders in increasing assembly span time. Using brainstorming and other *kaizen* techniques will help you find ways to reduce the wasted time and improve the flow.

Shortening Through Piece Production Time

Piece production time is the time it takes to produce an atomic unit of product. Knowing this amount makes it possible to detect when work stalls between stages (i.e., when its time in work goes beyond its piece production time). Having detected the stall, one can intervene quickly, before too much time is wasted and the schedule is overly impacted. The piece production time also provides a baseline against which to measure attempted improvements: If an improvement is tried and doesn't decrease the piece production time, this says that something is wrong with either the improvement or its execution.

Piece production time is different from takt time, which we will discuss under the lean pull principle in Chapter 21. Takt time tells you how quickly you must produce each atomic unit of work in order to keep up with customer demand. Subtracting takt time from piece production time gives the net improvement in assembly span time you must have to meet your demand.

To measure piece production time, you first identify your atomic unit of work. XP bases its piece production time on user stories. In Chapter 19, we mentioned a kind of piece that was a single procedure implementing an individual SCR table in an object of the requirements-hiding class. On the 382J and C-27J programs, for example, the team based its standard piece production time on a simple SCR REQ table of two columns (2 MONs) and one row, i.e., two cells, not counting those in the rightmost column. The rightmost column of the REQ table was accounted for by estimating the complexity of the functions it contained; in the standard piece production time, the relation deriving the CON was assumed to be simple. Implementation of this table into integrated and informally tested code would be expected to occur within four hours of work. Larger tables are expressed in multiples of the standard simple one; for instance, an SCR table of three rows with three columns (MONs), or nine cells, with no complicated functions would be 9 cells ÷ 2 cells = 4.5 times the standard piece production time, or 18 hours of work.

This method of estimating proved very accurate, much more so than traditional estimation methods. The main thing it didn't account for was when an entire new object of the requirements-hiding class had to be added to the build (the piece production time applied only to adding an SCR requirement to an existing requirements-hiding object, which happened much more commonly). Actually, in the 382J architecture, when a new requirements-hiding object needed to be added, so did a new hardware-hiding object. This was because the requirements were associated with a hardware interface device that either detected the MONs or changed the CONs. In that architecture, adding hardware led to adding both types of Parnas-criteria classes. Appendix A explains these and other 382J MC OFP architectural concepts. At any rate, in that project, when objects needed to be added to the software, additional time beyond the normal piece production time had to be added into the estimate.

Once you have established the standard piece production time, you can further break that up by production stages, e.g., into requirements analysis, design, code, and integration/test. This allows you to detect problems with the work on a piece or part before the end of its lifecycle. You can do something akin to an ongoing VSM on the piece, highlighting when it stalls, either in a stage or between stages. Having an expected span (the piece production time) makes it possible to know when progress has been unexpectedly slowed or stopped, especially on the stage transitions, which tend to be overlooked otherwise, since people are usually not assigned to the transitions like they are assigned to the work stages.

Whatever you choose as the basis for your atomic work unit, the starting estimate of piece production time on the first program in a domain will almost always be pretty uncertain. That's all right: After a handful of atomic units have been produced, e.g., full-cycle developments of tested code from the user stories, SCR tables, or whatever other atomic units you've chosen, the project team will have a much better idea of how long each atom is taking. Then, through techniques like value-stream maps and *kaizen*, you can identify and remove the wasted time in the process. Again, the biggest area of waste is typically the transitions between stages.

As you eliminate the causes of waste, the length of the work cycles and the average piece production time will shrink. By the end of the first project in the domain, they will be stable enough that future projects in the domain will be able to start with reliable estimates. Small deviations from this expected time can then raise an alarm about possible problems in the process, allowing earlier detection and correction of production problems, both in the lifecycle of each piece, and also in the span of the overall project.

The difficulty with many traditional development methods is that they provide no consistent atomic unit upon which to base piece production time. For instance, traditional textual requirements vary widely in the time they take to implement. It's clear that the more controlled requirements-modeling techniques and representations like tables, mathematical equations, and user stories create atoms whose scope is better understood, with all the benefits this brings in process consistency, estimation, and real-time tracking. This puts the emphasis back on adopting development methods and processes that can define consistent atoms and therefore useful piece production times. Once again, we see that an integrated lifecycle is important, because so many aspects of the lifecycle can (and should) reinforce and facilitate each other.

Reducing Backflows

When your production process inserts defects into a product, you must have a step for removing them. This necessitates a backflow between stages. The backflow begins where the process draws the line on the defect, saying "thus far and no farther!" Note that we did not say it begins where the defect is first detected, Software production, like automobile mass production, often says "keep the product moving; we'll fix it at the end." The backflow leads to the stage where work to repair the defect begins (this is typically the same stage of work as where the defect was originally inserted; e.g., the backflow for a requirements defect will lead back to the requirements-analysis stage).

The bigger the backflow, i.e., the further downstream the product goes from the stage where the defect is inserted to where the backflow begins, the greater the waste. For example, continuing to try to do correct work on a defective product can lead to more defects, just as pushing a car with a bent frame down an assembly line can cause the other parts to be misaligned as the workers do whatever it takes to fit them all together. Later, when they fix the frame, suddenly, the rest of the car doesn't fit and it all needs to be repaired. This work would never have had to be done if the frame had been straight from the beginning.

To minimize this kind of waste, you must shorten the backflows (the perfection principle takes this to the limit of eliminating them altogether). To shorten the backflows, you need to set up mechanisms to detect defects as early as possible; ideally, right after they occur. Then the backflow will be limited to the just-completed stage.

If your production process never introduces defects into the product, then of course, you can eliminate even the detection activities. But all production processes introduce defects, unless you've designed the process to make defects impossible, which comes under the lean perfection principle rather than flow. However, since most producers have never seriously pursued perfection, addressing backflows is still important to most organizations. The few producers who have put in place effective perfection mechanisms, however, have converted the detection and correction part of a flow program from type 1 or necessary *muda* to type 2 or unnecessary *muda*, making it possible to remove the associated work.

Toyota has removed so many backflows from its processes that it has approached perfection. Several software organizations are pursuing perfection sufficiently to eliminate almost all backflows. Perfection approaches are an alternative to the popular "test first" programming approaches, which institutionalize defect detection activities—even if they are as early as possible—and therefore must live with some resulting *muda*. In all fairness, test-first advocates point to other benefits that they believe counterbalance this cost, such as early requirements verification. However, it has been our experience that the perfection route provides the same positives without having to accept backflow-related *muda* (even minimally). We will have more to say about all this under the perfection principle, in Chapter 21.

Reducing Through QFD

One of the major benefits of using QFD is that it drastically reduces the number of backflows. By allocating customer value to specific design characteristics, you eliminate one of the main causes for backflows—design dead-ends that do not impart value.

Unanticipated changes in either the customer space or the producer space lead to backflows. Some unanticipated changes are unavoidable. The change from credit-card roller machine to card-swipe reader, discussed under domain engineering happened because the reader device worked better for all the customers: the card owners, the merchants, and the card companies who processed the data. When the original roller-machine system was designed, nobody could have reasonably been expected to anticipate magnetic card readers.

Nevertheless, many changes, perhaps most, can be anticipated or, in the producer space, even avoided. What we want to do in the lean world is to minimize needless change. Any work above the minimum required to handle necessary change is *muda*, and you need to head it off with preventative strategies.

Unnecessary requirements change often happens for any of the following reasons:

- The organization did an inadequate job of value resolution.
- People enjoy working on requirements while the organization doesn't have enough grip on its business goals to rein them in.
- The customer wasn't sufficiently folded into the development team and has no sense of ownership in the success of the product, or confidence in the company (and why would they, with no working relationship?).

Any given requirement in this situation may change many times, even returning to previous versions on its pilgrimage to some dimly perceived destination. Of course, requirements volatility due to customer requests can be slowed by ignoring the customer. However, requirements volatility of this type almost always occurs because the customer was never adequately consulted in the first place. They know it too, so they increase their demands to try to make sure they get something they can live with. Stiffing them only makes the situation worse.

About all one can say about this strategy is that it is better than complete failure due to out-of-control requirements creep. At least this way, the project will some-day finish, even if it's a business failure. Much better to do adequate value reso-lution from the start.

Unnecessary design change often happens for similar reasons. Technical people who are very good at their specialty, but who lack appreciation of how their actions affect their business, often drive unnecessary design changes. Many designers do appreciate business needs—the majority, in our experience—but it only takes one lower-level designer who doesn't care how his or her decision affects the business to compromise the design's overall performance. On one project for which Jim created the architecture, a detailed designer woke up on the wrong side of the bed one day and refused to fit his parts in anymore. His comment was simple and bold: "I won't follow the architecture, and you can have the boss fire me if you don't like it." The project was under intense time pressure, so he got to stay on.

Interestingly, the effects of the designer's resolution were both measurable and substantial. His subsystem took longer to verify and had more defects than the rest of the software program. It was also much less maintainable, which came back to haunt the project at a later date when other software engineers had a hard time understanding his unique approaches to things that were done consistently throughout the rest of the software program. Indeed, his refusal to cooperate was in the end, noticed even by the regulators. When it came time to deliver the sys-tem into service, his portion jeopardized their approval of the entire project, because the case for gaining their approval had leaned on the argument that the entire program was based on using a consistent development process that pre-vented errors from being introduced. Fortunately, the project leaders were able to show that this was an isolated incident and that the rest of the program had retained its integrity. Acceptance of his part though, had to rely on old-fashioned, brute-force, time-intensive verification techniques.

QFD works against all these causes of backflow by keeping everyone focused on producing products that embed customer values, eliminating all wasted efforts (including reinventing architectural decisions at the detailed-design level).

All the techniques we've covered thus far, or which we will cover through the end of Part III, are useful in a value-driven, QFD-planned and -controlled devel-opment project. The ones that are especially helpful with reducing backflows, however, are domain engineering, software DFMA, and meta-specification (cov-ered later in this chapter). Domain engineering is largely change-driven, and so anticipates most future design changes, minimizing their future impact. Software DFMA also minimizes change, since big parts tend to account for more of the likely changes to the system, and simple parts tend to focus on more fundamen-tal and stable abstractions. Meta-specification explicitly accounts for expected change and makes the design easier to modify and more robust when unanticipated changes need to be made. One additional, nontechnical technique for reducing backflows is to train developers in thinking about business concerns as well as the technical part of their job. Business-savvy developers become allies and can use their creativity to help minimize unanticipated change. The actual project leaders must be the ones doing the training, because developers don't normally pick up a business mindset from their formal schooling, and few have learned it from their peers or their previous experiences in the software industry. That training needs to be both academic and by the leader's example.

Other measures you can take to limit the backflows caused by unanticipated change are to delay the decisions that are the most likely to change until as late in the project as possible. Another tactic is to design the product and the processes in such a way that making unanticipated changes is as simple and practical as possible. While you might not be able to anticipate the changes themselves, you may be able to anticipate the aspects of the system where you think unanticipated change would be most likely to occur. Then, you could isolate those areas in the architecture (in a manner analogous to encapsulating secrets per the Parnas Information-Hiding principle). Actually, you should consider these criteria in all design and process decisions.

Reducing Through Design by Contract

Most controlled software development processes will have an inspection at the end of each major stage of production. For instance, requirements analysis will be followed by a requirements inspection, design by a design inspection, code by a code inspection, and so on. This train of inspections may be fairly rigorous, as in Michael Fagan's approach.

Inspections are good and useful; however, defects will still escape through these checkpoints and lead to future backflows. We need a tighter-meshed sieve than mere inspections to detect errors at their point of origin and avoid lengthy backflows. (The tighter sieve may replace the inspections, as well.)

One such development approach resembles a software method called "Design by Contract,"[1] developed by Bertrand Meyer, which revolves around the idea of assertions. Assertions are statements of the absolute, nonnegotiable truths about a piece of software. The Design by Contract technique has three kinds of assertions: preconditions, postconditions, and invariants. (Recall that the discussion of abstract interfaces in Chapter 15 touched on the idea of preconditions, under the interface item called *usage requirements*.)

Preconditions state what must be true before an operation is initiated. For example, a text editor could require that any text file passed to it must end in a ^Z.

Postconditions state what must be true upon completion of an operation; for instance, that an EBCDIC-to-ASCII text converter utility will have created an ASCII file that corresponds character-by-character to the original EBCDIC file.

Invariants state what will always be true about a class as a whole; as in a stack class that asserts the stack will never overflow. Meyer even developed a programming language with native constructs to support such assertions: It was (and is) called *Eiffel*.

Instead of applying Meyer-style assertions to the functionality of a piece of software, we can apply them to the functionality of a stage of a production line. The most useful type of assertion is the *postcondition*, because it can evaluate when a stage has completed a software product to the point of readiness to move on to the next stage of production. And since assertions are mathematically (formally) rigorous, you can machine-test them. This means that the developer can find any defects corresponding to these assertions, and in most cases, correct them in the stage in which they are introduced, that is, without backflows.

Let's look at the analysis stage of software development. If the stage product is a software requirement written in a formal representation like SCR, one postcondition could be that the requirement is complete across all subranges of its independent (MON) variables. With a method like SCR, a tool can automatically evaluate this (both the Naval Research Labs and Rockwell Collins have done this).

Next is the design stage of production. If the product is a UML model and if project standards call for capture of design in a formal subset like xUML, then tools can automatically evaluate the syntactic correctness of the model (the postcondition becomes "the design is syntactically correct"). Automation could also be created to check for inclusion of all design pieces required by the QFD mapping.

Following design, of course, is coding. If the code is implemented in a formal representation like SPARK Ada 95 with annotations, again the correctness can be checked by tool. At the code level, you will commonly find the following five types of errors that you can automatically check:

1. *Control flow.* Structure and "manners" of the code (e.g., "spaghetti," multiple loop exits)
2. *Data use.* Syntactic use of variables (e.g., data initialization; using inputs as outputs)
3. *Information use.* Output variables derived from the right input variables
4. *Semantic.* The actual mathematical relationship between output and input variables is correct
5. *Compliance.* Code corresponds directly and exactly to its specifications

Sometimes you can prevent code defects from ever occurring by choosing appropriate design criteria and checking them with design postconditions. For instance, you could use the xUML model syntax to eliminate the misuse of interface variables (the data use criteria above), then check this with xUML analysis tools and auto-generate the interface code. An approach like this is right on the transition line between lean flow and lean perfection. We include it with flow, however, because after-the-fact checking is still involved; it's just done a stage earlier. This is certainly an improvement, but it is not true error preclusion, as in the perfection principle. Even a project practicing perfection techniques, however, may have a political or customer need to confirm that the product is correct and error free. So, these kinds of flow techniques may still be needed in the most-advanced software projects.

While considering which postconditions to assign to a product at each stage, don't forget to assign postconditions to assure that value has been deployed. Comparing the elements put into the detailed design (when most specific values are assigned to the product), to the QFD-matrix value assignments is one way to do this at the design stage. Other values may need to be explicitly checked; for instance, if there are safety-related values, the code may need to be checked to ensure that it has not compromised safety (e.g., by allowing array overruns). Value-driven verification and resulting metrics can be even more important to a project's success than process-driven metrics. If one discovers early that value is leaking out of the product as it goes through production, you can improve the production processes to better retain value.

Meta-Specification and Meta-Design with XML

The foundation of a domain-based architecture software design is that which is common to all variants of the design.[2] Such a design isolates that which changes between variants away from the main structures of the design, so that changes have little effect on the rest of the software program. The domain or product-family designer makes choices of classes, interrelationships, major behavioral characteristics, and so forth. However, during the implementation stage, there are often still needs to change or add to the product-family design. The way this is usually done is very wasteful. For instance, a programmer may take a previous version of a software system and directly recode parts of it. During this recoding process, it is often not clear which parts of a module need to be changed and which are stable. The developer may reimplement things that don't need to be touched, because they are not part of the change. This kind of work is waste.

One way to reduce this waste is to use meta-specification and meta-design techniques. These techniques identify that which is common to all variants and that which seems likely to change (even if it will change in as-yet unknown ways) in future, hypothetical software products (e.g., requirements, detailed design, or code) of the product family. There are two approaches to preparing for this eventuality: 1) static (i.e., compile-time) and 2) dynamic (i.e., run-time).

In the static approach, you create a high-level metadocument for the requirements or code that explicitly identifies what is always present, i.e., common in any variant, as well as what is changeable, including all the alternatives discovered to date. XML is ideal for creating this document: Its tags can be used to identify both the common parts and alternatives for the changeable parts. One can then easily extract from the higher-level document a lower-level document composed of the common parts, and selections of any specific changeable parts that had been implemented before and included in the document as alternatives. It is then up to the developer to create any never-before implemented, changeable parts needed for a specific new product. Even these new changes can then be added back into the metadocument for future use by others creating products in the product family.

In the case of meta-code, all that remains to produce a given variant is to take the lower-level document (the source code), with its added bits, and recompile and relink it to produce a new object image. Of course, there will be a separate meta-specification for each major partition of the system, e.g., each class.

In the dynamic approach, the software system consists of a set of more general-purpose components. The developer uses interpreted macros and XML to construct glue that changes the external behaviors and interfaces of the compiled code (which does not change). The glue has been called structural and behavioral metadata in the main reference to this technique, "Software Development on a Leash."[3] In this case, the macros drive behaviors such as display and data handling, allowing you to customize software in the way it is most expected to change, without changing the compiled software at all. For the right domains, though not hard real-time embedded systems, this is claimed to be very productive. See the cited reference for more information.

Removing Production-Line Constraints

We've been looking mostly at positive ways of creating flow through the whole production line. Now we'll look at the flip side, removing active hindrances to good flow. One type of hindrance is called *constraints*.

Merriam-Webster's defines *constraint* as "the state of being checked, restricted, or compelled to avoid or perform some action."[4] Dr. Eliyahu Goldratt succinctly states that a constraint is "anything that limits a system from achieving higher performance versus its goal."[5] By either definition, a company needs to remove constraints on its production lines if they are ever to flow freely and quickly.

In the second half of the twentieth century, two major and very different approaches to removing constraints evolved. Oddly, the older of the two, TRIZ, which we discussed at some length in Chapter 12, is both less used and more radical. The newer of the two, Goldratt's Theory of Constraints, has already overhauled many production lines throughout many industries.

TRIZ Revisited

The last time we discussed TRIZ—the general creativity and problem-solving approach developed through scientific study of two and a half million patents and inventions—we examined how it can be used to improve our understanding of customer values.

Now we will specifically look at applying TRIZ to constraints. If you recall, at the heart of TRIZ is the idea that unsolved problems are essentially contradictions, which you confront and ultimately overcome through natural human creative thinking. TRIZ includes principles and techniques for accessing available knowledge, for breaking out of nonproductive thinking molds, for understanding problems, and for finding solutions.

In TRIZ, the idea of contradiction is synonymous with constraint. Contradictions restrict a production line from fully and freely performing its intended actions. For instance, earlier, we discussed the contradiction between the goals of DFM and DFA to both produce simpler and bigger parts. There are often contradictions between the need to work quickly within each stage and the need to move quickly between stages (e.g., a tool that makes work go the most quickly in one stage may be incompatible with the tool that makes work go the most quickly in another stage; adopting both into the production line forces the developers to convert products coming out of the first into a compatible format for entry into the second. Jim has seen this many times, such as when the requirements tool chosen for systems analysis is incompatible with the requirements tool chosen for software analysis, even though both were using the same requirements analysis methodology!).

There can be many contradictions on a line between competing and desirable goals towards achieving good flow. TRIZ techniques (e.g., based on its "Principles of Invention") reframe competing and contradicting goals in such a way that the contradictions disappear. The TRIZ method looks for genuinely creative breakthroughs rather than for workman-like improvements (not to downplay the latter: They are certainly also useful and can be pursued through such techniques as *kaizen*). TRIZ is likely to identify *kaikaku*, i.e., breakthrough changes in one's software production practices. Since genuine breakthroughs provide significant competitive advantages, TRIZ should reward those companies that give it a serious effort.

Goldratt's Theory of Constraints

One of the most creative minds in recent times is that of Dr. Eliyahu M. Goldratt. Not only has he rethought the way systems work, he has created methods for identifying what is broken, how to fix the breaks, and how to institutionalize the fixing process. These combined elements are called the Theory of Constraints or ToC. He has mixed all these principles with a folksy wisdom and the skill of a great storyteller. Indeed, much of his writing has been in the form of gripping novels, like his signature work, "*The Goal.*"[6]

Goldratt has focused most of his attention on the production line system. According to the ToC, any system or production line has just a few constraints . . . but always at least one. More importantly, the worst constraint masks the effects of the others, keeping the line operating slowly enough that you never discover the limitations posed by the other constraints. Of course, as one removes a constraint, performance improves and a new constraint becomes evident. Since no line operates at infinite speed, no matter how many constraints you remove, there will always be at least one more to limit performance.

In the customer space, the ToC begins by having the analyst identify the line's main goal, and the metrics that you can monitor to assess the effectiveness of suggested changes to the line. Metrics like piece production time (especially when it's broken out by production stages) can help here. Once this preparation work has been completed, the ToC counsels the analyst to make his or her intuition explicit by taking a series of five steps:

1. Identify the System's Constraints
2. Decide How to Exploit the System's Constraints
3. Subordinate Everything Else to the Above Decision
4. Elevate the System's Constraints
5. If in the Previous Steps a Constraint has been Broken, go back to Step 1

Restated in production terms, these steps could read:

1. Identify what is in such short supply that it limits the rest of the line: don't waste any of it.
2. Make sure the other resources do not limit production of the short resources.
3. Reduce the impact of the short resources on the rest of the line.
4. Improve production of the short resources.
5. Once the short resources are no longer short, i.e., not limiting line performance, start over.

The ToC then moves to the implementation space and places responsibility for improvement squarely on management. Goldratt states, "The first ability that we must require from a manager, is the ability to pinpoint the core problems . . . that once corrected, will have a major impact. Once a core problem has been identified, we should be careful not to fall into the trap of immediately struggling with the question of How To Cause The Change. We must first clarify to ourselves— What Shall Be Changed?—otherwise the identification of core problems will only lead to panic and chaos. Thus, we should also require that a manager acquire the ability to construct simple, practical solutions. In today's world, where almost everybody is fascinated by the notion of sophistication, this ability to generate simple solutions is relatively rare . . . what we have so harshly learned from reality, over and over again. Complicated solutions don't work, simple ones might."[7]

The ToC has a manager ask three questions about the production line's design space:

1. "What to change? Pinpoint the core problems!
2. To what to change to? Construct simple, practical solutions!
3. How to cause the change? Induce the appropriate people to invent such solutions!"[8]

The third question shows a possible convergence with TRIZ, in that the latter can help with generating inventive solutions to constraining problems. However, the ToC targets incremental improvement rather than breakthroughs and is complementary to TRIZ, rather than redundant.

The remainder of the ToC presents a set of techniques like Current Reality Trees (CRTs), Future Reality Trees (FRTs), and other logical and situational diagrams. These techniques help with identifying constraint problems and potential solutions, implementing the solutions, and systematizing this cycle. ToC's own materials clearly lay out explanations that you can easily apply to software. An oft-cited technical reference on the ToC is Goldratt's "*Theory of Constraints.*"[9] A good introduction is the Goldratt novel mentioned earlier, "*The Goal.*"

Building a Software "Flexible Manufacturing System" to Achieve Flow

Combining everything we've discussed about flow leads to what is known as a "Flexible Manufacturing System" or FMS. An FMS is "an integrated manufacturing capability to produce small numbers of a great variety of items at low unit cost; an FMS is also characterized by low changeover time and rapid response time."[10]

Making a production line into an FMS is the holy grail of the flow principle. It is also a radical departure from a traditional manufacturing system and from a traditional software process. We can summarize in four simple procedural steps the building of software a FMS (simple to state; challenging to do!) that applies to either a new or an existing production line and that is implemented using mostly the techniques we've studied under the flow principle. These steps, discussed in more detail below, are 1) identify essential production activities, 2) design for flow, 3) map production activities to stages and transitions, and 4) form integrated product teams (IPTs).

1. *Identify the absolute minimum and essential set of production activities needed to add the required value to the product.* Many things done in software

processes have nothing to do with adding value. Many steps in software processes exist simply to support mass production infrastructures (as in much of the CMM). Others are there only so developers can use technologies that are currently popular.

You should closely examine existing or planned processes and pare them down to the bare minimum required to add value. The only non-value-adding activities you should allow in the process are those that are imposed and unavoidable. Even the latter should be examined to see if there is another way to satisfy everyone, as a side effect of a value-adding activity. A *kaizen* event is a good venue for this kind of examination.

You also need to ruthlessly scrutinize technologies and justify them on the basis of adding value and improving flow. "One of the greatest impediments to rapid progress [in converting to lean production] is the inappropriateness of most existing processing technology—and many product designs as well—to the needs of the lean enterprise."[11] New technologies often distract from value and impede flow. You must not allow this to happen.

2. *Design the product (or amend an existing design) for flow, i.e., with characteristics that allow reducing the number of production stages, shortening the stages, and reducing backflows.* Any design should be highly producible, facilitating the most cleanly flowing production process possible. The previous quote cited product designs as well as processing technologies as major impediments to lean production.[12] Practically speaking, this often means that product designers must compromise on the absolute optimization of their designs in order to support improved flow.

One aircraft project on which Jim worked observed that the optimal spacing of bulkheads (reinforcing walls), from a weight standpoint, was too close together to allow human hands enough room to work effectively between them. Therefore, the bulkheads were moved further apart to improve manufacturability and greatly reduce overall product cost. Similar compromises are necessary in software as well. Parnas-criteria-based classes, for instance, do not make for the smallest or fastest code. However, they make for a system that is highly producible, quickly verifiable, easily certifiable, highly predictable to plan, and easy to explain to new developers—who become fully and independently productive in just a couple weeks (based on the experience of the 382J). Design for flow builds on such techniques as:
- Domain engineering
- Software DFMA
- Verification-Driven Development
- Meta-specification and -design

3. *Map and allocate the essential production activities from step 1 to stages, selecting the stages and the mapping for best balance between stage optimization and stage transitions.* There are two interconnected parts to this step: choosing stages and mapping activities to the chosen stages. The goal is that products flow as quickly and smoothly as possible from one activity to another, to deliver a product as quickly as possible end-to-end. The most important consideration is having the fastest, smoothest transitions between the chosen stages: "[The] greatest opportunities for performance improvement lie in functional interfaces—those points at which the baton (for example, 'Production specs') is being passed from one department to another."[13] Sometimes, different stages indeed belong to different groups (as in development and test in a mass production software house). Sometimes, they simply belong to different people. In either case, the handoff will break the flow, unless you take active measures to prevent it from doing so.

Tools can have a big positive or negative effect on transitions. When mapping activities to stages, you need to consider what development tools are available. The right combination of tools will support easier, smoother flow between stages, especially when the format of the output from a tool in one stage is a recognized format for input to the next stage. There is some give-and-take between defining stages and choosing tools. However, tool choice should only *influence* the definition of the stages, not *drive* them (the undesirable situation we touched upon in Chapter 18). Flow considerations still drive the selection of tools. However, tool availability is a constraint that feeds back into and influences process development.

Some factors you should consider in mapping activities to stages are:
- Minimizing assembly span time
- Reducing the number of stages, since fewer stages reduces the number of transitions, which are time consuming
- Having too few stages increases span time: Avoid overly ambitious stages, as they can become overly complex and slow down production
- Producing efficient big parts and simple parts, which also improves other cost drivers
- Removing line constraints (e.g., via TRIZ and ToC)

Other lean techniques and strategies that apply to this stage include:
- QFD
- The System Simulation–Emulation Lifecycle
- Takt time (discussed in Chapter 21)
- Process postconditions
- TRIZ
- ToC

A process that balances effective stages with good interstage flows resembles a good software design; it maximizes cohesion within stages and minimizes coupling between stages. It moves product through production, one piece at a time (more on this under the pull principle). There are minimal (preferably no) buffers between stages. At the end of each stage, there is a gate that immediately detects defects, elevates their visibility, and presents them for remediation. Tools are right-sized, flexible, and reconfigurable. In many cases, they will be self-developed for the specific needs of the production line. These include the expected types of product variants and the human nature of the workers. Regarding the latter, tools should be intuitive, with productivity-supporting interfaces. They should also be immediately on hand to allow the workers to begin doing their jobs the moment that product becomes available.

4. *Form Integrated Product Teams (IPTs)*. To maximize the benefit to the overall project, you should perform these four steps as early as practical. To the greatest extent possible, you should also do them in parallel, with those who are focusing on one concern having visibility into the thinking of those focusing on other concerns. This is needed because decisions made by one will affect the assumptions of another. For instance, changing the product design affects the production activities and potential wastes. Doing this well requires putting together a team that covers all the aspects of the production line and that can work together to trade them off to create a line that is optimized across all concerns. Because there is already much good literature on IPTs, we won't go into them further here.

This concludes our discussion of flow, the third lean principle. The next chapter covers the final two lean principles, pull and perfection.

ENDNOTES

1. B. Meyer, *Design By Contract*, Englewood Cliffs, NJ: Prentice Hall, 2002.
2. *Reuse-Driven Software Processes Guidebook*, SPC-92019-CMC version 02.00.03. Software Productivity Consortium, 1993.
3. D. Birmingham, V. Haynes Perry, *Software Development on a Leash*, APress, March 2002.
4. *Merriam-Webster Online Dictionary*, March 1, 2003. http://www.merriam-webster.com.
5. E. Goldratt, *Theory of Constraints*, pg. 4, Great Barrington, MA: North River Press Publishing Corporation, December 1999.

6. E. Goldratt, J. Cox, *The Goal: A Process of Ongoing Improvement*, Great Barrington, MA: North River Press Publishing Corporation, May 1992.

7. E. Goldratt, *Theory of Constraints*, pgs. 7–8, Great Barrington, MA: North River Press Publishing Corporation, December 1999.

8. E. Goldratt, *Theory of Constraints*, pg. 20, Great Barrington, MA: North River Press Publishing Corporation, December 1999.

9. E. Goldratt, *Theory of Constraints*, Great Barrington, MA: North River Press Publishing Corporation, December 1999.

10. http://www.nwlean.net/leanfaqs.htm, December 18, 2002.

11. *Lean Thinking*, pg. 95.

12. *Lean Thinking*, pg. 95.

13. Rummler, Brache, *Improving Performance: How to Manage the White Space in the Organization Chart*, San Francisco, CA: Jossey-Bass Management Series, pg. 9, 1995.

21

Pull and Perfection

THE ESSENCE OF THE PULL PRINCIPLE is just-in-time (JIT), the approach in which you "don't make anything until it is needed; then make it very quickly."[1] Ideally, a customer's order launches the final stage of production, which launches the stage before it, and so forth, back to the raw materials. More specifically, pull depends on demand to initiate production, then *kanban* to trigger demand for the inputs of the stages of development all the way back to value resolution. (A *kanban* is a card, ticket, or sign for managing and assuring the flow and production of materials in a pull system; this is discussed in general terms in Chapter 3.)

Pull: Turning the Software Lifecycle on Its Head

In software production, strong customer interest starts the ball rolling. Sometimes that interest is in the form of firm commitment, as in a contract. More often customer demand is soft, such as when a market survey indicates that customers will buy a product if it is available, or when a new concept is run by a focus group whose members are eager to obtain the product. In every case, however, lean production begins with the customer.

The final stage of production in most software production lines, and therefore the first activity triggered in a pull system after a customer shows strong interest, is verifying that the final product does what its requirements say it should do (this is often done with an acceptance test, though other means are possible). The materials or inputs required to perform this stage are:

1. A standard of verification
2. Executable software

These inputs are the outputs or products of earlier stages. Those stages can be conducted simultaneously or in parallel, since they have no dependencies on each other. Figure 21-1 shows a generic diagram for a pull-based software lifecycle.

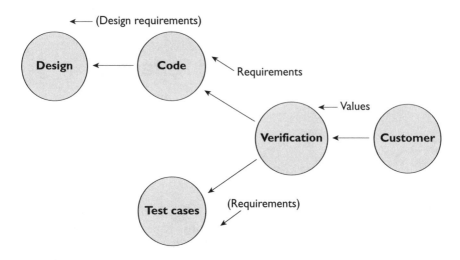

Figure 21-1. Generic Software Pull Systems

The stages in this example are simply the top-level stages of the software life-cycle. In a real software process, you would replace these generic stages with stages that are more specific to the actual project or business.

Note that verification here also encompasses requirements development. This is an inversion of the way most popular processes think of development, with the exception of XP and other Agile software approaches. They practice the same philosophy in their test-before-programming approach, an important area in which XP is more consistent with the lean paradigm than are other current software approaches.

To make a lifecycle process like that shown in Figure 21-1 possible, you must have in place the lean mechanisms of *kanban, takt* time, and one-piece flow. Now we will cover how these mechanisms work together to make the lifecycle in Figure 21-1 work. Chapter 3 describes these three mechanisms in a general way that applies to all lean production and provides the foundation for what we discuss here.

Kanban: Initiating Development Activities

The flow in the pull system of Figure 21-1 goes as follows. Products flow primarily from left to right, while control pulls exclusively from right to left. The first control starts with the customer. The customer expresses strong interest and provides values to the developers, though of course, project people work with the customer to develop that list of values (there is insufficient interest to trigger a project until you can find a customer or a suitable customer surrogate willing to support value resolution). These values are a *kanban* to the verification stage. You can think of their existence as the simple flag of traditional *kanban*, and their contents and form as the container being passed upstream to hold the product that will be returned.

Once the final verification stage has at least some values available, it begins working. The final verification stage produces product requirements from the values and passes them as a *kanban* to the code stage and test-cases stage. Requirements are both a control mechanism and a product, since validated requirements also kick off and constrain development. Indeed, in many ways, their role as a control mechanism is more important than their role as a product, which is why we show them as controls pulling from right to left, rather than products flowing from left to right.

When the code stage is notified to produce code by having received requirements, it knows that it needs a design into which to place its code. It passes upstream to the design stage a list of its non-negotiable needs, which such a design must accommodate if coding is to succeed at its job, such as what hardware platform and what programming language they are constrained to use. Hardware and language characteristics can, in turn, imply constraints on a design. This is why they are passed along as design requirements.

The design stage uses these design requirements along with the product requirements. However, design requirements are not to be confused with product requirements. Sometimes design requirements are derived, the difference between them and initial requirements being that the derived requirements are related to the producer space and not the customer space. This makes them design artifacts. The possibility that there may be no design requirements is why we show design requirements in parentheses. The design stage will use these design requirements, as well as the product requirements (flow not shown on the diagram), either to create a new domain design, or to use an existing domain design and perhaps modify it for the specific needs of this product development. (This work may include, for instance, updating of an existing meta-specification, or creating a new one.) Upon receipt of a usable design, coding commences and upon its completion, provides code to the verification task.

On the other branch of Figure 21-1, the test-cases stage works in parallel to the coding stage to convert requirements into test cases and provide them to the verification stage. We use the term "test cases" very loosely here. These could be traditional test cases; they could be code annotations for pre- and postconditions in a formal approach; or they could be empty, if requirements are used directly as the test cases as described in Chapter 17. The possibility of no need for test cases to come back is why we show requirements in parentheses.

Verification then integrates the new code (possibly with existing code, if this is a product modification) and applies the verification standard against the build, such as test cases, code annotations, or simply the requirements. Upon completion, the verification task delivers the product to the customer who initiated the work.

This is a simplified process. You could break out some of these stages, for instance, verification into acceptance and delivery, and add stages, especially upstream. Passing constraints upstream (such as the design requirements, from the coding stage to the design stage) gives earlier tasks in the lifecycle, at a higher level of abstraction, the opportunity to change their products to accommodate low-level issues.

For instance, one reason the coding stage might be forced to use a particular programming language is that the hardware platform specified in the system design is only supported by one compiler vendor. If that language choice harmed the project, the design stage would only have the option of working around it, not of eliminating the problem (hardware selection is outside its charter). However, if we extended Figure 21-1 to the left, i.e., further upstream into system engineering, this constraint could be passed to system design task (not shown in the current diagram), which could possibly select different hardware and avoid the constraint.

This means that, in principle, one could use the techniques of the Theory of Constraints (discussed in the previous chapter) to identify constraints in each stage and the *kanban* control flows of pull production to head off those constraints upstream, preventing them from ever becoming an issue on that project. We haven't had the opportunity to try this approach on a deliverable project yet, but experience in other lean industries indicates it has great potential to reduce *muda*.

In reviewing the pull system, we once again see the reasons why verification is so important and why development should be verification-driven, as we discussed in Chapter 17. Verification is literally the starting point of production (not unlike XP's outlook, though arrived at through different reasoning), and its ending point as well. That is, verification brackets and frames the entire production lifecycle.

Note also that, in a pull production system, stages may have to respond quickly to new demands, some possibly unprecedented. Therefore the tools in each stage should be flexible and reconfigurable. For instance, design tools should support quick updating of the product-family architecture to accommodate new kinds of needs.

Takt Time: Estimating and Managing Productivity

Takt time is the tool that links production to customer demand by matching the pace of production to the pace of final sales. That is, *takt* time determines how quickly you must produce each atomic unit of work in order to keep up with your customer demand. An organization cannot practice JIT unless it absolutely knows it can generate product quickly enough to keep the customer satisfied. Otherwise, the organization will have to work in a mass production batch mode and build inventory to stay ahead of anticipated or possible demand. In software, the latter makes nobody happy. It often corresponds to a heroic waterfall project that develops speculatively (i.e., without a good list of customer values), using company funds, and that delivers a large system all at once.

To review from Chapter 3, you calculate *takt* time by dividing how much product the customer is buying per elapsed calendar time (e.g., per day, per week, or per month), by however much work time (generally, in hours) is available for production in the same calendar time. For instance, if you had to deliver a build to a customer once a month (we'll assume for now that a month has four five-day work weeks), and each build contains, on average, sixty new atomic units (small SCR tables or whatever), then the *takt* time is 60 units/20 days or 3 units per day.

You then compare *takt* time to piece production time to determine how to run your software production line. For instance, if each development team produced the software and verifications for a small SCR table every four hours (the actual experience of the 382J MC OFP project), and if you had just one team, then assuming eight-hour workdays, this would mean you would produce two units per day. If your *takt* time was three units per day and your piece production time was one unit every four hours, you would need to increase production. You could then evaluate your options for meeting that demand. You could go to twelve-hour days. Or add some parallelism to the line so that one-and-a-half times the work is being done in the eight hours. Or improve your processes so that the piece production time decreases to one unit every two and two-thirds hours.

By knowing both your *takt* time and your piece production time, you will clearly understand your situation and options for meeting customer demand.

Level Scheduling: Smoothing the Ups and Downs

The Toyota idea of level scheduling applies to software mostly when you are a subcontractor to a customer who is producing a larger system that incorporates your software. In all likelihood, that customer will be working in batch mode, delivering large increments of its product to its own customer(s). This means your customer will present you with large and infrequent orders. If you can average the peaks in this demand, even if it means using your own business's money to do so, you can avoid the costs of staffing up and down, buying more expensive tooling to support staffing and production peaks, and so forth.

This is a case where using company money makes sense; it requires much less investment than does full-up batch development, and it is justified to reduce costs and improve profits on the project as a whole. Alternatively, if you keep up good relations with your customer, you may be able to negotiate an understanding that your software will be developed and delivered the lean way, and that the time may vary between deliveries of additions of major new areas of functionality, depending on the complexity of the particular functionality being added. If level work scheduling truly saves you money, you may be able to offer improved prices to your customer as an incentive for them to support your approach, thus partially or wholly eliminating the need to use your own funds to level the schedule. As in traditional manufacturing, however, level scheduling will only work if you have very accurate knowledge of customer demand.

One-Piece Flow and the Atomic Unit of Work

We alluded to the idea of one-piece flow in the earlier discussion of piece production time. At that time, we introduced the idea of an atomic unit of work. This could be a single user story (in the XP method), a small SCR table (in the Parnas-based approach), a Use Case (in the Rational Unified Process), or some other atom. The only restriction was that whatever representation you chose, it had to correspond to a predictable amount of work. Traditional textual requirements do not qualify, because they are so unstructured that there is no reliable way to identify how long a single requirement may take to implement.

One-piece flow is important to a pull system because producing single pieces eliminates batching and inventories, which shelter the production line from customer demand and make pull impossible. Pull is like a rope, with one end attached to the producer, and the other in the hands of the customer. Inventories are like a coil midway down the rope. When there are inventories, the customer pulls, but the producer does not feel it because the slack in the coil removes the tautness. One-piece flow removes the coil and allows the producer to feel the tug on the rope the instant the customer pulls on it. The ultimate lean goal is to apply one-piece flow to all business operations: product design, launch, taking orders, physical production, etc.

A Piece-Work Process

To work one piece at a time, you must institutionalize one-piece flow with a piece-work process. A piece-work process defines the entire lifecycle based upon a single atomic unit of work.

For instance, in a software organization working on an integrated hardware/software system, the systems engineering group may be the ones to initiate the development of a piece. They might create or modify a system-level requirement and pass it to the software group. Passing this requirement becomes the *kanban* that notifies the software group to get to work and make some software.

In a lean project, the requirements methods, architectural design, and so forth will have been chosen for their ability to isolate changes to as small a portion of the software system as possible. In an SCR-based project, for example, that incoming system requirement might correspond to just one SCR table. Even if a system requirement ultimately affects multiple or large SCR tables, the software group can estimate the multiplier of the amount of work for an atomic SCR table even before the new or changed SCR tables are developed. The software group uses this estimate of work duration for its *takt*-based planning.

The work that is initiated by arrival of the system requirement has a defined lifecycle, beginning with validation of the system requirement itself. This may result in the software group sending the requirement back to the system group (the customer) for more values or other clarification. Once the requirement has been validated, the next stage is to produce testable software requirements. Again, problems revealed by this effort may lead to sending the system requirement back to the customer.

Once validated software requirements (e.g., SCR tables) have been produced, work begins in parallel on the product and on the test scripts. On the 382J, this was not a pure pull system like the generic example in the previous section, but it came close. The difference on the 382J was that design came before coding. If no design was needed (as in simply extending the existing code by adding or modifying a requirement and its corresponding single code procedure), there was still the step of going through the design stage anyway. The extra transition added a certain amount of *muda* compared to a pure pull system, though much less *muda* than in a traditional nonpiece work software process.

If the software requirements are used as literal test cases, all that remains to be done on the verification-standard side is to create test scripts. On the 382J and its follow-on the C-27J, this was a semi-automated process: There was still some manual labor involved in the conversion from requirement to script.

When both code and test scripts are ready, verification completes its task of integration and testing. Then the software group hands the product to the customer who initiated it, in the case of our example here, the system engineering group. This is an example of a complete lifecycle process oriented around an atomic (or near-atomic) product unit. The top-level unit in this case is the system requirement and the software atom is the individual software requirement.

Interestingly, not everyone agrees that a single atom is the right-sized work target. "We often hear One Piece Flow pronounced as an absolute must for any work cell. Like the search for the Holy Grail, it is taken as a moral imperative. We find it more helpful to think of this question as the transfer batch or internal lot size. The issue is: 'What internal lot size will help the cell meet its performance goals?'"[2] One-piece flow remains, however, the ideal against which any divergence must be justified.

Another important point is that it is much simpler to execute piece-work if you design your architecture to support it. For instance, in the 382J MC OFP architecture, one requirement is implemented in exactly one procedure (see Appendix A; this rule is made possible by the well-defined characteristics of an

SCR requirement). This rule strictly limits the ripple effects on the rest of the system coming from changing any single requirement (i.e., only the parts of the system touching the MONs and CONs in the table can be affected). This, in turn, makes it easy to work on many requirements (work atoms) in parallel, which in turn makes it easier and cheaper to achieve shorter *takt* times.

Finally, looking at the XP approach, the reluctance of XP proponents to conduct a large, up-front, requirements-analysis effort, while a hindrance to lean practices on single-system development, is appropriate for products after the first in a domain. Full-up customer analyses on subsequent products off the production line would be unnecessary rework. Working one atom at a time supports this incremental working-out of products in an existing product family coming off the line.

Perfection: The Ultimate Goal

We come to the end of our lean journey with the lean perfection principle, the easiest lean principle to describe, but the most difficult to pull off. We will resort to history for a moment to help break into this subject. The ancient Greeks related one's position in society with one's character, and one's character with what one had studied and mastered. They identified a ladder of studies for young men to undertake (young women were not accorded the same opportunities). The lower rungs on this ladder were studies like military science and agriculture. Good performance on these subjects allowed one to move on to higher rungs.

At the top rung of this ladder was mathematics. The Greeks esteemed ideas as the ultimate reality and physical things as mere shadows of that reality. Mathematics mirrored their worldview: Mathematics described perfect things perfectly; physical things created from a perfect pattern always varied to some degree in dimension and shape. Thus, mathematics was the language for expressing the Greeks' highest ideals of perfection. The lean principle of perfection is to the other lean principles as mathematics is to the other rungs of ancient Greek education. It is focused on helping us meet our loftiest aspirations.

Lean perfection deals with two aspects of production: product and process.

Product Perfection: Entropy, *Poka-Yoke*, and *Jidoka*

With material goods, the laws of physics tell us that we can never attain true perfection. There will always be some disorder in the system, some effect of entropy on the results. The best we can do is continuously work to reduce the variance of actual products from the pattern that defines perfection. This is the main focus of the six sigma approach and when kept firmly in a lean context, provides various means (techniques, tools, etc.) for reducing variance. When we move into software, however, *the product* is the mathematics. The problem keeping us from attaining perfection with most software is that its underlying mathematics is very, very sloppy; usually so bad that it is essentially nonexistent.

We've discussed why most software professionals have rejected formal software development and why they have been right to do so. We also said (in Chapter 15) that a frontal assault on setting up mathematical software development is less likely to succeed than is an integrated approach. The integrated lifecycle uses other techniques—ultimately, other types of mathematics—to make production of a more thoroughly formal product possible. Domain engineering, for instance, relies heavily on the underlying mathematics of set and information theory. Dr. David Parnas said, "Correctness proofs for programs can become so complex that their own correctness is in question . . . . For large systems we would be forced to exploit the structure of the programs in producing the proofs . . . . We ask, 'What changes can be made to one part without involving change to other parts?' We may make only those changes that do not violate the assumptions that other parts make about the part being changed. In other words, a single part may be changed only if the 'connections' still 'fit'. . . we have a strong argument for making the connections contain as little information (in the information theoretic sense) as possible. Systems in which the connections between parts contain little information are termed well structured."[3] Structuring systems this way is the point of both domain design and also of building the design around the Parnas-Madey Four-Variable Model we used for software DFMA. *The software architecture will make or break whether you can pursue perfection any further in the final product.*

However, unlike material goods that are stuck with variance in their products, there is no absolute reason why designers and developers cannot make a software program mathematically perfect. Given a few presuppositions, the rules of entropy do not apply in the mathematical domain or in the digital domain in general. We do not prove a geometric theorem and then only expect our work to be valid some odd percent of the time. Either it is right or it is wrong. We do not just wish we could make a perfect copy of an audio CD, we go ahead and do it, reliably, predictably, every time.

It's clear that the goal of perfection in software development is different from the goal of perfection in other industries. Where they seek to reduce variance, we can seek to eliminate defects completely. Does software have the techniques and tools to pull off this definition of perfection? Not yet, at least not on a wide scale throughout all segments of the software industry.

But we can get very close and save money compared to our current costs by doing it. The techniques we have available today are good enough, in an integrated lifecycle, to produce software that has a tenth of the anomalies found in the highest-integrity software using traditional mass production techniques. An organization can achieve this while cutting costs to a fourth of those of normal safety-critical development, and by half those of non-safety-critical software. This was LM Aero's experience with the 382J and C-27J software process. The means of doing this is a goal—a way of looking at software development—which we've called "Correctness by Construction (CbC)."

There is much more the software industry can do with what it now knows. Perhaps the closest anyone has yet come to perfection on a commercially deliverable software system is the SHOLIS helicopter landing system developed by Praxis Critical Systems, Ltd., for the U.K. MoD (Ministry of Defence). Formal requirements, design, and coding were applied throughout the product, using the Z method for requirements specification and the SPARK high-integrity subset of Ada for code and static verification. Many have said that a fully formal lifecycle is impossible in commercial development, but SHOLIS has proven it is not only possible, but also practical.

On the other hand, Z, the SHOLIS requirements-specification language, is a mathematical representation readable only by trained experts. It is incomprehensible to customers and usually even to those in the same company that are outside of the software group using it. In this sense and others, SHOLIS is not fully lean. But the project is an impressive accomplishment that convincingly refutes conventional wisdom and points the way to the next round of progress towards lean perfection.

CbC seeks to replace all after-the-fact verification with measures that prevent defects from being introduced into the product. Such measures include using mathematically underpinned methods for requirements, design, and code; as well as more common process measures like Configuration Management and Process Control. The more common lean term for this idea is *poka-yoke*, which is Japanese for mistake-proofing.

Mistake-proofing is not an all-or-nothing proposition. It begins pragmatically. "A series of techniques commonly called *poka-yoke*, or mistake-proofing . . . make it impossible for even one defective part to be sent ahead to the next step."[4] Note that, at this stage, errors are not yet precluded, merely prevented from propagating to the next stage. This is not inconsistent with the ultimate goal of perfection. The paradox of this quest is that those undertaking it should be prepared to stick it out for the long haul: "Traditional management fails to grasp the concept of perfection through endless steps."[5] Even once you attain the ability to make a truly perfect product, process entropy continuously works to pull one back into defects, so you must always and continually pursue perfection.

Pragmatic *poka-yoke* utilizes automated means of defect detection, and manual means for the workers to stop the line until whatever in the process that allowed the defect to be introduced, has been corrected. This process is related to *jidoka*, the lean approach to error detection and correction discussed in Chapter 3. Recall the four steps of *jidoka*, which are equally applicable to software development:

1. "Detect the abnormality.
2. Stop.
3. Fix or correct the immediate condition.
4. Investigate the root cause and install a countermeasure."[6]

Using just such pragmatic means, the Lockheed Martin Aero GPSSUP program of the late 1980s produced a software system in which the customer has never reported finding an error. Even pragmatic *poka-yoke* works well, especially compared to systems in which this is not a high priority.

Eventually, however, *poka-yoke* graduates into error preclusion. "Error-proofing is a manufacturing technique of preventing errors by designing the manufacturing process, equipment, and tools so that an operation literally cannot be performed incorrectly."[7] The most productive eventuality for software would be to arrive at a test-not-at-all process, in contrast to the test-first process that is desirable in a lean pull system on a nonperfect software product.

Formal requirements are the foundation for CbC and *poka-yoke*. Without known-good requirements, by the GIGO (Garbage In, Garbage Out) principle, it doesn't matter what else you do. The game is lost. On the other hand, requirements that are mathematically consistent must be practical and usable by software professionals who are not formal methods experts, as well as readable by customers and other outsiders unfamiliar with software arcana. Most formal methods fail on this account. The SCR Method is an exception we have discussed repeatedly, though there is no reason for it to be the only one.

A final note on this subject: You can have a perfect CbC, *poka-yoke* approach that produces error-free software, but still completely miss the customer! To make sure you not only build the product right, but also build the right product, you need high-quality customer-space value resolution. In the end, becoming a lean-thinking organization with lean development, production, and learning is always the goal; not attaining perfection for perfection's sake. This ideal is what many authors have termed the *lean enterprise*.

Process Perfection

Process perfection is "the complete elimination of *muda*."[8] Thus, a perfect process will perfectly obey the value stream principle. The difference between the perfection principle and the value stream principle is that the perfection principle deals with *poka-yoke* techniques for driving all *muda* to zero. For instance, by applying CbC to the process, you are attempting to head off the introduction of *muda* to the process before it ever happens. This requires essentially domain-engineering the process, doing a change analysis of the possible ways that you anticipate where your process could degrade, and then designing measures into the process to prevent the degradation from occurring, or to at least detect degradation quickly when it happens and apply *jidoka* so the process is repaired immediately.

According to Sudhir Shah, the lean software manager of the LM programs, "Problem prevention is your best problem resolution. If you are facing ten problems, and you prevent nine of them before they happen, this is your best option." This is the perfection mindset at work. Of course, one endeavors to prevent all ten the next time. There has been little practical work on the subject of *muda*-proofing a software process. We raise the topic here to provoke more thought about how this might be done. In principle, however, many of the techniques used to create and to *poka-yoke* the product should also be useful to *poka-yoke* the process.

Last Thoughts on the Producer Space

Part III has discussed the producer space and the four lean principles the producer has available for implementing and producing a real product for the customer. The implementation part of the software lifecycle produces executable software systems that delight your customers and meet or exceed your business goals. The best way to achieve this is through an integrated lifecycle (value stream) that draws from the techniques of flow, pull, and perfection.

We've pointed out several software projects that have drawn on these techniques to achieve unusually strong performance on these goals. More are described in Part IV. These projects and the ones cited in greater detail in Appendix A were successful not just because they were productive, or that they produced a high-integrity product, or that they supported simultaneous production of multiple variants, or that they were reusable. Traditional mass production projects have accomplished each of these things individually.

Lean software projects to date are notable because they have achieved several of these results at once on the same projects. And though they have been imperfect and incomplete at best, with each lean journey, we have gained more understanding about how to apply the lean paradigm to our unique industry, an industry that is nevertheless similar to those lean industries that have paved the way. Pursuing lean software production is practicable, essential, timely, and that the benefits overwhelmingly justify the effort.

ENDNOTES

1. *Lean Thinking*, pg. 71.
2. http://www.strategosinc.com/onepieceflow.htm, January 15, 2003.

3. D. L. Parnas, *Some Software Engineering Principles*, pg. 259, from "Software Fundamentals: Collected Papers by David L. Parnas," Reading, MA: Addison-Wesley, 2001.
4. *Lean Thinking*, pg. 61.
5. *Lean Thinking*, pg. 91.
6. M. Rosenthal, "The Essence of Jidoka," *Lean Directions*, the e-Newsletter of Lean Manufacturing, a publication of the SME (Society of Manufacturing Engineers), 2002.
7. http://www.nwlean.net/leanfaqs.htm; from January 10, 2003.
8. *Lean Thinking*, pg. 90.

PART FOUR

Experiences of Lean Software Producers

22

Is Microsoft's Build and Synchronize Process Lean?

IN 2002, MICROSOFT HAD SALES REVENUE of $28 billion with profits of $12 billion. Worldwide, it employed over 50,000 people, spent over $5 billion on research and development, and had a cash pile of $40 billion. The Windows Operating System and Office Suite of programs had margins of over 80 percent, and the Office software had 300 million users. Microsoft's latest operating system, Windows XP, had sold 50 million licenses in the year since it was introduced.

Other software producers and regulators are critical of the business practices of the world's biggest and most profitable producer of software. This led to antitrust trials in the United States and Europe.[1] Ferguson indicates that Microsoft is unpopular because it tends to "develop products by licensing, acquiring, or copying the innovations of others . . ." and then using its financial muscle and dominant position to win new markets (p. 296). But Microsoft also has an effective software development model that is "disciplined and formalized" (p. 300).[2] Microsoft is remarkable in how well it aligns its organizational structure, strategies, and employee rewards. Microsoft does deliver great volumes of usable, low priced software every day. This indicates that Microsoft's current software development processes are working well. This chapter will attempt to evaluate to what extent their processes are lean.

The book *Lean Thinking* was published by Womack & Jones in 1996,[3] but many of the key lean ideas had been published in English well before this. For example, Schonberger's *Japanese Manufacturing Techniques* was printed in 1982.[4] Microsoft's approach was developed before the term 'lean' became popular. They did draw on the earlier quality literature and also learned from their experience gained from releasing so many software products. Microsoft does not therefore describe their processes using the now more familiar lean terminology.

Zero-Defects Code—The Beginning of
Microsoft's Improvement Initiative

The years 1987 and 1988 were Microsoft's dark days when "several key projects remained in chaos." The original Word program had "infinite defects" meaning that testers were finding bugs faster than developers could fix them, and each fix led to yet another bug. A key database program, which was supposedly three months from being finished in 1988, was cancelled a year and a half later because of these voluminous defects.[5]

In 1989, when Microsoft introduced its earliest version of Office, and in 1990, when it launched Windows 3.0, its software quality was widely felt to be poor. In 1988, experienced software engineers who joined Microsoft from Digital Equipment Corporation (DEC) called the company "Microslop." They felt the Microsoft developers were less experienced and approached problems "helter skelter."[6] Ferguson described it as "testosterone-based development" that often resulted in "disastrous results" and "tangled code."[7]

These unresolved and continuing problems and delayed products were reflected in crashes in the price of Microsoft's stock price. The frequent delays and recalls confused and frustrated customers. The running gag in the industry was that Microsoft products were in beta test until version 3.

Since 1990, Microsoft's products have significantly increased in reliability. The case of Microsoft's quality improvements and revised software process is invaluable in seeing how lean principles apply to software. A key turning point for Microsoft began with an internal memo entitled "Zero-defects code." Quotes from this document, written by Chris Mason in 1989, show the start of Microsoft's software improvement initiatives.

"There are a lot of reasons why our products seem to get buggier and buggier. It's a fact that they're getting more complex, but we haven't changed our methods to respond to that complexity . . . the point of enumerating our problems is to realize that our current methods, not our people, cause their own failure . . . . *Your goal should be to have a working, nearly-shippable product every day . . . .* Since human beings themselves are not fully debugged yet, there will be bugs in your code no matter what you do. When this happens, you must evaluate the problem and resolve it immediately."[8]

This approach has all the key elements of lean. Work in process (WIP), which was largely untested code, was to be significantly reduced by the insistence on building the code each day. No new code was to be written until the existing code base was stable. This had the effect of forcing the developers to resolve errors and the sources of errors when they occurred. This is a zero-defects goal where each defect is used as a way to improve process. By building the software on a daily basis, there were visual indicators of its condition—error messages if it failed to compile or run tests.

Microsoft reported using lean principles at a Software Quality conference in San Francisco, California. Tierney, a project manager, focusing on the interface between development and testing described Microsoft's practices:

"In manufacturing, it is very important to reduce inventory because mistakes can hide in the inventory (more units ruined before the mistake is detected). In software development, the same principle applies: Software inventory hides mistakes that can surprise you and ruin your schedule if you do not fix them early. Both testers and developers need to work together to enable code to be tested earlier, reducing software inventory. The developers need to write the code in stages that can be tested before the product is complete. The tester needs to be flexible enough to test whatever software is available thoroughly. This will provide a solid baseline for the remaining software to be built upon."[9]

In this quote, Tierney makes a direct comparison between lean manufacturing ideas and software processes. The focus is on a minimal work in process (WIP), in this case, code, flowing from the developer to the tester. Once software in development is conceptualized as inventory that flows, then the other lean ideas fit into place.

Microsoft, with its staff of 50,000, does not have a mandated methodology for developing software. It operates in many small groups and development approaches vary. This is necessary to tackle a range of markets, products, and constraints. To see if Tierney's approach was representative of Microsoft's practices, we reviewed Zachary's 1994 account of the development of Windows NT and other sources to see if the processes they described supported the five principles of the lean model: value, value stream, flow, pull, and perfection.

Value

According to Womack, value is providing a specific product that meets the customer's needs at a specific price at a specific time.[10] In 1993, Microsoft appointed Roger Sherman Director of Testing for Microsoft's Worldwide Products Group, which was responsible for producing all of Microsoft's Systems, Applications, Language, Database, and Consumer software. Sherman made it clear that reliability, defined as low defect rates in the implementation of the product specification, was only one aspect of quality for Microsoft.[11] Microsoft defined software quality as having three dimensions.

1. "The first is product definition, or what is sometimes called 'feature richness' within Microsoft.
2. The second dimension is shipping on time, which we will call 'schedule'. Schedule is often thought to be the enemy of quality, but at Microsoft, it is considered to be part of the quality of the product.

3. The third dimension is the traditional focus of Quality Assurance: low defect rates in the implementation of the product specification, which we will call 'reliability' in this paper. The term 'reliability' is defined by Microsoft as the rate at which an end user will encounter anomalies."[12] (See Figure 22-1.)

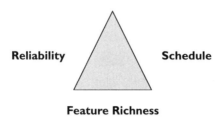

Figure 22-1. Microsoft's Three Aspects of Quality

While a high absolute level is the ambition for all three of these aspects of quality, their relative importance will vary. "For example, a low number of defects might be the most important in a mature market where competing products are not otherwise differentiated. In another situation, being first to the market may take precedence over reliability."[13]

The importance of this observation is that the software development process must adapt rapidly to the specific constraints and opportunities of particular markets and technologies. Therefore, a standard corporate, one-size-fits-all methodology is unlikely to be effective.

The objective is to provide value for the customers, by supplying the required mix of functionality, speed of delivery, and reliability. Note that reliability is measured in terms of "anomalies experienced by customers," which is a customer-focused measure, rather than using an engineering definition of reliability.

Zachary describes the value that was the objective behind Windows NT.[14] In 1988, when NT was conceived, it was to be a "Unix killer." Unix was attractive to customers because it had multitasking, connected easily with other computers, and could work on most kinds of hardware. It was also available free of charge. But Unix had a serious shortcoming: No common version existed. This meant application programs had to be modified to run on each of the different versions. This made it harder for applications writers to make money, as they had to tailor their products to fit different Unix variants. This raised costs and limited choice for customers. The task therefore was to write an operating system with more functionality and the portability of Unix, but which was only in one version.

Windows NT took 5 years to develop, has 5.6 million lines of code and cost $150 million. It required around 200 software engineers, although the numbers varied over the time of the project. While the specification evolved and fluctuated, the value driving the objective of the project did not change.

To try to ensure value was created, each software project had a program manager, "A messenger from the market place . . . the Program Manager studied competing products, gathered intelligence about forthcoming products from rivals and solicited suggestions from potential customers . . . . Gates valued strong Program Managers, believing that theirs counted among 'the most important jobs' in Microsoft because they 'own the vision of the product,'"[15]

Steve Maguire joined Microsoft in 1986 as a veteran software design engineer and spent several years at the company rescuing troubled software projects. His first ground rule was a focus on creating value:

"Any work that does not result in an improved product is potentially wasted or misguided effort. . . . I've found that groups regularly get into trouble because programmers are doing work they shouldn't be doing. They're spending too much time preparing for meetings, going to meetings, summarizing meetings, writing status reports, and answering email."[16]

Further, "Capturing what the customer values is a Vision Statement, which uses extensive customer input to identify and prioritize product features."[17] It is clear from all these sources, that *value is a primary and institutionalised focus within Microsoft.*

Value Stream

The value stream is activities that produce a specific product that an organization must precisely identify, analyze, and link together. This is so they can be challenged, improved (or eliminated), and eventually perfected. The need is to manage whole value streams for specific goods and services.[18]

Microsoft's successful process for developing and shipping products is to do everything in parallel, with frequent synchronization and daily debugging. By continuously testing the product as it is being built, fast feedback on quality is obtained.[19] Further, "The key idea is that one large team can work like many small teams if developers synchronize their work through frequent 'builds' and periodic 'stabilizations' of the product."[20]

Zachary describes this crucial process in operation for the development of the Windows NT operating system. Once the project had been running for nearly three years, there was enough code to allow the developers to use NT as their operating system for the completion of NT's own development. NT's architect and the project leader who led the programming was David Cutler.

"Cutler . . . was urging the team to 'eat its own dog food.' . . . The 'dog food diet' was the cornerstone of Cutler's philosophy. "We're going to run on the program we build," he insisted. "Eating dog food meant there would be no escape from facing the flaws and imperfections of NT . . . . If at first NT tasted no better than dog food, all the better. Code writers would feel an urgent need to raise the dietary level by quickly fixing the errant code and writing more durable code in the first place."[21]

The Build Laboratory, the place where Microsoft assembled the software from all the different teams, became the critical nerve center for the project. This was where Cutler based himself. The build process started off as a weekly event, before becoming biweekly and then daily. This process forced very fast feedback onto the developers on the quality of the software they were developing. Removing code inventory meant that errors were exposed within days or hours.

To ensure a value stream that focuses on producing reliable software, Microsoft has created a software process that highlights errors and problems that must be resolved very quickly. That is, it has a lean approach to reducing WIP. The features of the software that were actually working were always clear to Microsoft's developers and managers. Microsoft's value stream links the value-creating activities together and means the developers can focus on creating and managing value.

Flow

To have flow is to organize the process so work is done in a steady, continuous flow, with no wasted motions, no interruptions, no batches, and no queues.[22]

The build and synchronize process used by Microsoft differs significantly from a traditional sequential software process. In the sequential process, there are large batches of specifications or untested code. In Microsoft's process, work flows rapidly through the production steps of specify, code, build, and test. Wasted effort is minimized because the objective is so clear and visible. There will be many interruptions as the process uncovers faults, but this encourages developers to work with more care and learn from their mistakes because, not to be perfect means having their work immediately and constantly interrupted.

"Sequential approaches to software development may require very long periods of time because they schedule work in sequence, not in parallel. Managers may also find it difficult to assess progress accurately because they tend to schedule major testing very late—often too late—in the development cycle."[23]

Microsoft's build and synchronize process is a lean approach because it interrupts only to fix problems, removes the waste of unnecessary meetings or reports, and works with no batches or queues.

Pull

With pull, no one upstream should produce a good or service until the customer downstream asks for it. If an evolutionary approach is used, the software is grown gradually one piece at a time. The pieces that provide the most value are created first. This makes a process that is inherently more single piece than batch flow. It also makes it more capable of responding to changing customer requirements.[24]

". . . The real trick to avoiding massive delays was to test NT all along." Perazzoli, quoted in Zachary.[25]

This pull philosophy at Microsoft is summarized thus:

"Almost no one liked the interruptions, but Cutler considered them unavoidable. Practical concerns made him an incrementalist at heart. Even code based on the best specs and designs only improved a little at a time. This was tedious work, often avoided. So Cutler favored bothering code writers, whom he suspected always wanted to write new code and forget about yesterday's mistakes."[26]

The responsiveness to customer pull is well illustrated with Windows NT. Cutler gives one of many examples:

"NT is sort of a chameleon operating system. First we were doing OS/2. Then Windows started selling millions of copies." Perazzoli was proud of how quickly the team had made this about-face from OS/2 to Windows saying the adjustment took only three months.[27]

The important point here is that the change was required by an external shift in customer demand. This could not have been anticipated at the start of the project. It is the expectation that customer requirements will change and having in place a process to accommodate this makes lean particularly effective. An ever-shifting mix of functionality, price, and reliability defines quality. The fatal flaw in sequential processes is that it requires precise specifications before you start a project.

When Microsoft is developing software, the features that are required provide the pull. If these are prioritized, then a few core features go through the production process. The next features are not developed until the first ones are bug-free and stable. This evolutionary delivery of stable product is much easier to manage. A key metric becomes the daily bug count. The next new feature required and the bugs that needed to be fixed pull the developers to where their efforts should be directed. Microsoft has clearly implemented pull in their software development practices.

Perfection

Perfection requires endless steps because it is always possible to reduce waste by eliminating effort, time, space, and errors. The activity will also become progressively more flexible and responsive to customer pull. The key is not to do a one-off planning exercise, to obtain 'normal performance' and then simply manage it in a steady state. The goal is continuous radical and incremental improvement.[28]

Microsoft's process clearly does this. The build and synchronize process quickly forces errors into the open. Tierney gives examples of how once you standardize the process, you can optimize and automate it.[29] Sherwood also states specific tools were created to solve specific process problems.[30]

Tierney addresses the important issue of what to do when a problem emerges. He is guided by the work of Shigeo Shingo.[31] The key principle is to mistake proof the process. One of Shingo's favorite sayings was:

"Dissatisfaction is the mother of improvement. But don't let it get wasted as complaint, channel towards solutions."

The issue is to reduce the WIP, constantly testing each small part released. But the task is not just to correct errors discovered, but to also correct the process defect that caused the errors in the first place. The expectation has to be that whenever a tester finds a problem, they will also look for, and fix, the reason for the problem. As Tierney points out, it is not feasible to chase after every problem. Resources are finite so they must be targeted where the need is greatest. He recommends:

"Apply Pareto's principle: If there are a million problems bothering you, go after the most important ones first. Later on, you can tackle the minor ones, but put your effort into the ones that will save you the most grief."[32]

Tierney gives some examples from his work environment. Microsoft has developed a software testing tool, called Stress (stress.exe), to selectively limit hardware resources and so cause the software to fail.

"Stress verifies application behavior in low memory, low resource states. Application developers often neglect to consider the implications of system failure on their applications. Stress.exe allows you to selectively limit each resource needed by the application in order to make sure it fails in the proper manner: no loss or corruption of user data, no hanging of the system. Combining this with fully automated tests makes the bugs fly out of the software and makes these normally hard to reproduce bugs a snap."[33]

What is significant here is that Microsoft identified a frequent cause of software failure that was causing distress to their customers. They then allocated time and resources to develop a specific tool to tackle this problem. The overall result was a long-term reduction in problems experienced by their users. There was also a reduction in testing costs. Another example of using a specific tool to catch a whole class of potential errors was a utility called Diskinf.

"Diskinf verifies all correct files are on disk, no extras. During hand-offs from development to testing, it is not unusual for extra files to appear or other files to disappear. Sometimes the changes are necessary and sometimes they are mistakes, but Diskinf makes sure that *everyone* knows when a file is added or deleted so that they can establish whether the new configuration is correct or a mistake. Adding this to the Build Verification Tests greatly diminishes the odds of this whole category of error hitting you."[34]

Again a specific tool is built to keep a process on track and errors are reduced. This continuous improvement process is accelerated when only small chunks of software are released to testing at a time. It means the problems can be identified sooner and there is more time to devise and implement a solution. There is also less damaged inventory to correct, so scarce resources are not wasted on this. If you combine this with specific tools to address the problems identified, then a software process tailored to the specific project's challenges will rapidly emerge.

Even more importantly, as software is labor intensive, the developers are also encouraged and expected to have continuous improvement. The short cycle time helps to build a learning organization through continuous self-critiquing, feedback, and sharing.[35] Maguire describes how team members should be managed for 'constant, unceasing improvement,' by being continually challenged and setting goals for personal growth.[36]

Conclusion

Microsoft derived their software process largely through trial and error. The scale of their problems in 1989 forced them to find a more effective development method. Microsoft's software process was evolved before Womack & Jones' book *Lean Thinking* was published in 1996. Nevertheless, if their software development and business practices are examined, the lean principles are clear. Value became the organizing principle for their build and synchronize system. They focused on reducing WIP.

The principle of value was implemented by the role of a strong product manager, who is the messenger from the market place and owns the vision of the product. The lean principle of the customer pulling product from the producer is realized by the daily builds of software with incremental delivery. This means you are always addressing the most important customer needs first.

The big step for Microsoft was in 1989 with Chris Mason's memo. Here it was made explicit that the amount of inventory, i.e. untested code, had to be reduced to the bare minimum. As Zachary pointed out, the hardest challenge is that by reducing the (WIP), problems constantly arise that interrupt the workers. However, with lean thinking, this is exactly what you want to do, because these problems provide continual indicators as to where you need to improve the organizations' processes. Once there is a clear focus on value from a customer perspective combined with reducing WIP, then the other principles of value stream, flow, and perfection start to fall into place.

Whether it is in the manufacturing or software worlds, the lean approach to producing commercial success requires tailoring the organizations' processes to meet particular challenges. Specifically, it requires low levels of work in process to highlight quickly those areas that are causing problems. Only this will ensure effective and lean processes. Management's challenge is to negotiate and implement permanent systems and solutions to prevent these problems from emerging again.

This approach to production, as in manufacturing, makes Microsoft far more flexible and able to respond to external changes. This is because there is little inventory clogging up the development process. The rapid feedback loops that are created when work in process is reduced also build capability by rapidly increasing the rate of organizational learning. It is perhaps paradoxical that Microsoft's market dominance and strong finances gave it the time and opportunity necessary to learn how to develop software effectively.

ENDNOTES

1. Harvey, Fiona. "A Window to a Better Image," *Financial Times*, pg. 18, December 10, 2002.
2. Ferguson, Charles, H. *High St@kes, No Prisoners, A Winner's Tale of Greed and Glory in the Internet Wars*, London: Texere Publishing Ltd, 2001.
3. Womack, James, Jones, Daniel, and Roos, Daniel. *The Machine that Changed the World*, New York: Rawson Associates, 1990.
4. Schonberger, Richard. *Japanese Manufacturing Techniques: Nine Hidden Lessons in Simplicity*, New York: The Free Press, 1982.
5. Cusumano, Michael A. and Selby, Richard. *Microsoft Secrets: How the world's most powerful software company creates technology, shapes markets, and manages people*, pg. 40. New York: The Free Press, 1995.
6. Zachary, Pascal. *Show-Stopper! The Breakneck Race to Create Windows NT and the Next Generation at Microsoft*, pg. 38. London: Little, Brown & Co., 1994.
7. Ferguson, Charles, H., 2001.
8. Cusumano and Selby, p. 43.
9. Tierney, pg. 5, 1993.
10. Womack, Jones, and Roos, 1990.
11. Sherman, Roger. "Shipping World-Class Products on Time: A view of development and testing at Microsoft," pgs. 51–58. *7th International Software Quality Week*, San Francisco, May 17–20, 1994.
12. Ibid. pg. 51–58.
13. Ibid. pg. 2.
14. Zachary, pg. 31.
15. Ibid. pgs. 86–87.
16. Maguire, 1994.
17. Cusumano and Selby, pg. 194.
18. Womack, 1996.
19. Cusumano and Selby, pg. 261.
20. Ibid. pg. 262.
21. Zachary, p. 123.
22. Womack, 1996.
23. Cusumano and Selby, pg. 262.
24. Womack, 1996.

25. Zachary, pg. 126.
26. Ibid. pg. 126.
27. Ibid. pg. 125.
28. Womack, 1996.
29. Tierney, 1993.
30. Sherwood, 1993.
31. Shingo, Shigeo. *Zero Quality Control: Source Inspection and the Poka-yoke System.* New York: Productivity Press, 1986.
32. Tierney, 1993.
33. Ibid. pg. 5.
34. Ibid. pg. 6.
35. Cusumano and Selby, 1995.
36. Maguire, 1994.

Industrial Engineering Insights on Variance in the Software Development Process[1]

C REATING SOFTWARE REQUIRES A PRODUCT DEVELOPMENT SYSTEM that must deal with multiple tasks simultaneously. Even though many of the specific challenges are unique, much of the work, tasks, and sequences of tasks are common across projects. Lean principles are already being successfully applied to improving the complex product development process for cars,[2] it is therefore a small step to apply them to software development. You can then view the software development system as a knowledge work job shop, with multiple work centers and an integrated network of queues.

A job shop is defined as any operation not in the business of long run, proprietary, consistent, one-of-a-kind products. Job shops would generally be smaller, make-to-order operations that do not make the same product every day. Their business is likely to build unique products using perhaps thousands of parts, and they can never accurately predict which part number will get the call today or tomorrow.[3]

This chapter seeks to demonstrate that there are strong similarities between a manufacturing job shop and a software development operation. If this is accepted, then there are decades of lean manufacturing experience and literature for software developers to draw on. Current manufacturing books that have material that could be adapted for software include, for example, Baudin,[4] Allen et al,[5] and Standard & Davis.[6] They are valuable because they go beyond the general principles of Womack's *Lean Thinking* and describe specific, practical techniques in detail. Using these process management tools can reduce wasteful variation (*muda*) in software development while enhancing creativity.

Optimizing the Software Development Process

If we accept the premise that software development is a product development process (as the Capability Maturity Model and many other approaches to optimizing performance have already done), then the process management tools of queuing theory and lean manufacturing can be applied to optimize these processes.[7] Proceeding from this premise and analyzing these software processes from an industrial engineering perspective, there are two major determining factors for delays in any and every system:

1. Variability
   a. Task or Process
   b. Inter-Arrival or Flow
2. Capacity Utilization

These two concepts of variability and capacity utilization are the foundation for analyzing and improving the performance of any system. Repeated experience over years has shown there are simply no other starting points for improving system performance. It does not matter what the system does, variability and capacity utilization are fundamental.

You can mathematically analyze variability to show how it propagates in a system. For example, if one delivery date is missed in a system, the effect multiplies as hand-offs to other parts of the system occur. Variability compounds as it works its way through a system because erratic arrival times reduce the effective downstream capacity of a process. The same chain of events happens if the variability is caused by faulty work that is required to be redone.

Effects of Software Developers' Behavior on the System

If you visualize a single software developer's scope of work as a system where jobs; 1) arrive, 2) are worked on, and 3) passed on, then you can model the system as in Figure 23-1.

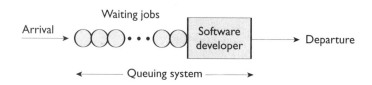

Figure 23-1. Software Developer's Scope of Work

From this model, it is now possible to demonstrate how different software developer behavior affects the system. For example, in Figure 23-2, consider a software developer who sometimes completes his or her jobs very quickly, but other times very slowly—has a high variance. Compare him or her with another developer who has exactly the same skills and productivity but who works consistently. If both work the same hours, there will be a significant difference in how much longer, on average, it takes the erratic developer's team to deliver their work. Note that their individual productivity is the same because over time, they will deliver the same amount of work. The only difference between them is that one is erratic and the other is consistent in delivery.

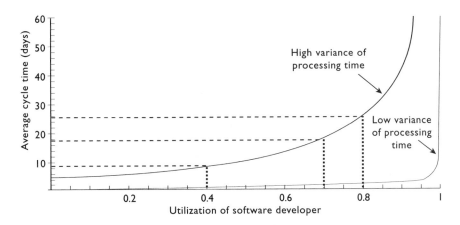

Figure 23-2. Comparison of Two Software Developers

Figure 23-2 shows the jobs arriving regularly, one each day. The X-axis indicates how heavily scheduled a software developer is. The Y-axis charts how long it will take him or her on average to complete a job. The time taken is referred to as average cycle time or customer waiting time; it consists of processing time plus the time before the job was started. The graph shows how higher variance dramatically increases average cycle time as utilization increases.[8] This graph, connecting resource utilization, variance, and average cycle time, is a standard widely used and relied upon in industrial engineering.[9]

Both developers are equally skilled and able to complete each job. But one developer is erratic in performance, and therefore, has a high variance of processing time. The effect of this is that if they both work, for example, 70 percent of their employed time, and their productivity is the same, a customer will have to wait about 16 times longer if their job is processed by the high variance, erratic developer.

Another significant point from this graph is that as these two software developers work longer hours, thus having higher utilization, the difference in average cycle time increases. For example, at 80 percent utilization, the absolute difference between the two software developers in the time taken for their work to arrive is considerably more than at 40 percent utilization. The precise numbers are not as important as the fact that there will definitely and always be significant deterioration in cycle time caused by higher variance at higher levels of utilization.

Capacity utilization and variability are tightly linked. A slight reduction in variation will greatly reduce customer waiting time. Visualize a road with two lanes. If a car breaks down in one lane when there is no other traffic, the system is running at low utilization and you can simply drive around the blockage with little delay. If, however, the breakdown occurs at rush hour when the road is highly utilized, the delay will be significant. This is because the actual capacity of the road is reduced by more than 50 percent when it is blocked. Variance has a much bigger impact when a system is highly utilized.[10]

There are a number of possible curves that you could select to illustrate the effect of variance on system performance. The precise curve for each specific programmer would be different, but the important point is that the impact of variability on average cycle time and the relationship to utilization would remain essentially the same. This is the underlying reason that lean thinking works in practice. Variability is far more damaging than is intuitively perceived. By implementing the lean principle of flow, you are, in effect, reducing variability, so greatly increasing the software development capacity that can be utilized.

The implication is that the way to improve software developer performance is to record and analyze all reasons contributing to performance variances. For example, interruptions, distractions, temperature fluctuations, lack of access to reference materials, low motivation, poor first line supervision, or limited availability of healthy food and drink could all cause variations. For example, DeMarco & Lister show how telephone interruptions can destroy an individual software developer's productivity, but they ignore the greater, total damage caused.[11] One developer's productivity declines due to the telephone interruption, but the impact of this variance is then multiplied. The above analysis from industrial engineering demonstrated that the variance in an individual's performance propagates throughout the system causing far more damage. By not appreciating the overall, significant, negative impact of variability, attention is not paid to reducing it.

If the problem is that the software developer's skills do not meet the job requirements, this needs to be addressed. Shingo gives insight into the techniques and attention Toyota uses to eliminate variances. For example, Toyota uses techniques to eliminate mistakes, prevent delays, improve flow, and facilitate workload balancing. If these approaches, combined with extensive training, are not sufficient to eliminate variances, then Toyota's practice is to redeploy any personnel that may be responsible and then finally, remove them if they cannot attain the required performance level.[12] This is the pursuit of the lean principle of perfection by complete elimination of waste through endless improvement steps.

Note that working longer hours will make some difference but is generally not enough to compensate for high variability, because as a system with high levels of variance works closer to capacity, its relative performance deteriorates significantly. Figure 23-2 shows the benefits of reducing variance to enable working smarter rather than harder.

Figure 23-2 also demonstrates that software developers should always have their work scheduled at less than capacity. In lean thinking, the objective is to be able to pull to meet customer demand, not to have the system always busy. This means the objective of full utilization, for its own sake, is misguided for the following reasons. First, it is impossible for any system to work at full capacity, so there is no point in trying. If a system is overloaded, all it does is generate queues. Second, unless there is slack or spare capacity in the system, it will not be able to handle any variances from an external or internal source in a timely manner. These variances will then propagate and compound as they work their way through the system. To enable flow without interruptions being experienced downstream, it is essential to ensure the presence of unplanned but inevitable interruptions is allowed for. There is no sense in planning by assuming everything in the external and internal environment will work perfectly and as expected. Third, there is no capacity remaining to actively seek out sources of variance and eliminate them, so the system rarely improves. This scenario describes many software organizations.

Morgan summarizes the lessons for the lean product development from queuing theory as:

- *Minimize task time variation:* Tasks are broken down into units that can be completed in a few days. If a task takes longer than anticipated, a variance has occurred. To prevent this from happening again, the source of the variance must be located and eliminated.
- *Minimize interarrival variation:* Variation in arrival time effectively reduces the capacity downstream. A task arriving late is a source of variation. The source of variation must be identified and eliminated to prevent future variations.
- *Minimize batches:* Releasing large amounts of work at one time into the software development system will cause queues to develop, thus reducing system capacity. Work should be released in small units at regular intervals.
- *Control capacity utilization:* Schedule the system below capacity so it can handle variances without propagating or compounding them. Pushing more work into a system than it has capacity to handle severely reduces output.[13]

Conclusion

The objective of lean thinking is to remove waste by eliminating effort, time taken, space used, and errors made. By doing this, a lean organization will become more flexible and responsive to customer pull. To achieve flow, perfection, and the other lean principles, the elimination of variation is essential. Software development is typically highly cyclical with lots of variation, which is the reason for slow throughput time. As can be seen from the above analysis, sources of variance must be actively identified and eliminated to reduce delays on software projects.

Past solutions, such as working longer hours, may be a short-term fix, but will not ultimately resolve the problem, and over-scheduling is counterproductive. Once software development is visualized as a process, proven industrial engineering techniques can show how to create a lean process. The credibility of these techniques is important because many of the lean ideas, such as scheduling below capacity and releasing work in small amounts into the development system, are counterintuitive and against conventional software wisdom.

ENDNOTES

1. Prof. Ho Woo Lee, Department of Systems Engineering, Sung Kyun Kwan University, Su Won, South Korea, and Dr. Shahrukh, Irani, Department of Industrial, Welding and Systems Engineering, The Ohio State University, Columbus, Ohio, USA, are co-authors of this chapter.

2. Morgan, J. (2003) "High Performance Product Development," *9th Annual Lean Manufacturing Conference*, University of Michigan, May 7, pgs. 1–31.

3. Connor, G. *Lean Manufacturing for the Small Shop*, Dearborn, Michigan: Society of Manufacturing Engineers, 2001.

4. Baudin, M. *Lean Assembly: the nuts and bolts of making assembly operations flow*, New York: Productivity Press, 2002.

5. Allen, J., Robinson, C., and Stewart, D., eds. *Lean Manufacturing: A Plant Floor Guide, Society of Manufacturing Engineers*, Dearborn, Michigan, 2001.

6. Standard, C. and Davis, D., *Running Today's Factory: A Proven Strategy for Lean Manufacturing*, Cincinnati, Ohio: Hanser Gardner Publications, 1999.

7. Morgan, J. "High Performance Product Development: A Systems Approach to a Lean Product Development Process to Drive the Lean Enterprise," PhD dissertation, University of Michigan, 2002.

8. George, M.L. *Lean Six Sigma: Combining Six Sigma Quality with Lean Speed*, New York: McGraw-Hill, 2002.

9. Hopp, W.J. and Spearman, M.L., *Factory Physics, 2nd ed.*, Boston Irwin McGraw-Hill, 2000.

10. Ibid.

11. DeMarco, T. and Lister, T. *Productive Projects and Teams, 2nd ed*, New York: Dorset House Publishing Co., 1999.

12. Shingo, S. *A Study of the Toyota Production System*, Portland, Oregon: Productivity Press, 1989.

13. Morgan, pgs. 1–31, 2003.

24

Why Culling Software Colleagues is Necessary and Even Popular[1]

*L*EAN *THINKING*, BY WOMACK & JONES, presents only three scenarios where employees should be laid off from a company. First, when a lean initiative is starting, often at a time of crisis and when overhead costs have to be dramatically reduced; second, if there is a collapse in sales at anytime in the future; and third, anyone, especially managers, who are resisting the changes to lean (p. 206).[2] Employees made surplus due to lean improvements should be redeployed. This should be feasible due to the growth that lean transformations generally bring.

Toyota's plants in the United States are lean operations that rely on great discipline and consistency from their workforce. If an employee is not performing as required, then their standard process is: retrain, so the person performs job as required; if this is not successful, redeploy to another more suitable position and lastly remove. This escalating process of retrain, redeploy, and remove is well understood and fair to all concerned.

Currently in software development, cutting staff is generally seen as an unpleasant duty a company carries out when its financial position deteriorates. This chapter explores the observation that regular culling of staff is necessary for optimal performance of the company and, surprisingly, is popular with the workforce. Poor performers cause much more damage than is apparent to management. By using queuing theory and running a simulation, a company can see the severe impact of poor work. In this context, the support for culling poor staff is logical. A simple questionnaire posed to the software developers can help companies quickly ascertain if culling staff would improve worker productivity. If the response is affirmative, a popular mandate to implement a rank-and-remove exercise would have been obtained.

In the chapter "Industrial Engineering Insights on Variance in the Software Development Process," the unseen damage of variance was highlighted. In this chapter, the argument is in software development, it is the developers who are a major source of variation. If this is the case, then measures to handle developer variance are necessary.

As part of a software research project, Peter recently spent a week with a 550-person software company. A few months ago, this company had cut a significant part of its developer workforce. This was to reduce its expenses to bring it in line with industry averages. This company had also implemented more streamlined software development practices that had increased its productivity and improved the reliability of its products. The culture of the company was particularly striking, being very open, candid, and deeply supportive of the employees individually and of the organization as a whole.

As part of a survey of the staff, the question in Figure 24-1 was included. The answers were to be given on a five-point scale from Strongly Agree to Strongly Disagree.

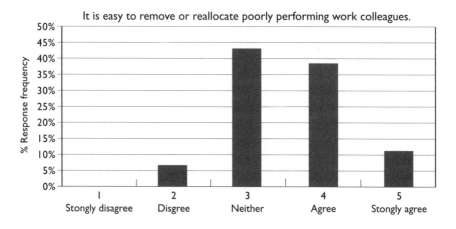

Figure 24-1. Culling Colleagues

Peter was were surprised at the feeling from 50 percent the developers that it wasn't easy to remove or reallocate colleagues perceived as poor performers—considering that recently so many had to leave the company. In follow-up informal discussions, there was a definite feeling that poor performers were being retained too long and that they were damaging the company. Given the positive nature of the company culture, this strength of feeling was unexpected. He had anticipated much more tolerance of weaker staff.

This reminded Peter of Jack Welch's management techniques at General Electric (GE). Welch visualized GE's talent pool of staff as a bell curve.[3] (See Figure 24-2)

The management task was then defined as moving the entire bell curve of talent to the right each year. This was done by identifying the bottom 10 percent and offering them coaching and training to improve their performance. If they did not improve significantly, they would be asked to leave the company. Similarly, the top

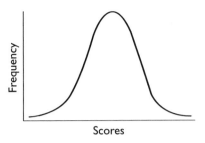

Figure 24-2. Bell Curve

10 percent would be identified for accelerated promotion. This process became harder to apply every year as only good people remained. It was also difficult to apply consistently across the company, as some areas were stronger than others. Nevertheless, in their anonymous annual staff survey, GE staff always reported that the weeding out process was not carried out stringently enough. This result surprised Welch, who had to fight hard to get his managers to implement this initiative.

How Well Employees Perform Depends on a Company's Work Philosophy

DeMarco and Lister produced data showing the wide spread of abilities among experienced software professionals. They also observed that how well you perform depends on the organization you are in. This data validates the idea of systematically working to improve or remove the bottom 10 percent very year.[4] But two questions remain:

- Why would culling fellow workers every year be popular with staff?
- Why does how well employees perform depend on the company they work in?

The answers lie in the dynamics of how the software development process works which we will illustrate with queuing theory. Visualize two software developers in an organization as in the following model (see Figure 24-3).

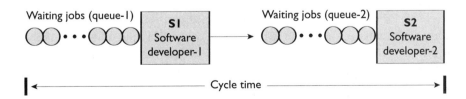

Figure 24-3. Two Software Developers

In this model, the team is made up of two developers, S1 and S2. They are reliant on each other; if one person's work is poor, it will degrade the productivity of the other. The most important variable affecting this team is the way jobs are added to queue-1.[5] Running a simulation of this situation with erratic delivery to the S1 developer and mildly erratic work by the S2 developer produces the following results for the S1 developer (see Figure 24-4).

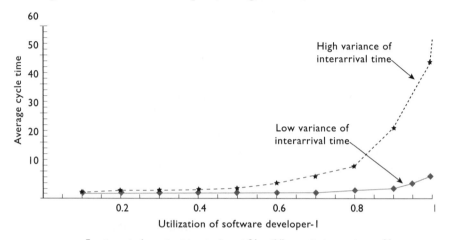

Erratic arrival, constant processing at S1, mildly erratic processing at S2

Figure 24-4. Running Simulation of Two Developers

The simulation shows that if the jobs are delivered with high variance to the S1 developer, that is, in large packages that arrive irregularly, the developer's productivity will be low. Alternatively, if the same amount of work is delivered, over the same time, with low variance, smoothly and in smaller chunks, the S1 developer's performance will significantly improve.

In this scenario, if you are the S1 developer and work productively for 80 percent of each day, the time it takes for you to deliver your work increases by a factor of four. The units of time are not important; it is the magnitude of the relative deterioration of the performance that is crucial. The S1 developer has not changed his or her work practices or effort at all—that is constant—what has changed is the erratic arrival of work.

The S1 developer is in a trap. If the S1 developer works harder, he or she may accomplish more, but the time it takes to deliver each task will increase rapidly. In a system with high variance, working harder and increasing your utilization will increase the time it takes to complete tasks. The big lesson from lean manufacturing is that, unless you remove the sources of variance from a system, it is simply not possible to run it effectively at high utilization. The same applies to software development. A bad system will defeat a good person every time.

The low productivity of the S1 developer is caused by erratic deliveries from upstream in the process. This could be due to a project manager, team leader, or marketing vice president causing work to be put into the system in large, irregular chunks, which destroys the productivity of people downstream. In this circumstance, the only way for the S1 developer to improve productivity and reduce frustrations is for the cause of the variance itself, either the project manager, team leader, or marketing vice president to either change the way in which they put work into the system or be redeployed or asked to leave the company. This would explain the support from staff for culling.

This also explains why how well an employee performs depends on the company's work philosophy. This simulation is consistently the same; variance introduced into a system degrades the entire system, not just the subprocess that introduced it. So a colleague who works erratically is going to bring everyone's productivity down. There is no alternative for improvement except to shape up or ship out. If you care about the organization, you are likely to support culling poor staff. Poor performance by coworkers prevents the implementation of the lean principle of flow.

In the lean approach, you steadily deliver work in small packages to increase your productivity. Lean software projects are not structured around large, irregular batches of work as in the traditional waterfall approach. It is therefore possible to break the work into small, regular packages that may reflect the increasing understanding of customer needs and the technology.

In software, you implement the lean principle of pull by seeking customer requirements and delivering solutions in an incremental, evolutionary way. This approach moves away from batches of requirements to more of a one-piece flow. This reduces work in progress, thereby, increasing flexibility and responsiveness. It also means poor quality issues are visible much more quickly and so are easier to resolve.

Management may be aware that a project is struggling, but it may not clearly see at what point in the process the variance and problems are being introduced. Assessing the contribution made by an individual team member is often opaque and distorted because of politics. To attain a sharper picture of who is the source of the problems (variance), management most likely would need to sound out team members.

Conclusion

Keeping the above observations in mind, there are a couple of things to remember when culling staff. First, do a simple staff survey to see if the retention of poor performers is perceived as an issue. If it is, work out how you are going to improve the bottom 10 percent and grow the top 10 percent. Second, rank comparable staff in each area using the bell curve: criteria of 10 percent exceeds expectations, 80 percent meets expectations, and 10 percent does not meet expectations. Third, follow through and repeat the process annually.

Lean development or manufacturing systems are much tauter and more disciplined than conventional ones. Any variance therefore becomes immediately noticeable. As DeMarco and Lister point out, the difference in productivity of software developers at the same experience level can be as much as 30 to 1. It is therefore essential that there is a regular process to steadily retrain, redeploy, or remove weak performers. This is how Toyota manages their production line workers in the United States and it is more critical for software developers.

General Electric found that their previous staff appraisal system was not working effectively. This is because nearly all staff received high ratings from their managers. This did not mean all staff were actually good, rather that the managers found it easier to carry them or pass them to another area. These ineffective appraisal systems are the norm. They are cruel in the long term. This is because the high variance of poor performers degrades the capacity of the entire organization. The means that a company becomes vulnerable and may well eventually have to implement panic layoffs. The solution is to routinely tackle variance at the source and so move to becoming lean.

ENDNOTES

1. Co-authors of this chapter are: Prof. Ho Woo Lee, Department of Systems Management Engineering, Sung Kyan Kwan University, South Korea and Dr. Shahrukh Irani, Department of Industrial, Welding and Systems Engineering, The Ohio State University, Columbus, Ohio, USA.
2. Womack, J. and Jones, D. *Lean Thinking: Banish Waste and Create Wealth in Your Corporation*, London: Simon & Schuster Ltd., 1996.
3. Welch, J. and Byrne, J., *Jack: straight from the gut*, London: Headline Book Publishing, 2001.
4. DeMarco, T. and Lister, T., *Peopleware: Productive Projects and Teams, 2nd ed.* New York: Dorset House Publishing, 1999.
5. George, M.L., *Lean Six Sigma for Service: conquer complexity and achieve major cost reductions in less than a year*, New York: McGraw-Hill, 2003.

25

XP and Lean Software Development—the Spare Parts Logistics Case Study

By Mark Windholtz

$59.5 BILLION IS WASTED EVERY YEAR.[1] That's a lot of *muda*! The United States gross domestic product loses 0.6 percent a year because of software defects. *Currently, over half of all errors are not found until "downstream" or during postsale software use.* This occurs even though vendors already spend 80 percent of development costs on defect removal. The software industry is becoming increasingly interested in removing defects *after they are created.* A focus on defect removal sounds like a good idea, but what if you didn't create defects in the first place? What would that be worth? Is it realistic to suggest that you can build software without defects?

The fact is, teams using lean software development are already demonstrating that they can reduce defects and cycle times while delivering a steady stream of incremental business value. Lean principles have developed over 50 years in manufacturing. Software developers recently created Extreme Programming (XP) to encapsulate practices that work. XP can be seen as a subset or implementation of lean thinking. Although coming from quite different starting points, their approaches have much in common. Therefore the experiences of XP illustrate elements of lean software development.

Lean Software Development—Expect Zero Defects

The software industry finds itself in a situation today similar to automobile manufacturers in the 1970s. Defects are sapping resources and angering customers. Defects and long cycle times are reducing its ability to respond to new business opportunities. The most heavily marketed solution is to add more bulky process steps and to do more testing at the end. This approach lengthens cycle times.

Feature cycle time for software development can be measured in the number of days needed between feature specification and production deployment. This is called *Software in Process* (SIP).[2] A shorter cycle indicates a healthier project. Lean projects can deploy to production every two weeks with a SIP of 10 working days. Some lean projects even deploy nightly. Going to production every two weeks may raise fears of introducing new defects. Good. In lean thinking, this is what you want to deal with, because to achieve short cycle times, you must identify and eliminate defects. With lean, a fundamental change in a company's thinking must occur—you start by expecting zero-defect software production. Does this mean that no single defect will ever occur? No. It means that you treat every defect as something truly useful. It is a signal from your process; you use it to continuously improve the process to prevent that class of defect from occurring again. This is very different from rhetorically claiming that defects are unacceptable and exhorting everyone to work harder with the same multiphase processes—and the same *muda*.

One way lean manufacturing production lines continuously eliminates defects is by allowing each assembly worker to stop the line if a defect appears. Paradoxically, lean production lines almost never stop. In "scientifically managed" production lines, only the manager can stop the line, yet the lines often end up crashing because defects are not reported until downstream, which creates bigger problems and more *muda*. Expect zero defects and you realize that the way you schedule, test, program, and release software needs to change radically to accomplish your goal. The good news is that, since 80 percent of traditional software project dollars are spent removing defects, the goal of zero defects is financially justifiable.

People in the software industry have recommended for a long time that before typing, programmers need to think about the problem at hand. Traditionally, this has resulted in using an analysis phase, which has two inefficiencies. The first is that it is a phase, which implies a substantial period of time with a long feedback loop, long cycle time, and large batch sizes. This is bad news when you are thinking lean. The second is that there is no definable goal or deliverable to analysis. That is, no one can clearly define the value of analysis. If your goal is to "think about the problem, rather than the solution," then there is no guarantee that you will ever complete this thinking. Often analysts write documents in special notation, and when the analysts think the analysis is complete enough, they simply stop. Another aspect of a definable goal that is missing is having definable quality measurements. What level of quality is acceptable for an analysis effort? How can you measure this? This is all very troubling, because to program correct code, you need to understand the problem first.

This is where lean begins. To become lean, you must translate (customer) requirements, one requirement at a time (to create small batch size), into repeatable automated tests. By delivering these requirements in small batches, you enable flow and pull, two of the five principles of lean.

The XP process practices *test-first coding*, which is fundamental to achieving the goal of zero defects. Test-first coding requires a programmer to write an automated unit test before the production code. The test-to-code cycle time is

5–15 minutes long. To support this style of programming, a standard unit test framework, called xUnit, is now available in over 50 programming languages.[3]

Additionally, automated upfront acceptance testing ensures that you deliver the correct business value. You build the acceptance tests directly from the requirements before writing the production code, and you build them one at a time immediately before each piece of production code. By moving the tests to the front of the process, you gain efficiencies by providing a tight discipline and direction to the team. A promising acceptance testing framework, called *fit*, is becoming popular for up front acceptance testing and is supported by a web interface called FitNesse.[4]

Lean and Extreme Programming (XP)

XP is a set of best practices that have been pragmatically developed, tested, and modified until they fit together. It is a bottom-up process developed by programmers that has worked in real projects. However, it has been difficult to explain to the uninitiated why it works. Michael Hill of ObjectMentor once remarked, "XP works in practice but not in theory." It is now apparent that *why XP works* is because it implements the principles of lean thinking.

Lean manufacturing also started as a bottom-up process when, in the late 1950s, Taiichi Ohno of Toyota Motors improved the time to change the manufacturing dies from one day to three minutes.[5] Ohno developed two basic concepts for the Toyota Production System: 1) Make what customers want when they want it, and 2) treat people with respect. These two concepts supported the two Pillars of the Toyota Product System: Just-in-Time (JIT) and autonomation (*jidoka*). Later, International Motor Vehicle Program (IMVP) researcher John Krafcik coined the term *lean* to explain why this new way of building cars worked so well. In the '90s, the theory of lean thinking matured and was applied to both manufacturing and also the design of new products.

Lean Thinking[6] defines the five principles: value, value stream, flow, pull, and perfection and has been applied to many successful businesses in fields from textbook publishing (AtomicDog.com) to travel (SouthWest Airlines). In many respects, the principles of lean closely match the practices of XP. (We will compare lean principles and XP practices at the end of this chapter.) Lean thinking also gives the XP practitioner added tools to explain XP productivity and integrate XP into the full range of business concerns.

It is the model of lean software development that explains why a business should program lean. For example, consider the expense of creating the artifacts of the software process. Could these artifacts be inventory? A major lean thinking tenet is identifying inventory as waste (*muda*). XP provides the techniques needed to minimize artifacts (reduce inventory) and reduce software in process (SIP).

Two Options to Increasing Business Value

There are two ways to increase the business value on a software project: *lower the cost* or *increase the value*. An organization could accomplish lower costs with off-shore development. Understandably, corporate executives are unhappy with paying high dollar rates for poor quality software built locally, so increasingly, they are moving projects offshore to reduce labor costs to increase payback. At least offshore programming gets lower-cost programmers to produce the same poor quality software as before.

An alternative way to increase payback is to *increase project value* by improving time to market, developing a closer understanding of the real customer requirements, and cultivating customer goodwill by providing defect-free applications. Lean software development provides the business rationale for this approach.

In the 1980s, Japanese lean auto manufacturer's established engineering and production facilities in the United States. Did they move development offshore for lower U.S. labor rates? No way! They now build cars in Ohio and Michigan in order to be closer to the customer, to ship quicker, and to understand more deeply. They moved closer to customers to produce more profitably. The same phenomenon occurs when companies adopt lean software development. Off-shore may be less expensive, but when software is business critical, software built locally with close customer communication, using lean software development with short cycle times and low defects, is the most cost-effective option. We will look at the Spare Parts Logistics (SPL) Project case study to examine this option.

The Spare Parts Logistics (SPL) Project

The SPL project was an 18-month project to extend a legacy 5 million lines of code logistics system. It was undertaken by a company we will call Big Software Inc. SPL was an extension of the Previous Logistics Project (PLP). (The names have all been changed.) The purpose of the SPL project was to manage depot stock levels of spare parts in depots worldwide. The customer organization, which we will refer to as The Depot Company, had millions of parts belonging to thousands of units of equipment that were moved frequently among depot locations. The Depot Company based the contract for the SPL project on time and materials, but they placed a strong emphasis on Big Software delivering on time and budget. Missing the date or budget would threaten additional contracts expected to provide years of future work for Big Software.

Motivation for Process Change

Big Software introduced lean software development because of the difficulty it had experienced in the Previous Logistics Project (PLP). The PLP had difficulty with code integration and poor software quality, resulting in a 700 percent cost overrun, a 200 percent schedule overrun, and a generally miserable experience for everyone. Big Software did not foresee these results, because the PLP project used a phased waterfall process and each phase taken alone indicated to upper management that the project had been going very smoothly. Phases were time-boxed and milestones were defined for the 12-month long project. Big Software set milestones for the phases of requirements, analysis, design, detailed design, code construction, in-house testing, and customer testing. It accomplished each milestone successfully, yet customer testing revealed that the code modules did not actually work.

While this was a nasty surprise for management, the programmers themselves had long been expressing concerns, but these were not addressed by the technical leads eager to push the project forward though hard work and extra effort. Because of these surprise defects, Big Software spent a second 12 months of development under very unpleasant, high-pressure conditions, reworking the application in order to pass the customer test phase. Eventually, PLP passed the customer tests and went into production. Even with this added rework, the system crashed repeatedly over the course of the first four weeks costing $1 million a day in system outage costs legal action was threatened. Apparently, even the customer tests were not sufficiently comprehensive. More importantly, the major defects first appeared in production.

How did this occur? Big Software geared its reward system toward delivering milestones. Further, they linked these milestones to individual compensation, making it in everyone's interest to push the product to the next phase. There are similarities here to how traditional automotive manufacturers, using mass production methods of projecting customer demand to produce inventory, then push this inventory onto their customer using various incentives. Developing and producing a product with a *push* philosophy often results in unpredictable processes and suboptimal behavior and creates waste. In the end, Big Software went through the expense of repairing PLP and continued running it in production.

After this debacle, management decided to take a lean software development approach based on XP for its next development project, which is when they contacted me at www.objectwind.com.

XP and Lean Software Development Approach

To begin the project, we had the Big Software SPL development team apply a highly controlled and disciplined approach to lean software development summarized by two imperatives: 1) working code and 2) conversing people—ensuring everyone talked to each other.[7]

Working code. This assures that you preserve flow in the software process. Specifically, this means that automated tests, test all code and that the whole team integrates all its work multiple times a day. Only this can assure that the code works and it all works together all the time. Furthermore, this feedback cycle gives project leadership a high degree of certainty on the true progress of the project. By the completion of the spare parts logistics (SPL) project, 2,400 automated unit tests were written and were run successfully over 30 times a day. Working code provided a medium for measuring flow of features though the team.

Conversing with people. This assures that you minimize waste by recognizing that the highest quality of communication is face-to-face.[8] All too often, committing issue details to paper slows down communication, prevents questions, and adds administrative work. Excessive reliance on intermediate documentation can easily become a source of process waste. In addition, documentation lacks a feedback cycle of question and answer, and when documentation becomes out of date, it can spread confusion and false information requiring added work to correct. The SPL development team included customers and testers that worked each feature from conception to functioning, clean, tested code. Planning took four to eight hours every two weeks and involved the whole team. In this way, the customer pulled the value from the team by specifying features during each iteration-planning meeting. Conversing people also gave the project a high level of transparency. When new Java programmers joined in the middle of the project (discussed later in this chapter), they often remarked how odd it was that the team told the customer on a daily basis the state of the project, even when the news was unpleasant. This transparency quickly helped improve The Depot Company's relationship with Big Software.

These two imperatives assured flow, minimized waste, defined customer value, created pull, and led to a project where everyone knew exactly what work had been completed. The ability to deliver features independently set the environment for a lean software process utilizing the concept of small batch sizes. Moreover, since the code was always working, the SPL team continuously improved requirements, designs, and code, which further enhanced flow . . . .

To further facilitate lean software development, we also had the SPL team members follow the XP practices. The practices can be divided into three loose groupings: customer practices, team practices, and programming practices.

XP Customer Practices

1. *Iteration planning.* At the beginning of an iteration (lasting two weeks), the whole team met with the requirements team and determined the exit criteria for a successful iteration. The requirements team determined what they needed to do next, which provided the pull of customer value. Then the programming team estimated the effort required, and the SPL team calculated what reasonably could fit into the allocated time frame. The meeting goal was to set clear, measurable, realistic, and attainable short-term goals.

2. *On-site customer.* During any software development effort, issues occur in layers. Often questions about requirements are not apparent until the programmers are writing the code, which forces them to either make assumptions or stop work until they find the correct answer. Wrong assumptions create defects and rework; stoppage creates waiting. Both are waste. By seating the domain experts with the team, the programmers are given answers as needed, so that programming can progress without work stoppage or interrupting flow. Also, by writing code using a small batch size, the team can handle all questions about the feature currently under development while it's fresh in everyone's mind.

XP Team Practices

1. *Open workspace.* Having the programmers, testers, and functional team sit together in the same workspace enhances communication about project issues. When development environment problems occur, they occur only once because the first programmer to encounter the problem immediately warns the rest of the team. This communication requires no training and it's simple. The first affected programmer lets out a spontaneous cry: *Oh no! The database is down again!* The other programmers overhear and shift to tasks that do not require the database. Sometimes another programmer in earshot knows the solution. *No, it's not. Just update your connection settings. They were changed at 2:00 PM.* At a minimum, you will not have individuals rediscovering the same problem for themselves. Problem rediscovery is avoidable waste. Open workspace encourages the formation of a team. Individuals working in solo in cubicles discourages team behavior.

2. *Pair-programming.* There is more to quality programming than typing speed. Programming is not bricklaying! Mistakes once committed to code are expensive. It is cheaper to review code while it is typed-in. Pair programming helps teams share insights about the design and the tools. Yet another benefit of pair programming is that no one person becomes an information bottleneck. At least two people work on each task. If someone is ill at home, the other person picks up the task and continues, preventing information bottlenecks and preserving flow.

3. *Collective code ownership.* Any pair can extend or fix any piece of code. On the other hand, under a system of individual code ownership, individual programmers become production bottlenecks. Collective code ownership, however, works only when you have unit testing in place. The tests support high code quality.

4. *Coding standard.* The SPL team strove to write standard code with the goal that all code in the system looks similar. The team partially wrote the

standard and partially used standards from the team culture. They talked freely about how to handle new challenges and how to code them clearly. The standard grew out of experience, and they updated it as new needs appeared.

5. *Sustainable pace.* Some software development projects oscillate between phases of boredom and panic. This becomes hard to manage because the productivity data swings wildly making scheduling of flow uneven. Sustainable pace means the team works consistent hours per week every week. This provides management with predictable outcomes, while the team is rested and alert on the job. Tired programmers write more defective code than rested programmers.

XP Programming Practices

1. *Simple design.* Overengineering can easily sidetrack a project by spending too much time on issues not directly related to customer needs. Simple design helped the SPL team focus on the simplest thing that fulfilled the requirements. One of the SPL programmers commented that this was the cleanest code he had ever worked on. The benefit of simpler code is that it is easier to extend and maintain. In other words, programmers can code faster with simpler designs. Simpler code is more modular. One indication that you have an overly complicated design is that it is hard to unit test. Occasionally in SPL, a code change caused multiple unit tests to fail, which indicated that the tests were not focused enough and that the design was not simple enough. Simple design is aided through continuous design improvement (refactoring), allows for smaller incremental improvements, and allows for an ongoing flow of features.

2. *Continuous integration.* A task is not completed until the code is integrated into the single code stream shared by the team. However, you can integrate code before completing the entire task. The SPL team would integrate at any point when all the unit tests passed. In C++, they were able to integrate every two to four hours of work. In Java, they would integrate every 20 minutes to two hours. As the length of time between integrations got longer, the pain in integrating became disproportionately greater. This encouraged the programmers to integrate frequently. Integration almost always occurred before end of day. Continuous integration works best in smaller two-hour cycles. The SPL team's daily integrations did cause some work to go slower when the time between integrations became too long.

3. *Test first.* SPL developed over 2,400 unit tests. With test-first programming, the test is written before the production code. The SPL team knew they were finished when the tests passed, which then gave clear exit criteria for tasks. The growing suite of tests provided reassurance as developers

added more features. The team did a great job in testing even though they struggled with an underpowered programming environment where compile cycle times were 20 minutes long. Such long cycle times forced the unit tests to grow bulkier than otherwise necessary. The Java part of SPL demonstrated how small and focused the tests could be. The Java team also showed how cycle times could occur in less than one minute.

4. *Refactoring*. Left unattended, software systems tend to slip toward disorder. As you add features, it often extends the original design in unforeseen ways, leading to ever more ugly and brittle code. Refactoring is the science of improving the design of existing code. Improving a design allows you to add new features more quickly. The SPL team minimally applied refactoring in the C++ parts of SPL. For the Java portion of SPL, refactoring was applied more aggressively and succeeded in exposing both dependency problems and coding errors. The best way to build flexible code is to flex it. Refactoring helped reveal design weaknesses early so the team could fix them. Refactoring on the C++ part of the project was greatly hampered by the long, 20-minute cycle time and the difficulty in creating and deleting classes in a difficult to use, heavily customized, source control system.

There were two XP practices not used for the SPL project: *small releases* and *metaphor*. *Small releases* is the practice of releasing to production in small pieces so that real-life production feedback is obtained. The SPL project contract was for a one-time big release after 18 months. When Big Software wrote the contract, The Depot Company was not aware of incremental approaches to project deployment. *Metaphor* provides conceptual integrity with a unifying mental picture of the application. By the time someone suggested an appropriate metaphor for the project, the programmers and The Depot Company had already become attached to the technical vocabulary used to describe the system parts. They were not interested in switching the names they were already happy using. To compensate for a missing metaphor, we introduced various techniques for understanding the core design of the system. One of those was the use of a Wiki (or collaborative web authoring tool) to document the high-level design elements.

SPL Case Study Highlights

Before discussing the highlights, it is important to note how all the above practices reinforced each other. For example, if programmers were asked to write test-first code alone, they usually did not write enough tests. If you write an insufficient number of tests, continuous integration becomes more difficult because the team doesn't know what is correct and what is broken. Without continuous integration, simple design is difficult to achieve because long integration cycles encourage big, elaborate, overengineered designs and so on. Now for the highlights:

On Time and On Budget

The 18-month SPL project was two weeks late and 108 percent of budget. In contrast, the previous project using a plan-driven phased-waterfall process with the same organization and technology was 200 percent of schedule and 800 percent of budget. Management and the customer were very pleased with the SPL project.

Kaizen *and the Final Sprint*

For the first 14 months, the team and Big Software management were open to the lean concept of continuous improvement (*kaizen*). The team made ongoing improvements both to the process and to the software design and held retrospectives every two weeks to reflect upon and improve team performance. The suppleness of software provided them with an added tool. When the team noticed that a repeated task took a long time, they would consider changes to the design as well as to the process. The ability to change the design quickly to support the work is not as common in standard manufacturing practices, but certainly proved valuable in lean software development. During the last four months of the project, the process and design seemed to solidify, which suggested improvements were fewer. Management also received suggestions for improvement ever more skeptically. During the final sprint to the end, improvement slowed and the focus turned back to working harder. The slow down in improvements may be related to the fact that the SPL team did not deliver small releases; but rather, they delivered all at once at the end. The approach of the end date raised fears and limited the creativity of the team. Smaller repeated releases would have increased the team's confidence that they could deliver.

Recovery Team

Halfway though the 18-month project, the SPL team had enough historical performance data to show that it would miss the deliverable date by two months. They calculated the slip nine months before the due date. This early warning provided enough time to react. Yet at the time, upper management was more concerned with a different project that was in crisis. Three months went by. Again, the team recalculated and presented the data to management. The project still had six months left to correct a two-month shortfall. The result was the creation of a separate recovery team to implement four of the remaining features separately. The fact that the SPL team had deferred design on these features allowed it to shift the design to a new technology for the recovery team. The recovery team is described later in the chapter.

Pulling Value

Early on in the project, the The Depot Company customer team said that a big architectural change would be needed to support a "big dreaded feature." During an early iteration-planning meeting, the SPL team talked about the details of the architectural change and the feature involved. It was truly a big change, and the programmers were concerned about how this would affect the schedule. There was some concern whether they could accomplish it with the current technology. The conversation with the Depot Company team was free flowing and wide ranging. To focus the conversation, we asked Depot Company representatives if they wanted this "big feature" implemented within the next two weeks. There was a quiet pause. Then the Depot Company team switched gears and suggested that since the SPL team needed something right now, it should work on a different feature. So the SPL team defined work for the next two weeks. After every few iterations, the big dreaded feature would re-emerge as an issue. Each time, we asked the Depot Company representatives to talk in terms of the next two weeks, and the big dreaded feature was delayed for a more pressing feature.

Some of the programmers were worried about this approach. They asked: "If this is so big, won't we be in trouble if we don't start to deal with it now?" But the SPL team continued to focus on providing an even flow of value as pulled by the customer during iteration planning. Eventually, Depot stopped mentioning the big dreaded feature. Months later, the SPL team was within two iterations of project completion and one of the programmers asked: "What about the big dreaded feature?" A Depot team member waved him away. "Well, we couldn't ever really figure out what that thing was supposed to do. So, we will just go to production without it." Having Depot pull value while the SPL team managed the flow was a huge triumph for this project . . . It may appear to be pure luck that the dreaded feature was not needed, but really, lean was at work. When you have the customer pull value, less-valuable features naturally fall to the end of the to-do list. And when they claim that everything is important, it's because they have not yet considered resource trade-offs. A pull approach offers a tool to allow those trade-offs to be made naturally and continuously.

Feedback and Customer Relationship

The project preceding SPL poisoned the relationship between Big Software and the Depot Company. Spending 800 percent of budget made Depot suspicious. This began to change, however, when the SPL team began delivering small bits of working code to Depot at regular two-week intervals. Within two months, Depot had warmed to the team. After eight months, the main Depot team representative requested office space near the SPL team, instead of having to work from a separate building. The Depot representative liked seeing the specified feature appearing in code a few days after he requested it. Though The Depot Company was detached and suspicious at the beginning of the project, the relationship improved as the SPL team delivered short feedback loops and the customer was able to pull their own defined value.

Managing Flow

In the early stage of the project, the team had been struggling with test-first programming but managed to work their way up to 178 unit tests. To encourage them, we had the SPL team write the total number of tests on a large whiteboard at the entrance to the shared workspace. Meanwhile, we left for three days to help another client. Upon returning, we noticed the number of tests was still stuck at 178. After three days! We were shocked. Had they stopped programming code using the test-first technique? No, they had stopped programming entirely. In our absence, the whole team attended meetings with the architect. Flow had stopped and they inserted an architecture phase. Architecture is an important element of software development, but it can and should be handled as a flow of delivering business value. We worked with the team to put practices in place so that future architecture was focused on the flow of value. As a result, they stopped having protracted, unfocused meetings.

Waste from Rework

The one thing that became clear only in retrospect was the waste caused by a lag of weeks between creating the code and the writing of the automated customer acceptance tests. There was a lag of about two weeks between the programmers finishing their tasks and the acceptance test completion. Inevitably, the team would find that even though the unit tests validated all the functionality on the small scale, a number of defects would occur when everything was put together. In order to correct the defects discovered in acceptance testing, the team members had to revisit the requirements. Meaning, acceptance testing at the end of the process caused rework. Figure 25-1 shows the number of tests completed per day. Acceptance tests are plotted in grey and use the scale on the right (0–400). Unit tests are plotted in the darker line and use the scale on the left (0–2,400). As you can see, the team started acceptance tests on day 53 of the project, whereas unit testing was applied from the first day of coding. In an XP approach, you should write acceptance tests immediately after the customer requests a feature and before the programmers begin work on the feature. In teams since the SPL project, a dramatic reduction in wasteful rework occurs when they write the acceptance tests first. A standard tool for acceptance testing before code is constructed is the fit framework.[9]

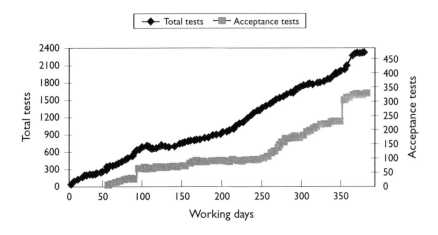

Figure 25-1. Number of Tests Completed Per Day

Bottlenecks and Small Batches

At the Big Software Company, the database administrator (DBA) shared time among a number of projects including SPL, which made it a typical bottleneck resource. Big Software gave project tasks to a DBA when a project work stoppage was imminent. A tech lead from another traditional project once asked: "When will SPL be blocked waiting for the DBA?" Unfortunately for DBA scheduling purposes, SPL rarely blocked because SPL programmers had small atomic tasks (small batches) to work on and could quickly shift to another small task when a needed resource was unavailable. The only unfortunate aspect of this was when the SPL team really did need timely DBA attention; they had to plead their case without the threat of work stoppage.

Supply Forecasting—Adding a New Team for the SPL Project

With six months to go in an 18-month schedule, the team calculated that the SPL project would be two months late. This was based on historical productivity data generated by the SPL team and on release-planning estimates for the C++ based programming team. The team determined it could separately implement the last four features having to do with supply forecasting, using Java technology. Since this was a new technology for Big Software, it added risk, but this risk was justified because the team believed it could find Java programmers quickly. As a result, the idea of creating a SPL-Forecasting (SPL-F) team became the plan to recover the two lost months on the schedule.

The manager was very happy with the high productivity and team spirit of the main SPL C++ team, and all agreed to keep the main team intact and to start a separate team from scratch. Adding a separate team to separate features of a late project would help avoid the perils of Brooks law: *Adding people to a late project will make it later.* This was possible only because the XP process handled one feature at a time, making the features independent enough for the SPL team to break them off and assign them to the new SPL-F team.

By the time the new Java programmers were available, the project had only two months to deliver the application. They were new to Big Software and to the process, but they had experience with Java and the development environment. The SPL-F team started writing tests and began to define the code integration cycle. The Depot customer team consisted of two in-house domain experts, a test coordinator, and a customer representative. The SPL-F team delivered the needed features to the SPL Team and made it possible to deliver the SPL on time and on budget. Two highlights of the SPL-F teams efforts are worth mentioning: 1) changing requirements and 2) rapid feedback, rapid learning.

1. *Changing (increasing) requirements.* Originally, the SPL team assumed it understood the requirements quite well. The four features were a re-implementation of an existing mainframe application. The goal was to move it to UNIX. However, when the SPL team held an exploration meeting with the new SPL-F team and gave a basic scope to the project, planned iteration #1 with the goal of planning work for one week, the Java programmers were a bit confused because so much was unclear at the same time. The new team had never used a lean process, had never programmed in test-first style, and had never integrated every hour. They were quite suspicious of the value of refactoring, and the SPL team was nervous since the time frame was short. The SPL-F team worried that one simple step at a time would not lead to completion in two months. Meanwhile, we worried that they may not learn the process in time for productivity to improve. The time it takes before the productivity boost begins is not related to programmer skill, but to programmer acceptance. Until the tests are being written with care, few programmers believe that refactoring can be effective. The effectiveness comes from not only simplifying the code, but also having confidence that complex features can emerge from simple features. The original list of four features grew to nine as the team broke them down into smaller features and added features to handle issues of concurrency and data clean-up that did not exist on the mainframe. It's common for requirements that appear well defined at the beginning of a project to need adjustment when the team finally investigates the details of implementation. Further, as the list of features grows, the work velocity of the team will, too. For these last two points, lean's agility becomes an important ally.

2. *Rapid feedback, rapid learning.* The timeline for the SPL-F team was very compressed, yet the team was organized and delivered the features in two months. The SPL team found that a one-week iteration schedule was very powerful for learning and feedback. Inside of this, the SPL team also held a brief meeting every morning for 15 minutes to review the previous day's progress and coordinated current tasks. The learning and course correction was very beneficial.

SPL Accomplishments

There were five broad accomplishments for the SPL project: 1) reduced cycle times, 2) reduced errors, 3) new team organization, 4) positive impact on staff, and 5) improved handling of process defections.

Reduced Cycle Times

Before the team was introduced to the XP process, the idea of cycle time was completely unknown to them. In adopting the process, the SPL team focused on speeding up the following cycles: 1) new class creation, 2) compile cycle, 3) requirements verification cycle, and 4) detection-correction cycle.

1. *New class creation.* This involved creating a new empty class and checking it in. The C++ class required four files: a source file plus header file, and a unit test file plus header file. The new class creation also required adding the test to the suite and checking all the changes into the source code control system. Initial time to accomplish this was one full day, which is shockingly long. However, since Big Software never considered it important to do this quickly, layer upon layer of paper-based procedures had evolved; making adding code to the source control system a wasteful bureaucratic exercise. One programmer joked that rather than a source code control system, we were really dealing with a source code prevention system! After a week of negotiating with various departments, the team reduced the time to four hours. This remaining time was due to the many technical steps needed to register and check in the four files. Over the next few weeks, the team invested time in building scripts and processes to eventually reduce this time to 20 minutes.

2. *Compile cycle.* At the start of the project, Big Software measured the compile cycle time in hours. The large base of legacy C++ code contained many dependency loops requiring multiple compile passes in the makefiles. The team addressed this by building the SPL extensions in a highly modular way that allowed separation of SPL compile cycle from the global compile cycle. Improvements were made to get a nightly global compile/

build, which shortened the SPL compile cycle to 20 minutes, much of which was linking to the global code.

3. *Requirements verification cycle.* The customer provides a requirement, the programmers implement it, and QA tests the implementation with the customer present. At the beginning of the project, this cycle took the entire length of any given project. After a few iterations, the team shortened the requirements verification cycle to three weeks, and by the end of the project, it was one week.

4. *Detection-correction cycle.* During the majority of the project, the team handled defects in real time and completed and released a feature to QA every three to six days. QA tested the feature and wrote any defects on 3" × 5" index cards and posted the cards on the task board for all to see. For emphasis, QA affixed a red sticker to the upper left corner. When a team member needed a new task, she would first choose a defect task. The two programmers working together would write a unit test to recreate the reported defect, fix the defect, run the full suite of tests to make sure nothing else was affected, and then check-in the changed code. They would initial the index card, place a yellow sticker on it to signify that the defect was ready for retesting, and place it again on the task board. A QA team member would notice the yellow sticker and retest the defect.

In lean thinking, it is imperative that you reduce the time between a defect's introduction, detection, and correction. But unfortunately, when the SPL project went into user testing, the team changed the process to the preexisting bureaucratic change control process. They also developed a two-track system: one track for the official, bureaucratic, automated tracking system and a lean one for the programmers. Testers would register the defect in the official automated tracking system, which maintained workflow control and routed the defect to various people for sign off and verification while simultaneously writing a simple index card and tacking it to the programmer's task board as before.

This led to a humorous episode. The first defect from customer release testing was reported as usual by index card. It was accepted by an enthusiastic programmer, tested, and fixed. Only then did the programmer realize that he was not authorized to check in the correction because the official automated workflow system had not yet assigned a defect tracking number. He waited four hours before the defect moved though the sign-off process and finally provided him with the required number. The point being that the administrative infrastructure was a drag on programmer productivity. This was pure waste and needed to be addressed.

Reduced Errors

The project previous to SPL required an additional 100 percent of schedule and 700 percent of budget just to rework the defects before going to production. SPL, however, sailed through three weeks of planned user testing with no level 1 defects and all discovered defects corrected within the normal testing schedule.

Lean Team Organization

The SPL team consisted of twelve programmers, a technical lead, a coach, and a manager. Three of the programmers were senior programmers, six were entry level. Every morning at 8:45 AM, the team assembled in a conference room. In a 15-minute "stand-up" meeting, they shared status reports of yesterday's work and the present day's plan with the team's manager. The manager recorded any organizational roadblocks that the team encountered so that he could work on them after the meeting. Directly after the meeting (after a stop for coffee), team members chose coding partners and worked two programmers per workstation on the tasks they chose for themselves that day. Every two weeks, the team held a day-long planning meeting to estimate, design, and commit to the tasks for the next two-week iteration. The planning meeting was the most strenuous part of the iteration for the team, so members often brought snacks and soft throwable objects like nurf balls to lighten the mood.

Positive Impact on Staff

The staff was generally enthusiastic about the lean approach to software development. The senior programmers felt rewarded by the balance they achieved between doing direct work and helping other team members. The junior programmers expressed excitement at the opportunity to work in a learning environment where they could get support when needed. A number of programmers were enthusiastic about the large and growing test suite because it gave them confidence in their work. Three people in a total of 34 did not enjoy the rapid pace and dynamic nature of this approach, so Big Software moved them to more traditional multiphase projects.

Using Lean Principles and XP Practices

We will now look more closely at how, in the SPL case study, the XP practices support lean principles. We'll see how the five lean principles and XP practices fit together and what is missing. The lean principles are: value, value stream, flow, pull, and perfection.

Value

On an XP project, the customer defines value. The XP customer refers to whoever provides the programmers with requirements. An XP customer can be the end user, a product manager, or a team of domain experts. The customer defines the value at three levels: 1) release planning, 2) iteration planning (collectively known as the *planning game*), and 3) during daily programming known as an *on-site customer*.

During *release planning*, the customer defines the features needed for the next small release, typically (one–three months of work). During *iteration planning*, the customer defines features for the next iteration (two–three weeks of work). The customer defines automated *acceptance tests* as the criteria for feature completion. Then, as an *on-site customer*, the customer answers fine-grain questions as they occur during the programming day. A strictly enforced protocol insists that the customer must make all business decisions no matter how small. The customer defines the value.

Value Stream

In lean manufacturing, the value stream identifies the entire step-by-step activities a specific product or product family must go through to be developed, produced, and delivered to the customer. That is, the value stream considers the needs of the customer in the broadest sense and examines how those needs are served from multiple sources and processes. XP focuses on the programming aspects of software development, so the programming team and its processes are just one part of that service. Though XP does not provide practices that directly support the principle of value stream, a fuller application of value stream could be a helpful addition to projects using XP to construct software. This would entail thinking about the project deliverables as part of the total value provided to the customer of the company sponsoring the software.

Flow

Flow is supported by many XP practices. With the XP approach, the team sits together in an *open workspace* so members can quickly share information. If one programming pair encounters an environmental problem (i.e., a failed global build or newly added operating system patch), other programming pairs do not repeat the effort of discovering the same problem. This frees up team members to devote their energy to maintaining flow in more productive areas of the project work. In traditional software projects, critical-path analysis is often used to find the shortest way to fit dependent tasks together. In XP, as well as in lean thinking, you remove dependencies, reduce batch size, and perform tasks in parallel. *Pair programming* lessens dependency on the knowledge of an individual.

Collective code ownership means that anyone can improve any part of the code, rather than stopping work until the designated code owner can make a requested addition to the code. *Sustainable pace* means that the team works a standard schedule to create more uniform output and allow for more accurate scheduling. An example of this was management's decision to recover the SPL schedule by spinning-off the SPL-F team.

Simple design helps a project avoid the ever-present temptation of over-engineering. Overengineering distracts the team with issues that have no customer relevance. Simple design keeps a team focused on the real requirements. *Continuous integration* provides a single stream of code that various programming pairs continuously update, ensuring that even intra-day changes are shared. In a traditional process, integration occurs every evening or every few weeks, which often causes broken global builds that interrupt the production flow. *Test-first* programming ensures that features added to the code do not cause rippling defects in other parts of the code. When the code is tested before it is integrated, integration becomes quick and secure. *Refactoring* or continuous design improvement encourages an ongoing simplification of the work product. The simplification makes defects resulting from overcomplicated code less likely and makes it easier to add future features.

Pull

The practices of XP that support pull are similar to the practices that support value as discussed above. At the same time the customer defines value, the customer also schedules it for production. XP's *release and iteration planning, on-site customer,* and *customer acceptance testing* are tools that pull the value from the team.

Perfection

XP teams strive for perfection in their ongoing efforts to improve the design and process. While not a defined XP practice, most XP teams use the *iteration-planning meeting* to conduct retrospectives to enhance continuous process and design improvement. *Collective code ownership* means that team members are expected to fix errors in the code, no matter where they might encounter them. *Open workspace* allows team members to share insights with one another immediately. *Coding standard* brings uniformity to the code and *test-first* programming assures that all code is tested. Finally, *refactoring* removes duplication and decreases variance, while *pair programming* ensures that all code is reviewed for correctness as it is typed.

Conclusion

The application of lean software development in the form of the XP process was a great success in the SPL case. SPL went to production on time and on budget with no major defects. In fact, it was four days in production before Big Software reported the first minor (level 4) defect. In the end, The Depot Company was happy, Big Software made a profit. The SPL software extension of a legacy 5 million lines of code logistics system was of high quality, and the programmers felt proud of their work. This is not to say there were not some challenges and adjustments. Lean thinking will require changes in culture, work habits, and workspace layout. It also will require a learning curve for many software professionals, since they are not versed in the practices of lean or XP. But, as the overwhelming success of the SPL project demonstrates, the wisdom of using XP and the lean approach is clear.

ENDNOTES

1. "The Economic Impacts of Inadequate Infrastructure for Software Testing," A report by the National Institute of Standards and Technology. www.rti.org/.
2. Kent Beck, Software-In-Process, A New/Old Project Metric, Three Rivers Institute www.threeriversinstitute.org/.
3. Kent Beck, Test-Driven Development, by Example, June 2003. The xUnit list of free implementations is available at www.xprogramming.com/software.htm.
4. Fit Acceptance testing framework by Ward Cunningham et al. http://fit.c2.com. FitNesse—The fully integrated stand-alone wiki, and acceptance testing framework—http://www.FitNesse.org.
5. Womack and Jones, *The Machine That Changed the World*, New York, HarperPerennial, 1991.
6. Womack and Jones, *Lean Thinking*, London, Touchstone Books, 1996.
7. Brian Marick, "Agile Methods and Agile Testing," www.testing.com/agile/agile -testing-essay.html.
8. Alistair Cockburn, *Agile Software Development*, Chapter 3: "Communicating, Cooperating Teams." Shows that the richest and most effective communication channel is "2 people at the whiteboard."
9. Fit Acceptance testing framework by Ward Cunningham et al. http://fit.c2.com.

26

Case Study: Timberline, Inc.— Implementing Lean Software Development

THIS CHAPTER[1] DESCRIBES THE FIRST FULL ADOPTION OF LEAN IDEAS to a commercial software development company. Timberline, Inc started their lean initiative in spring 2001, and this is an account of their journey, their results, and the lessons they learned until September 2003.

Company Background

Timberline is an American software company with all 450 staff based in Oregon. It employed 160 software developers that used C++ and object oriented techniques at the time of the lean implementation. The other people were in areas, such as telephone support, technical writing, administration, sales, and marketing. The company was founded in the early 1970s, and it is a market leader in software for the construction industry. In September 2003, the company was sold for approximately $100 million. During the period of the study, Timberline was NASDAQ-listed, but it is now privately held.

The catalyst for the lean initiative was a software problem that was delivered to customers and was costly to correct. The business context had also changed. Operating profit had fallen to around 3 percent from historically much higher levels. Their market was maturing with customers placing more emphasis on reliability; at the same time, competition was increasing. Due to past success and profitability, the software process had been neglected. But what worked in a high growth, profitable market was no longer perceived to be adequate in this new business environment.

The software development problems manifested themselves in several ways. There was little insight into how projects were progressing until near the end. This meant there was no predictability of output and they could suddenly find that a project needed an extra 60 calendar days to finish. The time from code-complete to ready-to-ship was unpredictable, due to the time taken to stabilize the completed code. Therefore, functions such as marketing and training could not prepare, so often their material was not ready when needed. This damaged the product when launched. Often the wrong mix of people and unnecessary people were assigned to projects because the exact nature of what was to be done was unclear. Quality assurance was testing the wrong things because it did not understand what the customer was trying to do with the product. Most importantly, features that customers needed were missed, yet money was poured into creating features that customers did not want. This was clear from customers' calls after products were launched.

Although the company had over 20,000 customers worldwide, development costs were too high at 27 percent of revenue. The use of nonstandard processes and tacit knowledge was not proving scalable to handle the growth experienced. When the processes in use were analyzed, some 900 discrete steps, 600 handoffs, and 275 review meetings were identified. Many of the 900 steps did occur in more than one process and were therefore counted more than once. Therefore the raw numbers overstate the complexity of the organization in spring 2001. Nevertheless, the teams charting the processes were routinely astonished at their convoluted and overly elaborate nature, which hindered flow. Waste in many forms, including rework, inventory, transportation, and searching, were commonplace.

For example, the practice was to have around six review cycles at each stage within a project. These were lengthy, political, and personality-driven meetings that were based on little data. There were no specific performance goals, just pushing for faster delivery and avoiding severe defects, which would damage a customer, e.g., by crashing their system or corrupting their data. The lack of specific goals meant that it was not possible to monitor progress.

To change a company that had been established for over 30 years and had a long record of profitability was a major challenge. In spring 2001, 92 percent of employees responded to a staff attitude assessment survey, which indicated that employees were very aware of the problems related to lack of process and poor communication. But awareness of a problem is different from taking responsibility for making change happen. There was resistance to change, which stemmed from people's natural discomfort with doing things differently. There was also a reluctance to adopt lean methods that had not been used in software before.

The CEO, Curtis Peltz, who, like many of the staff, had been working for the company for decades, decided to proceed with change. Consultants were selected on the basis of cultural fit and depth of change management experience. At this point, the company had no knowledge or interest in lean techniques. The consultants they selected had little knowledge of the software industry, but were experienced in using lean ideas to improve quality and productivity in service industries. To evaluate if the consultants would be effective, the initial fixed price contract was for two consultants for one month.

Lean Principles

The key lean concept is continuous-flow processing. In many software companies, it takes months or years to get a product out of the door. This represents a substantial amount of money tied up in work in progress, e.g. untested code or requirement documents written but not acted on. If the entire software development process is analyzed, there are queues and bottlenecks delaying product from being released to customers. Often requirements are put into the system in large batches, which is disruptive and hides errors. The solution is to handle the work in small batches, so with a small inventory of requirements, designing, coding, and testing are started earlier, and therefore, mistakes in requirements will be caught sooner.

To redesign the workflow, team members applied the design principles of lean manufacturing. These are principles, not prescriptions, so each lean implementation will be different depending on the context and constraints of the organization. Change management was handled by using *kaizen* events, which will be described in more detail. All processes were redesigned at the same time. The lean principles support each other, so there is no particular sequence or hierarchy for their adoption. The principles used were:

Customer Defined Value

Much more effort was allocated to the requirements definition stage. All members of the cross-functional team went to visit customers to see how they worked. If possible, they would do elements of the customer's work to experience it directly. Key people in the customer's staff would be identified so they could be interviewed in more depth and later shown early versions of the product. The team would then brainstorm to create a feature list and then survey customers to prioritize the features. This would be repeated to ensure the final set of requirements did not miss anything needed yet also contained attractive bonus features. Care was taken to omit any features that would have a negative impact on customers.

The work of Noriaki Kano, who developed the following model of the relationship between customer satisfaction and quality, was particularly useful (see Figure 26-1).

Kano identified three types of customer needs: basic, expected, and exciting. Basic needs are assumed from the product or service and will not be mentioned by the customer. Expected needs are those the customer already experiences, but would like them faster, better, or cheaper.

The exciting requirements are difficult to discover. They are beyond the customers' expectations. Their absence doesn't dissatisfy; their presence excites. These needs, which are tied mostly to adding value, are unspoken and thus

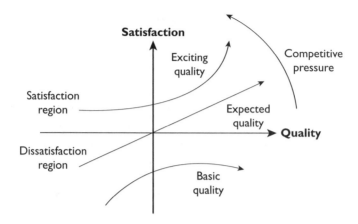

Figure 26-1. Relationship Between Customer Satisfaction and Quality

invisible to both the customer and the producer. Further, they change over time, technology, and market segment. This stronger customer orientation and the Kano techniques helped Timberline improve their delivery of products that reflected all three types of customer needs.

Design Structure Matrix (DSM) and Flow

With the Kano analysis, the voice of the customer is connected to data. This enables the scope/features trade-off decisions to be based on facts, not political power. Each requirement can then be broken down into the two to five day chunks of work needed to meet it. Once this was done, the skills needed to complete the work became clear. This approach resembles Function Point Analysis, which is a way of estimating work from breaking down requirements.

But by using the lean principle of flow, this could be taken one valuable step further. It was apparent that the work was not flowing smoothly between people with different skills, because some skill areas were overworked, while other areas were waiting for work. Therefore, load balancing was required to ensure, e.g., that sufficient quality assurance staff were allocated to a project and were not overworked, therefore, not becoming a bottleneck.

Design Structure Matrix is a systems analysis tool that provides a compact and clear representation of a complex system and a capture method for the interactions, interdependencies, and interfaces between system elements (i.e., subsystems and modules). More details can be found on www.DSMweb.org (see Figure 26-2).

This allowed the correct staff to be allocated to teams at the right time. This increased staff utilization and improved the flow of work through the project. The tool used was an Excel spreadsheet with a macro that allowed the entry of dependencies for each unit of work. The spreadsheet then sequenced the work

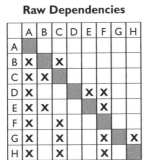

Raw Dependencies

	A	B	C	D	E	F	G	H
A	▓							
B	X	▓	X					
C	X	X	▓					
D	X			▓	X	X		
E	X	X			▓	X		
F	X		X			▓		
G	X		X		X		▓	X
H	X		X			X		▓

Sequencing

	A	C	B	F	E	D	H	G
A	▓							
C	X	▓	X					
B	X	X	▓					
F	X	X		▓				
E	X		X	X	▓			
D	X			X	X	▓		
H	X	X		X			▓	
G	X	X		X			X	▓

Figure 26-2. Design Structure Matrix

based on the dependencies. This tool was not easy to use and fell into disuse. But the idea of load balancing was retained and carried out successfully in conjunction with *takt* time.

Using *Takt* Time to Carry-Out Load Balancing

The eight steps below describe the use of *takt* time in conjunction with load balancing.

1. *Setting a common tempo or takt time was the heartbeat of this lean operation.* The objective was to pace work according to customer demand. A key problem was that too much work was being pushed into the software development system. While intuitively appealing, it caused the developers to 'thrash'. This meant that they switched tasks frequently, incurring many wasteful set-up times. The work would also accumulate in queues where no value was added and delivery would be erratic. This would cause further problems as other project schedules were impacted by the delays. The DSM in Figure 26-2, after sequencing, shows that activity F receives inputs from activities A and C. Activity F also delivers outputs to activities E, D, H and G. This enables activities to be scheduled to minimize delays and disruption.

   The solution was to break down projects into units of between two to five days of work. Tasks of unknown difficulty would also be assigned units, which broke them up into manageable chunks. This enabled tracking of progress. The total number of days available for each skill type is divided into the total amount of days work was to be done. If there was simply too much work allocated, then it could be cut back or extra resources identified. When this was done, the team was expected to meet their target date.

The generic *takt* time calculation is:

Takt time = (Net working days available ÷ no of units required)

Therefore, to determine the production rate, *x* number of kits should be produced in *x* number of days. It was therefore possible to use *takt* time to gauge the current production as an indicator of whether or not a project was on target for delivery (see Figure 26-3).

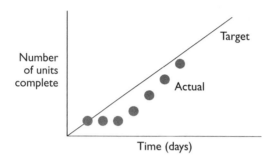

Figure 26-3. Visual Controls—Performance to *Takt* Time

This type of chart was posted in each team's workspace and used to indicate product delivery status. A green sticker indicated progress at 90–100 percent of *takt*, a yellow sticker at 80–90 percent of *takt*, and a red sticker at 70–80 percent of *takt*.

This approach of using Kano to really understand the customer, prioritize their requirements, and then identify the work necessary to fulfil them, worked well. The visual chart above, showing performance to *takt* time was very popular and was used with enthusiasm.

2. *Linked processes—located near one another.* In the company, different functions were located separately. This meant that even setting up simple meetings could take two weeks. Analysis showed that during the course of its life, a typical project moved over 20 miles within the office buildings. This traveling was pure waste, as it did not add value to the customer. This departmental structure was therefore complemented with the formation of cross-functional teams. This meant that meetings could be held quickly when needed to resolve any issues. A short stand-up meeting was held each morning, which was invaluable. Co-location made a considerable difference to productivity. Being such a well-established corporation with many long service employees, moving workplaces caused considerable agitation, but this did settle down.

3. *Standardized procedures (e.g., file storage, names, locations, workspace) to enable people to be moved around easily.* A key idea is to be able to move

people about between projects as they are needed. This raises productivity and speeds product delivery. This was being hindered by idiosyncratic work practices. This had nothing to do with creativity, but was the result of history. The presence of spaghetti legacy software can be a serious constraint on the implementation of new software processes. But, once the existing processes were looked at from the perspective of consistency, many simple improvements could be made.

4. *Eliminate rework by tracking the causes.* Rework severely disrupts current work schedules and contributes to delays and low productivity. The number of 'bounce backs' was tracked and had been halved. By investing more time in understanding customer need and context, much rework was eliminated. This also allowed the scope of a project to be cut where it did the least harm, if it was starting to run late. By analysis of the different software components to be built, ones that had high dependencies were identified as having the highest risk. These would be started early with particular care and more thorough testing. This also reduced rework.

5. *Balancing loads—eliminates necessary delays.* This follows from the *takt* time concept. What was happening was that a shortage of one skill would cause delays and hold up other people. A classic bottleneck was that quality assurance staffs were in short supply, so testing was not completed quickly enough. By looking at the skills needed per unit of work, the work and skills could be rearranged to eliminate the bottlenecks. This was done by assessing how many days people with a specific skill would be available, after allowing for holidays, training, and other commitments. The work to be carried out is captured in the 'units' it was broken down into. By comparing work to be done with the resources available, it becomes clear if there are any constraints. Often it indicated that some people are overloaded with work, while others have little to do. Multiskilling staff and reorganizing workload can achieve more balance. This raises productivity and improves predictability of delivery. It also creates a less stressful work environment. For example, the developers were cross-trained so they could carry out other tasks such as QA and interviewing customers. The people writing the training manuals were shown how to adapt and input their material into the software's Help feature. Previously, these two tasks were done separately, so much time and effort were duplicated and wasted. The QA team members who did manual testing were shown how to do automated testing. Support staff were shown how to do manual testing, which also increased their familiarity with the product (see Figures 26-4 and 26-5).

6. *Posting performance results.* Ideally, this would be each team's hourly productivity rate, but daily or weekly is also fine. This is vital. A key

Before work balancing:

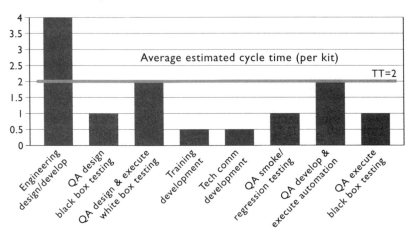

Figure 26-4. Balancing Workloads

After work balancing:

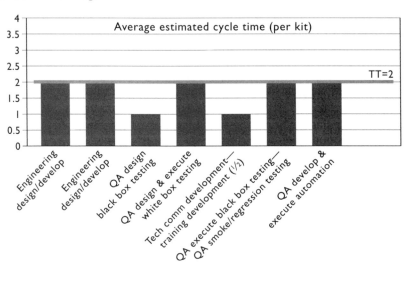

Figure 26-5. Balancing Workloads

advantage is to create a learning organization. To learn requires constant feedback as to where the problems and errors are. A basic test is that a complete stranger can walk into the work area and see the status of work.

Initially, this concerned the staff, but they quickly accepted it. The reason for this was that it indicated project progress and allowed sensible discussions about when work would be complete and how much capacity was available. This data enabled a team to become self-managing, allowing supervisors to focus on eliminating sources of variation. For example, by monitoring cycle times, it was seen on one occasion that manual tests were taking far too long. On investigation, it was found the person assigned did not want to do manual testing and was taking every opportunity to be distracted elsewhere. This person was therefore redeployed to writing automated test scripts that they were keen to do.

7. *Data driven decisions.* This was accomplished by collecting the data needed to make decisions so that the teams could be largely self-managing, which reduced supervision costs. It also greatly reduced the number and duration of meetings. For example, a customer survey showed that a new feature that the developers were convinced would be of great benefit to customers was dropped after it was given a low priority in a customer survey. Importantly, this decision could be taken quickly and without politics or rancour, as the data behind it was impartial. In another case, data showed that the work output rate needed to be doubled to meet the required ship date and that QA was the bottleneck. As the QA team was now familiar with the customers, they realized that the product was being planned for release on several extra operating systems that this type of customer was unlikely to use. They, therefore, suggested that the product be prepared to run on fewer operating systems, greatly reducing their need to create regression test suites. This enabled the schedule to be maintained with no loss of benefit to customers.

8. *Minimum inventory or work-in-progress.* Rather than having large requirements documents and batches clogging up the development process, only a small amount of work was allowed into the system at any one time. This was done by breaking major parts of the product into 'stories' made up of three to five 'features', which, in turn, were made up of 3–5 'units' of work. Each unit of work would be for 2–5 days and have multiple work types, e.g. coding, QA, marketing, within it. Teams could work only on a maximum of two features or feature-level integration at any one time. This also stopped teams cherry picking features they wanted to develop at the expense of the whole product.

The most frequent inventory problem was the build-up of untested code because QA was busy. Putting inventory limits in place limits staff in a discipline to work only so many kits ahead of the discipline who will be working next. For example, engineering would only be allowed to work three kits ahead.

Change Management

Change management was known to be key and was managed systematically. Nearly 100 people took part in designing the new process. The company was organized in functional departments, also known as 'stovepipes' or 'silos.' It was therefore essential that senior management be involved. It was only at senior management level that functional departments could be reorganized to focus on the entire horizontal process rather than just vertical command and control. To change from 'stove pipe' to process needed top management leadership—there was no other way.

The transition had to be made from a purely vertical, silo organization to a hybrid horizontal/vertical structure. Power passed to the teams led by program managers, with the vertical, functional departments being charged with supporting the horizontal teams. They did this by providing qualified team members and advancing technology in their respective areas, but staying out of day-to-day decisions on the projects.

Process has no value of its own; it must be linked to a vision, not a fantasy, of where the company strategically intends to go. When strategy is clarified, the key processes that need to improve to make it happen are selected for attention. Unless there is a clear business imperative, the investment needed to implement lean processes is not justified. To assist with this process, the consultants assessed the enterprise to find processes that could be refined to make a substantial difference. During this time, the senior team was constantly briefed and given insights into where problems were likely to arise. They were taken through a lean simulation to show them what was intended. The simulation was the decisive experience that convinced most, if not all, of the senior team to continue on. They proceeded to engage five consultants for a six-month period on a time and materials basis, but capped by a not-to-exceed amount.

The next step was to carry out a pilot project to provide the organization with experience and allow them to see for themselves the practical results. It was not realistic to expect them to take the ideas and change purely on trust. After this, a 'big bang' approach was taken and all the processes were changed.

For a process change, it is necessary to agree on goals, scope, and the agenda. It took up to four weeks to complete this preparation. They were then ready for a *kaizen* event. This is normally a five-day exercise, where people are pulled off their jobs for a week with a goal of implementing substantial change. The team is empowered to make changes and the senior managers have agreed this will happen. The team does need to get approvals during the week by way of report-outs to a management guidance team, but there are generally no major surprises because of the preparation work that is done prior to the *kaizen* event. This is a proven technique that will work even if there is low morale or considerable skepticism, but it may need to be refined to fit each situation.

At Timberline, the complex and political nature of the existing development process required a more circumspect approach. During the course of a five-day workshop, a team received two days of lean training. They then spent about a half-day mapping the entire existing process. They then created a vision of a new process. The new process map was displayed like a big mural around the change team's office. This map was then broken into chunks and delivered to two additional teams who spent another five-day workshop creating detailed task information.

To ensure the entire process was always kept in sight and that there was no suboptimization, there were multiple 'report outs' to a steering team to ensure a holistic view. There were many cases of suboptimization observed. For example: The analysts would skimp on requirements capture to finish their work quickly. This caused high rework due to the need to release a second version with the missed requirements. Quality assurance and engineering were in functional 'silos' so their focus was internal, rather than on customer needs. The voice of the customer was lost because no one focused on the customers by frequently checking on their needs. This caused products to drift away from customer needs.

The motivation of people working on the new process designs was high, and they really enjoyed the experience. People outside were concerned about what they were dreaming up and how it would impact them. Regular briefing meetings were held and a newsletter was published to try and reduce these fears.

The structure of a regular *kaizen* blitz week is on the first day to walk and record the existing process. On the second day, they use lean concepts to create a vision of how it could be improved. The remaining three days is used to implement the vision. This approach provides a mechanism whereby the senior team understands and drives the change, but it facilitates and encourages worker ideas. It therefore combines top-down direction with bottom-up initiative. This process is then repeated with different value streams. The deliverable of each *kaizen* workshop is an implemented documented process that will produce significant benefits. The objective is to create a 'dashboard' so the teams become self-managing and the supervisor's role grows into a continual improvement focus.

Results

After over two years of effort from May 2001 to September 2003, the following can be reported. To establish if lean software development provided significant advantages, six areas were looked at.

1. *Initial process analysis.* The complexity of the software development process in May 2001 is illustrated by the following findings. One process

involved 498 steps. In another process, only 1.4 percent of the steps served to add value to the product and a third process traveled 28 miles as it weaved its way through the company's offices. All these processes have now been substantially improved.

2. *Informal estimate of productivity gains.* The informal estimate by senior staff was that there had been about a 25 percent productivity gain over the two years. This was based on carrying out more work with fewer staff. As there was no baseline measurement before the work started, it is not possible to provide a more specific estimate.

3. *Staff survey.* This was carried out anonymously in September 2003, to provide insight into what the software developers, QA engineers, technical writers, and business systems analysts thought after experiencing over two years of lean software development. In the survey, 55 percent of the respondents either strongly agreed, or agreed, that lean ideas do apply to software development, while another 24 percent were neutral. When asked whether or not lean software had made things worse, 82 percent indicated that lean software had not made things worse, or were neutral. Another question was asked regarding whether or not employees thought that lean was just a passing fad. To this question, only 10 percent of respondents felt that lean was a fad.

4. *Quality metrics.* For each new feature, about 20–25 customers drawn from a representative sample were interviewed and many more were surveyed. This raised the quality of products, as no rework was required after release. Smooth progress to the next version could now take place, which was a significant benefit. Schedule slippage fell to at most four weeks, where previously, it had been months or years. There was a 65 to 80 percent decrease in time taken to fix defects during the development cycle. Defects needing to be repaired a second time, due to a faulty first fix, dropped by 50 percent.

5. *Process data.* A key test of whether a process is under control is if a person unfamiliar with a project can establish its status in a few minutes. To do this, there is a need for simple visual indicators. The *takt* time to actual chart shows the number of units of work completed over time, compared to a target. It easily allows the viewer to see where the project is relative to its time-related goals, as well as the overall trend.

6. *Customer satisfaction.* When the first product produced under the lean process was released at a trade show, the customer response was overwhelmingly positive. This was due to the continual focus on customer needs combined with the frequent, iterative development cycles. This approach delivered the functionality and ease of use the customers needed.

Lessons Learned

Software quality is impacted by all parts of an organization—sales, marketing, finance, strategy, and support. Therefore, the change management process must start with the premise that senior management is involved. It simply will not be effective without their leadership and power to work across the functional silos.

Organizational change is emotionally hard; it is a contact sport. Training to help people understand their feelings of loss of the old ways of working is important. But the senior people must be prepared to ask people who are not fitting in to leave, if necessary. It is not possible to have change, where everything stays the same. The Toyota approach to poor performers is to retrain, redeploy, and finally, remove them. This '3R' discipline is essential.

A lean simulation exercise is remarkably effective in providing an experience of the gains it is possible to accomplish. This is more powerful than presentations or written material for convincing people.

The change process must be actively and explicitly managed. People need a roadmap of what is going to happen and help understanding their feelings.

Having people walk a process they are involved with from end to end is a revelation. They will usually be shocked by the waste, delays, and bottlenecks they encounter. This will make them keen to suggest changes and so have ownership.

Co-location of all staff involved is vital. It speeds up communication and allows a richness of understanding that is generally not possible otherwise.

The timescale for change needs to be around two years. This is the level of commitment that is required. It is this long because people need time to adapt and internalize new ways of working. It also takes time to revise all the processes and implement the changes required. Rushed change where the people do not have ownership or buy-in is unlikely to be effective.

Conclusion

The evidence from Timberline's experience over the last two years is that lean thinking does transfer across to software development. As all sections of the company impact software quality, it is essential that it is a company-wide effort, rather than just confined to the software developers. The place to start is with the senior management team, with some training and a hands-on simulation. A software quality initiative only within software development will be severely limited in the benefits it can hope to achieve. The way forward is to take the lean ideas and adapt them to your culture and circumstances. Each lean implementation will be different.

Lean software development enormously facilitates short, frequent iterations, each with a minimum useful number of features delivered to the internal or external customer. When these frequent iterations are coupled with capturing the voice of the customer more effectively, the results can be excellent. The conventional approach of just gathering customer requirements is taken to a new level of customer intimacy and understanding. The extra effort to really connect with the customer pays off in less rework to correct skimped analysis and greater customer satisfaction.

For manufacturers whose products have high software content, lean software development does show a way forward. They can leverage their lean expertise into their software organizations. It gives a common company-wide language with which to address quality and productivity issues. The lean focus on customer needs helps to integrate the software people more closely with the rest of their corporation.

ENDNOTES

1. Chapter: written with Ms. Amy Flaxel, Timberline Inc., Mr. Ammon Cookson, Lean360, Dr. Mike Rowney, ETI Group.

CONCLUSION:
A ROADMAP FOR LEAN
IN *YOUR* ORGANIZATION

I N THIS BOOK, WE HAVE TALKED ABOUT almost every aspect of lean: what it is, ways of doing it, and examples from those who've tried it. What we've saved for last is how to get your organization to accept and even to embrace the transformation. While nobody can take away the human free will to support or to oppose change, we *can* work systematically to build a favorable consensus. Here we will cover a few techniques for gaining the needed support, a couple of arguments you can use for defusing common objections to lean, as well a few lessons learned and some lean activities you can immediately apply.

Building Support for Accepting Lean

The most essential needs for lean transformation are, first, the support of high-level management and other decisionmakers, and second, the acceptance of the culture.

Winning the Leaders Over

The only way an organization is going to convert from craft or mass production to lean is if the change is actively promoted by its leaders. That support will usually not already be in place, so you must work to gain it. To begin with, you'll need a list of everyone whose support might affect whether or not lean transformation can happen in your setting. You can use the brainstorming technique of Chapter 9 to build a candidate list of such people. At this point, you don't need to determine how influential to it they actually are, only find people who you think *could conceivably* be influential. The people on this list will include managers, to be sure, but will also probably include other types of people. In Part II, we saw how people like government regulators can be customers just as much as the people who take delivery. Similarly, you will probably have people outside the vertical chain of command who will still have a big impact on lean acceptance in your organization.

With your candidate list in hand, apply the Analytic Hierarchy Process or AHP (also discussed in Chapter 9) to prioritize your list. Create all possible pairs of the names in the list, and ask for each, "How important is A relative to B for getting the organization to support lean transformation?" Follow the AHP process and fill out the matrix as in Chapter 9, to develop a single, prioritized list of the names whose support you must win. In developing the list, be sure to consider not only how their positive support can help or even mandate the change, but how their opposition (direct or indirect, e.g., sabotage) can hurt it. You should cut the list off with the first person (going down the list from most important to least) whose AHP-ranking is low enough to you (a subjective call), and who your gut feel (equally important!) tells you, is not a major factor to success.

Now apply a simple technique called "political mapping" to estimate the amount and kinds of work you'll need to do to gain the support of each person on your list. First, create a page with a column down the left side. Fill that column with the list of names you've just developed, starting with the "most influential" name at top, and continuing down to the last name on your list.

Each name on the page begins a row. To the right of each name draw a line, labeled with a "1" above the left end, and a "5" above the right. This line signifies the level of support for lean transformation (from "1," intentional and committed opposition, to "5," enthusiastic and active support). Draw a small "square" on the line at the place where you (and those working with you on this exercise) believe that person's level of support needs to be. For instance, you may need complete support (a "5") from the CIO, but only good support (say, a "4") from the CEO. And you might get by with tolerance (a "3") from a middle-manager who can't OK your transformation, but who could torpedo it if he or she so chose.

Now go back through each row again, and draw a triangle on the same line for the level of support you believe they would give the initiative if you asked them right now, without their having already been approached or wooed in any way. You'll also need to record the reasons you determine for what you believe their position to be.

The best way to do this step is to treat it as essentially a form of "value resolution." You need to learn what each of them value and why. It also needs to be from their perspective, not yours. Some of the techniques we discussed under value resolution do come in handy here, such as using questionnaires (similar to surveys), interviewing, and so forth (see the techniques discussions in Chapter 11; you will want to "tone down" your adaptation of most of the techniques you might use from there, however). You can probably get by with recording values as simple text (something like SCR would probably be overkill).

Since most people who find their way onto your list are likely to be very busy, you'll need to strongly minimize your demands on their time. Surrogates are acceptable if you can't get any time at all. These might be people who have worked with the people on your list, or people who have worked in those positions before, or people who are getting close to the level or job that your target person has.

Especially focus on values that might motivate them to oppose changing the production systems. For instance, if they highly value on-time delivery—a terrific lean value—they might assume that something as major as changing production systems could lead to big delays in finishing existing programs. And that could indeed happen, if you didn't factor that concern into your plan for implementing lean. So, knowing their values and their concerns can help you win them over, as well as help you come up with a better plan for phasing in lean production. A true win/win for everyone. Their stickiest values—and the ones both most invisible and that you most need to know about to win them over—are those unrelated to business performance, such as political or personal concerns.

It may be best to frame your questions around your desire to know what they value so that you can find better ways to implement their priorities. This is true anyway; most people in such places highly value business performance, and that's what lean production is designed to improve. If you phrase some of the questions you ask in ways that are "open ended," you also allow them to express their "soft values." Choose for yourself whether it is wise at this point to raise the issue of possibly changing the production system. If they are open minded, knowing this might motivate them to answer you. Some of the thoughts in Chapter 7 on why it's time to change may prove helpful here.

If they are not open, raising the possibility of changing the production system may put up barriers in their minds before they've even heard what such a change could do to help them achieve what *they* want. Indeed, since many leaders in the software world aren't familiar with the concept of production systems, it may be more expeditious to keep the discussion in terms of process improvements (a much better-known and accepted concept) rather than of production systems or paradigms. The downside is that you don't gain the advantage of tying your leaders into the lean concepts and experiences of other industries . . . so this strategy also gives up something important. But if the "process improvement" is successfully made, you can conceivably backfill the knowledge of lean production later.

The width of the gap between the triangle and the square for a given person is how much work you need to do to win them over. The positioning of the square on the line tells you how completely you have to win them over.

Finally, develop a plan for how to bridge the gap between their current likely support level and the support level you need them to have if lean is to succeed. Take each "reason" you identified for them to oppose the change and turn it into a positive statement. The "on-time delivery value" mentioned above is a perfect reason *for* adopting lean. Lean leads to much better on-time performance than craft- or mass production. It's one of lean's guiding values. Identified negatives can often be turned into some of your greatest positives in winning over leaders.

Winning the Culture Over

Winning the leaders is the first half of the battle. The second half—and just as essential—is to successfully navigate the minefield of your culture.

Here, we apply a simple three-step process called "culture mapping." The steps are:

1. Identify what the resistances to the change will likely be.
2. Understand why the resistances exist.
3. Develop a plan to overcome the resistances.

For the first step, use the 7MP tools to develop your understanding of cultural resistances. Affinity Diagramming works well here (explained in Chapter 11). So does the Interrelationship Digraph and possibly others.[1]

In the second step, take the list of resistances, and look for the reasons they exist. Typically, a resistance will be based on a "story" held in common by many in the culture. A "story" is a "mental model" or belief about the culture, company, or even simply what works in the workplace. For instance, one cultural story could be "this company doesn't care about its employees. So, anything new is just another attempt to shaft us." The stories are the real key, rather than the stated resistances (you just need to know the resistances so you can identify the stories). Each negative story speaks of an underlying positive value. The "company doesn't care" story reveals an underlying set of values, such as "*I* care about my work; I wish the company recognized that and rewarded me for it."

Step three is to develop a plan to overcome the resistances. The last thing you want to do when you try to bring about lean production is to step into everybody's stories. If you know the stories, however, you can bring on the lean changes in ways that appeal to the values revealed by the stories. For instance, one of the first things you could implement would be a recognition system, and immediately begin recognizing people for everything they do that supports a lean principle. You'd also want to put some training in place, so they'd know which behaviors would get them the recognition.

Whatever you do with culture, you have to expect it to take time to change. That's another reason you need good leadership buy-in . . . so they'll support you as long as it takes to win over the culture.

Removing the Roadblocks to Lean

Your best efforts to win over leaders and the culture will be torpedoed if people have the wrong ideas about lean production. These ideas become objections, and the objections become roadblocks. We'll address the two main concerns we've seen people have and how you can defuse their worries.

Faulty Vocabulary—"Lean is Good," "Lean is Sugarcoating"

To the extent that software organizations have adopted the word "lean," it has been mostly misunderstood and misused. This usually comes out in one of two major ways, which we will call "lean = good," and "lean is sugarcoating."

"Lean = Good"

First, people often take the word "lean" as a synonym for "good." This makes the saying "we are <u>lean</u> software developers" another way of saying "we are <u>good</u> software developers." With such a definition of "lean," anyone with any pride in their work at all would, of course, use the word, especially those implementing positively recognized software practices like the higher SEI CMM Levels. Yet we saw early in this book that most such practices are not lean at all, but rather mass at best. This kind of misuse of the word "lean" is fairly widespread, yet relatively easy to correct. Just replace the wrong definition with a right one, and continue to support people's desire to be respected for their work (adopting lean will give them even more reasons to be proud of their wisdom).

"Lean is Sugarcoating"

The other misuse of the word "lean" is much harder to reverse because it sounds sweet at first, but leaves such a bad aftertaste. Some leaders have attached the word "lean" to the actions their companies take to address troubles during business downturns. We have heard "lean" used to justify actions like right-sizing (i.e., laying-off) and conserving resources (e.g., restricting the availability of office supplies). People have also attached the word "lean" to accounting strategies like stock buybacks and creative bookkeeping to boost short-term share prices (and not-so-incidentally, perhaps, the book value of executive stock options).

An organization may genuinely need to take some of these actions when times are hard. Nevertheless, borrowing words from the lean lexicon and attaching them to these types of actions does not convert such actions into lean practices! Indeed, experience has shown that the need for taking such measures might have been avoided, or at least minimized, if the organizations had become lean before the difficult circumstances arose. The Japanese were able to retain employees, for instance, far longer into their latest national recession than U.S. companies were. "[Lean] management must offer its full support to the factory workforce and, when the . . . market slumps, make the sacrifices to ensure job security. . . . It truly is a system of reciprocal obligation."[2]

The word "lean" is a worldview and a work paradigm, not a polite code word for belt-tightening. It is a way of thinking about production that is on the same plane as the ideas of mass and craft paradigms. "There is a better way to organize and manage . . . We labeled this new way *lean production* because it does more and more with less and less"[3] . . . not "less and less with less and less," nor "more and more with more employee overtime."

Becoming more competitive, rather than juggling numbers, is one's best defense during hard times. The lean paradigm is designed to make one more competitive in the most challenging of circumstances. Any benefit obtained from having a socially acceptable reason to point to for causing employee pain, is more than offset by the resulting discredit of lean concepts among the very people whose support would be required to implement the lean paradigm should the organization later decide to do so!

True lean production reduces, not intensifies, the suffering of workers. It doesn't stop there, however: It continues changing things until the worker's role is more fulfilling than ever. "Lean assembly plants will be populated almost entirely by highly skilled problem solvers whose task will be to think continually of ways to make the system run more smoothly and productively."[4] Both authors of this book have experienced this result of lean production, first-hand, on multiple projects.

Wrong Assumptions About Lean

The second major roadblock to implementing lean comes when people make two major and related wrong assumptions. They associate lean strictly with Japan. And they jump to faulty conclusions about what the Japanese depression of the 1990s and now the 2000s implies about the lean paradigm. Let's deal with the Japan association first.

"Lean is Strictly Japanese"

Despite the number of Japanese words used in lean production and its rich history in Japan, lean is not solely a Japanese invention. It is true that the Japanese, and more specifically Toyota, were the first to synthesize a complete approach and to apply it to large-scale production. However, many of the concepts of lean production had even earlier roots in the teachings of American experts like W. Edwards Deming and Joseph M. Juran, as well as in the writings of Henry Ford and his ideas on the practice of flow.

In the early 1980s, because of this assumption, people wondered if lean could be made to work on American soil. After all, as the thinking went, Japanese culture is, in many ways, opposite to American culture. The Japanese value the group over the individual, company welfare above individual career, and conformity in place of individualism. Surely a Japanese approach to production couldn't work in the United States. Yet, within a few years, Ford Motor Company had developed its own flavor of lean and was considered by many to execute certain aspects of lean (notably QFD) better than the Japanese. Though the Japanese have done a magnificent job with developing lean production, it began and now thrives far beyond Japanese borders.

"If Lean Was Valid, Japan's Economy Would Be Better Off"

Many people know that the Nikkei, or main Japanese stock index, free-fell 75 percent from its peak early in the 1990s, and has risen relatively little for over ten years afterward. At the time of this writing, their stock situation is roughly comparable to where the U.S. stock market would be if the American Dow dropped below 3,000.

Compounding the Japanese collapse has been the appearance of outright deflation. This mirrors, in various ways, the U.S. experience in the 1930s. Many people have assumed that this economic catastrophe comes from failures in Japanese industry. If that were true, it would point back to the lean paradigm, because lean production is so widely practiced in Japanese industry (though many Japanese companies still have far to go before they are truly "lean"). This would naturally reduce the credibility of lean production.

But the Japanese depression has nothing to do with its industry. John Mauldin is one of the most respected of international financial analysts. His business is built on serving high-asset investors, people with a net worth of at least one million dollars, by (among other things) vetting exclusive investment vehicles like hedge funds. The caliber of his clients and his success on their behalf is an indication of the caliber of his opinions. Mauldin sums up the causes of the Japanese depression this way:

> "I have often written that the Bank of Japan (and the Japanese government in general) is the only management group which can make Xerox management look competent. Xerox squandered more great inventions than any management team I know of. They should be bigger than both Microsoft and IBM combined, if they had properly exploited their research. Yet today their loans are considered junk.
>
> "The Bank of Japan, along with their government, has likewise made a bad situation into a disaster. They raised rates and kept them too high. They did not deal with corporate debt, moving to hide it and weakening the bank system while keeping brain-dead corporations on life support. They let deflation become a spiral by not directly monetizing debt or changing bank reserves. They raised taxes, ran huge deficits, and funded pointless work projects. Just about everything you could do wrong, they did.
>
> "In fact, they acted much like the U.S. Fed did in the 1930s when it was a case of wrong policies and then of too little, too late."[5]

The Japanese situation is due to macroeconomic factors at the level of the national government and the national bank, far above and largely unrelated to the level of industrial practices. One proof of this is that the share of the U.S. market held by the truly lean Japanese automobile manufacturers grew after the Japanese depression began. "The U.S. market share of the five main Japanese automakers has been rising steadily, hitting 24.7 percent this year, the highest since 23.8 percent reached in 1991."[6] Furthermore, the same figures show that the more lean the individual manufacturer, the better it faired.[7]

The success of the lean paradigm is one of the few bright points in the depressed Japanese economy. Who knows where the Japanese economy might be today had the Japanese government and banks—both by all accounts rife with *muda*—given the lean paradigm as serious a try as have many Japanese businesses? It's clear that the lean worldview did not cause the Japanese depression. It's just unfortunate that lean was never applied in the fields where it might have helped to prevent it.

Thus, the opposite of our starting false assumption is actually the truth. That is, "if lean *weren't* valid, the Japanese economy would be much worse off than it is."

Lean Lessons Learned

The following are some essential lean lessons learned that both authors have acquired in their experiences implementing lean software development.

Senior Management Participation and Buy-in

Garnering senior management team knowledge and commitment is essential. The best way we have observed to gain this is for them to take part in a lean manufacturing simulation. Senior management needs to experience firsthand the large gains made from implementing lean thinking. Without senior effort, it will not be possible to integrate all the different functional areas into a lean enterprise. For any lean organization to be truly successful, it depends on the integration of sales, marketing, production, support, accounting, and human resource functions.

Assessing Organizational Alignment

Developing organizational alignment is perhaps even more important than senior management commitment. Alignment means that the rewards and penalties available in an organization support the organization's goals. If done correctly, this means that people with energy and vision will be recruited and retained. Their innovation and creativity will be supported. Too often experimentation is discouraged on the basis that it might fail. Dissent is not welcome so the pool of ideas is limited. A well-aligned organization may seek out ways to achieve outstanding performance, even if the senior people are indifferent. The problem is, you still need to have discipline and care to maintain alignment.

Changing the Software Process

The software process must support an organization's strategy and recognize its constraints. The particular software process you evolve depends on what you want to achieve and at what point you are starting from. There is not a standard 'off the shelf' process that all organizations should implement. Once the organization's objectives are clear, you can use lean techniques to design and optimize the process necessary to achieve your objectives. Software quality is a shifting mix of functionality, reliability, and speed to market, tailored for a specific market segment at a specific time. You need to combine these with the strategic issues of how you beat your competition and lock in your customers. Understanding of these issues evolves over time, as does the implementation of lean techniques to construct the necessary software and related processes.

Specifying Incremental Procurement Procedures

Procurement procedures often cause difficulty. The instinct of purchasing officers and the regulations by which they are bound cause them to require a fully specified solution. The intention is that they can then judge delivery against clearly listed criteria. The problem is that many things change, thus rendering this 'waterfall' approach consistently ineffective. The technology, the competition, and customer requirements all evolve. It is also impossible to specify precisely a complex system *before* you start, so the contract specification will be riddled with ambiguities and contradictions. One way to deal with this is a procurement contract that specifies incremental delivery of working and usable subsystems. Rather than asking contractors to deliver a 'black box,' you need to focus more attention on matters like agreeing that the software architecture will be flexible. Deliverables can become, instead of hard-to-verify 'waterfall' phase documents about requirements or design, the actual usable subsystems.

Eight Useful Activities for Delivering a Lean Solution

If you are unable to change or influence your entire organization, here are some very useful things you can begin doing. These activities overlap and reinforce each other.

1. *Reduce WIP.* If there are big reports or programs, try to produce and release a little at a time. Inventory is harmful because it reduces feedback to whomever produced it. This means learning is reduced. Having inventory also reduces responsiveness if the market, technology, or competition changes. It makes an organization sluggish as it works the inventory out of its system, before it can respond. Inventory in software is typically a build-up of unused requirements, specifications, and code.

2. *Attain fast cycle times.* The easiest way to see if a process is wasteful is to ask how long it takes from start to finish. For example, determine how long it takes from the initial customer enquiry to that customer actually gaining benefit from your organization. If simple approvals are taking

weeks, it is a clear indication that a winding, inefficient process is in place. The solution is to track exactly where you are actually adding value. This may be politically difficult, and it will require access to the inner workings of other functional departments, but it is necessary to map your processes if you are to change how work gets done.

3. *Shorten feedback loops.* You need to design processes so they provide signals on the quality of the work rapidly and consistently. For example, a software metrics program can analyze faults reported by customers and try to analyze them. This could well be a feedback loop of months or years for the sales people, analysts, or developers who seeded the errors. Far better is a lean approach where you build the metrics into the daily work so feedback occurs in hours not months. Reducing the work in process is a common way to achieve this.

4. *Eliminate the variance enemy.* Anything that is erratic reduces productivity. If the capability or arrival time of any required information, component, or person is unreliable, then you must make allowances. The overall effect is that the software development system will run at significantly reduced capacity.

5. *Always go to where the work is and examine it.* You should never rely on verbal or written reports. The reason is that the reality of the situation will be massaged and reports cause delays. The distortion of relying on second- or third-hand information weakens understanding of the situation. Ask to see the code and have the developers walk you through it. Do the same for designs, test plans, strategy, business cases, and so on. If you don't understand, keep asking until you do. You may feel awkward, but 90 percent of the time, you will learn something that is essential to improving the process and project.

6. *See problems as welcomed messengers from the process.* Problems are not just things to be resolved, but are signals that you need to understand, that indicate a need to resolve deeper issues (wastes). Many will be out of your scope of control, but you can prioritize and tackle the most important ones. In lean thinking, you make progress with many small refinements (incremental improvement), and this usually starts with tackling the root causes of your problems.

7. *Don't overutilize people.* It seems intuitive to load work onto software developers—to utilize and keep them busy to their capacity. But the more important issue is that organizations often fail to use their people's abilities and time. Better to underutilize your people on occasion than to force full loading at all times. This doesn't mean simply giving them less to do. The target is to have a smooth flow of work with no queues or inventory. You want to avoid feeding big chunks of work into the system in one go

and instead, find a way to break it into small bits, steadily fed to your people. If a developer is not ready for more work, then there is no point in allocating work to them just to keep them "fully utilized." The work will just sit in a queue. The need is to work with him or her to find ways to clear the backlog. Trying to force more work through a system than it has capacity for will simply reduce its output further.

8. *Reduce waste by load balancing.* It often occurs that some people in a process are working very hard while others have little to do. This is wasteful and ensures low overall productivity. If you hire people with—or train people to have more—than one skill, you can reallocate them as needed which provides far more flexibility. This means you can reduce the constraint or imbalance of work so that it can flow again.

Prognosis for Improvement in the Software Industry

Even if a few businesses get the support of their company leaders and culture, overcome all the misunderstandings and wrongful uses of key lean words, and even implement a few lean concepts, the larger question remains: Will the software industry as a whole be willing to adopt lean production principles, grow a lean culture, and continuously implement the five principles of the lean paradigm? We may be tempted to affect a jaded and knowing pessimism about this, but other mass production industries have asked the question before, with encouraging answers.

> "We were greatly concerned that no one would listen. Perhaps the slumber of mass production was too deep to disturb? [but] far from ignoring our findings or resisting our advice, many audiences . . . told us they were anxious to give lean production a try. Their question was seemingly a simple one: How do we do it?"[8]

We believe that, once equally well versed and focused on the issues confronting software development, and informed about some of the fledging successes of lean software—like those discussed in this book—software professionals will be as disposed to adopt the lean paradigm as their counterparts have been in other industries. Indeed, lean thinking finally offers leaders and developers the renaissance mindset needed to transform the industry's maverick attitudes into a revolutionary but proven approach for developing and producing software.

ENDNOTES

1. M. Brassard, "The Memory Jogger Plus + Featuring the Seven Management and Planning Tools," GOAL/QPC, May 1996. A simple read, and simple techniques.

Highly recommended, since each technique works from a different perspective and can help find additional answers.

2. *The Machine That Changed the World*, pg. 102.
3. *Lean Thinking*, pg. 9–10.
4. Ibid, pg. 102.
5. John Mauldin's Weekly E-Letter, August 16, 2002. www.2000wave.com; www.johnmauldin.com; john@2000wave.com.
6. Yuri Kageyama, "Japanese dominate Tokyo show, gain market share across Pacific," Associated Press, October 25, 2001.
7. Analyses of statuses of all major Japanese automakers in http://autozine.kyul.net/Manufacturer/Japan.htm, August 20, 2002.
8. *Lean Thinking*, pg. 9–10.

APPENDIX A
THE LM AERO 382J MC OFP
SOFTWARE PRODUCT FAMILY

THE 382J PROJECT THAT WE'VE MENTIONED several times in Parts I through III of this book has been an ideal setting for trying out lean software ideas. The overall project, of course, covered a lot more ground than just software; it created a new version of an existing aircraft. The part of that project we're examining here is the development of the software called the Operational Flight Program (OFP), which runs on its two identical central integrating Mission Computers (MCs). The same group that created the MC OFP also created a similar but smaller program for two computers that backed up the MCs. Everything we'll talk about here applies to both the larger and smaller versions, and we've grouped them under the single heading of "MC OFP."

Being part of a larger vehicle project, the software development effort was driven by the project goals. Those goals were very challenging and demanded much better software cost and schedule performance than was (or is) typical in the software industry. The overall project grew in scope over time, without an equal growth in software budgets and schedules, putting more pressure on the software team. Senior project management recognized the difficulty of what was being asked of software and allowed the team unusual flexibility in choosing its lifecycle models, methods, tools, processes, and techniques.

Jim came onto the 382J MC OFP development project in its initial stage to be the architect of the software and of its high-level technical processes. The lean ideas implemented on that project came from a combination of prior software schooling he'd received; from working with Sudhir Shah, the innovative software manager mentioned several times throughout this book; from personal study of lean production; and from trying various lean ideas on prior projects. One other influence came from the writings of the revolution in management thinking that really began getting wide notice in the United States in the mid-1980s (it had quietly started much earlier), especially through the works of Deming and several other strategists who have been published particularly by the Goal QPC organization and many of whose training sessions he had attended over the same time period. Many of these sources are cited throughout the rest of this book, where you've also seen all the lean ideas that were used on the MC OFP software development.

The biggest factor in the success of the MC OFP development, more important than the ideas presented here, was enlightened management. The Software Project Manager, Mr. Sudhir Shah, supported the lean reforms noted above and also led the creation of a lifecycle-process framework that allowed them to be integrated with each other to reach their full effectiveness. That framework was a V-spiral resembling the one shown in Chapter 16. He also created many management mechanisms to handle challenges like a proliferation of simultaneous software configurations. Finally, he made the project a great place to work on a human level. Humanity is an important lean priority (workers are stakeholders, and as we've said, lean pays attention to stakeholders), which is perhaps the biggest reason why so many people have wanted to stay on lean software projects once they've ever been on one. Without his visionary oversight, the program not only would not have been lean, it would have been greatly delayed.

The various lean reforms and the domain architecture that we will describe here were acted on by the most consistently excellent group of leaders. Their execution of these ideas was responsible for the remainder of the success of this project.

Before getting into details, note that, throughout this book, you've also seen a lot of lean ideas that were *not* used on the 382J. The 382J MC OFP project was an early lean experiment. Much of what we learned from the 382J has gone into the thinking in the rest of this book about what can and should be done better. Indeed, since then, we've implemented on other projects many lean ideas that go beyond those on the 382J.

Despite the progress Lockheed Martin has made since that time, the MC OFP development still makes a good study in lean software production. There's several reasons for this. The software was large for a hand-generated (as opposed to, say, 4GL code) high-integrity system: approximately 350,000 lines of code, including both the larger and smaller variants of the OFP. The software is now complete, except for ongoing maintenance, modification, and extension as customers request them.

The software portion of the project has been scrutinized by many outside (non-Lockheed Martin) parties who have done their own analyses, reacted to the project in their own ways, and extensively published on the subject (as have several Lockheed Martin personnel from the inside). This gives the project a size, a maturity, and a depth of available analysis that makes it an ideal laboratory for evaluating lean techniques.

Above all, the 382J MC OFP software development shows how one can take individual lean ideas and turn them into a complete and reasonably lean software lifecycle in the context of a deliverable project coping with high business pressures. Along the way, we have seen how several different lean techniques worked in specific situations, like the shaping of a software architecture. Many of the references to the 382J through the body of this book have left out details of what was done for the sake of the flow of explanation. We look at many of those details here. But first, we'll review the background of the 382J project.

Background

As we said when we first introduced the project early in this book, the 382J was a billion-dollar plus commercial program to replace the avionics, engines, and many other systems of the C-130 Hercules aircraft. The Hercules had been incrementally (though significantly) updated several times since it first entered service in 1956. The 382J upgrade was designed to dramatically improve speed, range, payload, and cost of operation. It has succeeded at those goals to the outspoken approval of its customers and operators.[1]

The 382J project began in 1991 and was initially scheduled for delivery in 1997. Growth in overall project scope led to actual first delivery in 1998. It was a block-oriented development with several major releases. Block 1 was the initial flying configuration, block 2 the civil certification version and beyond the 382J, block 3 the military baseline version, and blocks 4 and beyond being adapted for particular customers. Software production in all blocks was done in a spiral life-cycle model. Block 1 preceded its production with a design-stream development of the software domain architecture that would be used throughout the project.

Mission Computer (MC) Operational Flight Program (OFP) software was (and still is) the integrating heart of the aircraft, coordinating and tying together nearly everything else in the aircraft, including avionics, engines, and support systems.

The MC OFP was created as a product family, with the intention that it be easily reusable both in upcoming variants of the 382J and also in completely different aircraft. The latter intention was fulfilled when the C-27J aircraft project began in the late 1990s, and completed with even better project performance than the 382J. We will briefly look at the C-27J project experience near the end of this Appendix.

We have abstracted and generalized many details of the MC OFP design. This is done to keep the information at a level that is most useful for illustrating lean principles, as well as to make the rest of the information available to you by protecting Lockheed's proprietary interests. All the technical contents of this appendix have been previously placed into the public domain through the many articles and conference papers discussing this project. However, they have never been correlated to each other and to the lean paradigm in one place as they are here.

We will begin by walking through the MC OFP lifecycle in terms of the phase activities of the software domain-engineering lifecycle. As we've discussed in the body of this book, the software was domain-engineered, rather than engineered as a single system, despite the fact that this was LM Aero's first time developing a centrally integrated avionics architecture for airlifters (the avionics architectures of earlier C-130s had used collections of largely standalone avionics devices). Jim and his colleagues were firmly convinced, based on our prior experience with creating and using integrated, lean lifecycles on other projects, that domain engineering would more than pay for itself within this one project. And it turned out to work this way on the 382J as well.

Phase 0: Software Project Planning

During block 1, not much was known about how well all the lean techniques being tried would work. Also, budgets and schedules were largely assigned to the software group based on the constraints of the overall project. Indeed, the main reason the team was allowed to change its development lifecycle so radically was that these assignments were more challenging than anything the company had attempted before. Either something would be done differently, or the project was virtually guaranteed to fall behind.

By block 2, the team had a much better idea of how quickly things would go in a lean production line. As we mentioned in Chapter 21, early experience showed that each simple SCR requirement took four hours to fully develop into verified code. Larger SCR requirements could be extrapolated based on the added number of cells in the SCR table and the relative complexity of the functions determining the CONs. This made estimation much more accurate than it had been on previous projects using traditional textual requirements, or even using graphical specifications like Schlaer-Mellor's. Progress on software work went more quickly and predictably. Indeed, the group continued to improve its processes and its piece production time throughout the project.

Phase 1: System Engineering

The overall project's system-engineering phase for block 1 focused on the integrated functionality of all parts of the aircraft, including computers, software, engines, avionics, and so forth. To orient its work in this larger world and to prepare for product-line engineering, the MC OFP team analyzed the domain of airlift, a huge subject with many functions and artifacts. As a result, the team broke it into software subdomains, using the important question, "what are the natural and stable divisions of the domain?" Things in the domain that tended to change together at a given change-triggering event would be grouped into a subdomain. This allowed taking advantage of some additional commonalities shared between items in a subdomain, but not shared at the overall level.

In the world of airplanes, through a long process of evolution, the customer space has become divided into well-recognized categories oriented around types of functionality and the parts of the airplane that implement them, i.e., categories like navigation, communications, engines, air data, and electrical systems.

As electronics began implementing more and more aircraft functions, each of these categories came to be (and still are) associated with certain types of avionics ("aviation-electronics") devices. For instance, the navigation category is served by equipment like GPS receivers and inertial navigation computers. "Communications" is mostly implemented through different types of aircraft radios. "Engines" has an "engine-controller" device that monitors and controls engines. The air data category covers information that is monitored by either a collection of standalone instruments or by an air data computer, reading parameters like air temperature, pressure, and aircraft velocity relative to the surrounding air mass. The electrical category has power-generation and conditioning boxes, as well as other types of devices. There are several other categories as well.

Each type of avionics box is almost completely independent of the others. If something fundamental changes in an aspect of the world of aviation, such as in technology, federal regulation, or standard flight operating procedures, the avionics boxes and their underlying responsibilities are separated in such a way that any single change usually affects only box. Thus, the categories underlying the boxes have been cleanly separated from each other based upon the types of changes that affect them.

Achieving such separation is the purpose of the changeability analysis step in domain engineering. Usually a lot of effort is required to do changeability analysis (as we discussed in Chapter 11). The domain of aircraft (under which airlifter falls) is unusual in that people did that analysis long ago, and standardized it for everyone working within the domain to use.

In a few cases, however, there were no existing avionics devices covering exactly what the MC OFP needed to do. For those, the team had to do domain analysis from scratch, identifying natural, and if possible, recurring structures in the customer's world.

For instance, the team found that, within the aircraft electrical systems, there was a need for many individual lighting systems, such as those for different displays or for input devices. Each lighting situation had characteristics common to other lighting situations, and each had unique needs. No one lighting system could handle everything, but multiple similar lighting systems could. The MC OFP team found that every lighting system needed to respond to both general cockpit situations like thunderstorms versus nighttime versus daylight operations, as well as unique situations like differing lamp brightnesses based on age and production variances. Moreover, the set of issues shared among all lighting systems, and the set that varied from system to system, never changed, unless possibly if something fundamental shifted in the whole field of lighting, such as the arrival of a new lighting technology. This meant that a lighting class could be expected to be very stable for a long time to come. That made lighting a natural and recurring structure in electrical systems. The team created several such sub-domains to augment the subdomains corresponding to classic avionics devices.

One other advantage of this type of subdivision, in a domain-engineering sense, is that the interfaces between such subsystems and categories tends to be based on customer-space abstractions, such as altitude or radio frequency. Such abstractions usually remain unchanged, even when events in the world of avia-tion necessitate changes to an avionics box (such as when an implementation technology like the means of lighting is replaced).

The one possible wrinkle to the MC OFP team's using the historic domain subdivisions as the main way to organize its software requirements was that the 382J integrated its avionics boxes and their associated information under the con-trol of its central computers, i.e. under the MCs. In some cases, a type of box would even be eliminated and its functionality directly incorporated into the MC OFP. Would this aspect of the system architecture somehow blur the subdivisions of the traditional aircraft domain?

It did not. The extra stability of the interfaces between the traditional avionics divisions (noted above) meant that, in most cases, the effect of any given need for change still stayed wholly within a single avionics-device cate-gory despite the highly-integrated software architecture. The MC OFP team therefore divided the airlifter domain into software subdomains according to the types of avionics boxes that had historically existed. The team used the avionics device names, in most cases, verbatim as the names of its software sub-domains. Later on in the project, this decision was validated when they found that almost every one of the thousands of software requirements fell cleanly into one of those categories.

Knowledge of the best domain subdivision helped the MC OFP team sup-port the overall system engineering effort. During every block, the MC OFP developers analyzed how the avionics team's system-design decisions affected the future software development. Where proposed system divisions and alloca-tions would make it more difficult to build a domain-oriented software system, the MC OFP team let the avionics team know. An IPT (Integrated Product Team) organizational structure facilitated this so that all parties worked together smoothly.

One other aspect of the systems-engineering phase would later have a large impact on the software development. Systems-level requirements engineering was very active and competent. However, not much prior value resolution, at the overall aircraft level and in the lean sense, had been done by the project. This led to quite a bit of system-requirements volatility later on. This in turn continued to impact software development throughout the project, as we shall note again when we look at the last stages of the software lifecycle. Nevertheless, lean pro-duction helped the team even with this challenge.

Phase 2: Software Analysis

In software analysis, the MC OFP team created software requirements from the system requirements it was given by the project systems engineers.

The software team developed its requirements using the SCR method discussed in Chapter 10. As you may recall, the SCR method identifies the scope of a software system versus its surrounding environment. In the SCR worldview, the purpose of the system is to change that environment based on the current and previous states of the environment.

The environment around the MC OFP software is the rest of the aircraft (outside of the MCs) as well as the surroundings with which the aircraft interacts. Thus, the system's MONs represent the current conditions in the aircraft and surrounding world. The CONs represent the ways the customer wants the 382J's MC software to change that environment. The REQs (requirement tables) express what the state of the environment around the MCs should become when that environment is in any current state ("no change" is a perfectly acceptable requirement). Chapter 10 discusses this aspect of SCR in much more detail.

Each traditional avionics device cleanly associates with a unique set of environmental MONs and CONs that it either monitors or affects. In the MC OFP project, the software subdomains assigned to these devices, and the ones created in the absence of corresponding traditional devices (such as lighting subdomain).

The naturalness of this way of partitioning the system made the transition from analysis into design much easier and quicker. We'll see some of the good effects of this when we explore how architectural design worked in the next lifecycle phase.

The team also assessed the probability that each software requirement would change over the course of the current program or in future programs. The software team had little access to the customers, as all its system requirements information came from the systems engineers. However, the team used the systems engineers and a few other people as surrogates to do some value resolution of its own. The software team identified the project's customers using brainstorming and the AHP, and continued using the AHP to prioritize its software requirements (as described in Chapter 8). However, on this project, there was no *kano* analysis, little QFD, and only the simplest risk analysis of the individual requirements.

Phase 3: Software Architectural Design

To change their environment as specified in the SCR tables, the MCs have to somehow interact with that environment. They do this through external interface devices. Some of these devices exist primarily to read the condition of the environment (e.g., sensor devices): These provide the MCs with knowledge of the MONs. Other devices primarily change the environment (e.g., actuators or cockpit displays): These provide the MCs with the ability to change the CONs.

The MCs communicate with these interface devices across data buses ... sending messages to the output devices and receiving messages from the input devices (or both, for devices that both monitor and control the environment). The data on those buses is of course encoded in the language of the interface devices. They are not MONs and CONs, which are the real quantities in the environment around those interface devices, but rather INs and OUTs in SCR terms (see Chapter 10), the actual interface variables. INs and OUTs are related to MONs and CONs through the SCR IN and OUT relations (also described in Chapter 10). Thus, the messages coming into the MC are mostly filled with IN variables, which the interface devices have set based on the MONs they observed in the environment. The messages leaving the MC for the interface devices are mostly filled with OUT variables, whose values are used by the interface devices to change the actual CONs of their surrounding environment.

The software architecture is structured mainly around the three major SCR relations; IN, OUT, and REQ. This was an intentional strategy to decrease the transition gap between the software requirements analysis stage and the software architectural design stage (see the discussions of "Assembly Transport" in Chapter 19 and "Shortening Forward Transitions" in Chapter 20). The output products of requirements analysis are usually very far from being ready to be used in a design. The goal here was to create a design into which the requirements (i.e., the REQ tables) and the interface conversions (i.e., the IN and OUT tables) could be dropped, essentially without modification.

The goal went further: There was to be only one procedure in the code for each requirement (REQ table). In most systems, requirements end up being split and distributed among several design parts. This practice makes it harder to develop, modify, or verify the product. Each time a requirement is implemented, it must be visited each time one of these activities is done. Having one place for each requirement would make initial production, modification, and verification quicker, less error-prone, and generally less wasteful.

The high-level classes we chose to accomplish this goal were derived from the Parnas criteria; i.e., requirements-hiding, hardware-hiding, and decision-hiding (see the "Parnas Criteria" section of Chapter 19). Based on these concepts, the team chose three major software classes:

1. *Device Interface:* Hides the details of interfacing to specific hardware in the system architecture. (It was called a "DI" on the Lockheed project.)
2. *Device Control:* Hides the requirements, one per method, updating CONs (output variables, but in customer-space terms).
3. *Device Current State:* Makes MONs (input variables, but in customer-space terms) available to users, and keeps users from interacting with the DI.

The third class was not a Parnas decision-hiding class, as you might assume. Rather, it was more like a UML <<interface>> stereotyped class. It was a mechanism to isolate most other objects and their programmers from touching objects of the DI class and potentially introducing new errors in the software. This makes introduction of the "device current state" class more a lean perfection-principle tactic than a value stream one, but it needs to be mentioned here to provide a complete picture of the class selection process. There were some decision- or implementation-hiding classes in the architecture, primarily to hide specific aircraft diagnostic algorithms, but they represented a smaller portion of the overall system, so we won't discuss them further here.

In the MC OFP, there was one instance of each class for each subdomain in the architecture. For instance, under the domain, airlifter, was a device called the "NIU" or "Nacelle Interface Unit." An NIU keeps track of engine telemetry, such as oil pressure and temperature. This kind of device is common on most aircraft, so a software subdomain based on its traditional responsibilities would be likely to remain stable on all versions of the aircraft for many years to come. Thus, in the MC OFP architecture, there was an "niu_di," an "niu_control," and an "niu_state" object, respectively.

Figure A-1 shows the simple class structure that covers approximately 70 percent of the MC OFP. The diagram omits some small subsystems, as well as a couple of minor support classes that nearly always accompany these, but whose contents are relatively trivial.

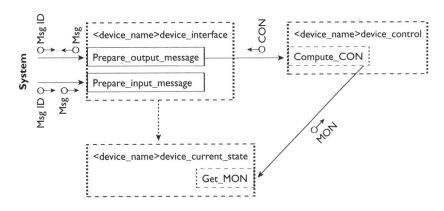

Figure A-1. Foundational Class Structure of MC OFP Software

We use a hybrid of the Buhr and Booch notations rather than the UML. This is what was used on the original project, but more importantly, it expresses a design concept that the UML does not model well. In this diagram, a dashed border means the enclosed structure is a generalization, and there will be from zero to multiple instances of it in the actual software. If the border is of a class, it means there will be zero to many instances (i.e., objects) of that class. In practice, there is always at least one instance of a class in this software. If a method or operation within a class has a dashed border, it means there will be anywhere from zero to many instances of that method or operation in any given instance of the class. For instance, all the requirements-hiding operations are represented generically in the design by one generalization method in the "device control" class.

Repetitions of class instances are common in OO. Repetitions of methods or operations in a class are not, and are something that the UML does not model well. Nevertheless, repeated operations facilitate a particularly powerful lean concept called *big parts* (discussed in Chapter 19 under "Software DFMA"). The arrows represent invocations, and the data flow symbols on the arrows are inputs or outputs for a given invocation. The combination of instantiating a class once for each subdomain, and instantiating an operation once for, say, each REQ table (or IN or OUT table) provides a tremendous expansiveness to this scheme. That is, a lot of the finished product comes from each part or class definition. Because both the objects and their operations were generalized, the MC OFP classes were also simple parts. This met the inherently conflicting demands of DFA—for fewer parts—and DFM—for simpler parts.

Figure A-1 shows the core of the architecture. It also provides a strong anchor for everything else in the software, giving logical places to attach other types of functionality that don't fit the basic SCR model as well (such as heavily algorithmic functions, which, in general, can't be represented as effectively with REQ tables; the MC OFP utilized a few additional classes to handle such situations).

Indeed, the part count of classes in the entire 350,000 line of OFP programming (including both the large and small versions) was in the tens, rather than in the hundreds. The classes proved exceptionally big in the sense that they could be used over and over again to derive the objects needed for practically every system expansion or modification. Usually, the only work needed was to implement the additions or changes themselves (i.e., there was almost never any need for redesign).

This diagram should primarily be read from left to right. A small portion of the software, represented by the word "SYSTEM" on the left, has a scheduling list for when to send and when to retrieve messages across the databuses between the mission computer and the other devices on the aircraft. When this software (dubbed the *system software* on the OFP) retrieves a message, it calls the "process_input_message" method of the DI, and passes it the data in the bus's format (along with an identifier of which message's data is being passed: there are many defined message formats for each device). This DI operation converts the physically encoded data into a set of internal variables representing the external MONs, in accordance with the IN relations. These "MONs" are usually standard programming language variables and generally concern some quantity in the environment of the customer space. The details of the IN-relation conversions are the "secret" of the "process_input_message" method of the DI. This ends the "input" flow.

When the system software reaches the time to send an output message to a device, it notifies the DI by calling its "prepare_output_message" method. The DI invokes the "Compute CON" method of the control object, which, in turn, invokes the "Get_MON" method of the current_state object for each device from which a MON is needed. Then the "Compute CON" method simply follows the directions of the REQ table for that CON, derives the appropriate value for the CON variable, and passes it back. The REQ relation is the secret of the "Compute CON" method. The DI calls "Compute CON" repeatedly (in implementation, some efficiency will be gained by inlining the code, so there is no calling overhead), getting every CON for every field in the outgoing message, until the message has been completed, and the DI passes it back to the system software.

When the system software has done this for every input message and every output message, the input and output cycles have been completed. Then, when the appropriate time has passed, it starts the cycle over again.

Once the classes and operations had received their initial quick and dirty definitions (without too much time being spent on them), it was time to refine them. Designs of specific objects of these classes were completed. *Narrow-slice scenarios* (*see* "Narrow-Slice Anticipatory Development" in Chapter 16) of system inputs and expected outputs were created and bounced off these specific objects.

This is somewhat analogous to the "Class-Responsibilities-Collaboration" (CRC) card approach developed by Ward Cunningham and Kent Beck of Tektronix in the 1980s, and advocated by many in the Smalltalk and UML camps. The CRC card approach captures some basics of a class on a 4×6 inch index card. In the CRC approach, you use a class name, a list of top-level responsibilities of that class (optimally around three to five), and a list of other classes with which this class must interact. As developers work through various use cases, they refine the CRC cards and classes to get the cleanest allocation of responsibilities.[2] Narrow-slice scenarios like those used on the 382J corresponded closely to use cases. The 382J went beyond the CRC approach when it developed abstract interfaces, however, because class responsibilities correspond only to the abstraction part (what the class encapsulates, from the user's view) of a class's abstract interface.

The narrow-slice scenarios on the 382J also helped identify secrets (what's likely to change) of the class abstract interface, like who's the manufacturer of a device (e.g., whose NIU is used in the actual aircraft). The domain architecture was then refined to limit the spread of changes throughout the software due to any postulated stimulus. Using scenarios in this way drove the design further towards domain orientation. Ten years with many 382J variants and other products reusing the software (such as the C-27J airlifter, another airplane and avionics suite completely) have proven the effectiveness of this approach. New releases of the software, even on other aircraft, continue to be accommodated easily and productively by this architecture.

As the reader can see, this architectural approach has elements of object orientation mixed with elements of functional orientation. We've long believed that OO was a tool in the developer's toolbox, not a religion. Each perspective has its place, and each has been useful in this particular architecture. Note that either approach can be lean. *It is conformance to the principles of lean development that matters, not the specific design approach.*

Not everything in a domain-structured program corresponds to repeatable classes. For those parts that are unique (i.e., not repeated), and which are primarily dynamic in nature (like the sequencer for MC OFP messaging), functional design can be a useful and resource-conserving strategy. Indeed, in the safety-critical MC OFP, regulators demanded absolute determinism in message sequencing and completion. A simple cyclic executive was just what they wanted to see, and a functional subsystem was the most straightforward way of designing it. Some OO methodologies incorporate the idea of "active objects" to service this type of situation, which is essentially a way of attaching a functional subsystem to an OO one. My own preference is for an explicit hybrid (not trying to make the functional part look like it is part of an OO design, but that comes from a personal bias towards being as explicit as possible, rather than directly from any lean principle).

Phase 4: Software Detailed Design

The team did the domain design at the architectural level just once, in the initial part of block 1 (though there were occasions to make a few slight tweaks during later spirals). However, part of a domain design is at the detailed-design level: In block 1, this was done for the block 1 devices; in later blocks, this was repeated every time a new device was added to the avionics suite and thus to the MC OFP.

On the first pass through detailed design, in block 1, the team developed a set of templates for each of the classes and methods identified in the architecture. These templates contained all the major parts that would be required in the actual final code—headers with specific information fields, interface definition sections, processing sections, and so forth—and helped guide all development from that point on to "cover the bases" as well as to be reasonably compatible in organization and style with other implementations throughout the system. Templates also helped with training and with productivity, because every time developers added a new device, they could reuse them and simply fill in the details of the device. During detailed design, the *objects* and *methods or operations* of architectural design became the *packages* and *procedures* of the targeted code (the MC OFP was developed in the Ada programming language, which uses these constructs).

To turn a DI template into the detailed design of a specific subdomain, the team would fill in the stubs and data references for the specific physical interfaces (INs and OUTs) and environmental variables (MONs and CONs). Also in this phase, they finalized the translation between the physical bus format data and the logical MON or CON variables. However, they left the details of coding the translation for the coding phase.

Likewise, for the device control package for that device, they stubbed a procedure for each REQ table assigned to that device. Each device owned a list of CON variables, parameters in the user's environment that it was responsible to affect. As explained in Chapter 10, each CON was derived in accordance with a REQ table. The team would insert the processing specified by the REQ table during the coding phase, but the interface for passing back the filled-out CON variable was stubbed during detailed design. The current_state package template was also filled in, but its contents were usually fairly trivial.

Phases 5 and 6: Implementation, Integration, Verification, and Conclusions

In the coding phase, for a given subdomain, the developers completed filling out the stubs of the instances ("packages") of the three classes of packages in the target programming language. The team verified the code against the domain structure in two ways. The first was compilation. Then, for the safety-critical parts of the system, SPARK annotations (comments to the compiler, but meaningful to the SPARK Examiner tool) were inserted, which stated what the code was supposed to do according to the requirements. Then the completed code with SPARK was run through the SPARK Examiner tool, which informed the developers whether the code did what it was supposed to do and how it departed if it didn't (SPARK also identifies many types of coding errors). The developers could then correct the code to conform to the SPARK annotations. Corrections were almost never needed at higher levels (like detailed design), since other measures—discussed under the lean perfection principle—had already limited the scope of mistakes.

Alignment—the DFMA term for ease of assembly or integration—was high. When, during the OFP's development, a new requirement was added to the architecture, an operation to compute the requirement's CON was added to that device's "device-control" object. Most new requirements referenced existing Monitored Variables (we found that understanding of a system's existing environment came sooner than the understanding of all its requirements). Therefore, the developers could usually write the procedure behind the "Compute CON" operation to invoke existing "device current state" operations to obtain those MONs. Finally, they would update the "device-interface" object to obtain the CON and to pack it into the appropriate field in an outgoing message. Only two locations needed to be modified—one for the logic of the requirement and one for the change to the message interface. Change did not propagate, and because of the Four-Variable Model, no side effects were possible (in the Four-Variable model, each CON is an independent quantity). Then the team could focus testing on the appropriate field of the outgoing message to verify that the field's corresponding CON had been calculated properly for the conditions on each row of the SCR table.

Another advantage of the Four-Variable model-based architecture is that alignment goes better than it normally would when you change the vendor of a given type of device. Having a "device interface" meant that a change to the hardware's interface could be addressed in just one place. Indeed, in most cases, you could accommodate a complete swap to a different vendor's box in just the one object, the DI, because all that would be affected would be the INs and OUTs, not the MONs and CONs of the other two major classes: The "device control" and "device-current-state" objects remained unchanged. The rest of the software system was also unaffected. And so it went for other change scenarios, which were all cleanly divided and aligned according to the Four-Variable Model and the assignment of the variables to different classes. New objects or operations on the MC OFP project almost always integrated successfully the first time, and with no need for active coordination between the part development and the development of the rest of the assembly beforehand. The "Lego" block-like interface took care of such concerns.

Again, a traditional architecture would have difficulties with these types of changes, for the same sort of reasons it had with requirements changes; extra efforts in analysis, implementation, and verification to bring about an acceptable part mating.

The major waste in the latter part of the lifecycle came about because of the lack of value resolution in the very beginning of the project (which we mentioned early in this appendix). Our estimation models showed that a software project of this size and complexity would normally release ten major builds. This is what the early software planning was based upon. To accommodate the continuing evolution of air vehicle requirements, the MC OFP development team, by the end, had to release *sixty* builds of the same scope. Yet, while the work increased by a factor of six, the schedule increased by only a little over a year: Instead of the original planned delivery in 1997, the first aircraft was delivered in 1998. Lean processes came close to recovering for the project the time that would have been lost under traditional software processes by the growth in work. Furthermore, at the same time, the number of configurations planned to be in work simultaneously grew from three to seven over this time period, increasing the complexity of managing the work (and the interrelated work products) tremendously. Yet lean production absorbed most of the schedule impact. The great independence of the subdomains, combined with the isolation of each REQ table in the architecture, allowed doing much more work in parallel than would normally be possible. The productivity of the lean production kept costs half the norm for the aerospace industry (industry norms at that time were three hours per delivered and qualified safety-critical source line of code).

The processes worked well enough that the cost to the project for adding functionality to the MC OFP was much lower than it was for adding functionality to the avionics devices built by other suppliers. This affected overall project planning: Many new functions that would normally have been added to the other devices were added instead to the MC OFP.

Because governmental regulators such as the FAA require thorough testing of code against requirements, tests based on the SCR requirements were developed and run against the MC OFP code. Such testing never revealed any safety-related errors. Only a handful of minor errors (errors that had no detrimental effect on either safety or functionality) were found. This level of quality was confirmed by the Independent Verification and Validation (IV&V) performed by the British company Aerosystems International (AeI), at the behest of the 382J's first customer, the U.K. Ministry of Defense (MoD). AeI found that the MC OFP had only $\frac{1}{10}$ the density of anomalies as the average safety-critical software on the aircraft, even though the average software had also been developed to the highest government standards for integrity. Anomalies, in the MoD's definition, included both outright errors and inconsistencies among the development artifacts (e.g., requirements, design, code, and test).

Testing, while required by the regulators and done more productively than was typical in this industry, certainly didn't prove to be cost effective given the small handful of minor errors that survived the software-creation portion of the development process. In the absence of an external mandate to do requirements-based testing and in a nonsafety critical application, most testing could have been eliminated. Furthermore, the MC OFP team had identified additional ways to prevent errors from entering the code, ways that the project schedule had not allowed them to pursue (such as auto-code and auto-test generation). The team was convinced that a little more tightening of error-prevention measures could have eliminated most of the few errors that did make it to the end. This is similar to the experience of lean manufacturers in other industries. The normal progression is to go from heavy reliance on after-the-fact defect detection and correction (e.g., the "rework men" of Ford and GM fame), to no rework needed at all. In that case, the product leaves the production line in perfect condition.

The MC OFP development showed that domain techniques provide an effective framework upon which you can build a lean lifecycle. Projects like the 382J and C-27J described below show that software development can be made lean right now, because lean has nothing to do with types of technologies and everything to do with strategies and lifecycle integration.

Phase "N+1:" The C-27J Reuse Project

The avionics hardware and software architectures of the 382J were designed to be reusable. The opportunity to reuse them came only in the late 1990s, in the form of the C-27J project. The C-27J is a two-engined airlifter that looks very much like a smaller version of the 382J. Alenia, an Italian aerospace manufacturer, built the airframe for this aircraft while LM Aero developed the avionics suite, engines, mission computers, and integrating software.

Figure A-2 shows the amount of software requirements reuse (essentially ⅔ of all requirements, since ACAWS was a subsystem for which requirements were not reused though part of its design was reused). Many of these requirements were, however, partially modified (i.e., rows and/or columns of the SCR charts were changed, many significantly). The team estimated that effective overall reuse, accounting for all products and stages of the development, was between 30 percent and 40 percent.

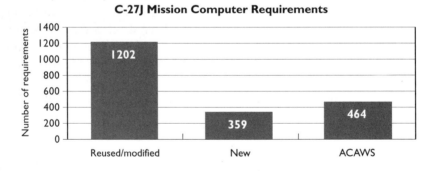

Figure A-2. C-27J Reuse from the 382J

As we stated in Chapter 10, productivity on the C-27J was over twice that of the 382J, or under 0.8 hours/SLOC compared to 1.6. The software industry's experience is that reuse typically saves less than the new development it replaces. In other words, if half of a new system was created through reuse, you would expect the overall system costs to total perhaps 70 percent of the cost of a completely newly developed system. This is because you always have overhead involved in obtaining and adapting reused parts to the new purpose. But the C-27J reversed that effect and saved a higher percentage of its costs than its percentage of reuse. The higher productivity occurred for four main reasons:

1. *Integrated lifecycle.* Both the 382J and C-27J used an integrated lifecycle of products and processes from all lifecycle phases (as discussed in Chapter 16).
2. *Reused both processes and products.* The C-27J reuse of processes was more like 80 percent compared to product's 30+ percent. Among other effects, this reduced the learning curve for the C-27J developers.
3. *Other improvements.* The remaining 20 percent of processes were improvements, such as to process control and lifecycle implementation.
4. *Greater integration of systems engineering and software engineering.* This made for an overall project lean production line.

Overall integration error rates have continued to be reduced. From an already-low base on the 382J when the C-27J began, they have dropped on the C-27J by ⅔. "IPRs," or "Integration Problem Reports," are issues noted mainly by the people doing final integration and testing of the aircraft. IPRs record problems in which the aircraft does not function in the way that the aircraft testers (both pilots and test personnel) expect. IPRs can be caused by problems with system requirements, software requirements, system design, hardware (e.g., avionics "box") operation, software design, or software code. Whether or not an IPR is caused by a software defect, however, it will frequently require a software change (for instance, to compensate for when a piece of hardware functions in a way different from what the aircraft integrators expected).

The estimate of the number of IPRs expected over the initial C-27J development program was based on figures from the 382J and follow-on C130J programs. This is the upper line shown in Figure A-3. It is already much lower than industry norms for a program of this size. However, the C-27J's improvements to its overall systems/ software lean production line anticipated problems earlier in the system lifecycle, and cut IPRs to one-third of the expected number. The lower line in Figure A-3 shows this.

The C-27J project has been on schedule for every software delivery, and always under budget. It demonstrates the potential of a lean production line even moreso than the original 382J project. The 382J project included both domain design (i.e., lean industrial design flow) and production (lean production flow). The C-27J is the first major LM Aero project to produce additional software products for a different aircraft model off essentially the same lean product design. The first major customer, the Italian aircraft-safety regulatory authorities, was very pleased with the software approach and expressed "full confidence in the LM Aero software-development process."

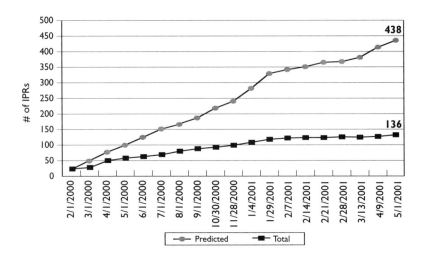

Figure A-3. C-27J System- and Software-IPRs Affecting Software

In the future, the C-27J team has estimated that the next project in the domain can be performed at twice the productivity of the C-27J, i.e., at 0.4 hours/SLOC for safety-critical software. They base this estimate partly on learning obtained during the C-27J on how to work within this type of lean production cycle in a reuse project, and partly on the assumption that the team will be allowed to devote some of its development funds to automating certain operations that are for now still conducted manually. Among these tasks are the adaptation of design templates to new requirements to generate code and the automatic generation of requirements-based test cases.

ENDNOTES

1. For instance, the "Air Force Link" online news magazine published the following assessments of the C-130J, derived from the 382J: Said Col. Paul Stipe, the deputy director of global reach programs for the Air Force . . . "This aircraft was developed by Lockheed Martin at its own expense, and the company contributed more than a billion dollars of its own money to develop (the C-130J) for the commercial market . . . and they were successful." According to Lt. Col. James Dendis, acquisitions deputy chief of tactical airlift, special operations forces and trainer division . . . "This looks like the older C-130s, but only on the outside. The avionics have been updated throughout, and the aircraft is arguably more complex now than our C-17 Globemaster III large cargo aircraft. It is a phenomenally complex, computer-driven, high-tech airplane." "The pilots love it, and the maintainers love it," Colonel Stipe

said. (Air Force Link, 7/28/04, http://www.af.mil/news/story.asp?
storyID=123008273.)

There have been a few detractors, but interestingly, none of them have been
customers, operators, or safety or acceptance regulators. In any event, none of the
issues raised apply to the MC OFP software-development portion of the project.

2. For an in-depth explanation of the CRC approach, *See* R. Wirfs-Brock, A. McKean,
"Object Design: Roles, Responsibilities, and Collaborations," Addison Wesley
Professional, November 2002.

Index

ABOUT THE AUTHORS

PETER MIDDLETON is a senior lecturer in computer science at Queen's University in Belfast, Northern Ireland. His research interests are software quality, lean software development, and how to successfully implement change. He received his PhD in computer science from Imperial College, London and an MBA from the University of Ulster. Before joining Queen's University, he worked in industry for 10 years, with 5 years as an information systems manager. He can be contacted on *p.middleton@qub.ac.uk.*

JAMES SUTTON is on senior staff at Lockheed Martin Aerospace and applies many of the lean strategies in this book to company and corporate projects. He recently advised the U.K. agency updating the London Air Traffic Control System software on how to meet competing integrity, cost, schedule, and political goals; most suggestions were adopted. He created lean software lifecycles as lead software and technical-processes architect for information-processing software for the C-5B, and central flight software for the 382J aircraft. Both projects doubled productivity and improved quality by an order of magnitude compared to industry norms. He has published numerous conference papers, been keynote and feature speaker at industry workshops, and in the 1980s, authored the software-engineering book *Power Programming.*